Essentials

Autodesk®
Navisworks® 2017 (R1)

September 2016

AUTODESK.
Official Training Guide

CONTINUING EDUCATION
AIA

Trademarks

The following are registered trademarks or trademarks of Autodesk, Inc., and/or its subsidiaries and/or affiliates in the USA and other countries: 123D, 3ds Max, Alias, ATC, AutoCAD LT, AutoCAD, Autodesk, the Autodesk logo, Autodesk 123D, Autodesk Homestyler, Autodesk Inventor, Autodesk MapGuide, Autodesk Streamline, AutoLISP, AutoSketch, AutoSnap, AutoTrack, Backburner, Backdraft, Beast, BIM 360, Burn, Buzzsaw, CADmep, CAiCE, CAMduct, Civil 3D, Combustion, Communication Specification, Configurator 360, Constructware, Content Explorer, Creative Bridge, Dancing Baby (image), DesignCenter, DesignKids, DesignStudio, Discreet, DWF, DWG, DWG (design/logo), DWG Extreme, DWG TrueConvert, DWG TrueView, DWGX, DXF, Ecotect, Ember, ESTmep, FABmep, Face Robot, FBX, Fempro, Fire, Flame, Flare, Flint, ForceEffect, FormIt 360, Freewheel, Fusion 360, Glue, Green Building Studio, Heidi, Homestyler, HumanIK, i-drop, ImageModeler, Incinerator, Inferno, InfraWorks, Instructables, Instructables (stylized robot design/logo), Inventor, Inventor HSM, Inventor LT, Lustre, Maya, Maya LT, MIMI, Mockup 360, Moldflow Plastics Advisers, Moldflow Plastics Insight, Moldflow, Moondust, MotionBuilder, Movimento, MPA (design/logo), MPA, MPI (design/logo), MPX (design/logo), MPX, Mudbox, Navisworks, ObjectARX, ObjectDBX, Opticore, P9, Pier 9, Pixlr, Pixlr-o-matic, Productstream, Publisher 360, RasterDWG, RealDWG, ReCap, ReCap 360, Remote, Revit LT, Revit, RiverCAD, Robot, Scaleform, Showcase, Showcase 360, SketchBook, Smoke, Socialcam, Softimage, Spark & Design, Spark Logo, Sparks, SteeringWheels, Stitcher, Stone, StormNET, TinkerBox, Tinkercad, Tinkerplay, ToolClip, Topobase, Toxik, TrustedDWG, T-Splines, ViewCube, Visual LISP, Visual, VRED, Wire, Wiretap, WiretapCentral, XSI.

NASTRAN is a registered trademark of the National Aeronautics Space Administration.

All other brand names, product names, or trademarks belong to their respective holders.

Disclaimer

Published by:

ASCENT Center for Technical Knowledge
630 Peter Jefferson Parkway, Suite 175
Charlottesville, VA 22911
866-527-2368
www.ascented.com

Contents

Introduction

Welcome to the *Autodesk Navisworks 2017: Essentials* Autodesk Official Training Guide (AOTG), training courseware for use in Authorized Training Center (ATC®) locations, corporate training settings, and other classroom settings.

Although this courseware is designed for instructor-led courses, you can also use it for self-paced learning.

This introduction covers the following topics:

- Course Objectives
- Prerequisites
- Using This Training Guide
- Downloading and Installing the Class Files
- Feedback
- Free Autodesk Software for Students and Educators

This training guide is complementary to the software documentation. For detailed explanations of features and functionality, refer to the Help in the software.

Course Objectives

After completing this course, you will be able to:

- Describe the main features and functionality of the Autodesk® Navisworks® software.
- Open and append 3D files of different formats and save in the Autodesk Navisworks format.
- Create links to object properties files and scheduling files in external databases.
- Perform visual project model reviews using the built-in review and reporting tools.
- Create construction simulations of a project model to check validity of construction schedules.
- Use Animator and Scripter to create interactive animations for presentations and demonstrations.
- Obtain 2D and 3D takeoff data from source models to create material estimates, measure areas, and count components.
- Perform interference detection tests between 3D files of different disciplines to check integrity of the design.
- Add true-to-life materials, lighting, and Environments to project models, to create photorealistic output.

Prerequisites

This course is meant for new Autodesk Navisworks users for the review, 4D simulation, clash testing, quantification, and presentation of existing 3D geometry files.

It is recommended that you have a basic understanding of 3D design and task scheduling software.

Using This Training Guide

The lessons are generally independent of each other, however, if a lesson is dependent on a prior lesson, a prepared class file is provided for you that includes the required steps completed. It is recommended that you complete these lessons in the order that they are presented unless you are familiar with the concepts and functionality described in those lessons.

Each chapter contains:

- **Lessons -** Usually two or more lessons in each chapter.
- **Exercises -** Practical, real-world examples for you to practice using the functionality you have just learned. Each exercise contains step-by-step procedures and graphics to help you complete the exercise successfully.

    - Exercise titles which finish with (C) include model examples of Construction/buildings, etc.
    - Exercise titles which finish with (P) include model examples of Plant projects, etc. It is suggested that you use the exercises that reflect your business type.

Feedback

We always welcome feedback on Autodesk Official Training Courseware. After completing this course, if you have suggestions for improvements or want to report an error in the training guide or with the class files, please send your comments to *feedback@ascented.com*.

Students and Educators can Access Free Autodesk Software and Resources

Autodesk challenges you to get started with free educational licenses for professional software and creativity apps used by millions of architects, engineers, designers, and hobbyists today. Bring Autodesk software into your classroom, studio, or workshop to learn, teach, and explore real-world design challenges the way professionals do.

Get started today - register at the Autodesk Education Community and download one of the many Autodesk software applications available.

Visit www.autodesk.com/joinedu/

Note: Free products are subject to the terms and conditions of the end-user license and services agreement that accompanies the software. The software is for personal use for education purposes and is not intended for classroom or lab use.

Exercise Files

To download the practice files for this student guide, use the following steps:

1. Type the URL shown below into the address bar of your Internet browser. The URL must be typed **exactly as shown**. If you are using an ASCENT ebook, you can click on the link to download the file.

    Address bar

    `http://www.ASCENTed.com/getfile?id=diceros`

    File   Edit   View   Favorites   Tools   Help

2. Press <Enter> to download the .ZIP file that contains the Practice Files.

3. Once the download is complete, unzip the file to a local folder. The unzipped file contains an .EXE file.

4. Double-click on the .EXE file and follow the instructions to automatically install the Practice Files on the C:\ drive of your computer.

    Do not change the location in which the Practice Files folder is installed. Doing so can cause errors when completing the practices in this student guide.

http://www.ASCENTed.com/getfile?id=diceros

Getting Started

Product Overview

The Autodesk® Navisworks® software revolutionizes design review. The software provides interactive visualization and real-time walkthrough of even the largest and most complex 3D models.

Navigating and exploring the design to improve quality and compress the review process is effortless with the Autodesk Navisworks software.

The post-production value of 3D models is significantly increased by the wide-ranging access that the Autodesk Navisworks software offers for investigating and examining a design.

The tool provides a way of communicating design intent by creating NWD files in which everyone can view and walk through the 3D models in real time, without specialist skills and free from the limitation of preprogrammed animation.

Compressed and secure for distribution, Autodesk Navisworks files are faithful to the original native 3D data from which they are created.

TimeLiner

Embracing a fourth dimension of time, the TimeLiner tool available in the Autodesk® Navisworks® Simulate and Manage products is aimed at satisfying the growing interest in affordable 4D construction simulation for building and site planning, and presentation of time-based modeling.

TimeLiner makes it easy to produce time simulations and "what-if" scenarios. While these can be set up solely in the Autodesk Navisworks software, you can also link to some major project software, such as Microsoft Project, Primavera (Sure Track/Power Project), Excel (CSV files), and Asta Power Project. TimeLiner also supports any project scheduling software that can export the common MPX format.

Animator and Scripter

With the Animator and Scripter tools available in the Autodesk Navisworks Simulate and Manage products, you can animate your model and interact with it. For example, you could animate how a crane moves around a site, or how a car is assembled or dismantled. You can also create interactive scripts, which link your animations to specific events, such as On Key Press or On Collision. For example, the doors opens as you approach them in your model.

You can also link Clash Detective, TimeLiner, and Object Animation together to enable clash testing of fully animated TimeLiner schedules. So, instead of visually inspecting a TimeLiner sequence to ensure, for example, that the moving crane did not collide with a work group, you can run a Clash Detective test.

Quantification

The process of measuring quantities of materials from models, drawings, and specifications prepared by architects, engineers, and other designers is known as takeoff. In the Autodesk Navisworks software, takeoff is carried out using the Quantification feature. Quantification gives you the tools to automatically create material estimates, measure areas, and count components using source 3D models or 2D sheets. You can accurately estimate construction and renovation projects, and spend less time counting and measuring items and more time analyzing projects. The Quantification feature is available for Autodesk Navisworks Manage and Autodesk Navisworks Simulate users.

Clash Detective

The Clash Detective tool available in the Autodesk Navisworks Manage product enables the effective identification, inspection, comment tracking, and reporting of interference in a 3D project model. Clash Detective can eliminate a tedious manual task, with the accompanying risk of human error, to significantly reduce the expensive consequences of incomplete, inaccurate, and poorly coordinated production information. Project Coordination is simplified with the use of Clash Detective by easily coordinating with the responsible parties to track the clash through the project lifecycle.

For those who seek to complete design projects on time and in budget, the business case for Clash Detective is clear and unequivocal.

Rendering

The Autodesk Navisworks Rendering tool available in the Autodesk Navisworks Simulate and Manage products, is a visualization solution dedicated to enhancing the real-time experience and the creation of compelling rendered output to communicate design intent.

With this tool, you can apply textures, materials, and lights quickly to 3D models, and is ideal for fast-moving collaborative review at every stage of the creative process. With Rendering, everyone can enhance the realism of the interactive environment, and create both still and animated photo-realistic rendered output to share a vision of a project and improve understanding and design quality.

Freedom Viewer

Freedom is a separate Autodesk Navisworks software that provides users with a free 3D viewer to look at Autodesk Navisworks NWD files. It is the answer for those without design software or specialist skills who want to explore a 3D project model. Easily open, view, and walk through NWD files, even those streamed across the Internet.

Objectives

After completing this chapter, you will be able to:

- Describe the key interface areas in the Autodesk Navisworks software.
- Use each of the navigation tools, related tools, and key actions.
- Open and dock the required windows, customize the workspace layout and Ribbon to personal preference.
- Open and append Autodesk Navisworks NWD files and other file formats in the Autodesk Navisworks software.
- Check and change file units.
- Manipulate the frame rate used in navigating a model and use options to improve frame rate. The Autodesk Navisworks Interface.
- Publish files as NWD files.
- Merge similar NWF files into one file without duplication.
- Refresh files that have been updated in source CAD software.
- Use Autodesk Navisworks to send models through email.
- Open and view the Selection Tree and re-order and expand the structure as required.
- Change the resolution of the selection tool to select items or groups of items.

Lesson: Getting Started with Autodesk Navisworks

Overview

This lesson describes the Autodesk Navisworks interface and how the navigation tools work. It also introduces you to the windows, methods of docking them, and customizing the Ribbon. To complete the chapter you will learn to open 3D files of multiple formats in the Autodesk Navisworks software and via a URL. It also introduces you to appending additional files in the scene and transforming file units.

Objectives

After completing this lesson, you will be able to:

- Describe the key interface areas in the Autodesk Navisworks software.
- Use each of the navigation tools, related tools, and key actions.
- Open and dock the required windows, customize the workspace layout and Ribbon to personal preference.
- Open and append Autodesk Navisworks NWD files and other file formats in the Autodesk Navisworks software.
- Check and change file units.
- Manipulate the frame rate used in navigating a model and use options to improve frame rate. The Autodesk Navisworks Interface.

The Autodesk Navisworks interface is intuitive and easy to learn and use. It contains several traditional Windows Ribbon elements, such as the Application Menu, Ribbon, Quick Access Toolbars, etc.

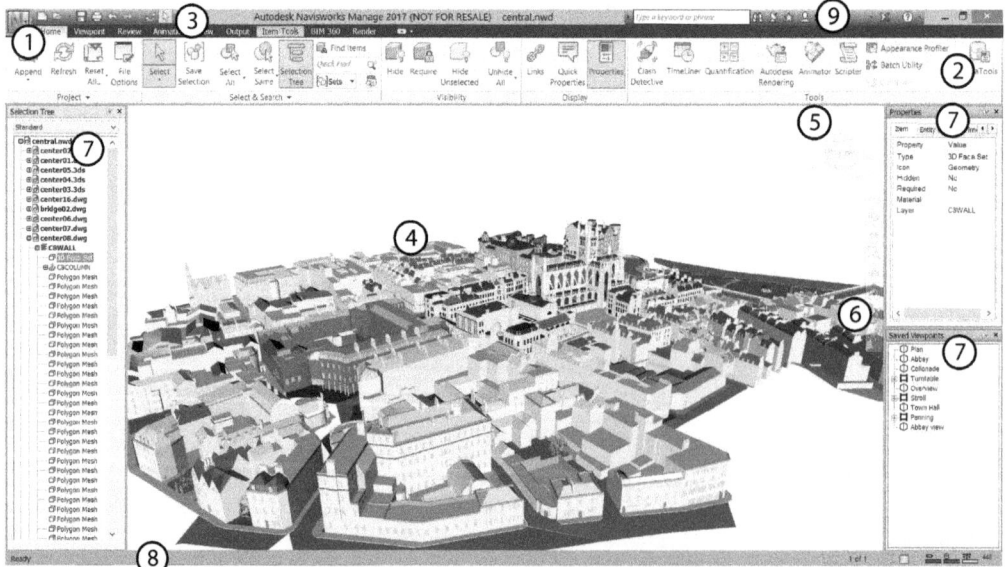

1 - Application Menu	4 - Scene View	7 - Dockable window
2 - Ribbon	5 - ViewCube	8 - Status bar
3 - Quick Access Toolbar	6 - Navigation bar	9 - InfoCenter

Application Menu (1)

The Application Menu provides access to commonly accessed tools. To access its commands, click

 in the top left corner of the Autodesk Navisworks software. The commands available in this menu include: file actions (New, Open, Save, and Save As), Export commands, the Publish command, the option to print or distribute it to other users by email, and Vault access options. In this menu, Options provides access to the Options Editor dialog box to customize your global settings.

Ribbon (2)

The Ribbon is a palette at the top of the application window that displays task-based tools and controls. The Ribbon is divided into tabs, with each tab supporting a specific activity. In each tab, tools are grouped together into a task-based series of panels.

To activate a command on the Ribbon, simply navigate to the tab and panel and select the command. Every command on a toolbar includes a tooltip, which describes the function the button activates. Placing the mouse over a button displays a brief instruction on how to use this feature. When some commands are activated, context-sensitive tabs might be added to the Ribbon. When active, the context-sensitive tab is highlighted in green to show tools that are only applied to the selected items. Once the objects are deselected, the context-sensitive tab is removed.

You can customize the Ribbon depending on your needs in the following ways:

- To specify which Ribbon tabs and panels are displayed, right-click the Ribbon and on the shortcut menu, click or clear the names of the tabs or panels.
- You can change the order of Ribbon tabs. Click the tab you want to move, drag it to the required position, and release.
- You can change the order of Ribbon panels in a tab. Click the panel you want to move, drag it to the required position, and release.
- You can control the amount of space the Ribbon takes in the application window. There are two buttons to the right of the Ribbon tabs, that enables you to choose the Ribbon toggle and Ribbon minimize states. Click to cycle between the minimized Ribbon states. Once fully compressed, click to resume the full Ribbon display state. The minimize Ribbon states enable you to minimize to tabs only, minimize to Panel titles only, and minimize to Panel buttons only. The drop-down enables you to control which of the states can be accessed as you are cycling.

Quick Access Toolbar (3)

At the top of the application window, the Quick Access Toolbar displays frequently used commands.

- A default set of commands have been included on the Ribbon, to enable/disable these defaults click ⬛ at the end of the Quick Access Toolbar, and select the commands that are to be included.
- You can add an unlimited number of buttons to the Quick Access Toolbar by selecting the command on its tab, right-clicking, and selecting Add to Quick Access Toolbar. New buttons are added to the right of the default commands.
- You can add separators between the buttons to subdivide the commands. To add a separator, right-click on the Quick Access Toolbar in the location where the separator is required, and select Add Separator. Separators can be removed by right-clicking on the separator and selecting Remove from Quick Access Toolbar.
- You can position the Quick Access Toolbar either above or below the Ribbon. To move its position, click ⬛ at the end of the Quick Access Toolbar and select either Show Below the Ribbon or Show Above the Ribbon.

> Only Ribbon commands can be added to the Quick Access Toolbar. Commands that extend past the maximum length of the toolbar are displayed as flyouts.

Scene View (4)

The Scene View window is used to interact with 3D models. You can control how much space the Scene View window uses compared to the dockable windows by dragging the edges of the windows as required. Alternatively, you could auto hide ⬛ the dockable windows, or switch on full screen mode (F11 to toggle).

The Scene View window can be split vertically, horizontally, or into four segments. Split views enable the user to set different viewing styles in each pane (i.e., wireframe in one, full render in one, and a transparent view in another)

- To split your current view horizontally, expand the Split View command in the Scene View panel on the View tab and click Split Horizontal.

- To split your current view vertically, expand the Split View command in the Scene View panel on the View tab and click Split Vertical.

- Resize a view by dragging the view borders or click Window Size ⬚ in the View tab and enter the required values.

- Views can be subdivided so that there are horizontal and vertical Scene View windows. This is done by selecting in a Scene View window to activate it and then splitting it again.

- Any of the sub-divided Scene Views have title bar headings. To float a Scene View, select its title bar heading and drag it away from its current location. To redock a floating Scene View, double-click on the title bar heading.

- Split Scene View windows can be set to Auto Hide by clicking Auto Hide ⬚ on the Scene View's title bar heading. Once auto hidden, it is listed above the Status bar.

ViewCube (5)

The ViewCube is used to reorient the current view of a model. You can reorient the view of a model with the ViewCube tool by clicking predefined areas on the ViewCube to assign preset views, click and drag on the ViewCube to freely change the view angle of the model, and define and restore the Home view.

- The ViewCube tool has twenty-six defined areas to click and change the current view of a model. The twenty-six defined areas are categorized into three groups: corner, edge, and face. Of the twenty-six defined areas, six represent standard orthogonal views of a model: top, bottom, front, back, left, and right. Orthogonal views are set by clicking one of the faces on the ViewCube tool. You use the other twenty defined areas to access angled views of a model. Clicking one of the corners on the ViewCube tool reorients the current view of the model to a three-quarter view, based on a viewpoint defined by three sides of the model. Clicking one of the edges reorients the view of the model to a half view based on two sides of the model.

> When the cursor is over one of the clickable areas of the ViewCube tool, the clickable face, corner, or edge highlights and the cursor changes to an arrow with a small cube to indicate that it is over the ViewCube tool. A tooltip is also displayed. The tooltip describes the action that you can perform based on the location of the cursor over the ViewCube tool.

- You can also click and drag the ViewCube tool to reorient the view of a model to a custom view other than one of the twenty-six predefined parts. As you drag, the cursor changes to indicate that you are reorienting the current view of the model. If you drag the ViewCube tool close to one of the preset orientations, and it is set to snap to the closest view, the ViewCube tool rotates to the closest preset orientation.

> The outline of the ViewCube tool helps identify the form of orientation it is in: standard or fixed. When the ViewCube tool is in standard orientation (i.e., not orientated to one of the twenty-six predefined parts) its outline is displayed as dashed. The ViewCube tool is outlined in a solid continuous line when it is constrained to one of the predefined views.

- When you view a model from one of the face views, two roll arrow buttons are displayed near the ViewCube tool. Use the roll arrows to rotate the current view 90 degrees clockwise or counterclockwise around the center of the view.
- When the ViewCube tool is active while viewing a model from one of the face views, four orthogonal triangles are displayed near the ViewCube tool. You use these triangles to switch to one of the adjacent face views.
- Clicking in the top right corner of the ViewCube reorients the Scene View to its default orientation and zoom level.

Additional ViewCube options can be accessed by clicking in the bottom left corner of the ViewCube. These options enable you to define the view setting, define the Home and Front orientations, and access its settings in the Options Editor.

The display of the ViewCube can be set in the View tab by enabling/disabling the View Cube command in the Navigation Aids panel.

Navigation Bar (6)

The Navigation bar is a user interface element where you can access both unified and product-specific navigation tools. Unified navigation tools (such as Autodesk® ViewCube® and SteeringWheels®) are those that can be found across many Autodesk products. Product-specific navigation tools are unique to a product. The navigation bar floats over and along one of the sides of the Scene View.

The Navigation bar is located on the right side of the Scene view. You can control the display of the Navigation bar on the View tab, in the Navigation Aids panel, by selecting/deselecting the Navigation Bar option.

Icon	Name	Description
	Full Navigation Wheel	The Navigation wheel contains common 3D navigation tools used for both viewing an object and touring a building. There are two sizes of wheels, full and mini. You can expand the current command on the Navigation Bar to gain access to and enable an alternate navigation wheel. Although the display of the two wheels vary, the commands on each are similar. You can zoom in or out, pan or orbit around a the model, rewind between views, or center around a selected point. Additional commands also enable you to walk through, look around a model, and adjust the view up or down.
	Pan	Drag in any direction to move the camera correspondingly. Press SHIFT and use the middle mouse button to temporarily switch to Orbit.
	Zoom	Drag up or down to move the camera in and out along the axis of the focal point.
	Zoom Window	Click and drag a box over an area on the scene to zoom into the bounding area.
	Zoom Selected	Zoom in to selected items in the scene window.
	Zoom All	Fit the complete model into the scene window. **Tip:** This can be useful if lost, in or outside the model.
	Orbit	Orbit the camera around the focal point; drag in any direction to orbit correspondingly. Orbit mode resets the world up vector. Press the middle mouse button to temporarily change to Pan.
	Free Orbit	Rotate the model around the focal point (similar to having the model in the palm of the hand). Drag in any direction to move the model correspondingly. Press and hold CTRL and select a new pivot location with the left mouse button. To temporarily change to Pan, press and hold the middle mouse button.
	Constrained Orbit	Spin the model as if it is sitting on a turntable. It resets the world up vector and it is always maintained. Press and hold CTRL and select a new pivot location with the left mouse button. Press the middle mouse button to temporarily change to Pan to adjust the camera height. **Tip:** Consider returning to the Classic Constrained Orbit option in the Options Editor > Navigation Bar area to set the model spinning on its own.
	Look Around	Turn the camera about the viewpoint (similar to moving your head around). Press CTRL to rotate the model.
	Look At	Looks at a particular face in the scene. The camera orients so that the selected face is centered and parallel with the screen.
	Focus	Focus an item to the center of the scene window. Select, then click on an item to center it.

Icon	Name	Description
	Fly	Fly the camera through the scene. Move up or down to ascend or descend and left or right to move correspondingly. If you find yourself flying too quickly, adjust linear and angular speeds by clicking Viewpoint tab > Edit Current Viewpoints. **Tip:** The Fly tool can be set to a speed that is suitable for the model size, etc. Select a viewpoint to navigate from, then click Tools menu > Global Options > Interface > Viewpoint Defaults. Add a checkmark to Override Linear Speed and then set the speed as required.
	Walk	Walk around and through the model scene. Walk mode resets the model to an upright position. Press SHIFT to increase walking speed or press CTRL to temporarily switch to Pan to adjust the camera height. Press SPACEBAR to temporarily crouch under an obstacle. **Tip:** The Walk tool can be set to a speed that is most suitable for the model size, etc. Select a viewpoint to navigate from, then click Tools menu > Global Options > Interface > Viewpoint Defaults. Click Override Linear Speed, then set the speed as required.

Dockable Windows (7)

Most features are accessible from the dockable windows. To display a dockable window, expand the Windows command in the View tab and choose from the list of available dockable windows. Alternatively, some of the windows can be enabled/disabled directly on tabs. For example, the Selection Tree and Properties windows are available on the Home tab.

All windows are dockable and resizable, and automatically lock to specific locations near to where they are moved.

Holding CTRL when moving a window, prevents it from auto docking.

Using the Docking Tool

When you drag a window from its current location towards a new destination on the interface, a docking tool is displayed. The docking icons point towards the four edges of the interface. The options that are available are dependent on the permissible locations for docking.

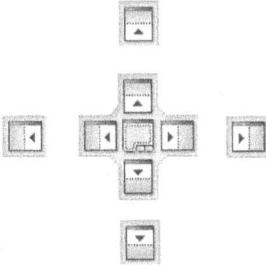

Note: These inner docking locations do not enable pinning/unpinning workspaces. Only the outside docking locations enable pinning.

When the window you are dragging is close to the place where you want it to dock, move the mouse over the corresponding area of the docking tool. An outline of the window displays on the interface. To dock the window, release the mouse button.

Tiling Windows

You can tile windows on the interface. To do this, drag the window you want to tile over the window where you want it to be placed. When a rectangular outline displays, release the mouse button.

Auto Hiding Windows

You can auto hide windows; this keeps them active while maximizing the amount of available screen space. If auto-hide is active, the body of the window disappears when you move the cursor out of it, leaving only the title bar visible. Move the cursor over the title bar to display the entire window again.

To toggle auto-hide on, click ▣ on the title bar. To toggle auto-hide off, click ▣ on the title bar.

Status Bar (8)

The Status bar is displayed at the bottom of the screen. The left corner of the Status bar displays short instructions for using the Autodesk Navisworks features. The right corner of the Status bar contains multi-sheet navigation controls, access to the Sheet Browser, and performance indicators that provide constant feedback as to how the Autodesk Navisworks software is performing on your computer.

Multi-Sheet Navigation Controls

Click the previous/next and first/last arrows to open the required sheet/model in the Scene View. This is equivalent to double-clicking the sheet/model in the Sheet Browser window. These controls are only available for multi-sheet files.

Performance Indicators

In the lower right corner of the workspace, there are four performance indicator bars that give constant feedback as to how the application is performing on the computer. The indicators are Scene Drawing, Disk to Memory, Web Server Download, and Memory Usage.

Icon	Name	Description
	Scene Drawing Indicator Bar	This progress bar indicates how much of the current view is drawn (for example, how much drop-out there is in the current view). When the progress bar is at 100%, the view is completely drawn, with no drop-out.
		While the view is being drawn, the Pencil icon changes to yellow. If there is too much data to handle and the computer cannot process this quickly enough for the Autodesk Navisworks software, then the Pencil icon changes to red, indicating a bottleneck.
	Disk to Memory Indicator Bar	This progress bar indicates how much of the current model is loaded from disk (for example, how much is loaded into memory). When the progress bar is at 100%, the entire model, including geometry and property information, is loaded into memory.
		While data is being read, the Disk icon changes to yellow. If there is too much data to handle and the computer cannot process this quickly enough, then the Disk icon changes to red, indicating a bottleneck.
	Web Server Download Indicator Bar	This progress bar indicates how much of the current model is downloaded when opening a file via a URL (for example, how much has been downloaded from a Web server). When the progress bar is at 100%, the entire model has been downloaded.
		While data is being downloaded, the Web Server icon changes to yellow. If there is too much data to handle and your machine cannot process this quickly enough, then the Web Server icon changes to red, indicating a bottleneck.
178 MB	**Memory Usage Indicator**	The field to the right of the progress bars displays the amount of memory currently being used by the Autodesk Navisworks software.

How the Autodesk Navisworks Engine Works

When working with large "supermodels" in the Autodesk Navisworks software, RAM capacity is required to load and review the data. The Autodesk Navisworks software employs technology that optimizes the usage of the available RAM.

Before running out of memory, the application pages unnecessary data to the hard disk, freeing up space for loading to continue. With the Autodesk Navisworks technology, you can start navigating the supermodel before it has completely loaded into memory.

InfoCenter (9)

The InfoCenter is located in the top right corner and provides a number of useful tools for getting to know and searching for help in the Autodesk Navisworks software.

| Type a keyword or phrase | 🔍 ⬆ ★ 👤 Sign In | ⋅ ✕ | ❓ ⋅ |

The InfoCenter can be used to search for keywords by typing directly in the entry field. The additional tools enable you to access product updates and announcements, sign in to the Autodesk A360 software, and to access the Autodesk Navisworks Help tool. The Favorites command also provides a convenient way of saving searched topics for future review.

Sheet Browser

The Sheet Browser is a dockable window, which lists all sheets/models that have been imported into the currently opened file.

> The Sheet Browser enables coordinators to group files together with various versions of the same file by interchanging them quickly and keeping them grouped. This functionality is also used for drawings that are prepared with phasing of the project in mind, since each phase can be separated into its own project. The ability to have several different elevations can also be beneficial in the clash detection process since the appropriate elevation can be opened and marked up when a clash is found and submitted as an RFI on the spot.

Procedure: To Open the Sheet Browser

There are two ways to open the Sheet Browser:

- On the View tab, in the Workspace panel, click Sheet Browser from the list in the Windows 🗗 command.

- On the Status Bar, click Sheet Browser 🗒.

The Sheets/Models palette is located at the top of the Sheet Browser and lists all sheets and models in the multi-sheet file. The label at the top of the palette indicates the file that is currently open. The sheets/models can be represented as a list view (🗔) or a thumbnail view (🗔). By default, the display order is the same as in the original file. The currently selected model/sheet is indicated with a shaded background, and the model/sheet currently opened in the Scene View is indicated with a black graphic border.

The Properties palette is located at the bottom of the Sheet Browser and is used to examine properties for the sheet/model selected in the Sheets/Models palette. You can view the properties for the currently opened file by clicking on its name. The properties are grouped by category, are read-only, and can be expanded/collapsed.

Some additional notes on the Sheet Browser include the following:

- To navigate between sheets/models you can either click the previous/next and first/last arrows on the Status bar or double-click the sheet/model in the Sheet Browser window.
- You can select several sheets/models at the same time with SHIFT and CTRL, but you cannot open more than one sheet/model in the Scene View.
- If more than one sheet/model is selected, the Properties palette only displays the number of selected items, and doesn't show any property information.
- Right-clicking on a filename in the Sheet Browser provides access to a menu that enables you to open, delete, merge, append, prepare, print, and rename sheets/models.

When you open a multi-sheet file, not all sheets/models might have been prepared to be used in the Autodesk Navisworks software. The sheets/models which require preparation are indicated with

Prepare ↻ . Only prepared models are found if a search is executed. A prepared file is one that has an .NWC file created for it.

> Refer to the Saving, Merging, Refreshing, and Publishing Files Lesson for more information on .NWC files.

Workspaces

The Autodesk Navisworks software comes with several default workspaces. You can use these workspaces as is or modify them for your own requirements.

With workspaces, you can work in a custom, task-oriented design review environment. Each workspace contains sets of toolbars and windows with the tools required to perform a certain job, making it easy to switch between layouts, as required. The workspaces can also be shared with other users. You could, for example, create separate workspaces for occasional and "heavy-weight" Autodesk Navisworks users, or set up your own corporate standard.

When you first start the Autodesk Navisworks software, a default workspace is displayed. You can choose a different workspace at any time by expanding the Load Workspace option in the View tab and selecting the required workspace from the list.

Note: Workspaces are saved and loaded using an XML file format.

Procedure: To Save a Workspace

1. Configure your workspace. You can customize which windows are displayed, their size, and the layout of the Scene View windows. Workspaces do not retain changes to the Ribbon or Quick Access Toolbar.

2. Select the View tab. In the Workspace panel, click Save Workspace.

3. In the Save Current Workspace dialog box, enter a name for the new workspace. You can also select the name of an existing workspace to overwrite it with your modified configuration.

4. Click Save.

Procedure: To Load a Saved Workspace

Select the View tab. In the Workspace panel, expand the Load Workspace option and select a saved Workspace from the drop-down menu.

Viewpoint & View Tab Commands

Viewpoint Tab

The Viewpoint tab contains all the commands that are available on the Navigation bar with a few additional viewing tools, as described below.

Icon	Name	Description
	Perspective (Camera panel)	View the model with a perspective camera (selected by default).
	Orthographic (Camera panel)	View the model with an orthographic camera.

Icon	Name	Description
	Collision (Navigate panel> Realism)	Prevent navigation through objects. You can walk or climb over objects in the scene up to half the height of the collision volume (viewer). This way, you can climb stairs. **Note:** Collision detection is only available in Walk or Fly modes. **Tip:** The collision volume (viewer) can be adjusted in height and radius. Click Application Menu ![N] > Options > Interface > Viewpoint Defaults > Settings (Default Collision Detection), and set the viewer radius and height as required.
	Gravity (Navigate panel>Realism)	Enable gravitational effect when walking (for example, being pulled downwards). You can ascend and descend stairs and slopes. Enabling the gravity tool automatically enables collision. This ensures that gravity stops moving downward once the viewpoint collides with the ground.
	Crouch (Navigate panel>Realism)	Enable automatic crouching while walking. (This function only works with Collision Detection switched on.)
	Third Person (Navigate panel> Realism) **Tip:** The Third Person, Collision, Gravity, and Crouch commands are also available on the Walk/Fly drop-down menu on the Navigation bar.	View from a third person's perspective. When activated, an avatar (which is a representation of yourself) is visible in front of the camera in the 3D model. Navigating tools control the avatar's interaction with the current scene. **Tip:** Collision Detection and Crouch, Gravity, and Third Person can all be switched on and off by pressing the shortcut keys, CTRL+D, CTRL+G, and CTRL+T, respectively. Using Third Person in connection with Collision Detection and Gravity makes this a very powerful function, giving an exact visualization of how a person would interact with the intended design. The Third Person settings can be adjusted. To change the settings for the current session, select the Viewpoint tab, and on the Save, Load & Playback panel, click Edit Current Viewpoint ![icon] and select Settings in the Collision area. Under Third Person, select Enable, then select Avatar (type), and the Angle and Distance if required.
	Align X (Camera panel>Align Camera)	Aligns the camera along the X-axis.
	Align Y (Camera panel>Align Camera)	Aligns the camera along the Y-axis.
	Align Z (Camera panel>Align Camera)	Aligns the camera along the Z-axis.

Icon	Name	Description
	Straighten (**Camera panel> Align Camera**)	You can straighten the camera to align it with the viewpoint up vector. When the camera position is close to the viewpoint up vector (within 13 degrees), you can use this function to snap the camera to an axis. **Tip:** Alternatively, enter **0** at the base of the Tilt window.
	Show Tilt Bar (**Camera panel**)	Use the scroll bar to tilt the camera up and down.

> Global settings for the default use of the Realism commands are set in the Application Menu > Options > Interface > Viewpoint Default > Settings. When the user assigns settings from this location they become the default for every model that is opened from this point on. To set and store the use of the Realism commands at the model level, click Edit Current Viewpoint on the Viewpoint tab and click Settings.

View Tab

The View tab provides access to a number of commands that affect the tools that are displayed in the Autodesk Navisworks interface, as described below.

- The Navigation Aids panel controls the display of the Navigation Bar, ViewCube, XYZ Axes orientation image, positional readout information line, and readout for the grid line location.
- The Grids & Levels panel enables you to toggle the display of grid lines off and on, control the active grid level in the file along with its display level, and control how they are displayed relative to the camera position.

> The Grid & Levels panel is only available when working with Autodesk Revit source files.

- The Scene View panel controls the display of the scene view. You can maximize the scene or control its size, split it into multiple viewports, and control the background color and title bars.
- The final panel is the Workspace panel, which is accessed to toggle the display of different windows in the Autodesk Navisworks Software (e.g., Saved Viewpoints, Selection Tree, etc.). Additionally, the Load and Save workspace commands enable you to save workspace customizations for reuse in a future sessions.

Absolute Coordinate Display

Displaying the XYZ position of the camera at the bottom left of the main view gives quick positional feedback. There are three formats in which the position can be displayed. Coordinates can be displayed as an XYZ positional readout, in a grid display, or as a compass that identifies a general direction. If an avatar (third person) is being used, then the displayed coordinates identify the position of the avatar's eyes.

Procedure: To Set Coordinate Displays

1.   Select the View tab. On the Navigation Aids panel, click the HUD drop-down menu.

2.   In the drop-down list, select the XYZ Axes, Position Readout, or Grid Location option. They can all also be selected at the same time. They are displayed at the bottom left of the main view, and update as the model is navigated.

Tip: Click the Third Person view on and off. At the same time, notice that although the camera position changes, the displayed coordinates do not, as the avatar's eyes are now positioned where the camera was in first person view.

About File Formats

When you open a model file or files in the Autodesk Navisworks software, you can save the file as either an NWF file or an NWD file.

NWD File

An NWD file is a fully published or saved Autodesk Navisworks file containing all geometry and review markups. An NWD file can be thought of as a "snapshot" of the current state of the model and can be viewed in both Autodesk Navisworks and Freedom (the Autodesk Navisworks free viewer). An NWD file can be created using the Publish command or using the Save As command.

NWF File

An NWF file contains the review markups, but no geometry. Instead, it includes links (acts as a pointer) to the original native CAD drawing files (as listed in the Selection Tree). This means an NWF is considerably smaller in file size than an NWD.

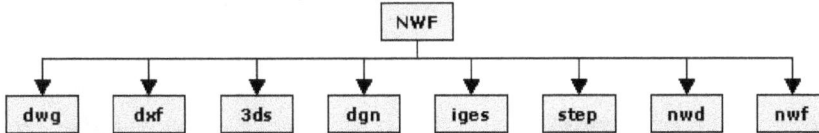

```
                          NWF
   ┌──────┬──────┬──────┬──────┬──────┬──────┬──────┐
 dwg    dxf    3ds    dgn    iges   step    nwd    nwf
```

Generally, you should use NWF files whenever multiple files are brought together to create the scene, such as xrefs in AutoCAD®. This way, whenever one file changes, the whole model does not have to be re-published, only the file that has changed needs to be re-read.

NWF files can also be used as the design review "buffer" for NWD files. Comments, views, redlining, animations, material overrides, and clash tests can all be saved and added to an NWF file. The NWD files might need to be re-published due to changes throughout the design process.

Procedure: To Save as an NWF or NWD File

1. Click Application Menu ![N] > Save As.

2. In the Save As dialog box, in the Save as type drop-down list, select NWD or NWF.

3. Browse to the required directory then add an appropriate filename and click Save.

   Tip: If a file needs to be read using an earlier version (2015 or 2016) of the Autodesk Navisworks software, it should be saved as that version type.

Cache Files

When the Autodesk Navisworks software opens a native CAD file, it first checks whether there is an Autodesk Navisworks cache file present with the same name as the CAD file, but with an NWC extension. If there is, and this cache file is newer than the native CAD file, the application opens this file instead, because it has already been converted to the Autodesk Navisworks format and opens more quickly. However, if no cache file is present, or if the cache file is older than the native CAD file, the application opens the CAD file and converts it.

Opening and Appending Files

The Autodesk Navisworks software provides file readers to support a variety of CAD file formats and laser scan file formats. When you open a CAD file in the Autodesk Navisworks software, an appropriate file reader is automatically used. If required, you can adjust the default file reader settings to improve the conversion quality. Once opened the file can be saved in an Autodesk Navisworks format.

New Files

Click New ⬚ on the Quick Access Toolbar to close existing files, and create a new file. Alternatively, you can also click Application Menu ⬛ > New.

Opening Existing Files

There are two ways to open files:

- In the Autodesk Navisworks software, click Open 🗁 on the Quick Access Toolbar, then browse to the required file. Ensure that you select the required file format. For example, Autodesk Inventor, Autodesk Revit, NWD, NWF, etc.

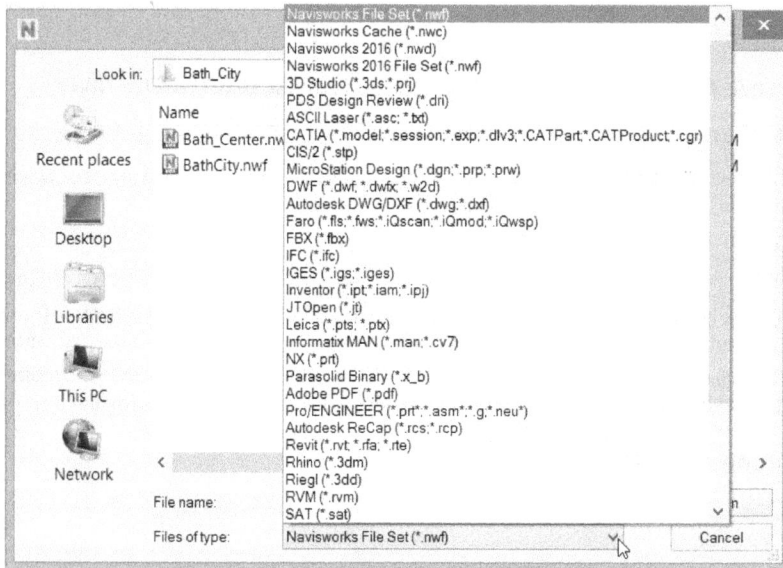

- In *My Computer*, select and drag the file into either the Scene View or the Selection Tree window. To display the Selection Tree window if it is not visible, select the View tab, expand the Windows option, and enable Selection Tree, or on the Home tab, enable Selection Tree 🗐 .

> To open multiple NWD files, select all the required files using CTRL and open them together.
>
> After opening a file, additional files can be opened in the existing file (appended). See Appending Files.

Appending Files

In the Autodesk Navisworks software, you can build a complex scene from smaller models by appending multiple model files together on the same sheet. They can be of any file format that the application supports.

Procedure: To Append Files to an Autodesk Navisworks file

To open additional files into a current scene:

- On the Home tab in the Project panel, click Append ⬜ and select the additional files as required. Press and hold CTRL to select multiple files at the same time.

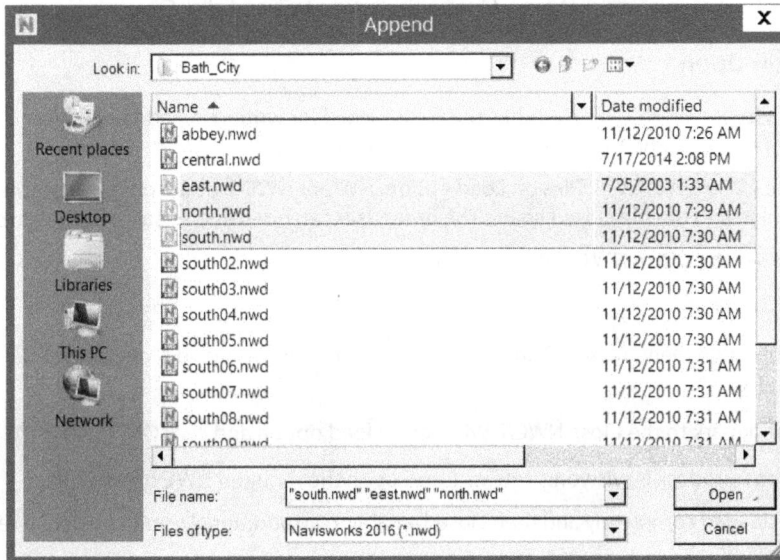

> The Interface > Appending and Merging category in the Options Editor enables you to control how files with multiple sheets are appended to a file. The options include never allowing the remaining sheets to be added, always allowing them to be added, or to be prompted whether they are to be added or not.

Importing Sheets and Models

As an alternative to appending models into an existing Autodesk Navisworks file, you can create a multi-sheet/model Autodesk Navisworks file by adding 2D sheets or 3D models. You can import multiple file formats, add all of its sheets/models into the currently opened file, delete any unwanted sheets/models, and then save the multi-sheet collection in a native NWD or NWF file format.

Procedure: To Import a Sheet or Model into an Autodesk Navisworks file

To import additional sheets/models into a current file:

- In the Sheet Browser, click Import Sheets & Models 🔲. In the Insert From File dialog box, use the Files of Type drop-down list to select the appropriate file format, and navigate to and select the file that is to be imported. Click Open. All of the sheets/models in the selected files are added in the order listed in the original file.

Open Files Via URL

With the Autodesk Navisworks software, you can open published NWD files via the Internet. Having uploaded an NWD file to a Web server, you can then open this file in the Autodesk Navisworks software. With Autodesk Navisworks technology, the entire file does not need to be downloaded before you can start navigating—between 10% and 50% of the file is sufficient for this, depending on the file structure. (The greater the hierarchical structure of the model, the closer to 50% of the file is required for navigation.)

Procedure: Opening Files via URL

- Click Application Menu > Open > Open URL. Enter a URL and click OK.

Close Files on Open

When a user is viewing an NWC or NWD file, the file is locked for writing (an additional user is prevented from re-saving the file while another user has it open).

By selecting the Close NWC/NWD Files on Load option, NWC or NWD files are opened completely on the user's machine and the file closed again. The other user can open and re-save the file as required.

Procedure: To Set the Close NWC/NWD Option

1. Click Application Menu > Options. In the Options Editor, expand Model and click Performance.

2. Add a checkmark to the Close NWC/NWD files on load option and click OK.

3. Restart the Autodesk Navisworks software and open the required NWC or NWD file.

   The file is loaded completely and then closed, enabling an additional user to open and re-save the file if required.

   Note: Using this feature might incur greater memory usage and the computer might not be able to open files that it could previously open with this feature disabled.

Reading Files into Autodesk Navisworks

The Autodesk Navisworks software has its own native file formats (.NWD, .NWF, .NWC), but the Autodesk Navisworks products can also read a combination of many popular 3D CAD formats. Exporter plug-ins are also available for certain applications; a file can be saved in NWC or NWD format. A number of readers exist where certain native file formats can be read directly into the Autodesk Navisworks software. These are the preferred methods by which to view files in the application.

The Autodesk Navisworks software also supports a number of additional file readers for applications without a native file reader or exporter. These applications can usually export to or save as one of these additional file formats.

File Units

Each file or sheet has its own units. When inserting additional sheets/models each sheet has its own units. The Autodesk Navisworks software understands the concept of what unit (scale) the scene is presented in. This is useful when measuring items, setting tolerances for clash detection, or sizes of textures.

Each file format has a default unit associated with it, which it uses when loading files of that type. There is a single scene unit that is set from the global Options Editor dialog box and this unit is used throughout as appropriate.

Procedure: To Set File Units

1. Click Application Menu ![icon] > Options. In the Options Editor, expand Interface and click Display Units.

2. In the Options Editor dialog box, in Linear Units field, select the unit (default setting is Meters), and click OK.

There is a default unit setting for each file format so that when files are opened, they are scaled appropriately to the scene's units. They can, however, be rescaled if the units are found to be incorrect for the scene.

3. In the Selection Tree, right-click the file to be rescaled and select Units and Transform.

4. In the Units and Transform dialog box, in the Model Units field, select the required units, and click OK.

Units and Transform	⊠

Model Units
Units   Meters ⌄

Origin
Origin (in):
[0.00]   [0.00]   [0.00]
☐ Reflected transform

Rotation
[0.00] ° about
[0]   [0]   [1]

Scale
[1]   [1]   [1]

[OK]   [Cancel]

Tip: When reading CAD files into the Autodesk Navisworks software, it is good practice to check that the model is displayed in the correct units. This not only ensures that the appended models align correctly, but more importantly you need to ensure that any measurements or clash detective results are accurate.

Frame Rate

User-Defined Frame Rate

An important feature of the Autodesk Navisworks software is that you can walk through any size model in real time.

The Autodesk Navisworks software guarantees a user-defined frame rate using a unique algorithm that automatically calculates which items to render first during navigation, based on the size of items and distance from the viewpoint center. Items that the application does not have time to render are therefore omitted ("dropped out") to aid interactivity. However, these omitted items are rendered when navigation pauses.

The amount of drop-out depends on several factors including hardware (in particular graphics card and driver performance). The size of the Autodesk Navisworks navigation window and the size of the model also affects the amount of drop-out.

To reduce drop-out during navigation, there is the option to reduce frame rate speed, which results in less drop-out.

Procedure: To Set Frame Rate

Select the Home tab. In the Project panel, click File Options ⌧ and select the Speed tab. Change the frame rate as required.

- The default setting is 6.
- Reduce the setting to reduce drop-out. This might cause jerky movement during navigation.
- Increase the setting to increase drop-out. This ensures a smooth navigation.

Making Objects Required

Although the Autodesk Navisworks software intelligently prioritizes objects for culling in the scene, sometimes it drops out some objects that need to remain visible while navigating.

Procedure: To Make Objects Required

1. Select the objects that must remain visible during navigation.

2. On the Home tab in the Visibility panel, click Require ⌧ to make the selected items required. The objects remains visible during navigation.

    Note: Items that have been set as Required are displayed in red in the Selection Tree.

3. To make items unrequired after navigation, select the objects (in the Selection Tree) then click Require ⌧ again.

Guaranteed Frame Rate

Being able to define and guarantee frame rate is a unique feature of the Autodesk Navisworks software.

By default, the Guarantee Frame Rate option is toggled on, so the engine maintains the user-defined frame rate (set previously in the Home tab > Project panel > File Options ⌧ > Speed tab) during navigation. When navigation is stopped, the complete model is rendered.

If Guarantee Frame Rate is toggled off, the complete model is always rendered during navigation, no matter how long it takes.

- To toggle the guaranteed frame rate off, click Application Menu > Options > Interface > Display and clear the checkmark from Guarantee Frame Rate.

OpenGL Hardware Support – Troubleshooting

The OpenGL rendering used by the Autodesk Navisworks software can take advantage of PCs with graphics cards that support OpenGL. The application automatically takes advantage of hardware support if it is available. However, some graphics card OpenGL drivers are not efficient and can cause operational problems. These problems might include:

- The model does not load.
- There is excessive drop-out.
- The window freezes or software closes down.

If you have these problems, toggle off Hardware Acceleration. To toggle off Hardware Acceleration, click Application Menu > Options > Interface > Display and clear the checkmark from Hardware Acceleration.

Exercise: Reset the Workspace and Default Options

If you are currently working in a training class environment, it is possible that your computer was used for a previous Autodesk Navisworks training class. This training guide continually has you modify the environment and the Autodesk Navisworks default options. Once set, the settings are maintained every time you launch the Autodesk Navisworks software. The intent of this exercise is to reset the defaults so that you can progress through the class using the default installation condition.

1. Select the View tab. In the Workspace panel, expand Load Workspace and select More Workspaces from the drop-down menu.

2. Browse to and open *C:\Navisworks 2017 Essentials Class Files\Navisworks Default Settings\ Default Workspace.xml.* This file was created for you to reset the workspace if a previous Autodesk Navisworks class was taught on your current computer.

3. Click Application Menu > Options. The Options Editor displays. Customization of the Autodesk Navisworks options are done in this dialog box. To reset all of the options to the default values you can individually go through each category and select Default. Alternatively, you can import a presaved options file.

4. In the Options Editor dialog box, click Import. Browse to and open *C:\Navisworks 2017 Essentials Class Files\Navisworks Default Settings\Default Options.xml.* Click OK to close the Options Editor.

Exercise: (C) Opening, Appending, Importing, and Navigating Navisworks Files

Opening and Adding Files to a Project

In this section of the exercise, you will open a project and append files to the existing sheet. In addition, using the Sheet Browser you will add additional sheets to the project.

1. Click Open 📁 on the Quick Access Toolbar and open *C:\Navisworks 2017 Essentials Class Files\Training\Examples\Bath_City\central.nwd*.

2. On the Home tab in the Project panel, click Append 📄 and select the following files from the *Bath_City* folder: *east.nwd, north.nwd, south.nwd,* and *west.nwd*. Click Open.

3. On the View tab in the Workspace panel, expand the Windows drop-down list. Select Sheet Browser and Selection Tree to display them, if not already displayed. In the Sheet Browser, click Import Sheets & Models 📑. In the Insert From File dialog box, press and hold CTRL and select the following files from the *Bath_City* folder: *east.nwd*, *north.nwd*, *south.nwd*, and *west.nwd*. Click Open.

4. On the Status bar, click ▷ to progress to the next sheet in the project. Continue to navigate through the files to see that all of the four files have been inserted as separate sheets and the first sheet contains the appended design with all files together.

5. Return to page 1, the sheet with the appended data.

Navigate a Project

In this section of the exercise, you will use the available navigation tools to manipulate and review a project.

1. In the Navigation bar, select ▭▾ associated with the Zoom command. Click Zoom All to obtain an overall view of the model. The button on the Navigation bar changes to 🔍 (Zoom All) and stays active until another one is selected.

2. Select ▭▾ again and click Zoom Window. In the Scene view, draw a box around an area on the model to zoom into this area. Continue to use the Zoom Window command to zoom as required. Press and hold the middle mouse button to pan the model, as required, while remaining in the Zoom Window command.

3. Click Walk 👣 on the Navigation bar to activate walk mode. Select ▭▾ under the Walk tool and select Gravity. Press and hold the middle mouse button and drag mouse downwards. With Gravity enabled you will immediately set yourself to a street level view when you start walking. Scroll the middle-mouse button to tilt head in the walk mode and use left mouse button to walk through the scene.

4. Select the Viewpoint tab. On the Camera panel, click Show Tilt Bar ⬚ (if it is not already displayed). Use the Tilt Camera slide bar to alter the line of view. Click Show Tilt Bar ⬚ to toggle off the Tilt bar. This is equivalent to scrolling the middle-mouse button when in Walk mode.

5. Press and hold the middle mouse button while moving up or down to pan the camera up or down. Press and hold the left mouse button while moving left and right to rotate. (For a two button mouse, use CTRL along with the left mouse button to pan up or down.)

6. Click Look Around ⬚ on the Navigation bar and drag the left mouse button to turn the camera around on the spot. This can be useful when in a narrow alley or road.

7. Select the Home tab. On the Select & Search panel, click Select ⬚ to select an object in the scene. In the Select Tree window, expand the central file and select the abbey from the Selection Tree.

    Tip: For more information on the Select tool, refer to the Selection Tree and Selecting Objects Lesson.

8. In the Navigation bar, click Zoom Selected in the zoom drop-down menu to zoom to the abbey. Press ESC to clear the selection.

9. In the Navigation bar, click Orbit ⬚ and press and hold the left mouse button to look around the model. Select ⬚ under the Orbit command and use the other Orbit options. Free Orbit rotates the model around the focal point in any direction and Constrained Orbit spins the model around the up vector as if it was on a turn table.

    Tip: To reset the pivot point in the scene, press and hold CTRL while selecting a new location with the left mouse button.

10. In the Navigation bar, select ⬚ associated with the Walk command and click Fly ⬚. Press and hold the left or middle mouse buttons to fly around and through the scene. The middle mouse button tilts the camera and the left mouse button rotates it. As you are flying through a scene, press and hold SHIFT to increase the speed. (If using a two button mouse you can press and hold CTRL to tilt.)

11. Select the Viewpoint tab. In the Realism ⬚ drop-down menu, click Third Person to see a 3D representation of yourself (an avatar) flying through the scene.

12. Change back to the Walk ⬚ command to see the avatar walk about the scene. In the Realism ⬚ drop-down menu, click Collision to prevent movement through objects (for example, walking through walls) and click Gravity to experience a gravitational effect when walking (e.g., pulled downwards), if not already selected. You can ascend and descend stairs and slopes.

    Tip: The Gravity option is only available with the Walk ⬚ command active.

13. In the Realism 🧍 drop-down menu, click Crouch to automatically crouch under an item in the scene that the avatar cannot normally walk under and would otherwise be in collision with.

> **Tip:** The avatar settings can be adjusted. To change the settings for the current session, select the Viewpoint tab, and on the Save, Load & Playback panel, click Edit Current Viewpoint 🖼 and select Settings in the Collision area. Under Third Person, select Enable, then select Avatar (type), and the Angle and Distance if required.

Change and Observe Display Settings

In this section of the exercise, you will make changes to the display settings and compare performance when navigating the model.

1. Select the Home tab. In the Project panel, click File Options 🖵 and select the Speed tab. Change the frame rate to 1 fps. Click OK.

2. Navigate around at this low frame rate setting and then at a high setting (60 fps) to observe the different effects. Reset to (6 fps), then navigate and observe the effect.

3. Click Application Menu 🅽 > Options > Interface > Display and clear the checkmark from Guarantee Frame Rate. Click OK. Navigate and observe effect.

4. Toggle Guarantee Frame Rate back on again.

Make Items Required

In this section of the exercise, you will mark required items in the project and compare performance when navigating the model.

Note: There might not be any noticeable difference if performed on a high performance computer.

1. In the Standard view of the Selection Tree, select *abbey.dwg*.

2. On the Home tab in the Visibility panel, click Require 🔒 to make the selected object required. Then press ESC to clear selection from the items.

> While you navigate around the model, the abbey will remain visible even though other objects might not be drawn.

3. In the Selection Tree, select *abbey.dwg* again. Click Require 🔒 to make the abbey unrequired.

4. Navigate around the model. There might be some drop-out of the abbey and other parts of the scene.

5. Close the file without saving.

Exercise: (P) Opening, Appending, Importing, and Navigating Navisworks Files

Opening and Adding Files to a Project

In this section of the exercise, you will open a project and append files to the existing sheet. In addition, using the Sheet Browser you will add additional sheets to the project.

1. Click Open 📂 on the Quick Access Toolbar and open *C:\Navisworks 2017 Essentials Class Files\Training\Examples\Clash.nwd*.

    Note: If prompted, do no save changes to any open files.

2. On the Home tab in the Project panel, click Append 🗋 and select the following file from the *Examples* folder: *Clash2.nwd*. Click Open. In this situation the two files were appended to compare changes made to the design, so they lie on top of one another.

    Alternatively, you can import each of these files as separate sheets/models into the current file using the Sheet Browser.

3. On the View tab in the Workspace panel, expand the Windows drop-down list. Select Sheet Browser to display it, if not already displayed. In the Sheet Browser, click Import Sheets and

    Models 🗗. In the Insert From File dialog box, select the file *Clash2.nwd* from the *Examples* folder. Click Open.

4. On the Status bar, click ▷ to progress to the next sheet in the project. The first sheet contains the two appended files and the second sheet only contains one file.

5. Return to page 1, the file with the appended data.

Navigate a Project

In this section of the exercise, you will open a larger model and use the available navigation tools to manipulate and review a project.

1. Click Open 📂 on the Quick Access Toolbar and open *C:\Navisworks 2017 Essentials Class Files\Training\Examples\Heating Plant.nwd*. Do not save the changes to the previous project.

2. In the Navigation bar, select ▾ associated with the Zoom commands. Click Zoom All to obtain an overall view of the model. The button on the Navigation bar changes to Zoom All

    🔍 and stays active until another one is selected.

3. Select ▾ again and click Zoom Window. In the Scene view, draw a box around an area on the model to zoom into this area.

4. Click Walk 👣 on the Navigation bar to activate walk mode. Scroll the middle-mouse button to tilt head in the walk mode and use left mouse button to walk through the scene.

5. Select the Viewpoint tab. On the Camera panel, click Show Tilt Bar 🎥 (if not already displayed). Use the Tilt Camera slide bar to alter the line of view. Click Show Tilt Bar 🎥 to toggle off the Tilt bar.

6. Press and hold the middle mouse button while moving up or down to pan the camera up or down. Press and hold the left mouse button while moving left and right to rotate. (For a two button mouse, use CTRL along with the left mouse button to pan up or down.)

7. Click Look Around 🔘 on the Navigation bar and drag the left mouse button to turn the camera around on the spot. This can be useful when in a narrow area.

8. Select the Home tab. On the Select & Search panel, click Select ▷ to select an object in the scene. Expand the Heating Plant.nwd file in the Selection Tree and select the red tank (DEAER81|STORAGE81) object.

9. In the Navigation bar, click Zoom Selected in the zoom drop-down menu to zoom to the red tank. Press ESC to clear the selection.

10. In the Navigation bar, click Orbit ⟳ and press and hold the left mouse button to look around the model. Select ▾ under the Orbit command and use the other Orbit options. Free Orbit rotates the model around the focal point in any direction and Constrained Orbit spins the model around the up vector as if it was on a turn table.

    Tip: To reset the pivot point in the scene, press and hold CTRL while selecting a new location with the left mouse button.

11. In the Navigation bar, select ▾ associated with the Walk command and click Fly 🖼. Press and hold the left or middle mouse buttons to fly around and through the scene. The middle mouse button tilts the camera and the left mouse button rotates it. As you are flying through a scene, press and hold SHIFT to increase the speed. (If using a two button mouse, you can press and hold CTRL to tilt.)

12. Select the Viewpoint tab. In the Realism 🚶 drop-down menu, click Third Person to see a 3D representation of yourself (an avatar) flying through the scene.

13. Change back to the Walk 👣 command to see the avatar walk about the scene. In the Realism 🚶 drop-down menu, click Collision to prevent movement through objects (for example, walking through walls) and click Gravity to experience a gravitational effect when walking (e.g., pulled downwards). You can ascend and descend stairs and slopes.

    Tip: The Gravity option is only available when the Walk 👣 command is active.

14.   In the Realism ♟ drop-down menu, click Crouch to automatically crouch under an item in the scene that the avatar cannot normally walk under and would otherwise be in collision with.

Tip: The avatar settings can be adjusted. To change the settings for the current session, select the Viewpoint tab, and on the Save, Load & Playback panel, click Edit Current Viewpoint 🗇 and select Settings in the Collision area. Under Third Person, select Enable, then select Avatar (type), and the Angle and Distance if required.

Change and Observe Display Settings

In this section of the exercise, you will make changes to the display settings and compare performance when navigating the model.

1.   Select the Home tab. In the Project panel, click File Options 🗇 and select the Speed tab. Change the frame rate to 1 fps. Click OK.

2.   Navigate around at this low frame rate setting and then at a high setting (60 fps) to observe the different effects. Reset to (6 fps), and then navigate and observe the effect.

3.   Click Application Menu 🅽 > Options > Interface > Display and clear the checkmark from Guarantee Frame Rate. Click OK. Navigate and observe the effect.

4.   Toggle Guarantee Frame Rate on again.

Make Items Required

In this section of the exercise, you will mark required items in the project and compare performance when navigating the model.

Note: There might not be a noticeable difference if performed on a high performance computer.

1.   In the Standard view of the Selection Tree, expand the Heating Plant.nwd file and select all of the objects between 3DSTRUCT|X-REF and EL_31325|3D_HANDRAIL using SHIFT.

2.   On the Home tab in the Visibility panel, click Require 🔒 to make the selected objects required. Then press ESC to clear selection from the items.

While you navigate around the model, the required items will remain visible even though other objects might not be drawn.

3.   In the Selection Tree, expand the Heating Plant.nwd file and select all of the objects between 3DSTRUCT|X-REF and EL_31325|3D_HANDRAIL again. Click Require 🔒 to make them unrequired.

4.   Navigate around the model. There might be some drop-out of the scene.

5.   Close the file without saving.

Exercise: Check and Set File Units

1. Click Open 📂 on the Quick Access Toolbar and open *C:\Navisworks 2017 Essentials Class Files\Training\Examples\Bath_City\center01.dxf* and *center02.dxf*.

    Tip: You will need to change the File of type to .DXF files.

2. On the ViewCube, select the Left face to reorient the model.

3. In the Selection Tree, expand *center01.dxf* and Door-C. Select the first instance of C1DOOR6. It highlights in blue.

4. In the Navigation bar, click Zoom Selected. If the Zoom Selected command is not displayed on the Navigation bar, select ▼ below the currently active zoom option and select Zoom Selected from the drop-down menu.

5. Press and hold the CTRL key and select the thin white frame surrounding the door.

6. Select the Review tab. In the Measure panel, expand the Measure command and click Point to Point 📏.

7. Select a point at the left of the door and a second point at the right of the door, to measure its width (include the white frame). The door should be approximately one meter wide, but the distance between the two points is only 0.001 meters.

    The reason for this error is the default unit settings for DXF files are set incorrectly for this model.

    Tip: Once a measure tool is selected, it will remain in this mode until another Navigation Mode is selected. If measuring an object that is larger than the current Autodesk Navisworks view, select the first point, then navigate to another part of the model, and select the next point selection.

8. In the Measure panel, click Clear 📏 to remove the measure lines from the view.

9. In the Selection Tree, right-click *center01.dxf*, and select Units and Transform. The file is currently set to Millimeters; that is why the door was only 0.001 meters wide.

10. In the Units and Transform dialog box, change the Units option to Meters. Click OK.

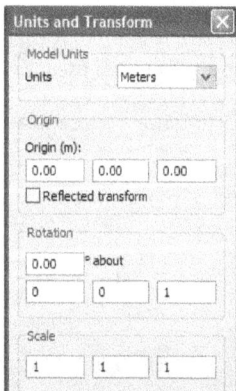

11. In the Selection Tree, right-click *center02.dxf* and follow the same steps as above to change its File Units to Meters.

Taking these steps has changed the model units from millimeters to meters (1 model unit now equals 1 meter). The model will no longer be in view, as it has effectively been scaled by 1000.

12. On the Navigator bar, select [⌄] below the currently active zoom option and select Zoom All to view the model again. Select the door again in the Selection Tree and use Zoom Select again

to zoom in on the door. On the Home tab. in the Select & Search panel, ensure that ⌖ is active. Select the thin frame around the door again.

Note: The selection of the door and the frame are not required for measuring. It was done to highlight the items for easier measurement.

13. Measure the width of the door again. It should measure approximately 1 meter, which is correct.

14. In the Measure panel, click Clear ✖ to remove the measure lines from the view.

15. If appending CAD files or importing models/sheets from a variety of formats, carry out the above check for each format and set the default units accordingly for each file format.

16. The remaining files to be appended in this example were all modeled in meters. Set all defaults to Meters so that all files will be read correctly.

17. Click Application Menu [N] > Options. In the Options Editor, expand File Readers, and click DWG/DXF. In Default Decimal Units, change the default to Meters.

18. In the File Readers section, select 3DS. In Default Units, verify the units are set to Meters and change the default to Meters, if not. Click OK.

19. Select the Home tab. In the Project panel click Append ⬜. Press and hold CTRL and select the *center03.3ds*, *center04.3ds*, and *center05.3ds* 3D Max files. Click Open.

Tip: You might need to change the File of type to .3DS files in the directory.

Tip: The Selection Tree lists each of the files opened/appended into the scene. Once a file has been appended and is no longer required, you can do either of the following:

- In the Selection Tree, right-click the file and select Hide, or select the file and click Hide in the Visibility panel on the Home tab. The file will be hidden (but retained). It can be displayed by selecting Hide again, either on the shortcut menu or on the Ribbon. The Unhide All option on the Visibility panel can also be used to unhide multiple files at one time.

- In the Selection Tree, right-click the file and click Delete. The file will be permanently deleted from the scene. (It can be re-appended if required.) **Note:** There is no Delete command available on the Ribbon.

20. Append ⬜ the *center06 - center16.dwg* and *abbey.dwg* Architectural Desktop (DWG) files (12 files).

21. Hover the cursor over the View Cube in the top right corner of the Scene View. Once the View Cube is active, Home 🏠 is displayed. Click Home 🏠 to return the model to its default orientation and zoom level to view the entire Bath City Center file.

22. Close the file without saving.

Lesson: Publishing, Merging, Refreshing, and Emailing Files

Overview

This lesson describes how to save opened files of multiple formats into a single Autodesk Navisworks file. It also introduces you to the purpose of the file formats and how to refresh and merge files.

Objectives

After completing this lesson, you will be able to:

- Publish files as NWD files.
- Merge similar NWF files into one file without duplication.
- Refresh files that have been updated in source CAD software.
- Use the Autodesk Navisworks software to send models through email.

Sharing Data

Publishing an NWD File

With Autodesk Navisworks Publisher, you can take a "snapshot" of the model at any time. This can then be issued to other members of the design team, who might not be CAD users, but who need to view the 3D model. NWD files can be viewed in the Autodesk Navisworks software for full design review, or with the Autodesk Navisworks Freedom free viewer for a simple real-time walkthrough.

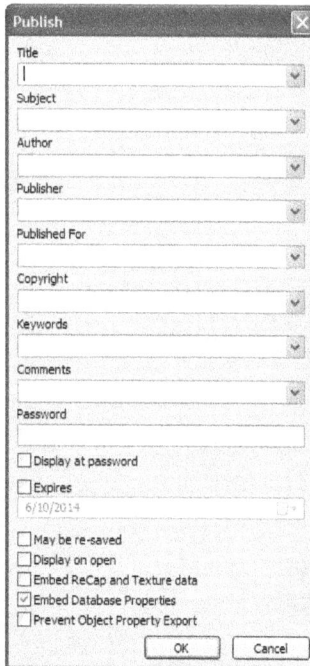

There is also the option for entering publication information that is saved with the file. This includes password protection and file expiration options.

Procedure: To Publish an NWD File

1. In the Autodesk Navisworks software, open the file that is to be published.

2. Click Application Menu > Publish or select the Output tab and click NWD on the Publish panel.

3. In the Publish dialog box, enter information in the Title, Subject, Author, Publisher, Published For, Copyright, Keywords, and Comments fields, as required. The additional commands described below can also be set, as required.

4. Click OK.

5. In the Save As window, browse to the required location, and enter a filename. (The name must be different if saved in the same folder as the original.) Click Save.

Publish Dialog Box Options

Option	Description
Password	Sets up a password if the file is to be protected and only accessed by certain personnel. (The password needs to be passed to those people.) By default, this dialog box, including the entered information, is not displayed until after the password has been entered and accepted. (See also Display on open option.)
Display at password	Specifies that the Publish dialog box, including the entered information, is to be displayed with the Password field.
Expires	Specifies an expiration date for the file. This can prevent the old files being used. After the expiration date is passed, the file cannot be opened.
May be re-saved	Enables further changes to be made to a file. By default, a published file cannot be re-saved. This prevents changes being added to this publication.
Display on open	Specifies that the Publish dialog box is displayed when the file is opened. By default, the Publish dialog box, with entered information, is not displayed unless the Display at Password box or the Display on open box is checked.
Embed ReCap and Texture data	Enables externally referenced ReCap and texture files to be embedded in the one project file. If textures have been added to the model, these can be embedded in the file or saved as separate files (in the same folder). You can choose how the ReCap files get embedded using the Options Editor. The benefits of using this option is that there is only one published project file, and the ReCap and texture files are included and benefit from password protection during publishing.
Embed Database Properties	Enables all the linked database properties to be embedded in the project file. This feature enables any object properties accessed via an external database to be embedded in the NWD as normal properties. This adds value to database linkage and NWD publishing, giving a quick and easy way of getting a large amount of database data into the model, which is then viewable by all.
Prevent Object Property Export	Prevents inclusion of the object properties from any native CAD package in the published file. This is intended primarily for protection of intellectual property.

Merging NWF Files

An NWD file might be sent by a project coordinator to multiple parties for review. Each party adds review markups and data to the model, which might include any combination of viewpoints, comments, redlines, Clash Detective results, TimeLiner schedules, Presenter materials, etc.

Each party can save their review session as an NWF file that references the original NWD file. The project coordinator can then merge all of the NWF files into a single file, duplicating neither the NWD file (referenced by all NWFs) nor any other review markup that is common to all NWFs.

> The Interface > Appending and Merging category in the Options Editor enables you to control how files with multiple sheets are merged to a file. The options include never allowing the remaining sheets to be merged, always allowing them to be merged, or to be prompted whether they are to be merged or not.

Merging TimeLiner Data

If two or more merged files contain TimeLiner data, limited merging can be done with this data. This can depend on various situations (for example, if the data sets are identical and if the data contains the same primary link).

For more information, see Chapter 3, TimeLiner.

Refreshing Files

When working on files in the Autodesk Navisworks software, others might be working on the linked CAD files. To ensure that the data being reviewed is current, the Autodesk Navisworks software provides a refresh function to reload any files that have been modified since commencing the review session.

- To refresh the data, click Refresh in the Project Panel on the Home tab.

This feature does not reload all of the files previously loaded, only those modified since last opening them.

Emailing Files

The Autodesk Navisworks software is also a communication tool. The Send by Email command makes it easy to send the current model along with its viewpoints by email. It uses the available mail exchange service. Sending a file as mail saves the current working file to ensure that the latest review is sent.

Procedure: To send a file by email

- Click Application Menu > Send by Email or select the Output tab and click Send by Email on the Send panel. This accesses available email software and sends the current file as an email attachment.

Receiving Files by Email

If an NWF file is received, the application searches for the appended files first using the absolute path with which the sender originally saved the file. This is useful if a team is on a local network and the files can be found using the Universal Naming Convention (UNC). Otherwise, a team not sharing a server can organize a project using the same file hierarchy and drive letter, and the Autodesk Navisworks software can find the files this way.

If the application is unable to find the files, then the recipient can save the attached NWF in a directory where all the appended files are located. The NWF can then look for these files relative to its own location.

This way, a whole sub-directory from the project's directory can be moved to a completely new location. Save the NWF file in this new place; it can search for the files from here.

Exercise: (C) Merging NWF Files

1. Open *C:\Navisworks 2017 Essentials Class Files\Training\Examples\Merge\gatehouse.nwd*.

2. To display the Saved Viewpoints window, if it is not visible, select the Viewpoint tab and select ⍟ in the Save, Load & Playback panel's title bar. Notice the available viewpoints that are listed.

   Tip: You can also open the Saved Viewpoints window by selecting the View tab, expanding the Windows option, and enabling Saved Viewpoints.

3. Select the Home tab. In the Project panel, expand the Append command and click Merge . Merge the file *Gatehouse_Design_Review.nwf* from the current directory.

   Notice that the *Gatehouse.nwd* file is not duplicated (as it would be if it had been appended). However, two new viewpoints have been added, including redlines and comments.

4. Close the file without saving.

Exercise: (P) Merging NWF Files

1. Open *C:\Navisworks 2017 Essentials Class Files\Training\Examples\Merge\heatingplant.nwd*.

2. If the Saved Viewpoints window is not displayed, select the Viewpoint tab and select ⬞ in the Save, Load & Playback panel's title bar. Notice that there are no viewpoints available.

   Tip: You can also open the Saved Viewpoints window by selecting the View tab, expanding the Windows option, and enabling Saved Viewpoints.

3. Select the Home tab. In the Project panel, expand the Append command and select Merge ⬞. Merge the file *Heatingplant_Presenter_Review.nwf* from the current directory.

   Notice that the *heatingplant.nwd* file is not duplicated (as it would be if it had been appended). However, a new viewpoint has been added that includes materials and lighting.

4. Select the Home tab. In the Project panel, expand the Append command and click Merge ⬞. Merge the file *Heatingplant_Design_Review.nwf* from the current directory.

   Notice the *heatingplant.nwd* file is not duplicated. However, additional design review viewpoints have been added.

5. Close the file without saving.

Exercise: Publish an NWD File

1. Open *C:\Navisworks 2017 Essentials Class Files\Training\Examples\Boiler Room\ Boiler Room_Publish.nwd*.

2. At the top of the Selection Tree, select Properties in the drop-down list. The *AutoCAD* and *Door Style* property folders are from the CAD application.

3. Select the Output tab and click NWD on the Publish panel or click Application Menu > Publish.

4. In the Publish dialog box, enter some information in the available fields.

5. Enter a password.

6. Add a checkmark to the following options

   - May be re-saved
   - Display on open
   - Embed ReCap and Texture Data
   - Prevent Object Property Export

7. Click OK. Enter the password again to confirm it, if you added a password.

8. In the Save As dialog box, save the file as **Desktop\Temp\Boiler Room_Published1.nwd**.

   Tip: Create the *\Temp* folder on your desktop to save temporary Class Files.

9. Close the current file and close the Autodesk Navisworks software. If you open the published file without restarting the Autodesk Navisworks software, you are not prompted for the password.

10. Launch the Autodesk Navisworks software and open the published file *Temp\Boiler Room_Published1.nwd*.

11. Enter the password, and click OK.

    Notice that the Publish dialog box is displayed with the information previously entered. This is because the Display on open option was selected when the file was published.

12. Click OK to open the file.

13. At the top of the Selection Tree, click Properties in the drop-down list, if not already active.

    Notice that the *AutoCAD* and *Door Style* property folders that are from the CAD application are not displayed. This is because the Embed Database Properties was not selected when published.

14. Open *C:\Navisworks 2017 Essentials Class Files\Training\Examples\Boiler Room\ Boiler Room_Publish.nwd*.

15. Select the Output tab and click NWD on the Publish panel or click Application Menu > Publish.

16. The drop-down menus in each field retain the previous information that you entered. Select any of the values as required and enter a password.

17. Add a checkmark to the following options:
    - Display at password
    - Embed Database Properties

18. Remove the checkmark from the following options, if they were retained from the previous publication:
    - May be re-saved
    - Display on open
    - Embed ReCap and Texture data
    - Prevent Object Property Export

19. Click OK. Enter the password again to confirm it, if you added a password.

20. In the Save As dialog box, save the file as **Desktop\Temp\Boiler Room_Published2.nwd**.

    Note: With Embed Database Properties selected, it could take a few minutes to extract the required data from the linked database and embed into the project file prior to completing the save operation.

21. Close the current file and close the Autodesk Navisworks software.

22. Open the file *Temp\Boiler RoomPublished2.nwd*.

23. Enter the password.

Notice that the *AutoCAD* and *Door Style* property folders that are from the CAD application are displayed in the Properties list.

Note: In order to see any folders that reference linked data, you must first link to its external database. For more information, refer to the Database Support (Data Tools) in the Appendix. Once linked you will have access to any folders that contained data originally linked from an external database if the Embed Database Properties option was selected.

24. Select the Output tab and click NWD on the Publish panel or click Application Menu > Publish.

25. In the Publish dialog box, click OK.

26. In the Save As dialog box, select a location and new name for the file. Click Save.

The file is prevented from re-saving because the May be re-saved option was not checked when previously published. You are now prevented from publishing this file. Use caution when disabling this option, because once the May be re-saved option is cleared the file cannot be published again.

27. Close the file without saving.

Lesson: Selection Tree and Selecting Objects

Overview

This lesson describes how to view items in the Selection Tree structure for files opened in the Autodesk Navisworks software. It also introduces you to the selection options, and how to sort the order of items in the Selection Tree.

Objectives

After completing this lesson, you will be able to:

- Open and view the Selection Tree and re-order and expand the structure as required.
- Change the resolution of the selection tool to select items or groups of items.

View the Selection Tree

As a model is opened, the filename is added to the Selection Tree window. The model's hierarchical structure can be expanded, revealing the files, layers, and objects used to build the model. This hierarchical structure is used to identify object specific paths (a unique path through the model data from the root partition, the filename, to a particular object).

- To display the Selection Tree window if it is not visible, select the Home tab, and on the Select & Search panel, enable Selection Tree 📇. Alternatively, you can control the Selection Tree's display on the View tab by expanding the Windows option, and enabling Selection Tree.

- A drop-down list is available at the top of the Selection Tree to provide access to alternate views. These other views include a compact view, properties view, and sets. Compact displays a simplified version of the hierarchy based on your customization of the level of complexity in the Options Editor. The Properties option displays the hierarchy based on the items' properties. The Sets option displays a list of selection and search sets.

Selection Tree Sorting

When working on large projects with many reference files, it can be difficult to locate the required file at a glance. With sorting, you can reorganize the Selection Tree alphanumerically, making it much easier to look for specific files.

Procedure: To Sort the Selection Tree

1.   Right-click on any item in the Selection Tree and select Scene > Sort.

      Note: A message is displayed indicating that this action cannot be undone.

2.   Click Yes to sort the Selection Tree. The Selection Tree is now organized alphanumerically.

Selecting an Object

There are two selection tools available on the Home tab in the Select & Search panel: Select and

Select Box . The use of these two tools controls the way you select geometry. Using either technique, you can clear any selection set by pressing the Esc key.

Select Tool

The Select tool ( ) enables you to select items in the Scene View with a single mouse click. Once an item is selected, its properties are shown in the Properties window.

Select Box Tool

The Select Box tool ( ) enables you to select multiple items in the model by using the left mouse button to drag a rectangular box around the area you want to make your current selection. All items completely within the box are selected. Additional controls include:

▪   Holding the Shift key while dragging the box to select all items that intersect the box and all items that are in the box.

▪   Pressing and holding the CTRL key to select multiple items by dragging multiple boxes in the Scene View.

> Holding the Space Bar when using the Select tool ( )switches the selection tool to the Select Box tool. When you release the space bar the selection tool reverts to the Select tool, retaining any selections that have been made. The reverse is not true when using the Select Box tool. To return to the Select tool you must select the option on the ribbon. All objects enclosed in the sketched box are selected.

The following are some key points about selection:

- Selecting an object in the Selection Tree also highlights it in the Scene View. Alternatively, selecting an object in the Scene View using the Selection tool ⬚ also highlights it in the Selection Tree.
- When making a selection, there is a default pick radius that is used. This value defines the distance from an item you have to be for it to be selected. To customize this value, click Application Menu

  ⬚ > Options > Interface > Selection and enter a pick radius. The valid values are between 1 and 9. This is useful when you select lines and points.

Selection Resolution (Level)

When an item in the scene is selected using the Selection tool ⬚, individual geometry or a group of geometry might be selected depending on the setting of the Selection Resolution.

Procedure: To Change the Selection Resolution using the Options Editor

1. To change the setting of the selection resolution, click Application Menu ⬚ > Options > Interface > Selection > Resolution.

2. Select the required option, and then click OK.

   Note: Any item in the Selection Tree can be selected regardless of the Selection Resolution setting for the Selection tool.

Procedure: To Change the Selection Resolution using the Ribbon

1. To change the setting of the selection resolution, expand the Select & Search panel on the Home tab and select a resolution setting from the Selection Resolution drop-down menu.

2. Select the required option.

   Note: Any item in the Selection Tree can be selected regardless of the Selection Resolution setting for the Selection tool. The Selection Resolution only affects selections made in the Scene View.

   Tip: Holding the Shift key while selecting items in the Scene View cycles through the selection resolution, enabling you to get more specific with your selection. The cycling does not affect the actual model setting that has been specified. This permits for a temporary overwrite of the setting.

The available selection options are:

- **File** – Selects the appended portion of the selected model.
- **Layer** – Selects all objects in a layer.
- **First Object** – Selects the first object in the path that is not a layer.
- **Last Unique** – Selects the most specific object (furthest along the path) that is unique (not multiple instanced).
- **Last Object** – Selects the most specific item (furthest along the Selection Tree path) that is marked as a composite object. If no composite object is found, the geometry is selected.
- **Geometry** – Selects the last object in the path (most specific, might be multiple instanced).

Selection Inspector Window

The Selection Inspector window provides a list of all selected objects in one convenient location. Additionally, the Quick Properties associated with each of the selected objects are also displayed. To open the Selection Inspector window, select the Home tab, and on the Select & Search panel, enable Selection Inspector ⊞ .

Using the options in the Selection Inspector window you can do any of the following:

- Zoom to a selected item in the list by selecting ▷ .

- Remove a selected item from the list by selecting ⊠ .

- Save a list of selections as a single selection set by selecting Save Selection. The saved selection is added to the Sets window.

- Export the entire list of selections by selecting Export CSV ⊞ .

> 💡 You must clear ⊠ objects if you want to exclude any of the selections in the exported CSV file.

- Modify the Quick Properties definition by selecting Quick Property Definitions. This option accesses the Options Editor to customize the Quick Property display. (See Lesson: Object Properties for more information on Quick Properties.)

Exercise: (C) Setting Selection Resolution and Sorting Structures

1.   Open the file *C:\Navisworks 2017 Essentials Class Files\Training\Examples\KLM\ Struct.nwf*.

2.   In the Selection Tree, select *roof.dxf* in the Standard list. The roof components are highlighted in the scene.

3.   In the Selection Tree, expand *roof.dxf* and select A216, which is highlighted in the scene.

4.   Select ⬛ below the Zoom command in the Navigation Bar and click Zoom Selected, if it is not already the active command, to view the selected item.

5.   Expand the A216 and select various 3D solid objects. They are individually highlighted in the scene.

6.   Expand the Select & Search panel on the Home tab and select the Geometry resolution setting from the Selection Resolution drop-down menu.

7.   Click Select ⬚ on the Home tab. In the scene, click where the 3D items were previously selected. You should be able to select individual 3D items in the scene the same as when selected in the Selection Tree.

8.   Expand the Select & Search panel on the Home tab again and select the Layer Selection Resolution setting.

9.   Click Select ⬚. In the scene, click where the 3D items were previously selected. The whole layer that the 3D items belong to is selected (highlighted).

10.   Collapse the *roof.dxf* file hierarchy in the Selection Tree so that only the layers are visible (≋). Notice that there is no alphanumerical order to the Selection Tree layers.

11.   Right-click on any Layer in the Selection Tree and select Scene > Sort.

12.   Click Yes to confirm that you will not be able to undo this operation. The Selection Tree is now organized.

13.   Close the file without saving.

Exercise: (P): Setting Selection Resolution and Sorting Structures

1. Open the file *C:\Navisworks 2017 Essentials Class Files\Training\Examples\Boiler Room\Boiler Room_Sort.nwf*.

2. In the Selection Tree, expand *Meadowgate – Services – Roof.nwd*, then select Packaged Plantroom no Foundation\Z-BOILER. The boiler components are highlighted in the scene.

3. Select [⬛▾] below the Zoom command in the Navigation Bar and click Zoom Selected, if it is not already the active command, to view the selected item.

4. In the Selection Tree, fully expand Packaged Plantroom no Foundation\Z-BOILER until the 3D solid geometry files are displayed.

5. Select various 3D solid objects. They are individually highlighted in the scene.

6. Expand the Select & Search panel on the Home tab and select the Geometry resolution setting from the Selection Resolution drop-down menu.

7. Click Select ⤺ on the Home tab. In the scene, click where the 3D items were previously selected. You should be able to select individual 3D items in the scene the same as when selected in the Selection Tree.

8. Expand the Select & Search panel on the Home tab again and select the Layer Selection Resolution setting.

9. Click Select ⤺. In the scene, click where the 3D items were previously selected.

   The whole layer that the 3D items belong is highlighted.

10. Collapse the *Meadowgate – Services – Roof.nwd* file hierarchy in the Selection Tree so that only the layers are visible. Notice there is no alphanumerical order to the Selection Tree layers.

11. Right-click on any Layer in the Selection Tree and select Scene > Sort.

12. Click Yes to confirm that you will not be able to undo this operation. The Selection Tree is now organized.

13. Close the file without saving.

3D Model Review

In this chapter you learn how to review a 3D model using the navigation and manipulation tools, create and mark up views, add comments, create animations, and communicate this information to other stake holders.

Objectives

After completing this chapter, you will be able to:

- Hide selected items or items not selected from view and make selected items always be displayed.
- Change the material appearance of objects.
- Open and view available object properties and add custom object properties.
- Open, view, and customize Quick Properties.
- Use the measuring tools to make linear, angular, and area measurements and visually move an object.
- Select objects, save as a selection set, and organize in folders.
- Use the Find tool to find objects that meet a criteria and save as a search set.
- Create, organize, edit, and export viewpoints, and prepare a viewpoint for navigation purposes.
- Add comments to viewpoints, animations, selection sets, and clashes.
- Markup a viewpoint using the Redline tools and create a Tagged comment.
- Record an interactive animation, then edit, and export it.
- Create an animation from viewpoints using automatic transitions.
- Create sectioned views from various planes and boxes.
- Link two section planes and set a sectioning range limit.
- Add links and define how they are displayed in the scene.
- Append two files, use the Compare tool to check for differences, and view the results.
- Select the lighting and rendering to achieve the required results.
- Select an object in the Autodesk Navisworks software, then use SwitchBack to view and edit the object in the original application.

Lesson: Hiding Objects and Overriding Materials

Overview

This lesson describes how to hide selected items or items that are not selected from view. It also introduces you to overriding object materials.

Objectives

After completing this lesson, you will be able to:

- Hide selected items or items not selected from view and make selected items always be displayed.
- Change the material appearance of objects.

Hiding Objects

The Autodesk Navisworks software provides tools that can be used to hide and display objects or groups of objects. This is useful when reviewing specific objects without needing to navigate around all the other objects in the model. All of these tools are located on the Home tab, in the Visibility panel of the Ribbon.

- Use Hide Unselected to hide all objects except the objects that have been selected.

- Use Hide to hide all selected objects.

- Use Require to ensure the selected objects are always displayed (not affected by drop-out).

> The Require command is also useful when navigating the model as the Autodesk Navisworks software ensures the objects that are set as Required are not affected by drop-out.

> When an item is selected in the Scene View, the Item Tools contextual tab displays. This tab provides additional options for working with the selected item. This includes hiding it, setting it as required, or holding it. The Hold option is only available on the Item Tools tab and enables you to set the selected item so that it remains stationary relative to other items in the scene when moved (orbit).

Overriding Object Materials

For models with unsupported materials and textures, an object is displayed in its wireframe color.

With the Autodesk Navisworks software, you can apply texture materials to objects in the scene. With any of the products, you can override the color and transparency of an object.

Procedure: To Override an Object's Color or Transparency

1. Select the item(s) to be changed.

2. Right-click on any of the selected items in the Selection Tree and click Override Item > Override Color. Select the required color. Click OK.

   Tip: Alternatively, you can also override a selected item's color on the Item Tools context-sensitive tab, by assigning a new color in the Appearance panel.

3. Press ESC to clear selection on the item(s) and view changes.

4. Right-click on any of the selected items in the Selection Tree and click Override Item > Override Transparency. In the Override Transparency dialog box, move the slider towards Opaque or Transparent as required. Click OK.

   Tip: Alternatively, you can also override a selected item's transparency on the Item Tools context-sensitive tab, by assigning a transparency value in the Appearance panel.

5. Press ESC to clear selection on the item(s) and view changes.

6. To reset all colors and transparencies to those of the original model, expand the Reset All command on the Home tab and click Appearances. Individual items can also be reset by right-clicking them in the Selection Tree and clicking Reset Item > Reset Appearance.

Tip: Alternatively, you can also reset all colors and transparencies on the Item Tools context-sensitive tab, by clicking Reset Appearance on the Appearance panel.

Note: The advantage of being able to reset everything to its original value is for security. Once an NWD file has been published, the issuer can guarantee that it can be returned to exactly the state it was in when published. (No other software can read NWD files and the Autodesk Navisworks software cannot export to any other 3D design file format.)

Exercise: Hide Items & Change Object Color and Transparency

Hide Items

In this section of the exercise, you will use the Hide tool to remove a selected item or all unselected items from display.

1. Open the file *C:\Navisworks 2017 Essentials Class Files\Training\Examples\Snowmobile.nwd*.

2. In the Selection Tree, expand Snowmobile.nwd and select *Rear Suspension-1*.

3. Click Zoom Selected in the Navigation Bar to view the selected item.

4. On the Home tab, click Hide Unselected . All objects in the screen, except the Rear Suspension, are hidden. Click ESC to clear selection.

   The Rear Suspension can be navigated and reviewed without the need to navigate around the other objects in the model.

5. In the Selection Tree, select *Rear Suspension-1* again.

6. Click Hide to hide the Rear Suspension and click Hide again to display it.

   Note: If other commands are used after the Hide or Hide Unselected commands were used, then clicking the command again will not undo the action. To undo the action, click

   Unhide All .

7. Click Unhide All to display all of the hidden items.

Change Object Color and Transparency

In this section of the exercise, you will override the existing color and transparency settings on objects in the mode.

1. To display the Saved Viewpoints window if it is not visible, select the Viewpoint tab and click on the Save, Load & Playback panel's title bar.

   Tip: Alternatively, select the View tab, expand the Windows option, and enable Saved Viewpoints.

2. Select the Dashboard saved viewpoint.

3. Expand the Select & Search panel on the Home tab and select the Geometry resolution setting from the Selection Resolution drop-down menu.

4. Press ESC to ensure that nothing is selected. On the dashboard, select the 4 cyan colored dial center covers, and then hide them by clicking Hide . Click OK to confirm that all instanced objects are hidden, if prompted.

5.   On the dashboard, select the 4 dials in the gauges. There is a center and edge part to each dial, so there are 8 selections in total.

6.   Change the color of the dials to red. Select the Item Tools tab. In the Appearance panel, change the Color to Red.

   Tip: Alternatively, you can also right-click on any of the selected items in the Selection Tree and click Override Item > Override Color. For the Color, select Red. Click OK.

7.   Press ESC to clear the selection of the dials and view the changes.

8.   On the Home tab, click Unhide All to unhide the original dial covers.

9.   Select the dial center covers again. Select the Item Tools tab. In the Appearance panel, change the Transparency percentage to 75.

   Tip: Alternatively, you can also right-click on any of the selected items in the Selection Tree and click Override Item > Override Transparency. Slide the bar towards Transparent to change the transparency to 75%. Click OK.

10.   Press ESC to clear selection on the dials covers and view the changes.

   Tip: If there is excessive drop-out, make the dials Required (always displayed). In the Selection Tree, expand the *Snowmobile.nwd* hierarchy and the Hood-2 group. Select the groups: 2 Inch Gauge-1, 5 Inch Gauge-2, 2 Inch Gauge-2, and 5 Inch Gauge-1, then click Require .

11.   Close the file without saving.

Lesson: Object Properties

Overview

This lesson describes how to view object properties that are embedded in the object files or in a linked external database. It also introduces you to creating custom object properties and Quick Properties.

Objectives

After completing this lesson, you will be able to:

- Open and view available object properties and add custom object properties.
- Open, view, and customize Quick Properties.

About Object Properties

The Properties window displays all the properties of a selected item. Properties are categorized (for example, Item and Material) with a tab for each category of the selected item. Whenever a single item is selected, this window is updated to show the properties of that item.

The Autodesk Navisworks software reports different CAD application object properties, such as those from Architectural Desktop, AutoCAD® Civil 3D®, or Autodesk® Revit® (MEP, Structure, and Architecture). Every property has a type associated with it, for example, an item's Name is a string, etc. For example, in AutoCAD Civil 3D you can bring in all the design data used to create a pipe network (inverts, slopes, rim elevation, structure connection names, etc.)

With the DataTools feature (described in Database Support), you can create a link between the stored data in a database and the object properties of the model.

Procedure: To Open and View Object Properties

1. To display the Properties window if it is not visible, select the Home tab, and in the Display

    panel, click Properties [icon]. As an alternate, you can also select the View tab, expand the Windows option, and enable Properties.

2. Select the required item in the scene or on the Selection Tree.

    All available properties for the item are displayed in the Properties window.

    Note: A model or item might not have any property information.

3. In the Properties window, click any available category tab for additional property information.

4. The Properties window is automatically pinned along the right side edge of the Autodesk

    Navisworks window. To set to AutoHide, click [icon] along the top of the Properties window. For

    the Properties window to remain open, click [icon].

Custom Properties

You can add custom properties or add additional property information to existing properties.

You can also add additional property tabs or additional fields to existing (custom) tabs without accessing the original CAD application.

Procedure: To Add a New Custom Property Tab and Property

1. With the Properties window displayed, select the required item in the scene or on the Selection Tree.

2. Right-click in the Properties window. Click Add New User Data tab.

3. Click the new User Data tab.

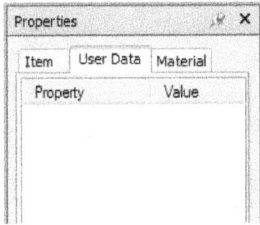

4. Right-click in the Properties window. Click Rename Tab.

5. In the Rename tab area, enter a new name for the tab. Click OK.

6. In the Properties window, click the Renamed tab.

7. Right-click in the Properties window. Click Insert New Property, and then click the following:

    - **String** – If the value is to be a string.
    - **Boolean** – If the value is to be Yes or No.
    - **Float** – If the value is a decimal value, for example 1.234.
    - **Integer** – If the value is a positive whole number (1, 2, 3,...), a negative whole number (-1, -2, -3,...), or zero (0).

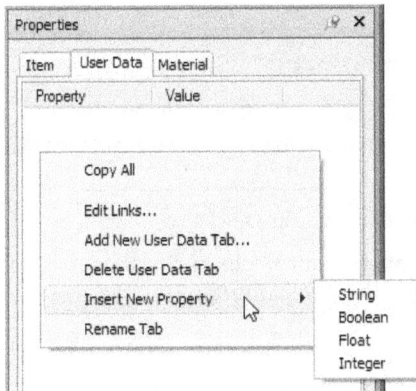

8. Click in the new property field under Property, and enter the name for the property (for example, Department). Press ENTER.

9. Right-click on the new property (Department). Click Edit Property Value.

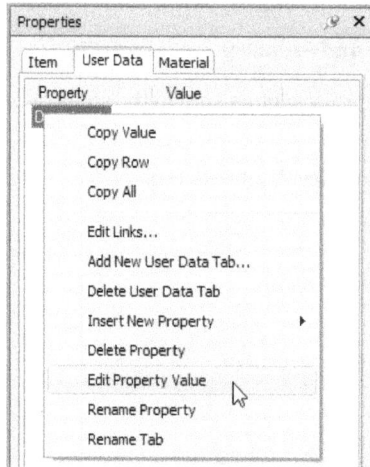

10. In the displayed Enter Property Value area, enter the value associated with this property name (for example, Salaries). Click OK.

11. Repeat the procedure to add additional properties in this custom property tab.

Quick Properties

Quick Property pop up information displays when the cursor is moved over an object, without having to select the item. It is displayed in a tooltip style window. The Quick Property disappears after a few seconds.

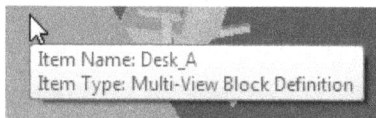

Procedure: To Enable and Customize Quick Properties

1. On the Home tab in the Display panel, click Quick Properties ⊟ to enable the display of Quick Properties in the model.

2. Move the cursor over the required object to display its Quick Property.

   This is a useful way to quickly get information about an object directly in the Scene View. The default information displayed is the name and type of the item, but the actual information displayed can be customized.

3. To control the display of Quick Properties, click Application Menu [▣] > Options > Interface > Quick Properties.

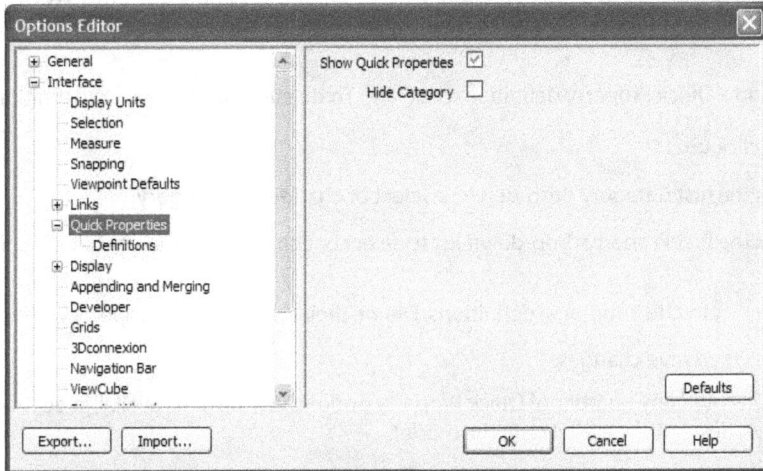

Options Editor

- ⊞ General
- ⊟ Interface
  - Display Units
  - Selection
  - Measure
  - Snapping
  - Viewpoint Defaults
  - ⊞ Links
  - ⊟ Quick Properties
    - Definitions
  - ⊞ Display
  - Appending and Merging
  - Developer
  - Grids
  - 3Dconnexion
  - Navigation Bar
  - ViewCube

Show Quick Properties ☑
Hide Category ☐

Defaults

Export...   Import...   OK   Cancel   Help

4. In the Options Editor, select the Hide Category check box if you do not want to see category names included in the Quick Properties tooltip.

5. In the left pane, expand Quick Properties and click Definitions.

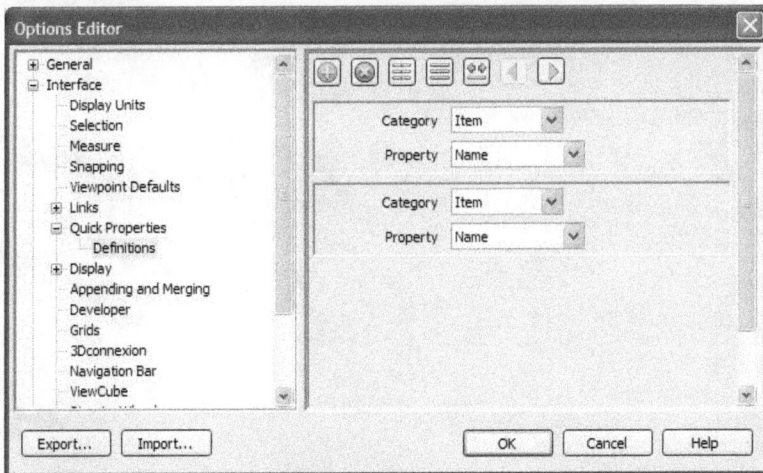

Options Editor

- ⊞ General
- ⊟ Interface
  - Display Units
  - Selection
  - Measure
  - Snapping
  - Viewpoint Defaults
  - ⊞ Links
  - ⊟ Quick Properties
    - Definitions
  - ⊞ Display
  - Appending and Merging
  - Developer
  - Grids
  - 3Dconnexion
  - Navigation Bar
  - ViewCube

Category Item
Property Name

Category Item
Property Name

Export...   Import...   OK   Cancel   Help

6. Choose the way Quick Property definitions are shown in the Options Editor:

- Click Grid View [▦] to display definitions in a tabular format.

- Click List View [▤] to display definitions in a list format.

- Click Records View [▤] to display definitions as records.

7. Use ⬛ and ⬛ to navigate between the definitions. If you selected Records View, this is the only way to move between the records.

    For every Quick Properties definition, you can change Category and Property by selecting an item and then selecting the relevant entry from the drop-down list.

8. To add a Quick Property definition, click ⬛. To delete a Quick Property definition, select it, and click ⬛.

9. Click the first Category drop-down to select or change the category.

10. Click the first Property drop-down list to select or change the property to be displayed.

11. Click ⬛ to add additional definitions. Define their Category and Property values, as required.

12. Click OK to save changes.

    You can add any number of Quick Property options. The options available depend on the properties that are available in the model.

Exercise: Add a New Custom Property Tab and Property

1.   Open the file *C:\Navisworks 2017 Essentials Class Files\Training\Examples\Meadowgate\Meadowgate.nwd*.

2.   Select the Office 2 viewpoint.

3.   On the Home tab, enable Properties ⊞ to display the Properties window.

4.   Expand the Select & Search panel on the Home tab and select the Last Object resolution setting from the Selection Resolution drop-down menu.

5.   Use ESC to clear all existing selections and use Select ⊵ to select any one of the desks.

6.   Right-click in the Properties window. Click Add New User Data Tab.

7.   Click the new User Data tab. Right-click in the Properties window and then click Rename Tab. In the Rename Tab window, enter **Personnel** as the Tab name, then click OK.

8.   Right-click in the Properties window again. Click Insert New Property > String.

9.   Click in the new property field under Property, and enter **Name** for the name for this property. Press ENTER.

10. Right-click the Name property, and then click Edit Property Value.

11. In the displayed Enter Property Value area, enter **David** (the name of a person who might sit at this desk). Click OK.

     This property is now attached to this item and can be saved with the model.

12. Close the file without saving.

     Tip: The custom property and its value might be used in search criteria or Quick Properties, like any other standard properties.

Exercise: (C) Enable and Customize Quick Properties

1. Open the file *C:\Navisworks 2017 Essentials Class Files\Training\Examples\KLM\ KLM.nwd*.

2. In the Selection Tree, expand *KLM.nwd* and select *Struct.nwd*.

3. Click Hide Unselected ⬚ to hide everything other than the building structure. Press ESC to clear selection from everything.

4. Zoom into the model to get a better view of the ends of the blue floor slabs.

5. On the Home tab in the Display panel, click Quick Properties ▭ to toggle on their display.

6. Move the cursor over one of the ends of the blue floor slabs. A Quick Property is displayed showing the Item Name and Item Type.

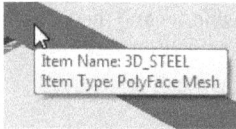

7. To control the display of Quick Properties, click Application Menu ▣ > Options > Interface > Quick Properties > Definitions.

8. In the Options Editor, click ⊕ to add an additional definition.

9. In the Options Editor, in the new definition, (the last entry in the Category drop-down list) select MultiSteel.

10. In the Property drop-down list, select Size.

11. Click OK to save changes.

12. Move the cursor over the edge of the blue floor slab again. This time the Quick Property displays the Item Name, Item Type, and MultiSteel Size properties (if each is available for the item that is hovered over).

13. Close the file without saving.

Exercise: (P) Enable and Customize Quick Properties

1. Open the file *C:\Navisworks 2017 Essentials Class Files\Training\Examples\Boiler Room\Boiler Room_Properties.nwf*.

2. In the Selection Tree, expand *Meadowgate – Services – Roof.nwd*. Select Packaged Plantroom no Foundation\Z-BOILER. The boiler components are highlighted in the scene.

3. Click Hide Unselected to hide everything other than the boiler unit. Press ESC to clear selection from everything.

4. To control the display of Quick Properties, click Application Menu > Options > Interface > Quick Properties > Definitions.

5. In the Options Editor, click to add an additional definition.

6. In the Options Editor, in the new definition click, in the Category drop-down list, select Entity Handle.

7. The Property drop-down list defaults to Value.

8. Click OK to save changes.

9. Expand the Select & Search panel on the Home tab and select the First Object resolution setting from the Selection Resolution drop-down menu.

10. If the Quick Properties are not displayed, on the Home tab in the Display panel, click Quick Properties to toggle on their display.

11. Move the cursor over one of the white boiler housings again. The Quick Property displays the other default properties along with the Entity Handle value.

12. Close the file without saving.

Lesson: Measuring and Moving Objects

Overview

This lesson describes how to use the measuring tools to measure dimensions, angles, and areas of objects. It also introduces you to using the measuring tools to visually move (transform) an object to a different location.

Objective

After completing this lesson, you will be able to:

- Use the measuring tools to make linear, angular, and area measurements and visually move an object.

Measuring Objects

Objects can be measured using the commands on the Review tab.

Procedure: How to Use Measuring Tools

1. Select the Review tab and expand the Measure command.

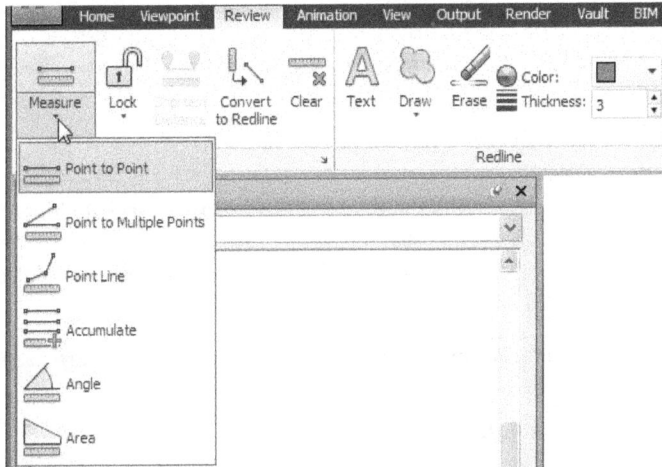

In the expanded Measure command there are six measuring tools that are available for use.

2. Point to Point ⟨icon⟩ measures between two points.

   - Click Point to Point ⟨icon⟩. Then click the start and end points of the distance to be measured. A line is displayed between the two points and the value is displayed on the model.

   - Click Clear ⟨icon⟩ or right-click to remove existing points and select a new base point.

3. Point to Multiple Points ⟨icon⟩ measures between a base and various other points.

   - Click Point to Multiple Points ⟨icon⟩. Then click on the start and first end point to be measured. A line is displayed between the two points and the value is displayed on the model.
   - Click the next end point to be measured. A line is displayed between the base point and the next end point and the value is displayed on the model.
   - Repeat to measure additional end points if required.

   - Click Clear ⟨icon⟩ or right-click to remove existing points and select a new base point.

4. Point Line ⟋ measures a total distance between multiple points along a route.

- Click Point Line ⟋. Then click the start and the second point to be measured. A line is displayed between the two points and the value is displayed on the model.
- Click the third point to be measured. The line extends to the third point.
- Repeat to measure the total distance between additional points if required.
- Click Clear ✖ or right-click to remove existing points and select a new base point.

5. Accumulate ▤ calculates the sum of several point-to-point measurements.

- Click Accumulate ▤. Then click the start and end points of the first distance to be measured. A line is displayed between the two points.
- Click alternately on additional start and end points as required. The sum of all the selected segments are displayed on the model.
- Click Clear ✖ or right-click to remove existing points and select a new base point.

6. Angle △ calculates an angle between two lines.

- Click Angle △. Then click on a point along the first line.
- Click on the first line at the point where the second line intersects. Finally, click on a point along the second line. The value is displayed on the model.
- Click Clear ✖ or right-click to remove existing points and select a new base point.

7. Area ◹ calculates an area on a specific plane.

- Click Area ◹. Then click on points along the perimeter of the area to be measured. Select as many points as required to obtain the accuracy you want. All the points added must lie on the same plane to be accurate.
- A line is displayed between the points and the value is displayed on the model.
- Click Clear ✖ or right-click to remove existing points and select a new base point.

The Measure Tools window can also be displayed when measuring to provide additional information on the measurements. To display this window, select the View tab, expand the Windows option, and enable Measure Tools or click ⇘ on the Measure panel title bar on the Review tab.

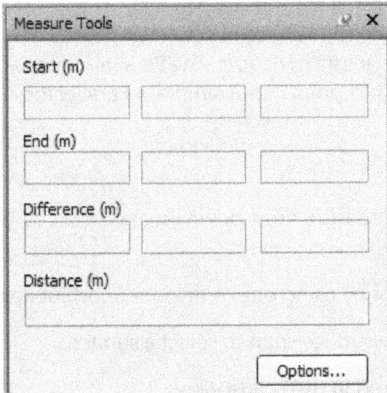

As selections are made on the model the locations of the start and end points are populated in the Measure Tools window and the Difference and Distance fields are calculated. The information in the Measure Tools window varies depending on the Measure command that is active. For example, when measuring an Angle or Area, the Distance field is changed to an Angle and Area field respectively.

Locking

When measuring, some object geometry may interfere with your ability to measure accurately. Locking ensures that your measured geometry maintains a consistent position in relation to the first measure point you create. The Lock command on the Review tab provides options to lock movement in the X, Y, Z, and a perpendicular or parallel direction to aid in achieving accurate measurements.

When a measurement is locked, the measure line changes color to reflect the type of lock. You can switch between different Locking modes when measuring multiple points using the options in the Lock drop-down list, or by using the shortcut keys.

Lock Type	Shortcut Key	Line Color
X Axis	X	Red
Y Axis	Y	Green
Z Axis	Z	Blue
Perpendicular	L	Yellow
Parallel	P	Magenta

The X, Y, and Z Axis locks enable you to lock each of these directions respectively. The Perpendicular lock enables you to lock in an alignment perpendicular to the surface of your start point. For example, a Perpendicular lock can be useful when measuring the height of a room. The Parallel lock enables you to lock in an alignment parallel to the surface of your start point. For example, a Parallel lock can be useful when taking perimeter measurements.

To use Lock while Measuring:

1. On the Review tab > Measure panel, expand the Measure drop-down list and select a Measure tool.

2. Select a lock option in the Lock drop-down list, or by using one of the lock Shortcut keys.

3. Move the cursor into the Scene View and use the surface snap to select a surface.

4. Click the start point of the distance to be measured in the Scene View.

5. Click the end point of the distance to be measured in the Scene View. The Lock setting remains active until it is changed or until you select None on the Lock drop-down list.

> When using 2D sheets, only X and Y axis locks are available. The Z axis, Parallel, and Perpendicular locks are not available for 2D sheets.

Measuring Tool Options

The Measuring tools have a number of options for obtaining accurate measurements. The options can

be accessed by clicking Options on the Measure Tools window or you can click Application Menu > Options > Interface > Measure. Select options, as required.

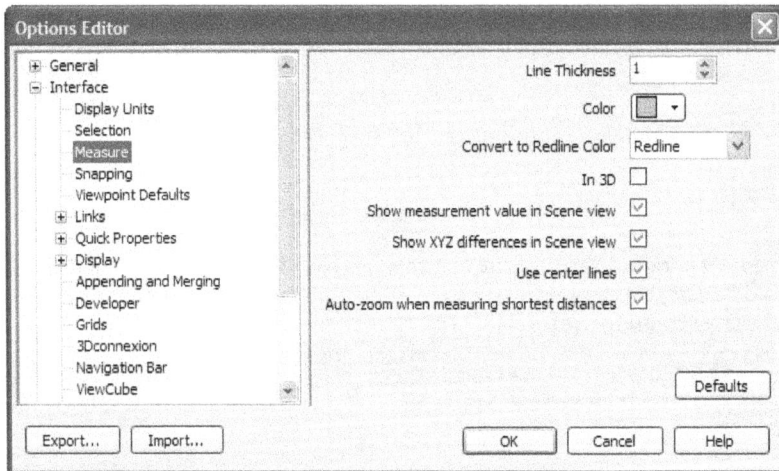

Snapping controls can be set in the Options Editor to precisely select vertices and edges while making measurements. These settings are in the Snapping group of the Options Editor dialog box. You can also specify the Tolerance for picking in this window.

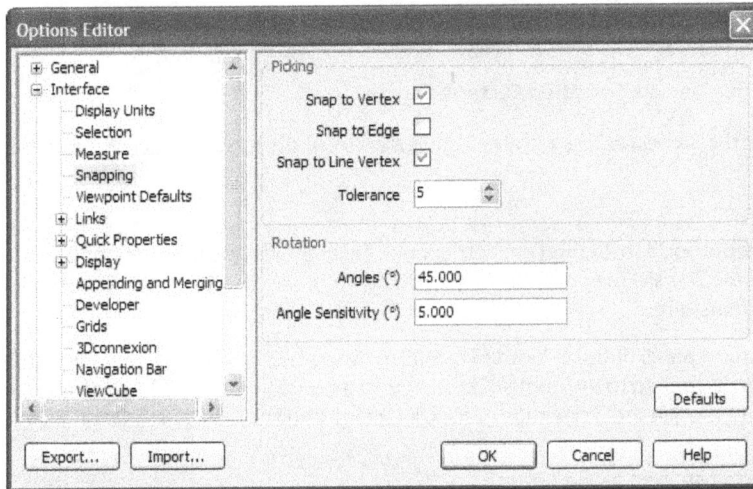

Enable Snap to Vertex, Snap to Edge, or Snap to Line Vertex, as required, to aid in making measurements. Snap settings can also help when moving, rotating, or scaling.

The cursor displays as a ✛ symbol if no reference is being snapped. The ✳ symbol identifies whether a vertex or edge is being snapped, and the ⊹ symbol identifies a surface snap.

> The geometry in the Autodesk Navisworks software is constructed with triangles, and therefore the cursor snaps to edges that might appear to be in the middle of a face.
>
> Viewing the model in Hidden Line ◻ mode clarifies which vertex or edge the cursor is snapping to.

Moving Selected Items

The position of an item in a model can be moved (transformed), thereby relocating it in the scene.

If the distance by which the item is to be moved is known, a transform can be applied directly to the item on the Selection Tree.

Procedure: To Move Items a Specified Distance

1.   Using either the Selection Tree or by selecting directly in the model, select the item to be moved.

2.   Select the Item Tools tab. In the Transform panel, ensure that the Move ⊕ option is active and expand the Transform panel title. Alternatively, right-click the item and click Override Item > Override Transform.

3.   In the Transform panel or the Override Transform dialog box, enter the XYZ values of the transform to be applied to the item(s). For example, a transform of (0, 0, 1) repositions an item by one unit (meter) in the Z direction. Click OK (Override Transform dialog box).

Procedure: To Move an Item by Freehandi

1.   Select the object to be transformed.

2.   Select the Review tab and expand the Measure command.

3.   In the Measure drop-down menu, click Point to Point ▭. Select a base point on the item to be moved, and another point where the item is to be moved to. This defines the transform distance.

4.   Expand the Measure panel and click Transform Selected Items 🗄 to apply the move.

      Tip: To move an item back to its original position, right-click the item in the Selection Tree or directly in the model and click Reset Item > Reset Transform. You can select multiple items and reset them all at once or you can select a top-level parent object to reset all objects in it.

Exercise: Using the Measuring and Move Tools

Conduct Measurements in the Design

In this section of the exercise, you will use the available measure tools to conduct measurements.

1. Open the file *C:\Navisworks 2017 Essentials Class Files\Training\Examples\Ship Complete.nwd*.

2. In the Saved Viewpoint window, select the saved view of the Door Hatch.

3. Select the Review tab. In the Measure drop-down menu, click Point to Point ▱. Select points on the hatch to determine the height and width. The hatch should measure approximately 2m high and 1.25m wide.

4. Experiment using the Point to Multiple Points ▱, Point Line ▱, Accumulate ▱, Angle ▱, Area ▱, and Clear ▱ tools. Use the Lock options to lock measurements in specific directions.

5. In the Saved Viewpoints window, select pressure vessels.

6. Navigate to the side of one of the yellow pipes coming from the right of the tanks.

7. On the title bar of the Measure panel, click ⬌ to open the Measure Tools window. Practice some additional measurements and notice how the Start, End, Difference, and Distance fields populate.

8. Click Options. In the Options Editor, select the Interface>Snapping category. Select Snap to Edge and click OK.

9. Use the Accumulate measure tool and navigate to follow and measure one of the yellow pipes coming from the right of the vessels. Notice that as you hover the cursor over edges the cursor changes to ✴ to indicate that you are snapping to an edge. Once this icon displays, select on the model.

    Tip: When following a piping system (for example) for measuring purposes, it might be useful to navigate to a side view of the system and use Pan ✋ to follow the pipes.

Move an Item in the Design

In this section of the exercise, you will use the Move tool to move an item in the design to a new location.

1. Click Clear ▱ or right-click to remove existing points and select a new base point.

2. In the Saved Viewpoints window, select pressure vessels to reorient back to the saved view.

3. Navigate to the side of one of the yellow pipes coming from the right of the vessels.

4. Select the first pipe tube.

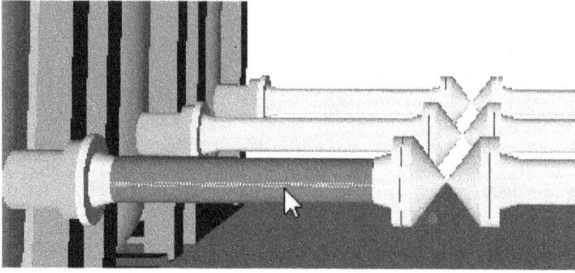

5. Select the Review tab and expand the Measure command.

6. In the Measure drop-down menu, click Point to Point ⊏⊐ . Click on the pipe tube near the top edge. This forms the base point of the transformation (item move).

7. Make the second measure point (target position) vertically down from the first point but still on the pipe tube. There should now be a line connecting the base point and the target point.

8. Expand the Measure panel and click Transform Selected Items ⊟ to apply the move.

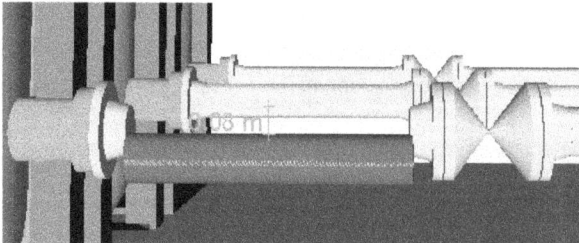

9. Close the file without saving.

Lesson: Selection and Search Sets

Overview

This lesson describes how to create and organize selection sets. It also introduces you to using the Find tool to search for items and save as search sets.

Objectives

After completing this lesson, you will be able to:

- Select objects, save as a selection set, and organize in folders.
- Use the Find tool to find objects that meet a criteria and save as a search set.

Selection Sets

Selection sets can be used to group a set of selected objects as a selection set, for reuse as required. Selection sets can be moved, reordered, or organized in folders if required.

Procedure: To Create and Organize Selection Sets

1. On the Home tab, in the Select & Search panel, expand the Sets drop-down and click Manage Sets to open the Sets window. Alternatively, select the View tab and on the Workspace panel, expand the Windows option, and enable Sets.

2. To create a selection set, select the first item to be saved, then hold CTRL, and select all the other items to be saved.

   Tip: Items can be selected on the scene, or in the Selection Tree. When selecting in the Selection Tree, you can use SHIFT to select a range of consecutive items.

3. On the Home tab, in the Select & Search panel, click Save Selection [icon]. Alternatively, right-click in the Sets window and select Save Selection or drag and drop the selection from the graphics window into the Sets window. The selection is created with a default name.

4. To save the selection set to an appropriate name, enter the new name and press ENTER. To rename an existing selection set, right-click the selection set and click Rename.

5. To move a selection set to a different position, drag to the new position.

6. To sort the list alphanumerically, right-click in the Selection Sets window, and then click Sort.

7. To create a folder, right-click in the Selection Sets window, and then click New Folder.

8. To rename a folder, right-click the folder, and then click Rename. In the Folder name field, enter a new name for the folder and press ENTER.

9. To move selection sets to a folder, select all sets to be moved, and drag to the folder.

10. To sort the list of folders (and sets) alphanumerically, right-click in the Selection Sets window, and click Sort.

Finding Items

The Find function can be useful when searching a model for items with a unique name or property. Searches can be saved as a search set for future reference or for use with Timeliner or Clash Detective.

The Autodesk Navisworks software also includes two additional search methods, Quick Find and Find Comments.

Procedure: To Conduct and Save a Search

1. On the Home tab, in the Search & Select panel, click Find Items 🔍 to open the Find Items window.

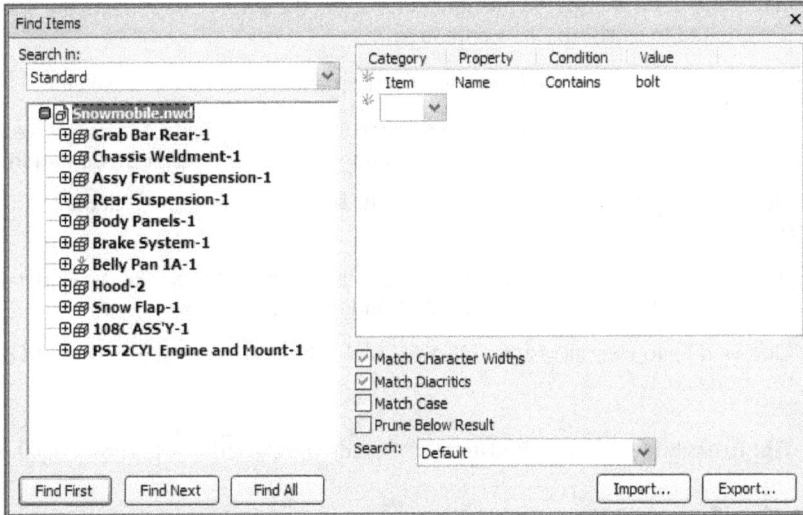

2. In the left pane select the file, layer, etc to be searched.

3. In the right pane, define the search criteria by selecting conditions in the following columns: **Category**, **Property**, **Condition**, and **Value**.

   Note: In Value, a criteria can be either entered in or selected from the drop-down list.

4. Remove the checkmark from Match Case unless you require the search to be case sensitive. Clear or enable the Match Character Widths and Match Diacritics

5. Click Find First then Find Next to view each result, which is highlighted in the Selection Tree and displayed as selected on the model.

6. Click Find All to view all results, which are highlighted in the Selection Tree and displayed on the model.

   Tip: To easily identify searched items, click Hide Unselected 🔲 to show only the results.

7. To delete a condition, right-click in the right pane of the Find Items window, and click Delete Condition.

8. Right-click in the Sets window, and click Save Search. Enter a name for the search.

   Tip: When a search is saved as Save Search, any additional items added to the model that meet the same search criteria are included next time the saved search is viewed.

Advanced Searches

Searches can include additional conditions and search options to enable a more refined result.

Procedure: To Create an Advanced Search

1. In the Find Items window, in the right pane, select the empty row beneath the first criteria that was created to establish a new criteria row.

2. In this new row(s), select/enter additional criteria to further refine the search.

3. By default, additional queries are interpreted as AND statements. To change the additional lines to OR statements, right-click the additional criteria and select OR Condition.

    Tip: To temporarily negate a condition in the search criteria, right-click the condition and select Negate Condition.

4. To delete a condition or all conditions, right-click in the right pane of the Find Items window, and click Delete Condition or Delete All Conditions, respectively.

5. Click Find All to view all results, which are highlighted in the Selection Tree and displayed on the model.

    Tip: To easily identify searched items, click Hide Unselected ⬚ to show only the results.

Exporting Search Data

The "search" or "search sets" can also be exported to use in another project. For example, if the models always have the same components, such as steel structure, ventilation ductwork, etc., then the Find function can be used to define generic search sets, which can then be exported as an XML file. The file of search sets can then be imported to other projects.

Procedure: To Export and Import the Current Search and Search Sets

1. To export a current search or search sets, select the Output tab and in the Export Data panel, click Current Search ⬚ or Search Sets ⬚. Alternatively, click Export in the Find Items window.

2. To Import the search or search sets into another project, click Import in the Find Items window.

Quick Find

Quick Find is simpler and quicker to use than the more comprehensive Find Items feature. It simply searches for the item you enter (case insensitive) in all property names and values attached to items in the scene.

Procedure: To Conduct a Quick Search

1. On the Home tab, in the Select & Search panel, use the Quick Find field ⬚ or press CTRL + F to open the Quick Find dialog box.

2.   In the Quick Find field or dialog box, enter the item to search for. Click in the Quick Find field or Find Next in the dialog box to view the first result. The result is highlighted in the Selection Tree and is displayed as "selected" on the model.

3.   To view the next result, continue clicking if you are using the Quick Find field on the Ribbon or click F3. Repeat as required.

Find Comments

Find Comments enables you to search for comments that are attached to viewpoints, items, clash results, and selection sets.

> For more information about adding comments, see the "Comments and Redlining" Lesson.

Procedure: To Find Comments

1.   On the Review tab, in the Comments panel, click Find Comments to open the Find Comments window.

2.   Click Find to search for all comments attached to the model. The search results are listed in the bottom pane.

3.   For a more defined search, select/enter details in the relevant fields in the Comments, Date Modified, or Source tabs, and then click Find.

4.   Select the required comment to display it in its associated view.

5.   Click View Comments to open the Comments window to display the comment details.

Selection Sets vs. Search Sets

Both Selection Sets and Search Sets are stored in the Sets window. Selections Sets are groups of items that have been selected in the model and are then saved as a group. Selection Sets are identified with in the Sets window. Search Sets are created based on the results of a search that is created and conducted in the model. Search Sets are identified with in the Sets window. Selection Sets are static, remaining unchanged as changes are made to the model, while Search Sets are dynamic and can be updated as any additional items are added to the model or changes are made that meet the search criteria used to create the Search set.

> For more information about Selection and Search Sets, see the "Create and Manage Selection and Search Sets" topic in Navisworks Help.

Exercise: Selection and Search Sets

Create a Selection Set

In this section of the exercise, you will create a Selection Set for quick access to commonly selected items.

1. Open the file *C:\Navisworks 2017 Essentials Class Files\Training\Examples\Snowmobile.nwd*.

2. On the Home tab in the Select & Search panel, expand the Sets drop-down and click Manage Sets to open the Sets window.

3. In the Selection Tree window, select Chassis Weldment-1, Belly Pan 1A-1, Hood-2, and Snow Flap-1.

4. On the Home tab, in the Select & Search panel, click Save Selection [⚙]. Alternatively, you can select Save Selection [⚙] in the Sets window.

   Selection Set is displayed in the Sets window and is active so that it can be renamed.

5. In the selection set name field, enter **Exterior**. To make a correction to the Set's name, right-click on it and click Rename.

6. Press ESC to clear the selection.

7. Select the Exterior selection set to highlight in the Scene view.

   Tip: You can also view selection sets in the Selection Tree. Select Sets in the drop-down list at the top of the Selection Tree. This list is only available if a selection or search set exists in the model. This display does not enable you to create new sets.

8. Select the seat of the model (Body Panels-1) directly in the scene window.

9. Press and hold the left mouse button on the seat and drag it onto the Sets window to create a new selection set.

10. Enter **Seat** as the name of the new set.

11. Select both the Exterior and Seat Sets using CTRL and click Hide 🔲 to hide the two Selection Sets. The interior of the snowmobile is now visible.

12. Click Unhide All 🔲 to unhide the items.

Conduct a Property Object Search and Save as a Set

In this section of the exercise, you will define the search criteria as a means of locating items and save it as a Search Set.

1. On the Home tab, in the Select & Search panel, click Find Items ![icon] to open the Find Items window.

2. In the Find Items window, in the left pane, select *Snowmobile.nwd*. In the right pane, do the following:

   - In Category, select Item.
   - In Property, select Name.
   - In Condition, select Contains.
   - In Value, enter **bolt**.
   - Ensure that a checkmark from the Match Case option is selected.

3. Click Find All. There are no objects found.

4. Clear the checkmark from the Match Case option.

5. Click Find All. Notice that the change in the objects found simply are based on the Match Case option.

6. Click Hide Unselected ![icon] to display only the results of the search. The selected items can now be viewed and examined.

   Tip: To display all items that have been hidden, click Hide Unselected ![icon] again or click Unhide All ![icon].

7. On the Home tab in the Display panel, click Properties ![icon]. The Properties window displays the number of items that were found.

8. In the Sets window, right-click and select Save Search.

9. Right-click the new saved search set and select Rename. Enter **Bolts** as the new name. Notice how the icons identifying the Selection Sets and Search Sets are different to differentiate them.

10. Close the Find Items window.

11. Clear all current selections using ESC and test that the Sets provide you with the required selections.

12. Close the file without saving.

Lesson: Viewpoints

Overview

This lesson describes how to create, organize, edit, and export viewpoints. It also introduces you to setting navigation commands in viewpoints.

Objective

After completing this lesson, you will be able to:

- Create, organize, edit, and export viewpoints, and prepare a viewpoint for navigation purposes.

About Viewpoints

Viewpoints are snapshots taken of the model as it is displayed in the scene.

The model can be navigated to a required view, items of the model can be hidden, and other items can be rendered with different materials and lighting. Then the finished scene can be saved as a viewpoint for future reference.

In addition, you can add a variety of comments and Redline tags to a saved viewpoint.

When a viewpoint is saved it contains information about the following:

- Camera position and focus point
- Section planes
- Navigation modes (the current Navigation mode is saved in the view)
- Speeds
- Rendering conditions
- Perspective/orthogonal modes

Procedure: To Display and Add a Viewpoint

1. To display the Saved Viewpoints window, select the Viewpoint tab and click ⬎ on the Save, Load & Playback panel's title bar. Alternatively, select the View tab, expand the Windows option, and enable Saved Viewpoints. The Saved Viewpoints window displays a list of the previously saved viewpoints.

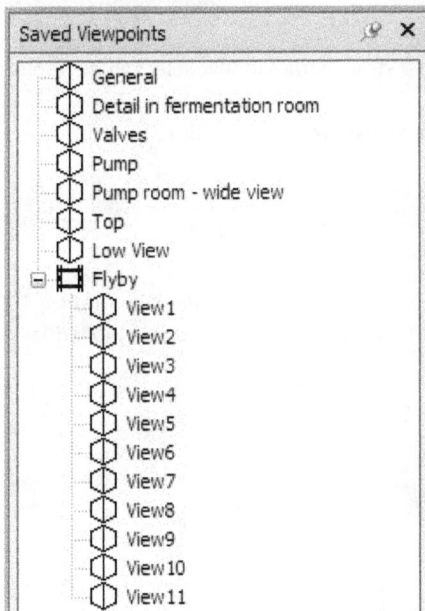

2. Click a viewpoint to display it.

3. To quickly view the whole model, click Zoom All on the Navigation Bar on the right side of the Scene View.

Note: Saved animations ⊟ are also located in the Viewpoints window. See "Animate Objects" for more information.

4. Navigate to the required position in the model.

5. Prepare the view (for example, apply rendering, lighting, comments, redlines, navigation modes, and tools).

6. Right-click in the Saved Viewpoints window, and click Save Viewpoint.

7. Enter a new name and press ENTER.

Tip: To rename a Viewpoint to an alternate name, right-click the viewpoint in the Saved Viewpoints window and click Rename.

Organizing Viewpoints

Viewpoints (and animations) can be moved, reordered, or organized in folders as follows:

- To move a viewpoint to a different position, drag it to the new position.
- To sort the list of viewpoints alphanumerically, right-click in the Saved Viewpoints window, and click Sort.
- To create a folder, right-click in the Saved Viewpoints window, then click New Folder.
- To rename the folder, right-click the folder in the Saved Viewpoints window, and click Rename. In the folder name field, enter a new name for the folder.
- To move viewpoints to a folder, in the Saved Viewpoints window, select all viewpoints to be moved and drag to the folder.
- To sort the list of folders (and viewpoints) alphanumerically, right-click in the Saved Viewpoints window, and then click Sort.

Editing Viewpoints

Viewpoint settings can be changed in Application Menu > Options > Interface > Viewpoint Defaults and affects all new viewpoints. Each viewpoint can also be edited individually.

Procedure: To Open the Viewpoint Editor

1. In the Saved Viewpoints window, select the viewpoint to be edited.

2. Right-click the selected viewpoint, and then click Edit.

    IMPORTANT: To save the changes after editing, click OK. Then right-click the viewpoint in the Saved Viewpoint window, and click Update.

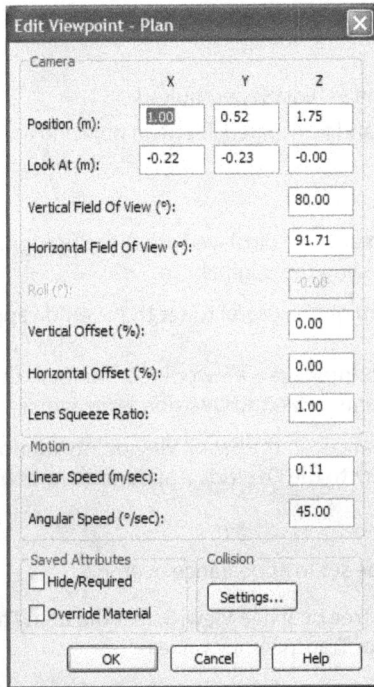

Camera Positions

- **Position** – X Y Z coordinates of the viewing position.
- **Look At** – X Y Z coordinates of the focal point.
- **Vertical Field of View** – Viewing perspective of the camera. This is not editable when in orthographic mode.
- **Horizontal Field of View** – Viewing perspective of the camera. This is not editable when in orthographic mode.
- **Roll** – Roll of the camera about its viewing axis. This value is not editable when the world up vector remains upright (in Walk, Orbit, and Turntable modes).
- **Vertical Offset** – The amount the camera position is positioned above or below an object.
- **Horizontal Offset** – The amount the camera position is positioned to the left or right (front or back) of an object.
- **Lens Squeeze Ratio** – The amount the camera's lens compresses the image horizontally. The default value is 1 as most cameras do not compress the image they record, and their Lens Squeeze Ratio is 1.

Motion Speeds

Editing the following motion settings takes effect when navigating from this viewpoint. When a different viewpoint is selected, the motion settings revert to the Global Option settings unless overridden in that viewpoint.

- **Linear Speed** – Navigation speed in a straight line.
- **Angular Speed** – Turning speed of a viewpoint (value in degrees per second).

Saved Attributes

- **Hide/Required** – Saves objects set in the scene as hidden or required.
- **Override Material** – Saves overridden colors and transparencies of an object in a viewpoint.

Overriding Existing Appearances

When a CAD model is opened, the appearances (materials) displayed are those brought in with the model. The materials can be edited, thereby overriding the original.

To override appearances in *all* new viewpoints, it might be useful to set the override appearances globally. Go to Application Menu > Options > Interface > Viewpoint Defaults. In the Options Editor, click Override Appearance. All new viewpoints default to Override Appearance.

To set an individual viewpoint to Override Appearances, in the Saved Viewpoints window, right-click the viewpoint, and then click Edit. Add a checkmark to the Override Appearance option.

Procedure: To Edit Material

1. Select the required viewpoint, which must be set to appearance override.

2. Select items to be changed in the Selection Tree or Scene View. Select the Item Tools tab and in the Appearance panel, change the Color or Transparency values.

   TIP: Alternatively, you can also right-click on any one of the selected items in the Selection Tree and click Override Item > Override Color/Override Transparency. In either the displayed Color or Override Transparency dialog boxes, make the changes you want, and then click OK.

3. In the Saved Viewpoints window, right-click the viewpoint, and then click Update.

   Changes have been made to this viewpoint only. Other viewpoints and the model materials remain unchanged.

   Note: When moving from a viewpoint with material overrides to a viewpoint without material overrides, some of the material overrides might temporarily carry over.

Collision

Click Settings in the Edit Viewpoint dialog box to open the Collision dialog box.

- **Collision** – Add a checkmark to switch collision detection on with this viewpoint.
- **Gravity** – Add a checkmark to incorporate gravity with this viewpoint.
- **Auto Crouch** – Add a checkmark to enable crouching in this viewpoint.

Make the required changes and click OK.

IMPORTANT: Right-click the viewpoint in the Saved Viewpoints window, and then click Update.

> Setting the Collision option in a viewpoint is only applied to the viewpoint that is being edited. To set Collision globally for all models opened in the Autodesk Navisworks software, go to Application Menu [N] > Options > Interface > Viewpoint Defaults > Settings and set the Collision option in the Default Collision dialog box. Alternatively, you can set the Collision option so that it is only on for a specific model by clicking Collision in the Realism drop-down menu on the Viewpoint tab. Gravity and Crouching can be controlled in the same way.

In the Collision dialog box you can customize the Viewer settings. The viewer is a 3D object with a default height and radius and with the camera set at a default eye level. These settings can be overridden as follows:

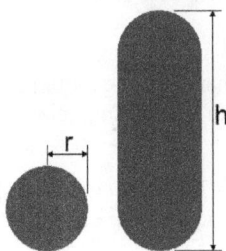

- **Radius** – Of the Viewer
- **Height** – Of the Viewer
- **Eye Offset** – Measured from top of the viewer

Third Person

With the Third Person view enabled, the 3D object (an avatar) type can be selected and the camera position relative to the avatar can be changed.

- **Enable** – Enable Third Person editing for this viewpoint.
- **Auto Zoom** – Enable for this viewpoint. With Auto Zoom enabled, the camera temporarily zooms closer to the third person, if separated by an object during navigation.
- **Avatar** – Select avatar type.
- **Angle** – Set camera angle to avatar.
- **Distance** – Set camera distance to avatar.

Make the required changes and click OK.

IMPORTANT: Right-click the viewpoint in the Saved Viewpoints window, and then click Update.

Exporting Views

Viewpoints can be exported to a 2D image, as an HTML report, or an XML file.

Procedure: To Export a Viewpoint Image

1. In the Saved Viewpoints window, select a saved viewpoint.

2. Select the Output tab and in the Visuals panel, click Image .

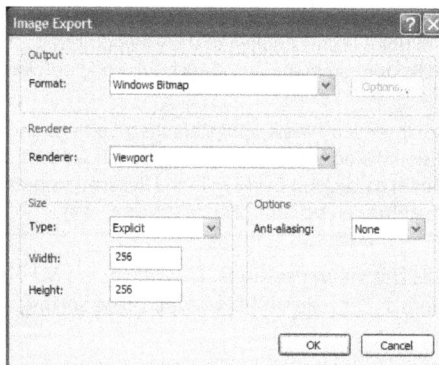

3. In the Image Export dialog box, under Output, select the image format.

4. In the Renderer area, set the image renderer. If using Autodesk materials and requiring a high quality rendering, select Autodesk. For a quick rendering, ideal for previewing, select Viewport.

5. In the Size area, set the width and height of the export image. The Type option enables you to keep the aspect ratio of the image the same while sizing it, or the image can be skewed using the Explicit option.

6. Under Options, for Anti-aliasing, select a level. Anti-aliasing reduces the jagged edges.

7. Click OK.

8. In the Save As dialog box, select a location and filename and then click Save.

Procedure: To Export Viewpoints as an HTML Report

Exporting viewpoints as an HTML report enables non-Navisworks license holders to benefit from a review session by providing them with access to viewpoints of problem areas, including any redlines, comments, and the coordinates of the camera position.

1. Select the Output tab and in the Export Data panel, click Viewpoints Report . Alternatively, right-click the saved viewpoint's name and select Export Viewpoints Report.

2. In the Export dialog box, select the location and filename for the viewpoint, and then click Save.

Procedure: To Export Viewpoints as an XML File

Exporting Viewpoints to XML could either be used to re-use common viewpoints in different projects, or they could be used to combine the viewpoints made by various reviewers of the same model.

1. Select the Output tab and in the Export Data panel, click Viewpoints . Alternatively, right-click the saved viewpoint's name and select Export Viewpoints.

2. In the Export dialog box, select the location and filename for the viewpoint, and then click Save.

Procedure: To Import Views

Viewpoints can be imported as an XML file.

1. Right-click in the Saved Viewpoints window and select Import Viewpoints.

2. In the Import dialog, select the location and filename of the viewpoint, and then click Open. The viewpoint is added to the opened file and listed in the Viewpoints window.

To Print a Viewpoint

A hard copy of a current viewpoint can be printed with a printer or plotter. When the print option is selected, the current viewpoint, scaled to fit and centered on the page, is printed.

Procedure: To Print the Current Viewpoint

1. Select the Output tab, in the Print panel, click Print . Alternatively, click on the Quick Access Toolbar or click Application Menu > Print.

2. In the Print dialog box, specify the printer settings. Click OK to print the viewpoint.

    Note: The maximum image size is 2048 x 2048 pixels.

    Tip: Before printing a copy of the viewpoint, it might be useful to preview it. On the Output tab, click Print Preview or click Application Menu > Print > Print Preview. Use commands (Zoom In, Zoom Out) to display the viewpoint the way you want it.

Procedure: To Conduct a Print Set Up

With this option, you can set the paper size and orientation options.

1. Select the Output tab, in the Print panel, click Print Settings or click Application Menu > Print > Print Settings.

2. In the Print Setup dialog box, make the changes you want, and then click OK.

Exercise: (C) Add and Organize Viewpoints

1. Open the file C:\Navisworks 2017 Essentials Class Files\Training\Examples\Bath_City\ West.nwd.

2. Using the navigation modes, navigate to one of the bridges that cross the river.

3. To display the Saved Viewpoints window, if it is not visible, select the Viewpoint tab and click ⌐ on the Save, Load & Playback panel's title bar.

    Tip: Alternatively, select the View tab, expand the Windows option, and enable Saved Viewpoints.

4. Save the view of the bridge. Right-click in the Saved Viewpoints window, and click Save Viewpoint.

5. Enter **Bridge1** for the new name and press ENTER.

6. Right-click in the Saved Viewpoints window, and then click New Folder.

7. Enter **My Views** as the name of the folder and press ENTER.

8. Move the saved view into the new folder. Drag Bridge1 into the *My Views* folder.

9. Close the file without saving.

Exercise: (P) Add and Organize Viewpoints

1. Open the file *C:\Navisworks 2017 Essentials Class Files\Training\Examples\Sample1.nwf.*

2. Zoom in to the four tanks at the top of the model.

3. To display the Saved Viewpoints window, if it is not visible, select the Viewpoint tab and click ⊿ on the Save, Load & Playback panel's title bar.

    Tip: Alternatively, select the View tab, expand the Windows option, and enable Saved Viewpoints.

4. Save the view of the four tanks. Right-click in the Saved Viewpoints window, and click Save Viewpoint.

5. Enter **Four Tanks** for the new name and press ENTER.

6. Right-click in the Saved Viewpoints window, and then click New Folder.

7. Enter **My Views** as the name of the folder and press ENTER.

8. Move the saved view into the new folder. Drag Four Tanks into the *My Views* folder.

9. Move the new folder by dragging it to a different location in the list.

10. Close the file without saving.

Lesson: Comments, Redlining, and Tags

Overview

This lesson describes how to add, view, and edit comments. It also introduces you to the functions of the Redline tools for adding markups on viewpoints, including the Tag tool.

Objectives

After completing this lesson, you will be able to:

- Add comments to viewpoints, animations, selection sets, and clashes.
- Markup a viewpoint using the Redline tools and create a Tagged comment.

About Comments, Redlining, and Tags

The following are tools that can be used in the Autodesk Navisworks software to communicate information in a file.

- **Comments** – Can be associated with saved viewpoints, viewpoint animations, selection sets, search sets, tasks, clashes, and TimeLiner tasks.
- **Redlining** – Annotation that can be added directly over a viewpoint when reviewing.
- **Tags** – Method for recording any findings during a review session. Combines the functionality of adding viewpoints, redlines, and comments.

Comments

Procedure: To Add Comments

1. Select the required selection set, search set, saved viewpoint, animation, or saved clash test that you want to add comments to.

2. On the Review tab, in the Comments panel, click View Comments to open the Comments window to display the comment details.

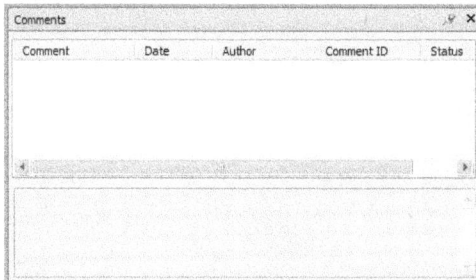

3. In the Comments dialog box, right-click in the Comments pane, and then click Add Comment.

4. In the Add Comment dialog box, enter your comments, and then select a Status option.

5. Click OK to save the comment. The comment is attached to the specific viewpoint and can be viewed when the viewpoint is selected or by conducting a search.

6. You can edit or delete a saved comment. Right-click on a listed comment, and then click Edit Comment or Delete Comment as required.

   Note: When a comment is saved, it includes the date it was added or edited and the user name of the person who was currently logged on.

> To quickly add a comment, right-click the selection set, search set, saved viewpoint, animation, or saved clash test in their associated windows and then click Add Comment. Comments in the selection and search sets need to be added like this from the Sets window. They DO NOT work from the Selection Tree window in the Sets tab.

Redlining

Redlining can be associated with saved viewpoints and clash detection result views. If a redline is added, a viewpoint is automatically saved if one is not already active.

1. On the Review tab, in the Redline panel, select the Draw drop-down menu to access the redlining tools. The Text and Erase commands are also used in redlining. The redlining tools are described below.

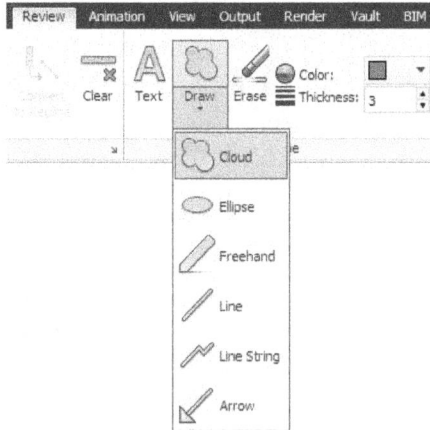

Icon	Name	Description
A	**Text**	Adds text in the viewpoint. Click the location where the text is to be placed. Enter text in the Text window, then click OK to add to the viewpoint.
	Cloud	Creates a cloud. Click in the viewpoint for each of the cloud base points. Select the start point to close the cloud.
	Ellipse	Creates an ellipse. Drag over the viewpoint and then release the mouse.
	Freehand	Creates freehand redlines. Drag in the viewpoint, then release the mouse.
	Line	Creates a single segment linear redline between a start and end points. Click in the viewpoint at the start and end points of the required lines.
	Line String	Creates linear strings of lines. Click in the viewpoint at the start, intermediate, and end points of the required lines.
	Arrow	Create an arrow. Click in the viewpoint at the start point and select again to end the line. The arrow displays at the endpoint.
	Erase	Erases redlines. Drag over the redline to be deleted, then release the mouse. The entire redline must be enclosed in the box for the erase function to be applied.

2. In the Redline panel, select settings for the line (Thickness and Color) before using the tools.

Tags

Tags combine the features of redlining, viewpoints, and comments into a single, easy to use review tool. This enables you to tag anything you want to identify in the model scene. A viewpoint is automatically created for you, and you can add a comment and status to the tag. For example, during a review session, you might observe an item in the scene that is incorrectly sized or positioned. You can then tag this item, identifying the problem. If a tag is added, the Add Comment dialog box is displayed and you can add a comment.

Procedure: To Add a Tag

1. On the Review tab in the Tags panel, click Add Tag . Click the object where the tag is to point to, then click where the tag label is to be located.

    The tag is added.

2. In the Add Comments dialog box, enter the text for the tag, and then select a Status option.

3. Click OK to save the comment. A tag viewpoint is created (you can rename it).

    Note: Additional Redline Tags can be added anywhere on the model. Each tag is numbered in the sequence that it was added.

Reviewing Tags

There are a variety of methods for finding Tags including the following:

- On the Review tab in the Comments panel, click Find Comments . Use the Find Comments dialog box to do the following:
  - Click the Comments tab to search for comments that are associated with tags. Search for a specific tag, text, author, ID, or status.
  - Click the Date Modified tab to search for comments within a date criteria.
  - Click Source tab to search for comments created in certain sources.
  - Click Find to search the model. **Tip:** Leave the search fields blank to search for all tags (this will also display any comments in the file).

- If viewpoints have been created for each tag, browse the Saved Viewpoints window for the required tag ID. Select the tag in the Saved Viewpoints window and review the comment in the Comments window.

- To navigate directly to a tag when you know its Tag number, select the Review tab and in the Tags panel, enter the tag number or select a number from the drop-down menu and click Go to Tag

- To renumber tags, select the Review tab, expand the Tags pane and click Renumber Tag IDs.

Exercise: Working with Comments, Redline Markups & Tags

Add a Comment

In this section of the exercise, you will add a comment to a saved viewpoint.

1. Open the file *C:\Navisworks 2017 Essentials Class Files\Training\Examples\KLM\ m&e\M&E.nwd*.

2. Expand the Selection Tree, and select 1PLUMB_A.DWG.

3. In the Navigation bar, click the View Selected Zoom option to focus on the plumbing system.

4. Save the current view as a viewpoint and name it **Plumbing System**.

5. If the Comments window is not already displayed, select the Review tab and in the Comments panel, click View Comments to open the Comments window.

6. In the Comments window, right-click and click Add Comment. Enter some text relative to the viewpoint, and click OK.

7. View the Comment data in the Comment window.

Add Redline Markups and a Redline Tag

In this section of the exercise, you will add redline markups to a viewpoint and create a tag.

1. Zoom in to a washbasin in the plumbing system. Save the viewpoint and enter **Washbasin** as its name.

2. Select the Review tab. In the Redline panel, experiment with each of the Redline tools to see how they work. Expand the Draw command to access the drawing tools.

   - Use Text to enter text directly onto the viewpoint.

   - Click Line String and select a starting point, with each additional mouse click create lines. Right-click to end the string, and start a new line.

   - Click Cloud and with each left mouse click, extend the cloud. Right-click to close the cloud.

   - Click Erase to remove a redline. Click and drag from the top left of the redline to be removed, encompass the redline in the eraser box, and release the mouse.

3. Clear the active viewpoint, and navigate to a different washbasin and click Add Tag on the Tags panel. Select an item in the viewpoint and select a location to place the tag. Add a comment in the dialog box and click OK.

   Notice that a viewpoint with a default tag ID has automatically been added and can be renamed. If you did not navigate to another viewpoint, the tag is added to the Washbasin viewpoint.

4. Close the file without saving.

Lesson: Animations

Overview

This lesson describes how to record, edit, and export animations. It also introduces you to creating animations from viewpoints and in the form of a slide show.

Objectives

After completing this lesson, you will be able to:

- Record an interactive animation, then edit, and export it.
- Create an animation from viewpoints using automatic transitions.

Creating Animations

Animations can be created, edited, and played back in the Autodesk Navisworks software, and also played back in the Freedom viewer. Animations can also be exported in AVI format to be played back in a variety of software including Windows Media Player.

There are two ways to produce an animation, either by recording interactive navigation, or by animated transitions between saved viewpoints. In addition, an animation can be created in the form of a slide show.

Animation Tab

Procedure: To View a Saved Animation

1. In the Saved Viewpoints window, select the animation.

2. Select the Animation tab.

3. On the Playback panel, click Play ▷ to view the animation.

4. Click Stop ☐ or Pause ⅠⅠ to stop play at any time.

5. Click Step Forward ⅠⅠ▷ or Step Backward ◁ⅠⅠ to advance or reverse by one frame in the animation.

6. Click Rewind Ⅰ◁ or Forward ▷Ⅰ to move to the beginning or end of the animation.

7. Drag the Animation Slider [Playback Ti◄═►] 30 % or the Time field [0:05.00] to view a specific point in the animation.

   Note: Animations can also be played back using the controls on the Viewpoint tab. The only difference is that the Animation Slider and the Time field are not available on this tab.

Procedure: To Record an Interactive Animation

1. Select the viewpoint where the animation is going to begin.

2. Select the Animation tab.

3. On the Create panel, click Record ⬤ to start recording movements in the scene.

4.   Navigate around the model as required.

5.   In the Recording panel, click Stop ☐ to end the recording. The Autodesk Navisworks software automatically saves the animation to the Saved Viewpoints window and names it Animation1.

6.   In the Saved Viewpoints window, right-click Animation1, and click Rename. In the animation name field, enter a new descriptive name, and press ENTER.

      Note: Any delay in navigation or delay due to switching navigation tools causes a cut frame to be added to the animation. This cut frame adds a controlled pause to the animation, or can be used as an identifier of where frames might need to be removed to make a more smooth video movement.

Procedure: To Create an Animation from Viewpoint Transitions

1.   Select the Animation tab.

2.   Right-click in the Saved Viewpoints window, and then click Add Animation.

3.   To rename the new animation, in the Saved Viewpoints window, right-click the animation, and click Rename. In the animation name field, enter a new name and press ENTER.

4.   Create all the viewpoints required for the animation and rename each if required.

5.   Drag the viewpoints into the empty animation. The animation is ready for viewing.

Procedure: To Edit an Animation

1.   To crop an animation, click the plus sign ⊞ 🎞 at the left of the animation to expand it and display all frames. Select any unwanted frames then press DELETE.

2.   To edit an animation (for example, change the duration), right-click the saved animation, and then click Edit. In the Edit Animation dialog box, you can change the total running time, select Loop Playback, or change the Smoothing option (see Note below).

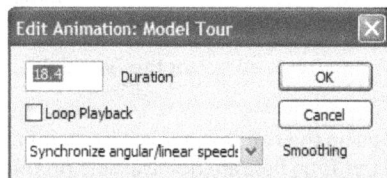

      Note: The speed of movement between frames of an animation is dictated by the angular and linear speeds of the individual frames and so selecting Synchronize angular/linear speeds (in the Smoothing drop-down field) smooths the differences between the speeds of each frame in the animation, resulting in a less jerky animation.

Combining Animations

Animations can be added together to make one extended animation.

Procedure: To Combine Animations

1. Click and drag one animation onto another animation; it is appended to the end.

2. Drag the appended animation to a different position if required.

3. To prevent the application from automatically creating an animated transition between the animations, add a cut (pause). To add a cut, right-click the animation and click Add Cut.

Creating a Slide Show

A slide show is created similar to creating transitions in animations; you add cuts (pauses) between viewpoints.

Procedure: To Create a Slide Show Animation

1. Follow the procedure for combining Animations and include the required viewpoints.

2. Expand the animation, and then right-click the second viewpoint. Click Add Cut.

3. Repeat for all the remaining viewpoints.

4. The default cut (pause) duration is one second. Right-click a cut and click Edit to change the duration.

Exporting an Animation

Animations can be exported out of the Autodesk Navisworks software, either as an AVI file, or as a series of static images (JPEG, PNG, or Windows Bitmap).

Procedure: To Export an Animation

1. In the Saved Viewpoints window, select the animation to be exported.

2. Select the Output tab and in the Visuals panel, click Animation . Alternatively, on the Animation tab, click Export Animation on the Export panel.

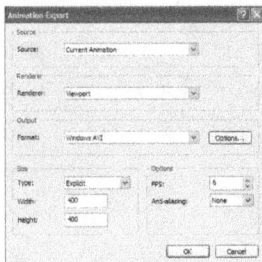

3. In Animation Export dialog box, for Source, select Current Animation.

4. In the Renderer drop-down list, select either Viewport (default setting) or Autodesk (available with Autodesk Navisworks Simulate and Manage only), depending on how the animation is to be rendered. (For quick rendering at lower quality, select Viewport.)

5. Under Output, for Format, select Windows AVI for an animation, or use the other options for a set of static images.

6. Click Options. In the Video Compression dialog box, select a video compressor from the drop-down list and other configuration settings as required. Click OK.

   Note: Any video compression tools loaded on your computer can be used by the Autodesk Navisworks software and is listed in the drop-down menu. If a video compressor is not available on your computer, Configure is grayed out.

7. In the Animation Export dialog box, under Size, select the width and height of the AVI display.

   Tip: Use the default size, view the results, then increase/decrease the size if required.

   Note: The larger the size, the larger the overall file size!

8. Under Options, select the FPS (frames per second) and Anti-aliasing settings.

   Tip: Anti-aliasing gives images smoother edges and does not affect the output file size. However, it does increase the rendering time, so it is best used for final AVIs.

9. Click OK to export the animation. The AVI file can be played back using Windows Media Player.

Exercise: (C) Working with Animations in Navisworks

Record an Interactive Animation

1. Open the file *C:\Navisworks 2017 Essentials Class Files\Training\Examples\Bath_City\ West.nwd*.

2. In the Saved Viewpoints window, select the Gas Cylinders saved view.

3. On the Navigation bar, activate either the Walk or Fly tools.

4. Select the Animation tab. On the Create panel, click Record to start recording movements.

5. Navigate between the Gas Cylinders.

6. In the Recording panel, click Stop to end the recording. The Autodesk Navisworks software saves the animation to the Saved Viewpoints window, and names it Animation1.

7. In the Saved Viewpoints window, right-click Animation 1, and click Rename. In the animation name field, enter **Gas Tour** for the new name, then press ENTER.

8. Select the Gas Tour animation in the Saved Viewpoints window. On the Playback panel, click Play to replay the Gas Tour animation.

Create an Animation from Viewpoint Transitions

1. In the Saved Viewpoints window, select the General View of city viewpoint.

2. In the Standard view of the Selection Tree, expand the file hierarchy, and then select *bridge07.dwg*.

3. Click Zoom Selected in the Navigation Bar to display the bridge in the main view.

4. Right-click in the Saved Viewpoints window, and click Save Viewpoint. In the viewpoint name field, change the name to **Bridge 7** and press ENTER.

5. In the Selection Tree, select *bridge08.dwg*, and use Zoom Selected in the Navigation Bar to display the bridge in the main view. Save the viewpoint as **Bridge 8**.

6. Repeat this procedure for the remaining bridges, *bridge09.dwg* and *bridge10.dwg*, saving viewpoints for each of them.

7. Right-click in the Saved Viewpoints window, and click Add Animation. Rename it **River Tour**.

8. Drag each of the saved views of the bridges (in order) to the River Tour empty animation.

9. Ensure that the bridges are not selected. Press ESC.

10. Select River Tour and click Play on the Animation tab to view the animation.

    The Autodesk Navisworks software navigates between each viewpoint.

11. Reorder the animation's viewpoints from Bridge 10 to Bridge 7. Replay the animation.

Edit an Animation

1. In the Saved Viewpoint window, right-click the Gas Tour animation (previously created) and click Edit.

2. In the Edit Animation dialog box, change Duration to 10 seconds, add a checkmark to Loop Playback, and set the Smoothing option to Synchronize angular/linear speeds, if not already set. Click OK.

3. In the Saved Viewpoint window, select the Gas Tour animation, and click Play ▷ .

4. Click Stop ☐ .

Combining Animations

1. In the Saved Viewpoints window, drag the River Tour animation onto the Gas Tour animation. This is appended to the end.

2. To avoid an animated transition between the two animations you can add a cut. Right-click the first view in River Tour and click Add Cut.

3. Select Gas Tour, and then click Play ▷ .

4. If required, click Stop ☐ to stop the animation before it is complete.

5. Save this file with the name **West** and your initials, to a new location (for example, *C:\Temp\WestJMD.nwf*).

Exporting an Animation

1. In the Saved Viewpoints window, select the Gas Tour animation.

2. Select the Output tab and in the Visuals panel, click Animation ◇ .

3. In the Animation Export dialog box, for Source, select Current Animation.

4. For Renderer, select Viewport.

5. Under Output, for Format, select Windows AVI.

6. Under Size, for Type, select Use Aspect Ratio. For Height, enter **200**.

7. Under Options, for FPS, select 6. For Anti-aliasing, select None.

8. Click OK. Save the file in your temporary folder (for example, *C:\Temp\WestJMD-Gas Tour.avi*).

9. Use Windows Media Player to play back the AVI.

Exercise: (P) Working with Animations in Navisworks

Record an Interactive Animation

1. Open the file *C:\Navisworks 2017 Essentials Class Files\Training\Examples\Process Plant.nwd*.

2. In the Saved Viewpoints window, select the Section Z saved view.

3. On the Navigation bar, click Walk. Select ⏷ below the Walk command and disable Collision if it is enabled.

4. Select the Animation tab. On the Create panel, click Record to start recording movements.

5. Navigate along the top of the plant.

6. In the Recording panel, click Stop to end the recording. The Autodesk Navisworks software saves the animation to the Saved Viewpoints window, and names it Animation1.

7. In the Viewpoints window, right-click Animation1, and then click Rename. In the animation name field, enter **Top Tour** for the new name, then press ENTER.

8. Select the Top Tour animation in the Saved Viewpoints window. On the Playback panel, click Play to replay the Top Tour animation.

Create an Animation from Viewpoint Transitions

1. In the Selection Tree, expand the *Process Plant.nwd* hierarchy (0 > SOLVAY_MODEL > SOLVAY_MODEL > MODEL1).

2. Click Zoom Selected in the Navigation Bar to display MODEL1 in the main view.

3. Right-click in the Saved Viewpoints window, and click Save Viewpoint. In the viewpoint name field, change the name to **Model1** and press ENTER.

4. In the Selection Tree, select MODEL2, and use Zoom Selected in the Navigation Bar to display Model2 in the main view. Save as a viewpoint as **Model2**.

5. Repeat this procedure for the remaining models, MODEL3, MODEL4, and MODEL5, saving and renaming viewpoints for each of them.

6. Right-click in the Saved Viewpoints window and click Add Animation. Rename it **Model Tour**.

7. Drag each of the saved views of the models (in order) to the Model Tour empty animation.

8. Ensure that the models are not selected. Press ESC.

9. Select Model Tour, and then click Play to view the animation. The Autodesk Navisworks software navigates between each viewpoint.

10. Reorder the viewpoints in this order: Model 4, 1, 2, 3, and 5. Replay the animation.

Edit an Animation

1. In the Saved Viewpoints window, right-click the Model Tour animation (previously created) and click Edit.

2. In the Edit Animation dialog box, change Duration to 10 seconds, add a checkmark to Loop Playback, and set the Smoothing option to Synchronize angular/linear speeds, if not already set. Click OK.

3. In the Saved Viewpoints window, select the Model Tour animation, and click Play ▷.

4. Click Stop ☐.

Combining Animations

1. In the Saved Viewpoints window, drag the Model Tour animation onto the Top Tour animation. The application appends this to the end.

2. To avoid an animated transition between the two animations, you can add a cut. Right-click the first view in Model Tour and click Add Cut.

3. Click the Top Tour animation, and then click Play ▷, to stop the animation before it is complete, if required.

4. Save this file with the name **Plant**, plus your initials, to a new location (for example, C:\Temp\PlantJMD.nwf).

Exporting an Animation

1. In the Saved Viewpoints window, select the Top Tour animation.

2. Select the Output tab and in the Visuals panel, click Animation ◇.

3. In the Animation Export dialog box, under Source, select Current Animation.

4. For renderer, select Viewport.

5. Under Output, for Format, select Windows AVI.

6. Under Size, for Type, select Explicit. For both Width and Height, enter **400**.

7. Under Options, for FPS, select 6. For Anti-aliasing, select None.

8. Click OK then save in your temporary folder (C:\Temp\PlantJMD-Top Tour.avi).

9. Use Windows Media Player to play back the AVI.

Lesson: Sectioning

Overview

This lesson describes how to create sectional views of a model. It also introduces you to linking section planes and setting a section range.

Objectives

After completing this lesson, you will be able to:

- Create sectioned views from various planes and boxes.
- Link two section planes and set a sectioning range limit.

Sectioning a Model

Section Planes

With sectioning, you can make up to six sectional cuts in any plane and still be able to navigate around the scene. You view models inside without hiding any item. Viewpoints of section planes can be saved and used in animations to show a dynamically sectioned model.

Slices can also be created using multiple section planes and linking them as a slice. In this way the model can be navigated and the scene viewed as a slice in real time, and used in viewpoints and animations.

Procedure: To Create Sectioned Planes

1. Select a saved viewpoint or manipulate the model to an orientation to begin sectioning from.

2. Select the Viewpoint tab and click Enable Sectioning in the Sectioning panel. The Sectioning Tools context-sensitive tab displays.

3. In the Mode panel, ensure that Planes is enabled to define planar sections in the scene.

4. In the Current drop-down menu in the Plane Settings panel, select a plane to activate it. By default Plane 1 is activated. Verify in the drop-down menu that Plane1 is enabled as indicated by the yellow lightbulb icon. Select the lightbulb icon to activate if required. The remaining planes are not initially active.

5. By default, each plane has a default Alignment already assigned (e.g., Top, Bottom, Front, etc.). To change this alignment, select the Alignment drop-down menu in the Planes Settings panel. The alignment options correspond to the faces of the ViewCube along with the following options:

    - Click Align to View to section through the model, parallel to the current viewpoint regardless of its viewing angle.
    - Click Align to Surface to section through the model aligned with a selected surface.
    - Click Align to Line to section through the model aligned to a selected line.

6. To change the location of the sectioning plane in the model, select either the Move or Rotate commands in the Transform panel.

7. Use the gizmo that displays on the plane in the Scene View to move/rotate the position of the plane in the viewpoint. To enter an exact positioning value, expand the Transform panel and enter coordinates or angular values.

8. Enable additional planes by selecting them in the Current drop-down menu. Once enabled you can change their alignment or Move/Rotate them, as required.

9. To disable a plane once it is displayed, select ⌦ on the Planes Settings panel header and disable the plane's display in the Section Plane Settings window that displays.

10. On the Save panel, click to save the Viewpoint. Enter a descriptive name.

Linking Section Planes

Use Link Section Planes to link two or more section planes together, forming a slice, and then use the gizmo or the Transform fields to move the slice through the model.

Procedure: To Link Section Planes

1. Create all of the individual section planes that are going to be linked together.

2. With the Sectioning Tools tab active, enable the appropriate planes that are required in the slice. The planes can be either parallel or perpendicular to one another.

3. On the Planes Settings panel, click Link Section Planes to link the planes together.

4. Use the gizmo that is displayed on the linked section planes or the Transform fields to move the slice through the model.

5. Repeat the above steps for other planes if required.

6. On the Planes Settings panel, click Link Section Planes again to disable the link.

7. On the Save panel, click to save the Viewpoint. Enter a descriptive name.

   Tip: Record the model as it is progressively sectioned, either using the gizmo or by setting up two views of the model in different states of section and then adding them to an empty animation.

Section Boxes

As an alternative to using multiple planes and linking them to define a sectioned area, you can use the Box mode.

Procedure: To Create a Section Box

1.   Select a saved viewpoint or manipulate the model to an orientation to begin sectioning from.

2.   Select the Viewpoint tab and click Enable Sectioning in the Sectioning panel. The Sectioning Tools Contextual tab displays.

3.   In the Mode panel, ensure that Box is enabled to define the section in the scene using a three-dimensional box.

4.   To change the location of the sectioning box in the model, select either the Move or Rotate commands in the Transform panel.

5.   Use the gizmo that displays on the box in the Scene View to move/rotate the position of the box in the viewpoint. To enter an exact positioning value, expand the Transform panel and enter coordinates or angular values for the X, Y, and Z axes.

6.   To change the size of the sectioning box in the model, select Scale in the Transform panel and use the gizmo to drag the size of the box or enter values in the expanded Transform panel.

7.   On the Save panel, click to save the Viewpoint. Enter a descriptive name.

Exercise: Section Planes

Section Planes

1. Open the file C:\Navisworks 2017 Essentials Class Files\Training\Examples\KLM\KLM.nwd.

2. Orient the model to its default Home view using 🏠 on the ViewCube. Zoom in on the model, as required, to achieve a satisfactory view.

3. Select the Viewpoint tab and click Enable Sectioning 🔲 in the Sectioning panel. The Sectioning Tools context-sensitive tab displays.

4. In the Plane Settings panel, ensure that Plane 1 is displayed as the currently active plane in the Current drop-down menu. Drop-down the menu and notice that Plane1 is enabled as indicated by the yellow lightbulb icon. If not enabled, select the lightbuld adjacent to Plane1. The remaining planes are not active.

5. By default, the Alignment option for Plane 1 is set to Top as shown in the Plane Settings panel. Ensure that Top is set as the alignment option. Reselect Top in the drop-down list if the plane is being displayed vertically through the building.

6. In the Transform panel, ensure that the Move ✥ command is enabled so that you can access the move gizmo on the section plane.

7. Select the gizmo that is displayed with the plane. Drag the gizmo upwards by selecting and dragging the red axis to change the position of the plane in the model.

8. To accurately position the section plane, expand the Transform panel and enter **3.000** as the Z position value. The X, Y and Z values in this field define the position of the section plane.

9. In the Plane Settings panel, select the Current drop-down menu and select Plane 2 to enable it. Expand the Current drop-down menu again and notice that Plane 1 is also still displayed as indicated by the yellow lightbulb icon.

    Tip: To disable a plane once it is displayed, select 📋 on the Planes Settings panel header and disable the plane's display in the Section Plane Settings window that displays.

10. By default, the Alignment option for Plane 2 is set to Bottom. Maintain this setting.

11. In the Transform panel, ensure that the Move ✥ command is enabled. Using the expanded Transform panel, enter **.33** as the Z position value.

12. In the Plane Settings panel, click Link Section Planes 🔗 to link section planes 1 and 2 together, forming a slice of the first floor.

13. Use the gizmo on the model to move the slice through the model.

14. On the Save panel, click Save Viewpoint ⬚ to save the Viewpoint. Enter **Section1** as the name of the viewpoint.

    While using section planes, you can use the navigation modes to review areas of interest in the model.

15. To disable the section planes, select ⬚ on the Planes Settings panel header and disable the plane's display in the Section Plane Settings window that displays.

Section Box

1. Orient the model to its default Home view using ⬚ on the ViewCube. Zoom in on the model as required, to achieve a satisfactory view.

2. The Sectioning Tools tab should still be active, if not, select the Viewpoint tab and click Enable Sectioning ⬚ in the Sectioning panel.

3. In the Mode panel, select the drop-down menu and click Box ⬚. A box displays around the entire model.

    Note: The Plane Settings panel is not available when using a Box section.

4. In the Transform panel, ensure that the Move ⬚ command is enabled so that you can access the move gizmo on the box.

5. Select the gizmo that is displayed with the box. Drag the planes and axes on the gizmo to change the location of the box.

6. To accurately position the box, expand the Transform panel and enter **0** as the X, Y, and Z position values. The X, Y and Z values in this field define the position of the box.

7. To accurately resize the box, expand the Transform panel and enter **10** as the X, Y, and Z size values. The X, Y and Z values in this field define the size of the box's shape.

8. On the Save panel, click Save Viewpoint ⬚ to save the Viewpoint. Enter **Box1** as the name of the viewpoint.

    While using Box sections, you can use the navigation modes to review areas of interest in the model.

9. Click Enable Sectioning ⬚ in the Enable panel to disable sectioning.

10. Select the Section1 and Box1 saved viewpoints to display them again. Once a section or box view has been selected, you must disable sectioning or return to a non-sectioned viewpoint. Simply returning to the Home view will not disable sectioning.

11. Close the file without saving.

Lesson: Links

Overview

This lesson describes how to add links to objects in the model. It also introduces you to the link options for how links are displayed in the scene.

Objective

After completing this lesson, you will be able to:

- Add links and define how they are displayed in the scene.

Using Links

Links can be attached to any object(s) in the model and linked to external files, exported viewpoints, selection sets, clash tests, and URL's.

Procedure: To View and Add Links

1. On the Home tab in the Display panel, click Links 🔗 to switch on the Links feature. Any previously added links are displayed pointing to the attached object.

2. Move the cursor over the link to display the link name or address.

3. Click the link to open the file, etc.

4. To add a link, select the object in the scene (or in the Selection Tree) that the link is to be attached to.

5. Right-click on the object and select Links > Add Link from the pop-up menu.

6. In the Add Link dialog box, in the Name field, enter an appropriate name.

7. Click ⬚ to browse and add a link to the required external file or URL.

8. Select a Category.

   Tip: Manually enter an alternative category name, if required, from the following options: Viewpoints, Selection Sets, Redline Tags, Clash Detective, or TimeLiner.

9. To point to a specific part of the object, click Add, and then click on the object.

10. Click OK. The link is displayed in the scene. If the link is not visible refer to Links options in the Options Editor dialog box.

Note: If the object that was selected when the link is placed is Hidden, the link is also hidden.

Link Options

The Links feature has many options which can be set based on user preference.

Procedure: To Change Link Options

1. Click Application Menu ![N] > Options > Interface > Links.

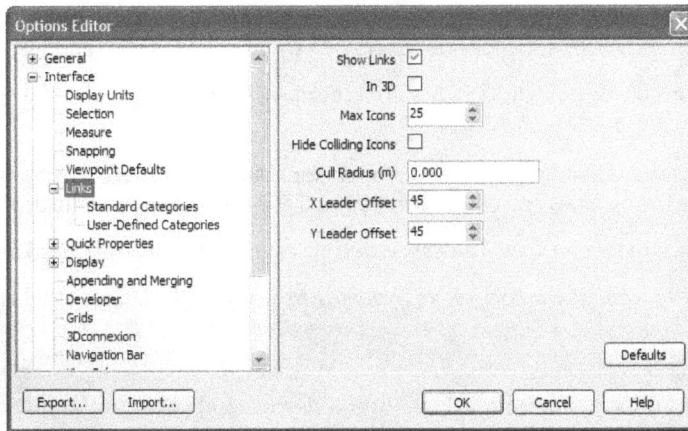

2. In the Options Editor, select In 3D for the link to float in front of the attached item in the scene.

Note: In 3D mode, a link can become hidden by other objects in the scene when navigating.

3. In the Max Icons field, set the maximum number of links visible in the scene. This might need to be increased if an added link is not visible.

Note: If the scene becomes too cluttered with links, add a checkmark to Hide Colliding Icons. Icons that appear overlapped in the main view can be hidden if the Hide Colliding check box is selected.

4. In the Cull Radius box, enter the distance for how close links should be in order to be drawn in the main view. Any links further away than this distance are not drawn. The default value of 0 means that all links are drawn.

5. In the Leader Offset fields, change the angle of the link arrow. The default is 0. The recommended angle is 45.

6. In the Links category, in the Options Editor, select Standard Category. To reduce the clutter of links, scroll through the list and clear the Visible option on any category (i.e., Hyperlink, label, clash detective, etc.) that is not required in the display. If there are custom categories included, you can disable them from displaying using the options in the User-Defined Category.

7. Click OK to save and close the dialog box.

Exercise: View and Add Links

1. Open the file *C:\Navisworks 2017 Essentials Class Files\Training\Examples\Bath_City\ Central.nwd*.

2. On the Home tab in the Display panel, click Links 🔗 to switch on the Links feature and display any links previously added in the model.

3. In the Selection Tree, expand the *Central.nwd* hierarchy. Select *abbey.dwg*.

4. Click Zoom Selected in the Navigation Bar to view the selected item.

5. In the Selection Tree, right-click abbey.dwg, and then select Links > Add Link.

6. In the Add Link dialog box, in the Name field, enter **Photo**. Click [...] and browse to *\Training\Examples\Bath_City\Abbey.bmp* and click Open to add the link address.

7. In the Add Link dialog box, click OK. The link is displayed in the scene.

8. If the arrows are not pointing to the abbey, click Application Menu [N·] > Options > Interface > Links. Select Show Links and enter **45** in both the X and Y Leader Offset fields. Click OK.

9. Click the link in the Scene View. The *Abbey.bmp* file should open in an appropriate software.

10. In the Saved Viewpoints window, select Overview. Notice all of the link tags that are displayed across the scene.

11. To control the display of these links in the Scene View, click Application Menu [N·] > Options > Interface > Links > Standard Categories and clear the Visible checkmark in the Viewpoints section. Click OK.

    Note: Consider using any of the sections in the Standard Categories category to customize the display of links.

    Note: If the object that was selected when the link is placed is Hidden, the link is also hidden.

12. Close the file without saving.

Lesson: Comparing Models

Overview

This lesson describes how to open and compare items, files, or models that should be the same but have some differences.

Objective

After completing this lesson, you will be able to:

- Append two files, use the Compare tool to check for differences, and view the results.

About the Compare Tool

The Compare tool becomes available when two items that should be exactly the same are selected. These can be any type of item, but the Compare tool is most useful when comparing two versions of the same model. During the comparison, the Autodesk Navisworks software starts at each item and travels down each path, as seen in the Selection Tree, comparing each item that it comes across in terms of the criteria requested.

Procedure: To Compare Two Model Files

1.   Open the model file to be compared.

2.   Append the other model file to be compared. Ensure that the models are displayed and can be distinguished in the Selection Tree.

3.   Hold CTRL and select both files to be compared in the Selection Tree.

4.   On the Home tab in the Tools panel, click Compare .

5.   In the Compare dialog box, under Find Differences In, add a checkmark to all the required find options.

6.   Under Results, add checkmarks to the required options.

     Tip: Add a checkmark to all the options except Save as Selection Sets. This is a good way to review the results of the comparison.

7.   Click OK to perform the comparison. Only the items of the model, where differences are found, are displayed.

Exercise: Compare Two Model Files

1. Open the file *C:\Navisworks 2017 Essentials Class Files\Training\Examples\Compare\ Clash.nwd*.

2. Append the file *C:\Navisworks 2017 Essentials Class Files\Training\Examples\Clash.nwd*.

3. Hold CTRL and select both files in the Selection Tree.

4. On the Home tab in the Tools panel, click Compare .

5. In the Compare dialog box, in the Find Differences In area, clear all but the checkmarks adjacent to the Geometry and Overridden Transform options.

6. In the Results area, leave all of the options selected, except Save as Selection Sets. Click OK to perform the comparison.

7. Display the Sets window if it is not already displayed. Sets have been created with the results.

   In this example, the entire section of the plant has been moved.

8. Click a selection set that has been added. Two items are highlighted—one in the original position and one in the new position. Use the Zoom Selected option to review the selected set.

   This function could be useful to determine what changes have been made between revisions of the same model.

9. Close the file without saving.

Lesson: Navisworks Real-Time Rendering

Overview

This lesson describes the lighting modes. It also introduces you to the rendering styles and how to select the required effects.

Objective

After completing this lesson, you will be able to:

- Select the lighting and rendering to achieve the required results.

Real-Time Rendering

The Autodesk Navisworks software provides four lighting modes and four rendering modes with which a model can be viewed in real time.

> It is useful to split the screen when rendering to compare effects. To split your current view horizontally, expand the Split View command in the View tab and click Split Horizontal. To split your current view vertically, expand the Split View command in the View tab and click Split Vertical.

The Render Style panel is available on the Viewpoint tab.

Lighting Modes

Lights come through from various CAD file formats as scene lights. The following controls can be used to achieve the required appearance, with further adjustments available in File Options. The spheres below demonstrate the effect the lighting styles have on them. In order from the left, are full lights, scene lights, head lights, and no lights.

Icon	Name	Description
☼	**Full Lights**	Uses lights that have been defined with the Rendering tool (Autodesk Rendering).
🔦	**Scene Lights**	Uses whatever lights are defined in the source CAD model. If there are none available, two default opposing lights are used. To change the intensity of the scene lights, click File Options ⬚ in the Project panel on the Home tab. In the File Options dialog box, select the Scene Lights tab. Move the slider to adjust the ambient intensity.

Icon	Name	Description
	Head Lights	Uses a single directional light located at the camera (viewer) in addition to an ambient light. To change the effects of the head lights, click File Options ☐ in the Project panel on the Home tab. In the File Options dialog box, select the Head Light tab. The Ambient slider changes the overall brightness of the scene and the Head Light slider changes the brightness of the directional light.
	No Lights	Switches off all lights including any defined in the model. The model is shaded with flat rendering.

Rendering Mode

The four render modes affect how the items in the scene are rendered. The spheres below demonstrate the effect the render modes have on their appearance. In order from the left these are full render, shaded, wireframe, and hidden line.

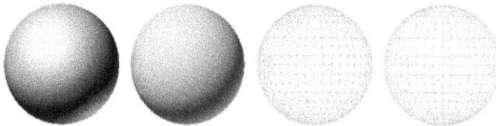

Icon	Render Mode	Description
	Full Render	Renders the model with smooth shading including any materials that have been applied, or have been brought through from the CAD file.
	Shaded	Renders the model with smooth shading and without textures.
	Wireframe	Renders the model in wireframe. As triangles are used to represent surfaces and solids, all triangle edges are visible in this mode.
	Hidden Line	Renders the model in hidden line. This requires two-pass rendering, so it is equivalent to rendering shaded and wireframe at the same time. The output is low quality, as all the facet edges in the model are visible.

Primitive Display

You can enable and disable the drawing of Surfaces, Lines, Points, Snap Points, and 3D Text in the Scene View. These options are all controlled on the Viewpoint tab in the Render Style panel.

Icon	Primitive	Description
	Surfaces	Controls the display of Surfaces in the model. Surfaces are the triangles that make up the 2D and 3D items in the scene.
	Line	Controls the display of Lines in the model. **Tip:** You can change the width of the drawn lines using the Options Editor.
	Points	Controls the display of Points in the model. **Tip:** You can change the size of drawn points using the Options Editor.
	Snap Points	Controls the display of Snap Points in the model. Snap points are implied points in the model. Points are "real" points in the model, whereas Snap Points mark locations on other primitives, for example the center of a circle, and are useful for snapping to when measuring. **Tip:** You can change the size of the drawn snap points using the Options Editor.
	3D Text	Controls the display of 3D text in the model.

Exercise: Setting Lighting and Rendering Options

1. Open the file *C:\Navisworks 2017 Essentials Class Files\Training\Examples\Dodge_Viper.nwd.*

2. To split your current view horizontally, expand the Split View command in the View tab and click Split Horizontal.

3. Click in the top pane. Expand the Split View command in the View tab and click Split Vertical. The top pane splits vertically.

4. Click in the lower pane. Expand the Split View command in the View tab and click Split Vertical. The lower pane splits vertically.

5. The Rendering mode in each pane can be adjusted individually. Click on a pane to make it active.

6. Select the top left pane.

7. Select the Viewpoint tab. In the Render Style panel, click Head Light from the Lighting drop-down menu.

8. Select the Home tab. Click File Options in the Project panel. In the File Options dialog box select the Headlight tab. Adjust the Ambient and Headlight slide bars and view the effect. Click OK.

9. Select one of the other panes.

10. Select the Viewpoint tab. In the Render Style panel, click Scene Lights .

11. Select the Home tab. Click File Options in the Project panel. In the File Options dialog box, select the Scene Lights tab. Adjust the Ambient slide bar and view the effect. Click OK.

12. Experiment with the Render modes and navigating in the different panes. Notice that each pane remembers its last render style (Lighting and Mode setting).

13. To exit the split screen mode, click Close X at the top of each pane.

14. Close the file without saving.

Lesson: Switchback

Overview

This lesson describes how to use the SwitchBack feature to view and edit 3D geometry in the original application, while reviewing the model in the Autodesk Navisworks software.

Objective

After completing this lesson, you will be able to:

- Select an object in the Autodesk Navisworks software, then use SwitchBack to view and edit the object in the original application.

The SwitchBack Feature

SwitchBack is designed to improve the workflow of design review by significantly reducing the time taken finding and altering original designs.

When reviewing a model, the SwitchBack feature enables an instant switch back from the Autodesk Navisworks software, to the CAD application that the model was created in. Furthermore, when an object is selected in the Autodesk Navisworks software and then SwitchBack is selected, the same object is displayed in the CAD application, in the same camera position.

This means that when reviewing an object in the model that then requires changes, by using SwitchBack, you can access the object easily in the CAD application and make changes. When the file is saved in the CAD application, and the model in the Autodesk Navisworks software refreshed, the effect of the altered object can be reviewed.

> For this feature to be used to full benefit and to significantly increase workflow efficiency, the model being reviewed in the Autodesk Navisworks software should be an NWF file.
>
> This feature requires the CAD application to be on the same computer and running at the time. Only AutoCAD® (version 2013 or later), Autodesk® Revit® (version 2013 or later), Autodesk® Inventor® (version 2014 or later), and MicroStation® based applications (/J and v8.9) are currently supported.

Procedure: To Use the SwitchBack Feature

1. For AutoCAD (or products based on it), first open the product in the usual manner, and type: **nwload** in the command line to load the nwexport plugin.

    Note: If SwitchBack needs to be available every time AutoCAD is run, nwexport can be added to the set of startup applications in AutoCAD.

2. Once the CAD package is running and nwexport has started, return to Autodesk Navisworks.

3. Click Application Menu > Options > File Readers > DWG/DXF. On the DWG/DXF page, ensure that the Convert Entity Handles option is selected.

4. Select an object in the Scene View, and on the Item Tools tab click SwitchBack on the SwitchBack panel. Alternatively, you can right-click on the object being reviewed in the Selection Tree and click SwitchBack.

    The current Autodesk Navisworks camera view is taken back to the CAD package, and the same object is selected. Selection of objects is done by entity handle.

    Tip: Alternatively, in the Clash Detective window, on the Results tab, you can click SwitchBack. The Clash Detective feature is available for Autodesk Navisworks Manage users only.

5. Make the changes in AutoCAD, then save the changes.

6. Return to the Autodesk Navisworks software and on the Home tab in the Project panel, click Refresh ✍.

The changes made to the object can now be reviewed in the Autodesk Navisworks software.

Tip: When using the Switchback feature it is important that the CAD file (e.g., AutoCAD) is the same version (release year) as the version of the Autodesk Navisworks software. If they are not, it can present problems with the workflow producing the correct result.

Note: Some objects cannot be selected in AutoCAD (for example, blocks), which may mean that running SwitchBack may be unsuccessful with a given selected object. If this is the case, try selecting further up the object tree and trying again.

TimeLiner

Autodesk® Navisworks® TimeLiner creates 4D simulations (a simulation that includes time) of the construction of 3D models. By attaching items in the model to tasks with a start and end date/time, you can create a simulation that shows sections of the model being added or removed over time, according to the scheduled tasks.

With TimeLiner, you can also link the objects to tasks in an external scheduling file, and synchronize the simulation with the actual status of the project. Actual and planned dates can be associated with the tasks, simulating actual against planned schedules.

Objectives

After completing this chapter, you will be able to:

- Open the TimeLiner window in the Autodesk Navisworks software.
- Effectively use the simulation controls to review the simulation in detail.
- Understand the data displayed during a simulation.
- Create tasks with start and finish dates.
- Use a variety of methods to attach tasks to objects on the 3D model.
- Create tasks automatically.
- Open and display the Gantt View for your project.
- Control the display of tasks in a Gantt View.
- Import tasks from an external file.
- Use shortcuts to speed up attaching tasks to objects on a 3D model.
- Synchronize the task data in TimeLiner with data in the linked external file.
- Configure how objects are displayed at each stage of a simulation.
- Customize existing or create new appearance definitions.
- Export a simulation in AVI format.
- Use the export options to create a suitable quality AVI.

Lesson: TimeLiner Overview

Overview

This lesson describes how to open and use the TimeLiner simulation controls to effectively review the construction or demolition process. It also describes the various information displays in the simulation window.

Objectives

After completing this lesson, you will be able to:

- Open the TimeLiner window in the Autodesk Navisworks software.
- Effectively use the simulation controls to review the simulation in detail.
- Understand the data displayed during a simulation.

TimeLiner Overview

The TimeLiner tool adds schedule simulation to Autodesk Navisworks. TimeLiner imports schedules from a variety of sources. You can then connect tasks in the schedule with objects in the model to create a simulation. This enables you to see the effects of the schedule on the model, and compare planned dates against actual dates. Costs can also be assigned to tasks to track project cost through its schedule. TimeLiner also enables the export of images and animations based on the results of the simulation. TimeLiner will automatically update the simulation if the model or schedule changes.

Opening the TimeLiner Window

To open the TimeLiner window, select the Home tab and click TimeLiner in the Tools panel. The TimeLiner window displays and can be docked in the Autodesk Navisworks window by dragging it to the required position.

> TimeLiner is only available if you have an Autodesk® Navisworks® Simulate or Manage license. Otherwise, you can only use TimeLiner playback.

Creating a Timeliner Simulation

A Timeliner Simulation can be created in the following ways:

- Manually create individual tasks that have a name, start date, end date, and a task type.
- Import tasks from an external source, such as Microsoft Project™.

> To learn how to manually create tasks and import tasks from an external source, refer to the Creating Tasks and Import Tasks from External Project File Lessons.

Simulation Control Bar

The Simulation control bar is located on the Simulation tab.

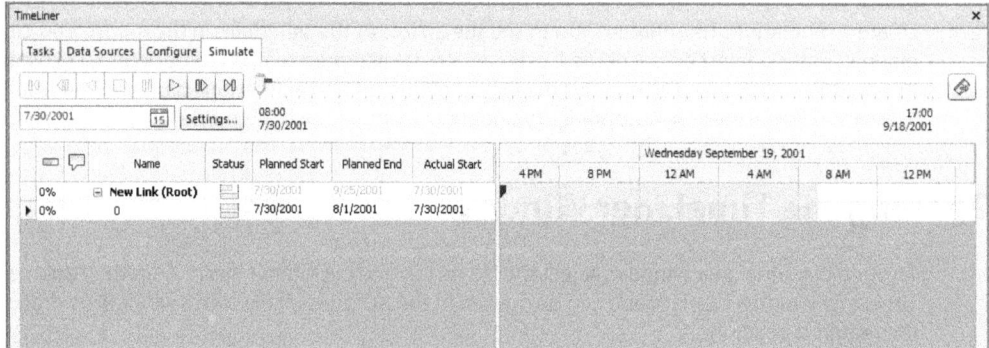

The tools on this tab include the main simulation control tools to play, stop, and navigate to any point in the simulation. There are several additional controls and settings to further increase the effectiveness of the simulation.

Icon	Name	Description
	Rewind	Rewind to start of simulation
	Step Back	Step back one step size in simulation
	Reverse Play	Play simulation in reverse
	Pause	Pause simulation
	Stop	Stop simulation
	Play	Play simulation
	Step Forward	Step forward one step size in simulation
	Forward	Forward to end of simulation

Use Pause [⏸] at any time or the slider bar ⎯⎯〇⎯⎯ to review task information at any point in the simulation.

The start and end dates of the simulation are displayed at each end of the slider bar.

The Date field [8/6/2001 📅] displays the date position of the slider bar. Click the drop-down list calendar to set and move the simulation to a specific date.

Active Tasks Pane

The Active Tasks pane is located in the lower portion of the Simulation tab and displays all active tasks. It also displays the Gantt View at any point of the simulation and includes available information about each task.

🔲	💬	Name	Status	Planned Start	Planned End	Actual S	Monday August 06, 2001			Tues
							12 PM	4 PM	8 PM	12,
0%		⊟ New Link (Root)		7/30/2001	9/25/2001	7/30/2001				
▶ 50.57%	1	S_DEEP_FOUNDS_E10		8/6/2001	8/6/2001	8/6/2001				

- **Simulation Progress %** – Displays progress of the task as a percentage.
- **Comments** – Number of comments associated with this task.
- **Name** - Displays the name of the task.
- **Status** – A quick reference graphical display of actual against planned dates. Each task has two bars. The top bar represents the planned dates The lower bar represents the actual dates. If the actual start and finish dates are the same as the planned start and finish dates, the bars are displayed in green. Any variations between planned and actual dates are displayed in red. If there are no planned dates, the actual dates bar is red.
- **Planned Start/End Dates** – Planned (or scheduled or base line) start and end dates of the task.
- **Actual Start/Actual End Dates** – Actual start and end dates of the task.
- **Task Type** – If the task is to construct the attached objects the task type should be Construct. If the task is to demolish the attached objects the task type should be Demolish etc.
- **Gantt View** – The Gantt Chart displays a colored bar chart illustrating the project status. Each row displays only one task. The horizontal axis represents the time span of the project, broken down into increments (such as days, weeks, months, and years). Tasks can run sequentially, in parallel, or overlapping.

Exercise: Run a Basic TimeLiner Simulation

Simulating the Tasks

1. Open the file *C:\Navisworks 2017 Essentials Class Files\Training\Examples\Gatehouse\ Gatehouse_TimerLiner.nwf.*

2. On the Home tab in the Tools panel, click TimeLiner ⏰ if it is not already displayed.

3. Select the Simulate tab and click Play ▷ to view the simulation.

   The 40 second animation displays an example of TimeLiner in action, with the model being constructed in the Scene View according to the task time schedule. At the same time, the tasks are displayed at the bottom of the Simulate tab as they are carried out.

   The default view for TimeLiner simulations is:

   - At the start of the simulation no items of the model are displayed.
   - When a task start date is reached the items attached to a task, are displayed in transparent green to indicate the task has started.
   - When a task end date is reached, the task items are displayed in their normal colors to indicated the task is complete.

   This example contains both actual and planned dates. There are options available to define how the schedule is simulated, which are described in Configuring and Defining a Simulation.

4. During the simulation, in the Active Tasks window, observe the task's Status, Progress %, start and end dates, and the Gantt View.

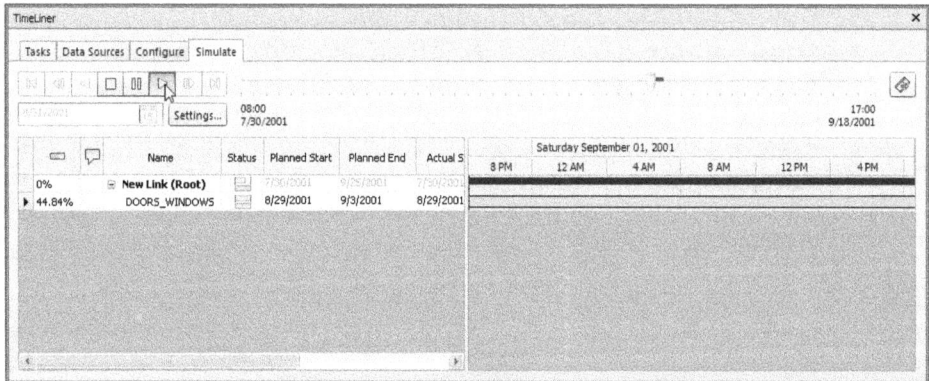

5.   Use the following controls:

- Stop   ▢
- Pause   ▯▯
- Reverse Play   ◁
- Rewind   ◁◁
- Forward   ▷▷

6.   Use the slider bar ⎯⎯ to move to any part of the simulation.

7.   Use Step Forward ▷▷ and Step Backward ◁◁ and notice that at some points there are no active tasks displayed even though the model has changed from the previous step.

8.   Notice the tasks in progress are displayed in transparent green until completed.

9.   Close the file without saving.

Lesson: Creating Tasks

Overview

This lesson describes how to create tasks manually and automatically in TimeLiner. It also describes different methods of attaching each task to objects or groups of objects on the 3D model.

Objectives

After completing this lesson, you will be able to:

- Create tasks with start and finish dates.
- Use a variety of methods to attach tasks to objects on the 3D model.
- Create tasks automatically.

About Creating Tasks

TimeLiner tasks can be created manually from layers, selection sets, etc., or imported from external scheduling software such as Microsoft Project.

Procedure: To Create Tasks Manually

1. Open the model.

2. On the Home tab in the Tools panel, click TimeLiner ⏱, if the TimeLiner window is not already displayed. In the TimeLiner window, click the Tasks tab.

3. On the Tasks tab, click Add Task or right-click and click Add Task. A task is added.

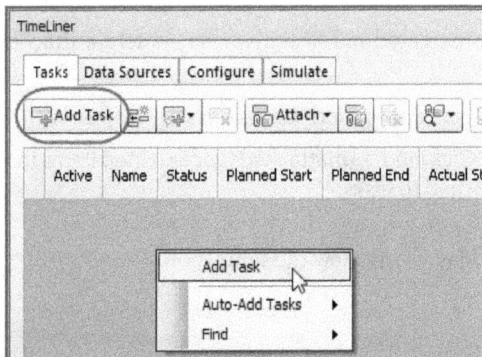

4. Select in the task name field and enter the task name. Press ENTER after entering the task name to create a new task.

5. By default, the checkbox in the Active column is enabled. Enabling/disabling this checkbox controls whether the task is on or off. If a task is toggled off, it does not appear in the simulation.

6. By default, the Planned and Actual start and end dates are enabled for use. To disable these dates, right-click in either the Planned Start or Planned End date cells and clear the Enable Planned Dates option. Alternatively, right-click in either the Actual Start or Actual End date cells and clear the Enable Actual Dates option to disable these fields.

7. The Status column displays two separate bars for each task, displaying planned relationships and actual relationships. The color is used to differentiate the early (blue), on-time (green), late (red), and planned (gray) portions of the task. Dots mark the planned start and end dates.

    Tip: Placing the mouse over a Status icon displays a tooltip explaining the task status.

8. Select a Task Type in its associated drop-down to determine how objects are displayed during a simulation.

    Tip: Use Demolition for tasks such as site clearance. Use Temporary for temporary tasks such as Scaffolding. Additional, customized task types can be created if required, see Configuring and Defining a Simulation, for further information.

9. Before a simulation can work, each manually created task needs to be attached to items in the model. In the Attached column you attach the required items to the relevant task using one of the following options:

    ■ In the Scene View or the Selection Tree, select the items to be attached to the task. In the TimeLiner task, right-click in the Attached cell for the task that is being created and click Attach Current Selection. The selected items are now attached to the task.

    ■ In the TimeLiner task, right-click in the Attached field for the task that is being created, click Attach Set, and then click the required selection or search set from the displayed list.

    Tip: If additional items in the model need to be attached to a task that already has items attached to it, the additional items can be appended to the existing selection. Select the additional items, right-click in the Attached column for the relevant task, and click Append Current Selection.

10. Repeat the process until all tasks are created and all items in the model are attached to relevant tasks.

11. Verify that the start and end dates are appropriate for each task.

    Tip: Right-click in the Task pane. Click Find > Unattached/Uncontained Items to display any items that have not yet been attached to tasks.

12. Select the Simulate tab and click Play ▷ to view the simulation.

Creating Tasks Automatically

Tasks can be created automatically in TimeLiner from the Selection Tree or from selection sets.

1. Open the model files.

2. On the Home tab in the Tools panel, click TimeLiner 🕐, if the TimeLiner window is not already displayed. In the TimeLiner window, click the Tasks tab.

3. On the Tasks tab, click Auto-Add Tasks 🔲 and select one of its expanded options. Alternatively, right-click, select Auto-Add Tasks, and select an option.

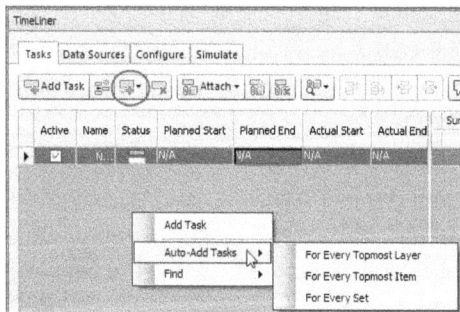

Select one of the following options:

- **For Every Topmost Layer** – Creates tasks with the same names as each topmost layer in the Selection Tree and automatically attaches each layer to the relevant task.
- **For Every Topmost Item** – Creates tasks with the same names as each topmost item in the Selection Tree and automatically attaches each item to the relevant task.
- **For Every Set** – Creates tasks with the same names as each selection and search set in the Selection Sets window, and automatically attaches each set to the relevant task.

4. Sequential Planned dates are automatically added to all tasks; edit as required. You can add Actual dates or disable these fields by right-clicking in either the Actual Start or Actual End date cells and clearing the Enable Actual Dates option.

   Tip: When tasks are created automatically, they might not be in the same order as the correct construction sequence. To reorder the tasks according to the dates, set the correct dates for each task, then click the relevant column header to reorder.

5. Edit the Active and Task Type fields for each task, if required.

6. Select the Simulate tab and click Play ▷ to view the simulation.

Exercise: Creating Tasks Manually

1. Open the file *C:\Navisworks 2017 Essentials Class Files\Training\Examples\Dodge_Viper.nwd.*

2. On the Home tab in the Tools panel, click TimeLiner ⌚ if it is not already displayed.

3. In the TimeLiner window, click the Tasks tab, if it is not already active.

4. In the Tasks pane, select Add Task or right-click and select Add Task. A task is added.

5. In the task name field, enter **Chassis** as the task name. Do not press ENTER, which creates a new task.

6. Select the Active checkbox, if it is not already enabled.

7. Right-click on the Planned Start cell and clear the Enable Planned Dates. This disables the two planned date cells.

8. Set the Actual Start Date as 01/02/2015 and set the Actual End Date as 01/04/2017.

9. Scroll to the Task Type column and select Construct from the drop-down menu.

10. Expand *Dodge_Viper.nwd* in the Selection Tree window and select DODGE_VIPER_CHASSIS.

11. Return to the Chassis task in TimeLiner, right-click the Attached cell and select Attach Current Selection.

12. Click Add Task or right-click below the first task and click Add Task. Rename the task as **Body**.

13. Select the Active checkbox, if it is not already enabled.

14. Right-click on the Planned Start cell and clear the Enable Planned Dates. This disables the two planned date cells.

15. Set an actual start date of 01/04/2017 and an end date of 01/06/2017.

16. For Task Type, select Construct.

17. Right-click in the Attached cell, and click Attached Set > Body.

    Note: The Attached Set drop-down list includes selections sets and search sets, as listed in the Sets window.

18. Click Add Task or right-click below the two tasks and click Add Task. Rename the task as **Wheels**.

19. Select the Active checkbox, if it is not already enabled.

20. Disable the planned date cells.

21. Select an actual start date of 01/06/2017 and an end date of 01/10/2017.

22. For Task Type, select Construct.

23. Right-click in the Attached field and click Attached Set > Wheels.

24. Right-click below the first three tasks and click Add Task. Rename the task as **Lights**.

25. Select the Active checkbox, if it is not already enabled.

26. Disable the planned date cells.

27. Select an actual start date of 01/10/2017 and an end date of 01/12/2017.

28. For Task Type, select Construct.

29. Select the Home tab. In the Select & Search panel, click Find Items .

30. In the Find Items window, set the following criteria in the drop-down lists in the pane on the right:

    - In Category, select Item
    - In Property, select Name
    - In Condition, select Contains
    - In Value, select DODGE_VIPER_LIGHTS (Hint: you may need to expand the width on the Value column to see the full value name in the drop-down list.)

Category	Property	Condition	Value
Item	Name	Contains	Dodge_Vi...

31. Clear the checkmark from Match Case and click Find All. The searched items are selected.

32. Return to the Lights task in TimeLiner, right-click the Attached cell and select Attach Current Search. The searched items are attached to the Lights task.

33. Close the Find Items window.

34. Click the Simulate tab, and then click Play to view the simulation.

35. Save this file with the same name plus your initials to a new location, for example, *C:\Temp\ Dodge_ViperJMD.nwf.*

Lesson: Gantt View

Overview

This lesson describes how to access and display a Gantt View of your project schedule.

Objectives

After completing this lesson, you will be able to:

- Open and display the Gantt View for your project.
- Control the display of tasks in a Gantt View.

Displaying and Controlling the Gantt View

A Gantt View of the projects timeline can be displayed in the Tasks tab of the TimeLiner dialog box. This view provides a read-only graphical representation of your project schedule. Tasks are represented as bars on the Gantt chart and you can switch between Planned, Actual, and Planned vs Actual display dates. You can also use the Zoom control to set the resolution of your Gantt View.

Procedure: To Display and Control a Gantt View

1. On the Home tab in the Tools panel, click TimeLiner ⬚, if it is not already displayed.

2. Select the Tasks tab, if not already displayed. The Gantt View is displayed in the pane on the right. You can control the display of the Gantt View in the Tasks tab by enabling or clearing the

   Show or hide the Gantt chart ⬚ option.

   Tip: All of the information in the Gantt View tab is read-only. Changes made in the tasks update automatically in the Gantt View.

3. Using the display dates options ⬚ ⬚ ⬚, select either the Show Planned Dates, Show Actual Dates, or Show Planned vs. Actual Dates options to change the display. These options determine which dates are shown in the Gantt View. In the Planned vs. Actual display, the planned dates are shown as gray bars and the actual dates are blue bars.

4. Use the Zoom bar to control the zoom level of the Gantt View. Scrolling to the right expands the view to show days and hours, while scrolling to the left compresses the view to show weeks.

Exercise: Working with a Gantt View

Working with a Gantt View

1. Open the file *C:\Navisworks 2017 Essentials Class Files\Training\Examples\Gatehouse\ Gatehouse_TimerLiner.nwf.*

2. On the Home tab in the Tools panel, click TimeLiner 🕐 if it is not already displayed.

3. On the Tasks tab the Gantt View is displayed in the right hand pane. If it is not displayed, click

    Show or hide the Gantt chart 🗔 along the top of the Tasks tab.

4. Using the display dates options 🗔🗔🗔 , select either the Show Planned Dates, Show Actual Dates, or Show Planned vs. Actual Dates options to change the display. Review the changes to the Gantt View.

5. Select the Show Planned vs. Actual Dates 🗔 option. Review the changes to the Gantt View. The planned dates are shown as gray bars and the actual dates are blue bars.

6. Scroll the Zoom bar at the top of the Tasks tab. Notice how the Gantt View changes from a weekly display to a daily and hourly display. Manipulate the Zoom bar so that only a daily display is shown.

7. Close the file without saving.

Lesson: Import Tasks from External Project File

Overview

This lesson describes how to import tasks previously created in an external scheduling file. It also describes shortcut methods of attaching each task to objects or groups of objects on a 3D model.

Objectives

After completing this lesson, you will be able to:

- Import tasks from an external file.
- Use shortcuts to speed up attaching tasks to objects on a 3D model.
- Synchronize the task data in TimeLiner with data in the linked external file.

Linking to a Project File

One of TimeLiner's most powerful features is its integration with project scheduling software. A list of tasks, including their start and end date/times, can be imported from a project file directly into TimeLiner.

Procedure: To Link to a Project File

The typical scheduling software that is supported includes MS Project, Asta, and Primavera. The relevant software should be installed on the same computer as TimeLiner. However, if the schedule is saved in the MPX or .CSV format, then the relevant software does not need to be installed on the same computer.

1. Open the model files.

2. On the Home tab in the Tools panel, click TimeLiner ⏲ if the TimeLiner window is not already displayed.

3. Select the Data Sources tab. Click Add and select the project software file format. TimeLiner looks for relevant project scheduling software, which might take a few moments.

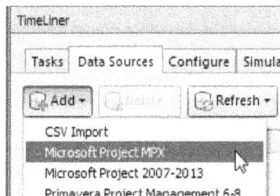

4. Browse for and open the scheduling file.

5. The Field Selector dialog box is displayed, where you can link any unrecognized, additional fields. Click in the External Field Name field at the right of a TimeLiner column field name, expand the drop-down list and select from the list of available column names in the external file. The available options might be different for each type of link source and, in some cases, may not need to be linked at all.

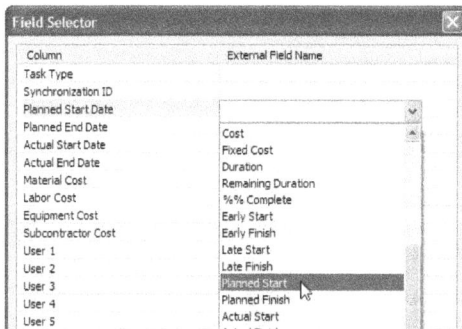

Tip: The Field Selector dialog box is used to map fields from external software so that the data from those are placed into the correct location in the Autodesk Navisworks software. For example, if the external file includes Baseline Start and End dates that need to link to the Planned Start and Planned End dates in TimeLiner.

---

6. Click OK.

7. The established link displays in the Data Sources tab in the TimeLiner. Notice that no tasks are currently listed in the Tasks Tab.

8. In the Data Sources tab, right-click the New Link and click Rebuild Task Hierarchy to extract the task data from the external file into TimeLiner.

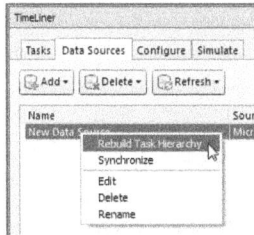

This imports all of the tasks from the project file including their Planned Start and Planned End dates, and any additional fields that were linked in the Field Selector dialog box.

9. Review any warnings that may appear, as there may be issues corresponding the columns in the external file with the Navisworks fields. For example, the import may recognize that task types are not corresponding. Since task types can be explicitly assigned, this is not an issue. In other cases you may want to import again and reassign the columns.

10. Click the Tasks tab to view the listed tasks.

11. Although the tasks have been imported into TimeLiner, they still need to be attached to objects in the model.

Note: Each task can be manually attached to a layer, selection set, search set, etc. However, this could take a long time. It is good practice to either use task names that correspond to layer names or to build selection and search sets that correspond to the task names. If this is the case, then a simple rule can be used so TimeLiner automatically (and instantly) attaches all the tasks to objects in the model.

12. Click Auto-Attach using Rules ⬛ to attach the tasks to items in the model.

13. Add a checkmark to a suitable rule then click Apply Rules or click New to create a new rule and Apply it. Close the TimeLiner Rules window. All the items that comply to the rule are attached to the correct task.

Tip: To understand how a new rule should be written, select an existing rule then click Edit to view that rule's formulation.

14. In the Tasks tab, review the Attached column. All attachments should now display Explicit Selection.

15. To identify any items that have not been attached to tasks, expand Find Items ⟨🔍▾⟩ and click Unattached/Uncontained Items.

16. If any unattached items are found, they are highlighted in the Selection Tree and on the model.

Click Hide Unselected ⟨🔲⟩ to display only these unattached items.

Tip: An item might not be attached because a task in the project scheduling file is omitted, or the item has not been included in a selection or search set.

Tip: Consideration should be made regarding the task name. You must either spell it the same and have matching case to the item group it is to attach to or you must setup rules to account/discount case sensitivity.

17. If required, re-apply the rules using the Auto-Attach using Rules ⟨🔳⟩ option.

18. Assign the Task Type, as required.

Tip: If all tasks have the same task type, select the Task Type field for the first task, press and hold SHIFT, and select the Task Type field for the last task. This selects all of the cells together. Right-click and select Fill Down to assign the same status to all tasks.

19. Select the Simulate tab and click Play ⟨▷⟩ to view the simulation.

Tip: You might need to configure the Settings for the simulation to ensure that the View options are set appropriately. For example, if there have been no Actual dates imported into the Timeliner, the Simulate settings must refer to something other than the actual dates in order to play the simulation. See Configuring and Defining a Simulation, for further information on Settings.

Synchronizing with Project Changes

One of the benefits of linking the model to an external project schedule file, such as MS Project, is that any changes to the schedule can be easily updated in TimeLiner.

Procedure: To Synchronize with Project Changes

1. Make any required changes to the project schedule in the scheduling software and save it.

2. On the Home tab in the Tools panel, click TimeLiner, if it is not already displayed.

3. Select the Data Sources tab. Right-click on the Link name and select one of the following options:

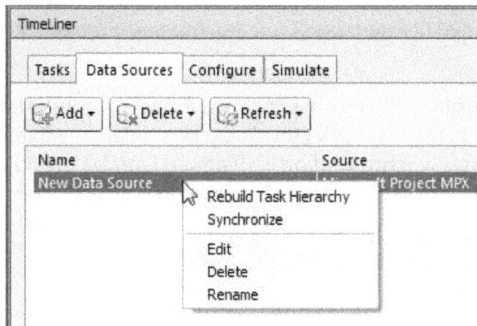

- **Rebuild Tasks Hierarchy** – Re-imports all tasks and associated data (as defined in the Field Selector window) from the selected project file and rebuilds the task hierarchy on the Tasks tab. Select this option to synchronize with the selected project file when new tasks have been added to the project file. This rebuilds the task hierarchy in TimeLine with all of the latest tasks and data.
- **Synchronize** – Updates all existing tasks in the Tasks tab with the latest associated data from the selected project file such as start and end dates.

> It is recommended that you recheck for uncontained items in case a new task has been added and items not attached to it.

Exercise: (C) Importing Tasks

1. Open the file *C:\Navisworks 2017 Essentials Class Files\Training\Examples\Gatehouse\Gatehouse.nwd*.

2. On the Home tab in the Tools panel, click TimeLiner ⏱, if it is not already displayed. Notice that no tasks are listed on the Tasks tab in this file.

3. Select the Data Sources tab. Click Add > Microsoft Project MPX.

   Tip: Microsoft Project MPX is a common format and does not require any scheduling software to be installed on the computer.

4. Browse to and open *C:\Navisworks 2017 Essentials Class Files\Training\Examples\Gatehouse\gatehouse_timeliner.mpx*.

5. The Field Selector dialog box is displayed to link the columns in the Autodesk Navisworks software to those in the .MPX file. In the Field Selector dialog box, select the External Field Names shown to map the Task Type, Synchronization ID, Planned Start Date, and Planned End Date to columns in the .MPX file. Click OK. The new link is listed in the Data Sources tab.

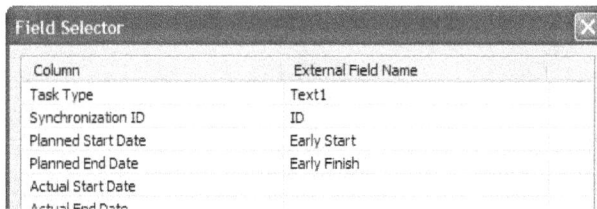

6. Select the Tasks tab and notice that there are still no tasks listed.

7. Select the Data Sources tab. Right-click the New Link and click Rebuild Task Hierarchy to extract the task data from the external file into TimeLiner.

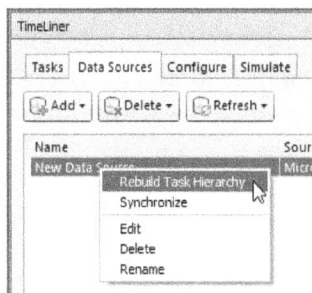

8. If warned that there are problems with the imported data, click OK. The import is recognizing that task types are not corresponding. This is not an issue as task types can be explicitly assigned.

9. Select the Tasks tab. The imported tasks appear, including their Planned Start and Planned End dates.

10. Click Auto-Attach Using Rules to attach the tasks to items in the model.

11. Add a checkmark to the rule Map TimeLiner Tasks from Column Name to Layers with the same name, Matching case. Click Apply Rules and close the TimeLiner Rules dialog box.

12. In the Tasks tab, verify that the Attached column fields now display Explicit Selection.

13. Expand Find Items and click Unattached/Uncontained Items to check if there are any items in the model not attached to tasks. There are no uncontained items in the model.

14. In the first task, select Construct as the Task Type.

15. Select the Task Type field for the first task, press and hold SHIFT, and select the Task Type field for the last task. This selects all the cells together. Right-click and select Fill Down, to assign the construct status to all tasks.

16. Select the Simulate tab and click Settings. Set the View settings as Planned. As no Actual dates were imported with this project, if you set the View settings to Actual, no tasks would display in the Simulate tab. Click OK.

For further information on Settings, refer to Configuring and Defining a Simulation.

17. Click Play to view the simulation.

18. Save this file with the same name plus your initials to a new location, for example, *C:\Temp\GatehouseJMD.nwd*.

Exercise: (P) Importing Tasks

1. Open the file *C:\Navisworks 2017 Essentials Class Files\Training\Examples\Plant\ Sample1.nwd*.

2. On the Home tab in the Tools panel, click TimeLiner ⏱, if it is not already displayed.

3. Select the Data Sources tab. Click Add > Microsoft Project MPX.

   Tip: Microsoft Project MPX is a common format and does not require any scheduling software to be installed on the computer.

4. Browse to and open *C:\Navisworks 2017 Essentials Class Files\Training\Examples\Plant\ Sample1_TimeLiner.mpx*.

5. The Field Selector dialog box is displayed. No additional fields need to be linked. Click OK. The new link is listed in the Data Sources tab.

6. Select the Tasks tab and note that no tasks exist.

7. Select the Data Sources tab. Right-click the New Link and click Rebuild Task Hierarchy to extract the task data from the external file into TimeLiner.

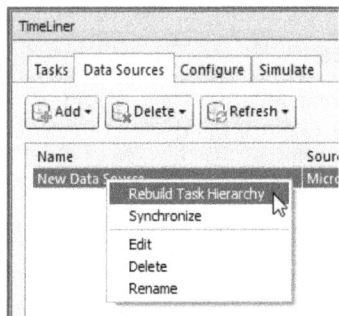

8. Select the Tasks tab. The imported tasks appear, including their Planned Start and Planned End dates.

9. Click Auto-Attach Using Rules 🖳 to attach the tasks to items in the model.

10. Add a checkmark to the rule Map TimeLiner Tasks from Column Name to Layers with the same name, Matching case. Click Apply Rules and close the TimeLiner Rules dialog box.

11. In the Tasks tab verify that the Attached column fields now display Explicit Selection.

12. Expand Find Items ⬚ and click Unattached/Uncontained Items to check if there are any items in the model not attached to tasks. There are no uncontained items in the model.

Planned End	Actual Start	Actual End	Task Typ	
10/9/2003	N/A	N/A		Attached Items
8/1/2003	N/A	N/A		Contained Items
8/5/2003	N/A	N/A		Unattached / Uncontained Items
8/6/2003	N/A	N/A		Items Attached to Multiple Tasks
8/12/2003	N/A	N/A		Items Contained in Multiple Tasks
8/13/2003	N/A	N/A		Items Attached to Overlapping Tasks
				Items Contained in Overlapping Tasks

13. In the first task, select Construct as the task type.

14. Select the Task Type field for the first task, press and hold SHIFT, and select the Task Type field for the last task. This selects all of the cells together. Right-click and select Fill Down to assign the construct status to all tasks.

Move Up
Move Down
Indent
Outdent
Attach Current Selection
Attach Current Search
Attach Set ▶
Append Current Selection
Clear Attachment
Add Comment
Fill Down
Dates ▶

15. Select the Simulate tab and click Settings. Set the View settings to Planned, if not already set. As no Actual dates were imported with this project, if you set the View settings to Actual, no tasks would display in the Simulate tab. Click OK.

For further information on Settings, refer to Configuring and Defining a Simulation.

16. Click Play ▷ to view the simulation.

17. Save this file with the same name plus your initials to a new location, such as *C:\Temp\Sample1JMD.nwd*.

Lesson: Configuring and Defining a Simulation

Overview

TimeLiner can be customized so that certain simulation processes can be easily identified. This lesson describes how to create a customized simulation.

Objectives

After completing this lesson, you will be able to:

- Configure how objects are displayed at each stage of a simulation.
- Customize existing or create new appearance definitions.

The Configure Options

The Configure tab enables you to define Task Types, Appearance Definitions, and the Default Simulations Start Appearance.

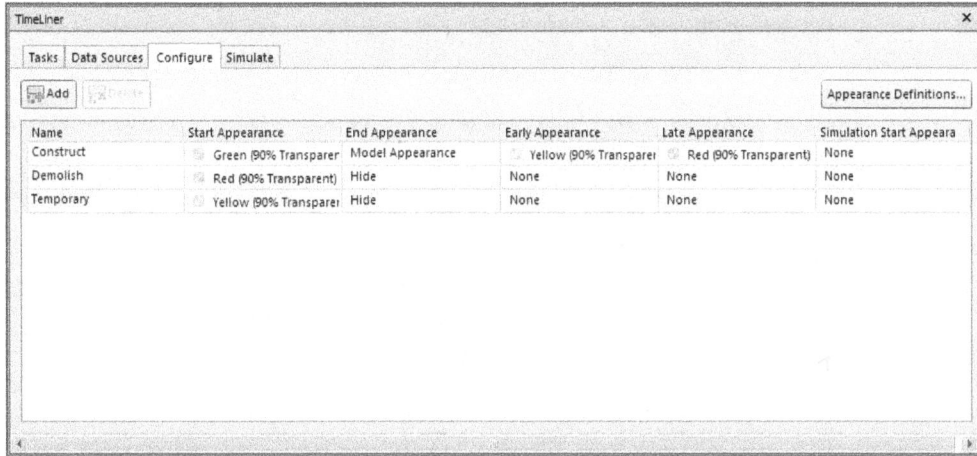

Name	Start Appearance	End Appearance	Early Appearance	Late Appearance	Simulation Start Appeara
Construct	Green (90% Transparer	Model Appearance	Yellow (90% Transparer	Red (90% Transparent)	None
Demolish	Red (90% Transparent)	Hide	None	None	None
Temporary	Yellow (90% Transparer	Hide	None	None	None

TimeLiner dialog box showing Tasks, Data Sources, Configure, Simulate tabs with Add, Delete, and Appearance Definitions... buttons.

> Further options are also available in the Simulate tab. See Simulation Settings.

Task Types

The available task types are listed in the Name column. Each task type has a set of conditions which can be individually defined:

- **Start Appearance** – Appearance of tasks at the start of the task (for example, green).
- **End Appearance** – Appearance when the task is completed (for example, task items displayed).
- **Early Appearance** – Appearance of task items if the task is started before the planned time (for example, yellow means needs Planed Start data).
- **Late Appearance** – Appearance of task items if the task is started later the planned time (for example, red means needs Planned End data).
- **Simulation Start Appearance** – Appearance of items at the start of a simulation (for example, if the task is demolition, then the task items would initially need to be displayed until the demolition task begins).

> A Default Simulation Start Appearance can be defined if required, by clicking Appearance Definitions. In the Appearance Definitions dialog box, select the Default Simulation Start Appearance drop-down arrow, and select from the list.

Procedure: To Add a Task Type

New task types can also be defined. Once created, these user defined tasks are available when assigning task types to scheduled tasks. The corresponding start and end appearances must match the task type.

1.   Select the Configure tab and select Add.

2.   To rename the new Task Type, select the task's Name and enter a descriptive name.

3.   Click the drop-down arrows associated with all of the task columns to fully define the new Task Type.

      Note: The appearance definitions in the drop-down list can be added to or edited as required.

Procedure: To Add or Change an Appearance Definition

The appearance definitions can be changed or new definitions added. Select Appearance Definitions on the Configure tab to access the Appearance Definitions dialog box.

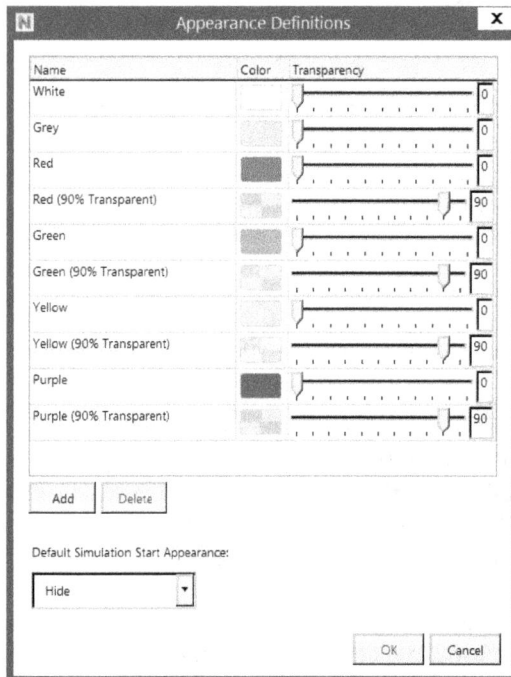

- To add a new Appearance Definition, click Add. A new appearance definition entry is added to the existing list of definitions, which you can edit as required.
- To rename an Appearance Definition, select the Name field and enter a new name.
- To edit an Appearance Definition transparency, enter a new transparency value or drag the Transparency slider to set the appropriate value for the selected appearance.
- To edit an Appearance Definition color, select the Color field for an appearance to display its color palette. Select the color you want to use and click OK.
- To delete an Appearance Definition, select the appearance definition row and click Delete.

Simulation Settings

Changes made to the definitions and the configuration of a simulation might not be apparent, due to the simulation settings. The Simulation settings enable you to further customize the simulation.

Procedure: To Use the Simulation Settings

1. In the TimeLiner window, select the Simulate tab and click Settings to display the Simulation Settings dialog box.

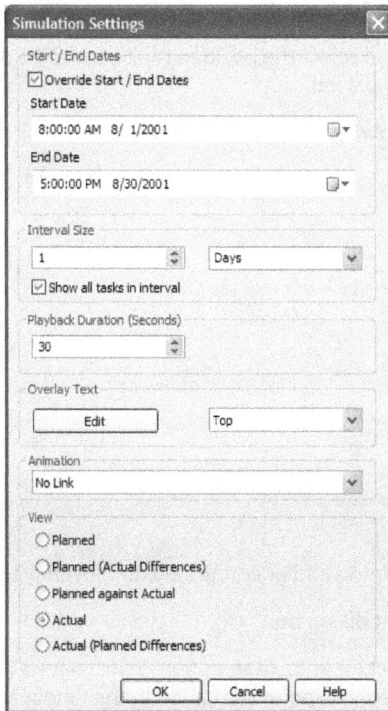

2. Add a checkmark to Override Start/End Dates, otherwise the simulation starts at the start date of the first task and finishes at the end date of the last task.

    Tip: Use this to start the simulation with a blank scene, or to set to a specific viewing period.

3. Set the Start Date and End Date fields.

    When using the Step Forward ⏭ and Step Back ⏮ tools, the interval size defines how the intervals are measured.

4. In the Interval Size area, click the right field drop-down arrow to set the interval to percentage, weeks, days, etc.

5. Click the left field drop-down arrow to set the interval value.

    Note: When using the Step Forward or Step Back tools, any tasks that start and finish between the intervals are not displayed. Add a checkmark to Show all tasks in interval to ensure that all tasks during the interval are displayed.

The playback duration of the simulation defines the total duration of the tasks. This value can be changed.

6. Click the field drop-down arrow and set to the required duration in seconds.

The simulation can display overlay text if required. The overlay text can include a combination of information including, date, time, cost, and information on tasks. The overlay text can be displayed in various colors and font type, and at different positions on the simulation screen.

Tip: Consider how it is going to look when played back on a different resolution (for example, too large or too small), and set the font size and color for best effect.

7. Click the Overlay Text drop-down arrow and select the position the text is to be displayed on screen or select None if text is not to be displayed.

8. Click Edit to display the Overlay text window.

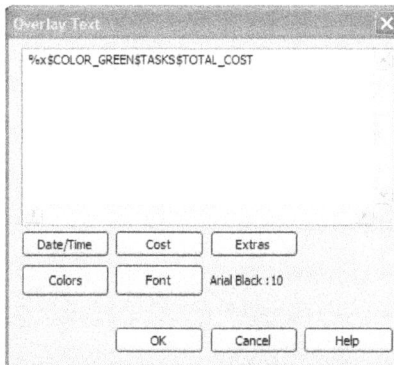

9. Click Date/Time, Cost, Extras, Colors, or Font to add or edit the existing overlay text.

10. Click OK to save and close the Overlay Text dialog box.

11. In the Simulation Settings dialog box, select an Animation option. Select Saved Viewpoints Animation to use a previously created saved viewpoint animation in the timeline or select No Link to not use a viewpoint animation.

12. In the View area, select options as required. The following description is based on this key.

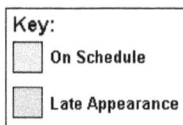

- **Actual** – Displays task items using actual start date/time and end date/time only.

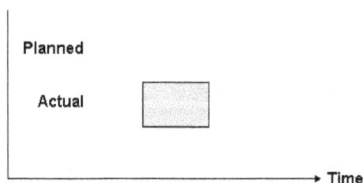

- **Actual (Planned Differences)** – Displays task items using actual start and end date/times. If this period is outside the planned period, it is displayed using the early start and/or late end appearances (for example, yellow/red.)

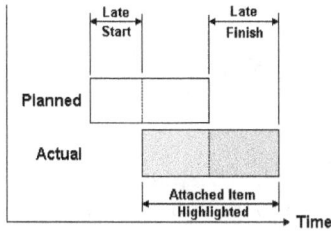

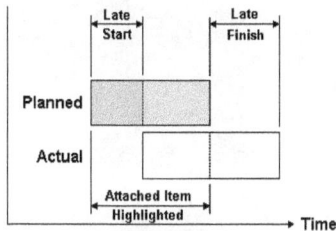

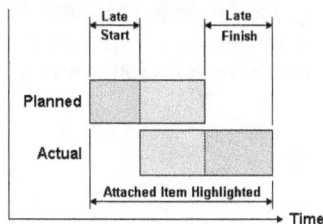

Late Start · Late Finish · Planned · Actual · Attached Item Highlighted · Time

- **Planned** – Displays task items using planned start date/time and end date/time only.

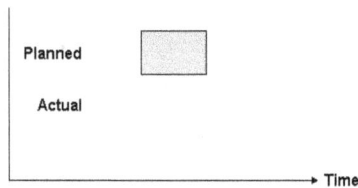

Planned · Actual · Time

- **Planned (Actual Differences)** – Displays task items using planned start and end date/times. If the actual period is outside the planned period, it is displayed using the early start and/or late end appearances (for example, yellow/red).

Late Start · Late Finish · Planned · Actual · Attached Item Highlighted · Time

- **Planned against Actual** – Displays task items using earliest actual or planned start and using earliest actual or planned end dates/times. If the actual period is outside the planned period, it is displayed using the early start and/or late end appearances (for example, yellow/red).

Late Start · Late Finish · Planned · Actual · Attached Item Highlighted · Time

Exercise: Customizing a Simulation

1. Open the file *C:\Navisworks 2017 Essentials Class Files\Training\Examples\Gatehouse\Gatehouse_TimerLiner.nwf.*

2. On the Home tab in the Tools panel, click TimeLiner 🕒 if it is not already displayed.

3. Click Settings in the Simulate tab.

4. In the Simulation Settings dialog box, add a checkmark to Override Start/End Dates. Change Start Date to 8:00:00 AM 8/1/2017 and End Date to 5:00:00 PM 8/30/2017.

5. Set Interval Size to 1 day, and add a checkmark to Show all tasks in interval.

6. Change Playback Duration to 30 seconds.

7. In the Overlay Text area, click Edit. In the Overlay Text dialog box, delete the current settings.

8. Click Date/Time and select Date representation for current locale.

9. Click Colors and select Green.

10. Click Extras and select Currently active tasks.

11. Click Font and select Arial Black 10pt. Click OK.

12. Click OK in the Overlay Text dialog box to save and return to the Simulation Settings dialog box.

13. Change Overlay Text to Top.

14. Select No Link in the Animation drop-down menu.

    Tip: Alternatively, you can also use the Saved Viewpoints Animation option in the drop-down to include a link to an existing animation. If using this option you must preselect the animation in the Saved Viewpoints window so that the Autodesk Navisworks software recognizes which animation to link.

15. In the View area, select Actual (Planned Differences).

16. Click OK to save these settings.

17. Play the simulation and observe the effect of the changes.

18. Save this file with the same name plus your initials to a new location, for example, *C:\Temp\Gatehouse_TimeLinerJMD.nwf.*

Lesson: Simulation Export

Overview

This lesson describes how to export a TimeLiner simulation.

Objectives

After completing this lesson, you will be able to:

- Export a simulation in AVI format.
- Use the export options to create a suitable quality AVI.

Exporting a TimeLiner Simulation

By exporting a TimeLiner simulation, it can be played and viewed using standard media player software, without the Autodesk Navisworks software installed, enabling simulations to be viewed by all stakeholders.

Procedure: To Export a Simulation

1. Select the Output tab and in the Visuals panel, click Animation .

2. In the Animation Export dialog box, under Source, select TimeLiner Simulation from the drop-down list.

3. Under Renderer, select either Viewport (default setting), or Autodesk (if Autodesk materials are being used) depending on how the simulation is to be rendered.

   Note: Overlay text is only available with Viewport rendering.

4. Under Output, in the Format drop-down list, select the export format as a movie file, AVI, or as a series of static images (JPEG, PNG, or Windows Bitmap).

5. Under Size, specify the screen size of the AVI.

   Tip: Use the default size of Width 640 and Height 642, view the results, then increase/decrease the size as required.

   Note: The larger the size, the larger the overall file size! Many PCs do not have enough memory to display large AVI files.

6. Under Options, specify the settings for FPS (Frames Per Second) and Anti-aliasing.

   Tip: Anti-aliasing gives the image smoother edges and it does not increase the output file size. However, it does increase the rendering output time, so it is best to only use anti-aliasing for the final finished AVI.

7. Click OK to export the animation.

   The AVI file can be played back using Windows Media Player, or as a series of static images (JPEG, PNG, or Bitmap).

Exercise: Exporting a TimeLiner Simulation

1. Open the file *C:\Navisworks 2017 Essentials Class Files\Training\Examples\Gatehouse\Gatehouse_TimerLiner2.nwf*.

2. Select the Output tab and in the Visuals panel, click Animation .

3. In the Animation Export dialog box, for Source, select TimeLiner Simulation.

4. For Renderer, select Viewport.

5. For Output Format, select Windows AVI.

6. Click Options. In the Video Compressor dialog box, for Compressor, select the Microsoft Video 1 compressor and set the compression Quality to 100. Click OK.

7. Under Size, select Explicit as the Type. Set the Height and Width to 400.

8. Under Options, set FPS (Frames Per Second) to 6.

9. Set Anti-aliasing to None.

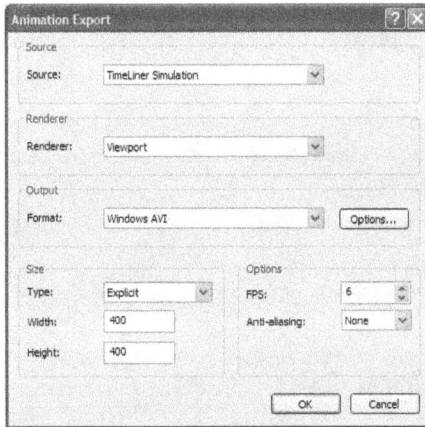

10. Click OK to export the animation.

11. Save the animation in a temporary directory.

12. Use Windows Media Player to play back the AVI.

13. Close the Media Player.

14. Close the file without saving.

Animator

With Autodesk Navisworks Animator you can animate your model and interact with it. For example, you could animate how a crane moves around a site, or how a car is assembled or dismantled. You can also create interaction scripts, which link your animations to specific events. For example, the doors open as you approach them in your model, or a conveyor belt moves when you pull a lever.

Animations created in Autodesk® Navisworks® can be played in all Autodesk Navisworks products, including Freedom. Combining the Rendering tools functionality with Object Animation enables you to greatly enhance the realism of your exported AVI movies, whether for marketing purposes or for instructional training.

This chapter begins with how to create a basic object animation, then advances to describe the more complex animations. This chapter is followed by a chapter on Scripter, which provides essential information about how to make animations interactive.

Objectives

After completing this chapter, you will be able to:

- Open Animator and understand the purpose of the Animator window and its tools.
- Add a new scene in the Animator window.
- Add a camera to a scene and use viewpoints or capture new views as keyframes for the Camera.
- Add an animation set to a scene using the current selection or current search/selection set option.
- Use the manipulation controls to modify position, rotation, size, color, and transparency of geometry objects in animation sets, and capture these changes in keyframes.
- Add a section set and use the section plane tools to create keyframes in a section set in an animation.
- Play back an animation scene using the playback options to achieve a required effect.

Lesson: Animator Overview

Overview

This lesson describes how to open the Animator window in the Autodesk Navisworks software. It also introduces you to the Tree and Timeline panes, tools, and Manual Entry bar.

Objective

After completing this lesson, you will be able to:

- Open Animator and understand the purpose of the Animator window and its tools.

About Animator and Tools

To open the Animator window, select the Home tab and click Animator in the Tools panel, or on

the Animation tab, click Animator in the Create panel. The Animator window displays at the bottom of the Autodesk Navisworks window and consists of two panes with the Animator toolbar at the top of these panes.

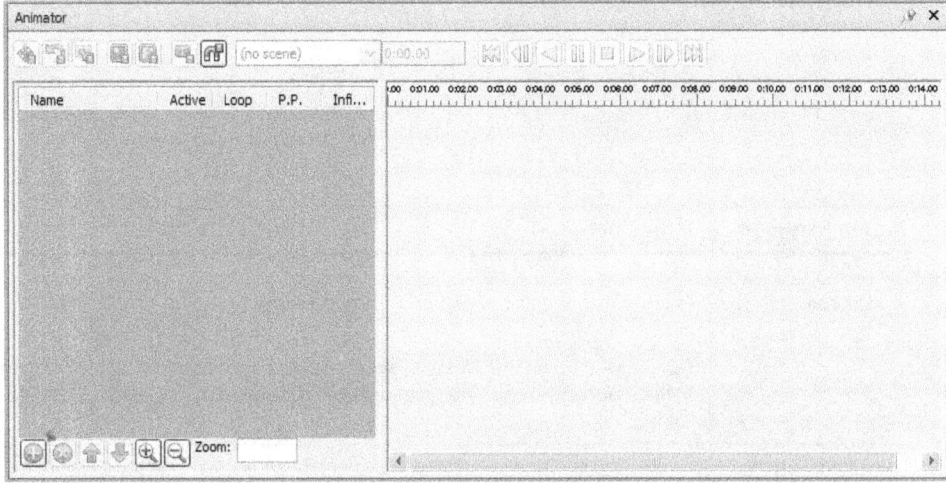

Tree

The Tree pane lists all scenes and scene components. It is used to create and organize animation scenes. A scene can include:

- Animation sets of objects to be animated
- Cameras
- Section plane for sectional views

Timeline

The Timeline pane displays the timeline for each animation set, camera, and section plane in a scene. It can be used to visualize and edit the animations.

A timeline has a colored animation bar, which is used to visualize the duration of an animation of the scene component. The animation start and end times can be edited by dragging the diamond shaped keyframe at each end of the animation bar.

Tree Pane Controls

The Tree pane controls are located at the bottom of the Tree pane window and are used to add, reorder, and view scene components. Additional options are available as checkboxes for each Tree component.

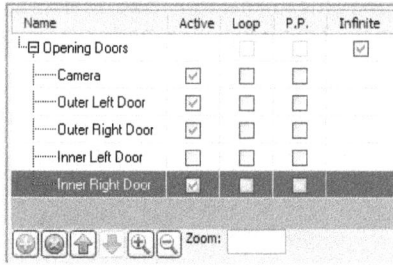

Action Required	Procedure
Add Scene	To add a new scene, click Add ![icon] > Add Scene. **Tip:** Depending on the situation, additional Add options are available when the ![icon] option is selected (e.g., Add Camera, Add Section Plane, Add Folder, and Add Scene Folder).
View Component	To view the components of a scene, select the plus sign (+) at the left of the required scene.
Delete	To delete a scene or a scene component, select the scene or component and click Delete ![icon].
Change Scene or Component Order	To change the order of a scene or scene component, select the item to be moved and click Up ![icon] or Down ![icon].
De-Activate	To make a scene component inactive in a scene, clear its Active checkbox.
Loop Play	Select the relevant Loop checkbox for a scene or any scene component to loop the animation playback back to the beginning once finished.
P.P. (Ping-Pong Mode)	Select the relevant P.P. checkbox for a scene or any scene component to set the playback to run forwards till it finishes and then run back to the beginning of the animation.
Infinite Play	Select the Infinite checkbox to make the scene play indefinitely or until explicitly stopped. If this checkbox is clear, the scene plays until its end point is reached.

Keyframe

A keyframe is a snapshot of a change to the model. Keyframes are shown as black diamonds in a timeline. The duration of each keyframe (shown at the right of the keyframe) can be adjusted by dragging the keyframe.

Capture keyframe ⬛ on the Animator toolbar is used to create a keyframe from the current view of the model. Keyframes for the camera, capture a snapshot of the camera position. Keyframes for Animation Sets or Section Planes capture a snapshot of the object's movement in the scene. Right-click a keyframe to display the following commands that can be applied to a keyframe:

- **Edit** – Enables you to edit the selected keyframe.
- **Go to Keyframe** – Moves the black time slider to this keyframe.
- **Cut, Copy, Paste** – Provides standard cut, copy, and paste commands. They only work inside the selected timeline. **Note:** Paste is only available once an item has been copied.
- **Delete** – Deletes the selected keyframe.
- **Interpolate** – Determines whether the Autodesk Navisworks software automatically interpolates between the current and the last keyframes. This is the default option. When disabled, the animation instantly jumps to the position/view of the second keyframe.

Timeline Pane Controls

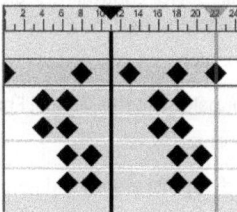

- **Timescale Bar** – The timescale bar at the top of the Timeline pane starts at 0 and is displayed in seconds. Use Zoom In ⬛ and Zoom Out ⬛ at the bottom of the Tree pane, if required.

- **Time Slider** – The time slider ⬛ is the black vertical line that represents the current position in the animation playback. To move the current playback position, drag the slider left or right in the Timeline pane, or use the controls on the toolbar. As the time slider is moved, the model in the Scene View updates to reflect movements caused by keyframes in the current scene as if the animation were playing back.

- **End Slider** – The red vertical line is the end slider ⊤ representing the end point of the current active scene.

> The end slider is hidden if the Infinite checkbox is selected for the current scene in the scene view.

The end slider is set to the last keyframe in the scene but can be manually overridden. Right-click on the end slider, and then click Manually Position Endbar. Drag the endbar left or right.

> The end slider is used as the animation end point when scenes are set to Loop or Ping-Pong.

Animator Toolbar

The Animator toolbar is located at the top of the Animator window and includes controls to create, edit, and play animations.

Icon	Name	Description
	Translate animation set	Enables Translation mode and displays the visual tool for controlling translation operations in the main Autodesk Navisworks window. You can modify the position of the geometry objects.
	Rotate animation set	Enables Rotation mode and displays the visual tool for controlling rotation operations in the main Autodesk Navisworks window. You can modify the rotation of the geometry objects.
	Scale animation set	Enables Scale mode and displays the visual tool for controlling scale operations in the main Autodesk Navisworks window. You can modify the size of the geometry objects.
	Change Color of animation set	Enables Color mode and displays the color palette in the Manual Entry bar. You can modify the color of the geometry objects.
	Change Transparency of animation set	Enables Transparency mode and displays the transparency slider in the Manual Entry bar. You can modify the transparency of the geometry objects.
	Capture keyframe	Takes a snapshot of the current change to the model, to use as a new keyframe in the Timeline pane.
	Toggle snapping	Toggles snapping to snap to the start and end positions of the translation, rotation, or scale operation to a relevant point in the animation set. **Note:** The snap only comes into effect when moving objects by dragging the visual tools in the main Autodesk Navisworks window, and has no effect on numerical entry or keyboard control.
Scene 1	**Scene Picker**	Displays the available scenes where you can select the scene to make active.

Icon	Name	Description
0:10.00	**Time Position**	Displays the current position of the black time slider in the Timeline pane. To change the position, enter the required value.
	Rewind	Rewinds the animation back to the beginning.
	Step Back	Steps back through the animation a single keyframe at a time.
	Reverse Play	Plays the animation backwards.
	Pause	Pauses the animation at the keyframe. To resume playing select Play again.
	Stop	Stops the animation playing and rewinds it back to the beginning.
	Play	Plays the animation in the currently active scene.
	Step Forward	Steps forward through the animation a single keyframe at a time.
	To End	Fast forwards the animation to the end.

Lesson: Creating a Basic Animation

Overview

This lesson describes how to create a basic animation in Animator. It also introduces adding scenes, cameras, animation sets, and key frames.

Objective

After completing this lesson, you will be able to:

- Add a new scene in the Animator window.
- Add a camera to a scene and use viewpoints or capture new views as keyframes for the Camera.
- Add an animation set to a scene using the current selection or current search/selection set option.

Creating an Animation

The Animator window enables you to animate objects. Animations consist of a parent scene that contains cameras and selected objects that can be manipulated to create the animation.

Procedure: To Create an Animation

1. On the Home tab in the Tools panel, click Animator 🖎 , or on the Animation tab, click Animator 🖎 in the Create panel. The Animator window displays at the bottom of the Autodesk Navisworks window.

2. To add a scene, from the Tree Pane controls, click Add ⊕ > Add Scene.

3. Double-click the new scene name. In the scene name field, enter a new name for the scene and press ENTER.

About Cameras and Viewpoints

Once a scene has been created, a single camera can be added to it. A camera can contain a series of viewpoints, or keyframes, to dictate how the scene is going to change. If no camera keyframes are defined, the scene uses the current views in the Scene View. If a single keyframe is defined, the camera moves to that viewpoint, and then remains static throughout the scene. Finally, if multiple keyframes are defined, the camera is animated accordingly.

Camera movement can be added using one of two methods. You can add a blank camera and then manipulate it to the required views, Alternatively, you can copy an existing viewpoint animation into the camera.

Procedure: To add a Blank Camera and set Keyframes

1. Select the Scene name. From the Tree Pane controls, click Add > Add Camera > Blank camera.

2. Select the Camera in the Tree pane.

3. Use the controls on the Navigation Bar or select a saved viewpoint that is going to be used as the first viewpoint in the animation.

4. On the Animator toolbar, click Capture keyframe to create a keyframe with the current viewpoint.

5. In the Timeline pane, move the black time slider to the right or enter a time value in the Time Position pane to set a time for the next keyframe.

6. Use the controls on the Navigation Bar or select a saved viewpoint that is going to be used as the next viewpoint in the animation.

7. To capture the current viewpoint changes in a keyframe, click Capture keyframe on the Animator toolbar.

8. Continue to change the time slider, viewpoints, and save keyframes, as required, to define the full animation for the Camera.

Procedure: To Add a Camera with an Existing Viewpoint Animation

1. In the Saved Viewpoints window, select the viewpoint animation.

2. Right-click the required scene name, and click Add Camera > From current viewpoint animation. The Autodesk Navisworks software automatically adds all of the required keyframes to the Timeline pane.

About Animations Sets

An animation set contains a list of geometry objects to be animated and a list of keyframes that describe how it is to be animated. A scene can have multiple animation sets and you can also have the same geometry objects in different animation sets in the same scene. The order of animation sets in a scene is important and can be used to control the final object position when the same object is used in multiple animation sets.

Procedure: To Add an Animation Set to a Scene

1. In the Scene View or the Selection Tree window, select the geometry objects to be animated.

2. Select the Scene name and use one of the following:

- Click Add ⊕ > Add Animation Set > From current selection to add the animation set based on the current selection.

- Click Add ⊕ > Add Animation Set > From current search/selection set to add the animation set based on a current search set or selection set.

Note: if you are adding an animation set based on a selection set, the contents of the animation set are automatically updated if the contents of the source selection set change.

Note: If the model changes so that objects in a particular animation are missing, they are automatically removed from the animation set when the model file is resaved.

Note: If the selection or search sets are deleted, the corresponding animation set becomes a static selection of objects based on what it last contained.

3. Click the new animation set, then press F2 to rename.

4. Repeat steps 1 to 3 to add additional animation sets for all the geometry that is to be animated.

5. Save the file.

See Manipulating Geometry Objects for more information.

Tip: When creating keyframes for a camera or animation set, change the timeline to the correct time before setting the keyframe.

Exercise: Create an Animation

1. Open the file *C:\Navisworks 2017 Essentials Class Files\Training\Examples\Animations\ KLM 1.nwf.*

2. On the Home tab in the Tools panel, click Animator ⊙. The Animator window displays at the bottom of the Autodesk Navisworks window.

Add a Scene

1. From the Tree Pane controls, click Add ⊕ > Add Scene.

2. Select the new scene name and rename it **Opening Doors**. Press ENTER.

Add a Camera

1. Select the Opening Doors scene, click Add ⊕ > Add Camera > Blank camera. A Camera entry should be displayed under the Opening Doors scene.

2. Open the Saved Viewpoints window, if not already displayed, and select the Entrance 1 saved viewpoint.

3. Select the Camera entry and click Capture Keyframe ⊞ on the Animator toolbar. This captures a keyframe of the current view and places it at the beginning of the camera timeline.

   Tip: Ensure that the view does not change as you are selecting the Camera entry. Selecting the entry in a column other than the Name column helps.

Add Animation Sets to a Scene

1. Select the viewpoint Entrance 1.

2. In the Scene View, select the left outer door, which is to be to be animated. Ensure that the selection filter is set to Geometry.

   Tip: It might be easier to select the door by moving closer to it or navigating through the Selection Tree to select the correct 3D Solid door in the *gclad.dwg > A315* file.

3. In the Animator window, select the Scene Opening Doors and click Add ⊕ > Add Animation Set > From current selection.

4. Click the new animation set and rename it **Outer left door**.

5. Repeat these steps to add additional animation sets for the Outer right door, Inner left door, and Inner right door.

6. Save this file in a temporary location with your initials. (For example, *C: \Temp\Animations\ KLM 1JMD.nwf.*)

Exercise: Adding a Camera and Camera Viewpoints

1. Continue to work on the file from the previous exercise. Alternatively, if you did not complete that exercise, open the file *C:\Navisworks 2017 Essentials Class Files\Training\Examples\Animations\ KLM 2.nwf.*

2. On the Home tab in the Tools panel, click Animator ⟨icon⟩ , if it is not already displayed.

3. An initial Keyframe was created for the Camera using the Entrance 1 saved viewpoint. Select the Camera entry. In the Timeline pane, drag the black time slider to 8.

4. Using the Walk ⟨icon⟩ navigation tool, walk towards the entrance doors and proceed until you are between the outer and inner doors.

5. Click Capture keyframe ⟨icon⟩ on the Animator toolbar. This captures a keyframe of the current view and places it at the current Camera timeline.

6. In the Timeline pane, drag the black time slider to 13 or enter the value in the Time Position field.

7. Walk through to the far end of the desk, then click Capture keyframe ⟨icon⟩ .

8. In the Timeline pane, drag the black time slider to 18.

9. Use the Look Around ⟨icon⟩ Navigation tool and turn around to view the doors you have just walked through, and click Capture keyframe ⟨icon⟩ .

10. In the Timeline pane, drag the black time slider to 22.

11. Using the Walk ⟨icon⟩ navigation tool, walk backwards from the entrance doors a few paces and click Capture keyframe ⟨icon⟩ .

12. Click Stop ⟨icon⟩ then click Play ⟨icon⟩ on the Animator toolbar to view the animation you have created. The animation should walk through the doors, turn around to view the doors, then move backwards away from the doors. Notice how the doors were not animated. Only the camera has been animated.

13. Save this file in a temporary location with your initials. (For example, *C:\Temp\Animations\ KLM 2JMD.nwf.*)

Lesson: Manipulate Geometry Objects in an Animation Set

Overview

This lesson describes how to manipulate the selected geometry in an animation set and capture the changes as a keyframe. It also introduces you to the various manipulation controls.

Objective

After completing this lesson, you will be able to:

- Use the manipulation controls to modify position, rotation, size, color, and transparency of geometry objects in animation sets, and capture these changes in keyframes.

Geometry Manipulation Controls

Snapping Control

When you manipulate geometry objects by changing their position, rotation, or size you can use snapping to control the precision of your operations in the Scene View. To toggle on snapping mode, click Toggle snapping on the Animator toolbar.

The snap control works like "gravity" around the snap points. Snapping makes sure your translation, rotation, and scaling of an animation set, starts and ends at a point defined by the user. This is usually a specific point on the animation set geometry.

Further Snapping options are available in Application Menu > Options > Interface > Snapping.

Highlighting Objects

When animation sets are selected in the Tree pane, they are also highlighted in the Scene View.

To get a clearer view of an object as you animate it, there are three different highlighting methods available: Shaded, Wireframe, and Tinted.

Go to Application Menu > Options > Interface > Selection to select the preferred option.

Keyframes

Keyframes are like snapshots and are used to define position and properties of the changes to the animation sets. New keyframes are created by clicking Capture keyframe on the Animator toolbar. The captured keyframe is added to the currently selected animation set, camera, or section plan, at the position of the black time slider in the Timeline pane.

Keyframes are used to capture the relative translation, rotation, etc., of objects in the model compared to the previous keyframe. Combined with the interpolate function in Animator, an animation is created that displays the object moving from its position in the previous keyframe to its position in the next keyframe.

Procedure: To Perform Object Manipulation by Linear Movement

1. Expand the required scene in the Animator window, and then select the required animation set. The corresponding geometry objects are highlighted in the Scene View.

2. Click Capture keyframe on the Animator toolbar to create a keyframe in the initial object state.

3. In the Timeline pane, move the black time slider to the right or enter a value in the Time Position field to set the time.

4. Click Translate animation set on the Animator toolbar.

5. Use the translation tool to change the position of the selected objects. The translation tool displays three colored axes at the correct angles relevant to the current camera position.

6. To move all objects in the currently selected animation set use the translation tool with one of the following techniques:

    ■ Place the mouse over the required axis and when the cursor changes to a hand , drag to increase/decrease the translation along that axis.

    ■ To move along two axes at once, drag the square planar frame that is located between the required axes.

    ■ Drag the white circular handle in the center of the translation tool to move the geometry freely in all planes.

    ■ To snap the tool to other objects, press and hold CTRL while dragging the white circular handle in the center of the translation tool. These additional features provide more ways of controlling the items being translated more precisely.

    ■ For point-to-point translation, press and hold CTRL and use the center square to drag the tool to the start point. Then, with CTRL released, drag the square again to move the object to the end point. These additional features provide more ways of controlling the items being translated more precisely.

    Tip: To move the translation tool rather than the actual animation set, hold CTRL while dragging the white circular handle in the center of the translation tool.

    Tip: To move the selected animation set using exact values, select Move on the Item Tools tab, expand the Transform panel, and enter exact translation values in the Transform type-in fields.

7. Click Capture keyframe on the Animator toolbar to create a keyframe in the current object state.

Procedure: To Perform Object Manipulation by Rotation Movement

1. Expand the required scene in the Animator window, and then select the required animation set. The corresponding geometry objects are highlighted in the Scene View.

2. Click Capture keyframe on the Animator toolbar to create a keyframe in the initial object state.

3. In the Timeline pane, move the black time slider to the right to set the time.

4. Click Rotate animation set on the Animator toolbar.

5. Use the rotation tool to rotate the selected objects. The rotation tool displays three colored axes at the correct angles relevant to the current camera position.

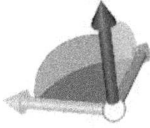

6. Before you can rotate the objects in the currently selected animation set, you need to move the white circular handle in the center of the translation tool to the required axis (center point) of the object to be rotated using one or both of the following techniques:

   ▪ Drag the white circular handle in the center of the translation tool so that it snaps to objects in the Scene View. This option enables you to move the objects freely. Alternatively you can press and hold CTRL to snap.

   ▪ Place the mouse over the required axis and when the cursor changes to a hand , drag the axis (with the rotation tool) along the axis to the required position. This option enables you to lock the movement of the object in a single direction.

   Tip: To rotate the selected animation set using exact values, select Rotate on the Item Tools tab, expand the Transform panel, and enter exact rotation values in the Transform type-in fields.

7. Once the rotation tool is positioned correctly, place the mouse over one of the curves between any of the axis, select it, and drag it to rotate the objects in the selected animation set to the required position. The curves are color-coded, and match the color of the axis used to rotate the object around. For example, dragging the blue curve between the X and Y axes rotates the object around the blue Z axis.

8. Click Capture keyframe on the Animator toolbar to create a keyframe in the current object state.

Procedure: To Perform Object Manipulation by Scaling

1. Expand the required scene in the Animator window, and then select the required animation set. The corresponding geometry objects are highlighted in the Scene View.

2. Click Capture keyframe on the Animator toolbar to create a keyframe in the initial object state.

3. In the Timeline pane, move the black time slider to the right to set the time.

4. Click Scale animation set on the Animator toolbar.

5. Use the scale tool to resize the selected objects. The scale tool displays three colored axes at the correct angles relevant to the current camera position.

6. To resize all objects in the currently selected animation set, place the mouse over one of axes or planes that are displayed on the scale tool. When the cursor changes to a hand 🖑, drag the square on the screen to modify the size of the objects. The dragging options include the following:

   - To resize the objects across a single axis only, use the axes.
   - To resize the objects across two axes at the same time, use planes that connect two axes.
   - To resize the objects across all three axes at the same time, use the white circular handle in the center of the scale tool.
   - To modify the center of scaling, place the mouse over the white circular handle in the center of the translation tool, and hold CTRL while dragging the square.

   Tip: Typically, dragging a square up or right increases the size. Dragging it down or left decreases the size.

   Tip: To scale the selected animation set using exact values, click Scale ⬚ on the Item Tools tab, expand the Transform panel, and enter exact scale values in the Transform type-in fields.

7. Click Capture keyframe 🖼 on the Animator toolbar to create a keyframe in the current object state.

Procedure: Object Manipulation by Changing Color

1. Expand the required scene in the Animator window, and then select the required animation set. The corresponding geometry objects are highlighted in the Scene View.

2. Click Capture keyframe 🖼 on the Animator toolbar to create a keyframe in the initial object state.

3. In the Timeline pane, move the black time slider to the right to set the time.

4. Click Change color of animation set 🖼 on the Animator toolbar. A Manual Entry bar displays at the bottom of the Animator window.

5. Press and select a color from the color drop-down menu ▣▾ or manually enter RGB values on the Manual Entry bar to define the color.

---

6. Click Capture keyframe ⬛ on the Animator toolbar to create a keyframe in the current object state.

Procedure: Object Manipulation by Changing Transparency

1. Expand the required scene in the Animator window, and then select the required animation set. The corresponding geometry objects are highlighted in the Scene View.

2. Click Capture keyframe ⬛ on the Animator toolbar to create a keyframe in the initial object state.

3. In the Timeline pane, move the black time slider to the right to set the time.

4. Click Change transparency of animation set ⬛ on the Animator toolbar. A Manual Entry bar displays at the bottom of the Animator window.

5. Use the transparency slider or enter a percentage value on the Manual Entry bar to adjust how transparent or opaque the selected objects are.

6. Click Capture keyframe ⬛ on the Animator toolbar to create a keyframe in the current object state.

Exercise: Manipulating Geometry Objects in an Animation Set

1. Continue to work on the file from the previous exercise. Alternatively, if you did not complete that exercise, open the file *C:\Navisworks 2017 Essentials Class Files\Training\Examples\ Animations\KLM 3.nwf.*

2. On the Home tab in the Tools panel, click Animator ⬡ , if it is not already displayed.

3. In the Opening Doors scene, select the Outer left door animation set.

4. In the Timeline pane, drag the black time slider to 4 or enter the value in the Time Position field.

5. Click Capture keyframe ⬛ on the Animator toolbar. This captures a keyframe of the current view and places it at the current position of the timeline for the Outer left door.

6. In the Timeline pane, drag the black time slider to 7 or enter the value in the Time Position field.

7. Click Translate animation set ⬛ on the Animator toolbar. The translation handles should be displayed near the selected door.

8. Move over the green axis handle and drag to the left until the sliding door has moved left to an open position.

9. Click Capture keyframe ⬛ on the Animator toolbar. This captures a keyframe of the current view and places it at the current position of the timeline for the Outer left door.

10. Right-click this new keyframe, and then click Copy.

11. Drag the black time slider to 18 (or enter the value), then right-click, and click Paste. This pastes a copy of the last keyframe at 18, which means the door remains open between 7 and 18.

12. Right-click the first keyframe at 4, and then click Copy.

13. Drag the black time slider to 21, then right-click, and click Paste. This pastes a copy of the first keyframe at 21.

14. Click Stop ⬛ , then click Play ▷ . As the entrance is approached, the left door should open, then the door should close as you move away from the door at the end of the animation.

15. Repeat steps 4 to 13 to animate the other 3 doors.

16. Select the Opening Doors scene and click Play ▷ on the Animator toolbar to view the animation with the animation sets you have manipulated. The doors should now open as you approach them and close as you move backwards away from the doors at the end of the animation.

17. Save this file in a temporary location with your initials. (For example, *C:\Temp\Animations\ KLM 3JMD.nwf.*)

Lesson: Section Plane Sets

Overview

This lesson describes how section sets with sectioned viewpoints are used in animations. It also introduces you to adding a section plane set and creating keyframes of sectioned views in an animation.

Objective

After completing this lesson, you will be able to:

- Add a section set and use the section plane tools to create keyframes in a section set in an animation.

About Section Plane Sets

A section plane set contains a list of sectional cuts, and a list of keyframes to describe how they move. Each scene can only have one section plane set in it.

> To correctly use the Add Section Plane feature, it is recommended you understand how the sectioning tools work. See Sectioning in Chapter 2.

Procedure: To Add a Section Plane Set

1. On the Home tab in the Tools panel, click Animator, if it is not already displayed.

2. Right-click the required scene name and click Add Section Plane.

3. On the Viewpoint tab > Sectioning panel, click Enable Sectioning. The Sectioning Tools contextual tab becomes available for you to manipulate sectional cuts.

Procedure: To Capture Sectioned Views

1. In the Animator window, in the scene view, select the Section Plane set.

2. Select the Sectioning Tools tab. Using standard sectioning functionality, ensure that the settings on the Mode and Plane Settings panels provide the required section plane for the animation.

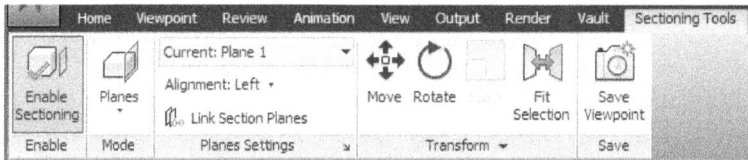

3. In the Transform panel on the Sectioning Tools tab, select Move to access the move gizmo on the section plane. Drag the axes on the sectioning gizmo or enter values in the Transform drop-down panel to define the initial location of the section plane for the animation.

   Tip: To begin the sectioning animation it is recommended that the sectioning plane begin outside the model.

4. Click Capture keyframe on the Animator toolbar. This captures a keyframe of the current view and places it at the beginning of the timeline.

5. In the Timeline pane, move the black time slider to the right to set the time or enter the value in the Time Position field.

6. In the Transform panel on the Sectioning Tools tab, ensure that Move ✛ is still enabled. Drag the axes on the sectioning gizmo or enter values in the Transform drop-down panel to define the next location of the section plane for the animation.

    Note: You can find more information about how to create plane cuts when sectioning a model under Sectioning in Chapter 2.

7. Click Capture keyframe 🔲 on the Animator toolbar. This captures a keyframe of the current sectioning view and places it at the current location on the timeline.

8. Repeat Steps 5 through 7 to capture the required keyframes.

9. Click Stop 🔲 and then click Play ▷ on the Animator toolbar to view the animation.

Exercise: Adding a Section Plane Set and Captured Sectioned Views

1. Open the file *C:\Navisworks 2017 Essentials Class Files\Training\Examples\Animations\ Heating Plant 1.nwf*.

2. Open the Saved Viewpoints window, if it is not already displayed, and select the Section saved viewpoint.

3. On the Home tab in the Tools panel, click Animator , if it is not already displayed.

4. In the Animator window, click Add > Add Scene.

5. Select the new scene (Scene 1) and rename it **Sectioned View**. Press ENTER

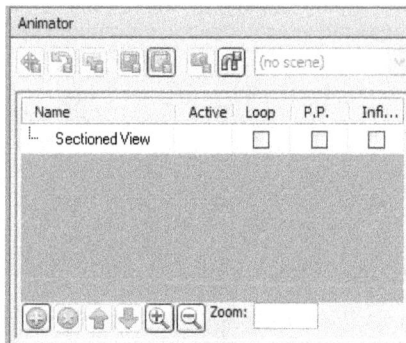

6. Right-click the Sectioned View scene and click Add Section Plane.

7. Press ENTER to accept the default name.

8. On the Viewpoint tab in the Sectioning panel, click Enable Sectioning .

9. In the Sectioning Tools context-sensitive tab in the Ribbon. Confirm that Plane 1 is listed in the Current field to ensure that it is active.

10. Confirm that the Alignment for Plane 1 is set to Left.

11. In the Transform panel, select Move to access the move gizmo on the section plane. If the full model is not already showing, select and drag the blue axes on the sectioning gizmo to display the full model.

12. Click Capture keyframe on the Animator toolbar. This captures a keyframe of the current view and places it at the beginning of the section plane timeline.

13. In the Timeline pane, drag the black time slider to 5 or enter the value in the Time Position field.

---

14. Expand the Transform panel and enter **X=5.00** to move the section slider.

15. Click Capture keyframe ⊞ on the Animator toolbar. This captures a keyframe of the current view and places it at the current camera timeline.

16. In the Timeline pane, drag the black time slider to 10 or enter the value in the Time Position field.

17. Move the section slider to approximately **X=10.00** and click Capture keyframe ⊞.

18. In the Timeline pane, drag the black time slider to 15 or enter the value in the Time Position field.

19. Move the section slider to approximately **X=15.00**, then click Capture Keyframe ⊞.

20. In the Timeline pane, drag the black time slider to 20 or enter the value in the Time Position field.

21. Move the section slider to approximately **X=20.00**, then click Capture Keyframe ⊞.

22. In the Timeline pane, drag the black time slider to 25 or enter the value in the Time Position field.

23. Move the section slider to approximately **X=25.00**, then click Capture Keyframe ⊞.

24. In Timeline pane, drag the black time slider to 30 or enter the value in the Time Position field.

25. Move the section to approximately **X=30.00**, then click Capture Keyframe ⊞.

26. In Timeline pane, drag the black time slider to 35 or enter the value in the Time Position field.

27. Move the section to approximately **X=35.00**, then click Capture Keyframe ⊞.

28. Click Stop ⊡ and then click Play ▷ on the Animator toolbar to view the section plane animation you created. The animation should progressively section the whole model.

29. Save this file in a temporary location with your initials. (For example, *C: \Temp\Animations\ Heating Plant1JMD.nwf.*)

Tip: Clear the Move ✛ tool to remove the sectioning plane from the animation.

Tip: This task could have been accomplished with only two keyframes. One keyframe at the beginning and one at the end. A camera movement could also have been added to further enhance the animation.

Lesson: Controlling Animation Scene Playback

Overview

This lesson describes how to use the animation controls to play back an animation scene. It also introduces you to the available playback options and when to use them.

Objective

After completing this lesson, you will be able to:

- Play back an animation scene using the playback options to achieve a required effect.

Animator Playback and Adjustments

The Tree pane contains checkbox options that can be used to customize the playback of an animation.

Name	Active	Loop	P.P.	Infi...
⊟ Opening Outer Do⊦		☐	☐	☐
Outer left door	☑	☐	☐	
Outer right door	☑	☐	☐	
⊟ Opening Inner Doc		☐	☐	☐
Inner left door	☑	☐	☐	
Inner right door	☑	☐	☐	

Option	Description
Active	Select the Active checkbox to disable sets in the animation.
Loop	Select the Loop checkbox if you want the scene to play back continuously. When the animation reaches the end, it resets to the start and runs again.
P.P	Select the P.P checkbox if you want the scene to play in ping-pong mode. When the animation reaches the end, it runs backwards until it reaches the start. This only happens once, unless you also select the Loop checkbox.
Infinite	Select the Infinite checkbox if you want the animation to play indefinitely along the timeline (i.e., until Stop is pressed). If this checkbox is clear, the animation plays to the scene end point. **Note:** Selecting this checkbox disables the Loop and P.P. checkboxes.

> If required, use the Active, Loop, and P.P. checkboxes to adjust the playback of the individual scene components.
>
> **Note:** Only the active animations play.

Procedure: To Play an Animator Scene and Adjust the way it Plays

1. On the Home tab in the Tools panel, click Animator ⌖, if it is not already displayed.

2. Select the scene in the scene view.

3. If you want the scene to play back continuously, select the Loop checkbox. When the animation reaches the end, it will reset back to the start and run again.

4. If you want the scene to play in ping-pong mode, select the P.P. checkbox. When the animation reaches the end, it will run backwards until it reaches the start. This will only happen once, unless you also select the Loop checkbox.

5. If you want the scene to play indefinitely (for example, until Stop is pressed), select the Infinite checkbox. If this checkbox is clear, the scene will play to the end point.

   Note: Selecting this checkbox disables the Loop and P.P. checkboxes.

6. If required, use the Active, Loop, and P.P. checkboxes to adjust the playback of the individual scene components.

   Note: Only the active animations will play.

Exercise: Adjust the Way an Animation Scene Plays

1.   Continue to work on the file from the previous exercise. Alternatively, if you did not complete that exercise, open the file *C:\Navisworks 2017 Essentials Class Files\Training\Examples\ Animations\ Heating Plant 2.nwf.*

2.   Open the Saved Viewpoints window, if it is not already displayed, and select the Section saved viewpoint.

3.   On the Home tab in the Tools panel, click Animator , if it is not already displayed.

4.   Select the Sectioned View scene, then click Play on the Animator toolbar to view the section plane animation. The animation should progressively section the whole model and stop.

5.   Select the P.P. checkbox on the Sectioned View scene. Click Play to view the animation. The animation should progressively section the whole model to the end, then play backwards to the beginning and stop.

6.   Select the Loop checkbox on the Sectioned View scene. Click Play to view the animation. The animation should progressively section the whole model to the end, then play backwards to the beginning and repeat continuously until you click Stop or Pause.

7.   Save this file in a temporary location with your initials. (For example, *C: \Temp\Animations\ Heating Plant2JMD.nwf.*)

Scripter

With Autodesk® Navisworks® Scripter you can add interactivity to your model. By combining "scripts" with animations created in Animator, an animation can be triggered by an event created in Scripter. For example, doors open (animation) as you approach them (script) in your model. You could animate how a crane moves around a site, or how a car is assembled or dismantled. You can also create interaction scripts, which link your animations to specific events.

By linking TimeLiner and Scripted Object Animation together, you can trigger and schedule object movement based on start time and duration of project tasks. This can help you with workspace and process planning. For example, a TimeLiner sequence might indicate that when a particular site crane moves from its start to end point on a particular afternoon, a work group causes an obstruction along its route.

This chapter begins with how to add a script and how to add and configure events. It then describes how to add and configure actions, and finally how to enable the scripts to work with animations.

> As the functionality of Scripter relates to animation scenes as described in Chapter 4, Animator, it is important to understand how to create animator scenes.

Objectives

After completing this chapter, you will be able to:

- Open Scripter and understand the functions of the Events and Actions panes and the tools available in the window.
- Add, rename, and organize scripts in folders.
- Add and configure events.
- Create and configure actions to achieve specific results.

Lesson: Scripter Overview

Overview

This lesson describes how to open the Scripter window in the Autodesk Navisworks software. It also introduces you to the Events and Actions panes, and Scripter tools.

Objective

After completing this lesson, you will be able to:

- Open Scripter and understand the functions of the Events and Actions panes and the tools available in the window.

About Scripts

To add interactivity to your model, you need to create at least one animation scene, into which you add certain events and actions that are carried out when those events take place.

Each script can contain the following components:

- One or more events
- One or more actions

To open the Scripter window, select the Home tab and click Scripter in the Tools panel, or on the Animation tab, click Scripter in the Script panel. The Scripter window displays at the bottom of the Autodesk Navisworks window. The Scripter window consists of four panes.

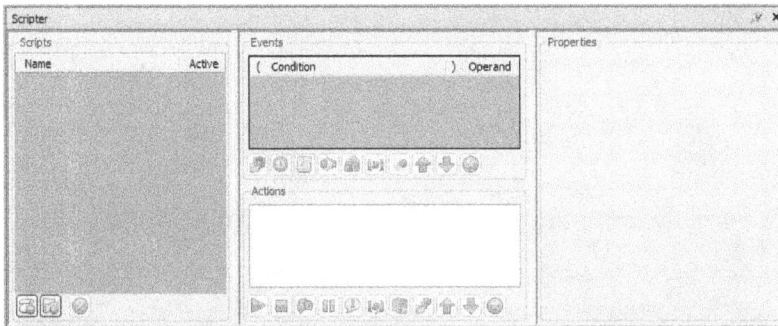

Scripts

The left pane lists the available scripts and is where new scripts can be added. Scripts can be organized in folders if required. This pane includes controls to add a new script or folder, or delete an item.

Events

The center top pane lists the events for the selected script. New event types can be added, managed, and reordered using buttons located at the bottom of the pane.

Actions

The center lower pane, lists the actions for the selected script. The action pane also includes VCR controls, action types, and reorder buttons located at the bottom of the pane to manage new and existing actions.

Properties

The right pane displays the properties of the selected event or action. This pane displays the properties and options used to configure events and actions added that were in the central panes.

Lesson: Creating and Managing Scripts

Overview

Creating interactivity in a model begins with adding a script. Events and actions are then added to the script, and each event and action is configured for the interactivity that you want. The scripts are then set up to work with the animations that you created in Animator. In this lesson, you learn how to create, delete, and organize scripts.

Objective

After completing this lesson, you will be able to:

- Add, rename, and organize scripts in folders.

Creating Scripts

Scripts can be added, renamed, or deleted. You can also group scripts in folders.

Procedure: To Add and Rename or Delete a Script

1. To add a new script, click Add New Script ⬚ in the Scripts pane or right-click in the Scripts pane and click Add New Script.

   Note: When scripts are disabled ⬚ is grayed out in the Scripter window.

2. Enter a new descriptive name for the script to help identify it and press ENTER.

3. To delete a script, select it and click ⬚ or right-click the script and click Delete Item.

> When scripts are enabled, you cannot create or edit scripts in the Scripter window. To disable scripting, select the Animation tab and click Enable Scripts ⬚ on the Script panel to clear the option.

Organizing Scripts

You can group scripts into folders. This has no effect on their execution, except that the contents of a folder can be easily switched on and off to save time.

Procedure: To Add a Script Folder

1. To add a new folder, click Add New Folder ⬚ in the Scripts pane or right-click in the Scripts pane and click Add New Folder.

2. Enter a new descriptive name for the folder and press ENTER.

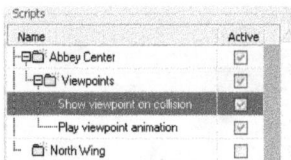

Procedure: To Move a Script

1. Select the script you want to move. Drag the script using the left mouse button to the destination folder so that the black arrow head is displayed on the folder.

2. Release the mouse to move the script into the folder.

Exercise: Create and Organize Scripts

1. Open the file *C:\Navisworks 2017 Essentials Class Files\Training\Examples\Animations\ KLM 4.nwf*.

2. On the Home tab in the Tools panel, click Scripter ⎙.

3. In the Scripts area, click Add New Script ⎙.

4. Enter **Outer Doors Open** as the new script name and press ENTER.

5. Repeat step 3 and 4 to add another script and name it **Outer Doors Close**.

6. In the Scripts area, click Add New Folder ⎙.

7. Enter **Entrance Outer Doors** as the new folder name and press ENTER.

8. Hold the left mouse button on the Outer Door Close script and drag to the folder so the arrow head is on the folder. Release the mouse to move the script into the folder.

9. Move the Outer Door Open script into the same folder.

10. Repeat Steps 3 to 9 to create scripts and folders for the inner doors. Alternatively, you can first add the folder, select it and create the two scripts in the folder.

Tip: When adding a new folder, it is created at the same level as a selected item, or at the top-level if no item is selected.

11. Save this file in a temporary location with your initials. (For example, *C:\Temp\Animations\ KLM 4JMD.nwf*.)

Lesson: Creating and Configuring Events

Overview

An event is the occurrence of an incident or a situation, such as a mouse click, key press, or collision, which determines whether your script is run or not. Your script can have more than one event in it.

When you use several events in the same script, the event structure becomes very important. That is, you need to ensure the Boolean logic makes sense, the brackets are correctly closed, etc. Additionally, until the combination of all event conditions in the script is satisfied, your script is not going to be executed.

Objective

After completing this lesson, you will be able to:

- Add and configure events.

About Events

There are seven event types available, which are displayed at the bottom of the Events pane. When an event is added, the properties view displays the properties for that event type and can be configured immediately or at a later time.

Event Types

On Start Event

On Start Event triggers a script as soon as scripting is enabled. If scripting is enabled when a file is loaded, then any start events in the file are triggered immediately. This is useful for setting up the initial conditions of your script, such as giving initial values to variables, or moving the camera to a defined start point. You do not need to configure any properties for this event type.

On Timer Event

On Timer Event triggers a script at predefined time intervals. You can specify the following properties for this event type:

- **Interval** – Enter the length of time in seconds between timer triggering.
- **Regularity** – Select the event frequency:
    - **Once After** – An event happens once only. Use this option when you want to have an event that starts after a certain length of time.
    - **Continuous** – An event is continuously repeated at specified time intervals. You can use this, for example, to simulate cyclic work of a factory machine.

On Key Press Event

On Key Press Event ⬚ triggers a script with a specific button on the keyboard. You can specify the following properties for this event type:

- **Key** – This is a read-only box showing the currently selected key.
- **Trigger On** – Select how the event is triggered:
  - **Key Up** – An event is triggered after you press the key, and let go (that is, when your finger releases the key).
  - **Key Down** – An event is triggered the moment you press the key (that is, when your finger hits the key).
  - **Key Pressed** – An event is triggered while the key is pressed. This option enables you to use a key press event together with Boolean operators. For example, you can use AND to connect this event to a timer event.

On Collision Event

On Collision Event ⬚ triggers a script when the mouse collides with a specific object. You can specify the following properties for this event type:

- **Selection to collide with** – Click Set, and use the shortcut menu to define the collision objects:
  - **Clear** – Clears your currently selected collision objects.
  - **Set From Current Selection** – Sets the collision objects to your current object selection in the Scene View.
  - **Set From Current Selection Set** – Sets the collision objects to your current search set or selection set.
- **Show** – This is a read-only box showing the number of geometry objects selected as collision objects.
- **Include the effects of gravity** – Select this option if you want to include gravity in collision detection. If this option is used, hitting floor when walking across it, for example, triggers your event.

On Hotspot Event

On Hotspot Event ⬚ triggers a script when the mouse is within a specific range of a hotspot. You can specify the following properties for this event type:

- **Hotspot** – Select the hotspot type:
  - **Sphere** – A simple sphere from a given point in space.
  - **Sphere on selection** – A sphere around a given selection. This option does not require you to define the given point in space. This hotspot moves as the selected objects move in the model.

- **Trigger When** – Select how the event is triggered:
  - **Entering** – An event is triggered when you cross into the hotspot. This is useful for opening doors, for example.
  - **Leaving** – An event is triggered when you leave the hotspot. This is useful for closing doors, for example.
  - **In Range** – An event is triggered when you are inside the hotspot. This option enables you to use a hotspot event together with Boolean operators. For example, you can use AND to connect this event to a timer event.

The remaining options appear depending on which Hotspot option is selected.

- **Position** – Specify position of the hotspot point in millimeters. If the hotspot type you select is Sphere on Selection, this field is not available.
- **Pick** – Pick the position of the hotspot point. If the hotspot type you select is Sphere on Selection, this button is not available. Click this button, and then click a point for the hotspot in the main Autodesk Navisworks window.
- **Set** – Select the hotspot objects. If the hotspot type you select is Sphere, this button is not available. Click Set, and select an option:
  - **Clear** – Clears the current selection.
  - **Set From Current Selection** – Sets the hotspot to your current object selection in the main Autodesk Navisworks window.
  - **Set From Current Selection Set** – Sets the hotspot to your current search set or selection set.
- **Show** – This read-only field displays the number of geometry objects linked to the hotspot. If the hotspot type you select is Sphere, this field is not available.
- **Radius** – Set the radius of hotspot, in millimeters.

On Variable Event

On Variable Event ⬚ triggers a script when a variable meets a predefined criterion. You can specify the following properties for this event type:

- **Variable** – Specify the alphanumeric name of the variable to be evaluated.
- **Value** – Enter an operand to use. Enter a value to be tested against your variable. Alternatively, enter a name of another variable. Its value is tested against the value in your variable.
  - If you enter a number (for example 0, 400, 5.3), the value is treated as a numeric value. If it has a decimal place, the floating-point formatting is preserved up to the user-defined decimal places.
  - If you enter an alphanumeric string between single or double quote marks, such as "hello" or "testing," the value is treated as a string.
  - If you enter an alphanumeric string without single or double quote marks, such as "counter1" or "testing," the value is treated as another variable. If this variable has never been used before, it is assigned a numerical value of 0.
  - If you enter the word true or false without any quotes, the value is treated as a Boolean (true = 1, false = 0).

- **Evaluation** – Enter an operator used for variable comparison. You can use any of the following operators with numbers and Boolean values. However, comparing strings is limited to the 'Equal to' and 'Not equal to' operators only.
  - Equal to
  - Not Equal to
  - Greater than
  - Less than
  - Greater than or equal to
  - Less than or equal to

On Animation Event

On Animation Event 📇 triggers a script when a specific animation starts or stops. You can specify the following properties for this event type:

- **Animation** – Select an animation that triggers the event.
- **Trigger On** – Select how the event is triggered:
  - **Starting** – An event is triggered when the animation starts.
  - **Ending** – An event is triggered when the animation ends. This is useful for chaining animations together.

Procedure: To Add and Create an Event

1. In the Scripts pane, select the script.

2. At the bottom of the Events pane, click an event type button to define the event. For example, click On Key Press 🔲 to create a start event.

3. Review the properties in the Properties pane and change the property values, as required.

When scripts are enabled, you cannot create or edit scripts in the Scripter window. To disable scripting, select the Animation tab and click Enable Scripts 📜 on the Script panel to clear the option.

Exercise: Create and Configure Events

Outer Doors Open Script

1. Continue to work on the file from the previous exercise. Alternatively, if you did not complete that exercise, open the file *C:\Navisworks 2017 Essentials Class Files\Training\Examples\Animations\KLM 5.nwf*.

2. In the Saved Viewpoints window, select the Entrance 1 saved viewpoint.

3. In the Scripts pane of the Scripter window, expand Entrance Outer Doors and select the Outer Doors Open script.

4. In the Events pane, select (On Hotspot).

5. In the Scene View, select both outer doors.

6. In the Properties pane, select Sphere on selection in the Hotspot drop-down menu.

7. Click Set and select Set From Current Selection to attach the hotspot to both doors.

8. In the Trigger when drop-down menu, select Entering.

9. In the Radius field, enter **1.500**.

Outer Doors Close Script

1. In the Scripts pane, select Outer Doors Close script.

2. In the Events pane, click On Hotspot .

3. In the Scene View, select both outer doors, if not already selected.

4. In the Properties pane, select Sphere on selection in the Hotspot drop-down menu.

5. Click Set and select Set From Current Selection to attach the hotspot to both doors.

6. In the Trigger when drop-down menu, select Leaving.

7. In the Radius field, enter **1.500**.

Scripts for Inner Door

1. Repeat the steps to apply events to the two Entrance Inner Door scripts.

2. Save this file in a temporary location with your initials. (For example, *C: \Temp\Animations\KLM 5JMD.nwf*.)

You have now added hotspot events to the four entrance doors. In the next lesson you attach actions to these hotspots so that when the doors are approached and the hotspot triggered. The hotspot event starts the associated action. This action plays the opening doors animation.

Lesson: Creating and Configuring Actions

Overview

An action takes place when triggered by an event. Your script can have more than one action in it. Actions are executed one after another, so it is important to get the action sequence right. However, Scripter does not wait for the current action to be completed before moving on to the next action.

In this lesson you learn how to create and configure actions.

Objective

After completing this lesson, you will be able to:

- Create and configure actions to achieve specific results.

About Script Actions

Action Types

There are eight action types. When an action is added, the Properties pane displays the properties for that action type and can be configured immediately or at a later time.

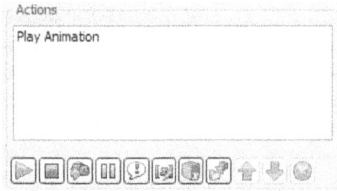

Play Animation Action

A Play Animation Action specifies which animation to play back when a script is triggered. You can specify the following properties for this action type:

- **Animation** – Select the animation to play. If you do not have any object animation in your Autodesk Navisworks file, this field is not available.
- **Pause at End** – Select this checkbox if you want the animation to stop at the end. If this checkbox is clear, the animation snaps back to the starting point when it ends.
- **Starting at** – Select where the playback starts:
  - **Start** – The animation plays forwards from the beginning.
  - **End** – The animation plays backwards from the end.
  - **Current Position** – The animation plays from its current position if the playback has already started. Otherwise, the animation plays forwards from the beginning.
  - **Specified Time** – The animation plays from the segment defined in the Specific Start Time field.
- **Ending at** – Select the playback end from the drop-down list:
  - **Start** – The playback ends at the beginning of the animation.
  - **End** – The playback ends at the end of the animation.
  - **Specified Time** – The playback ends at the segment defined in the Specific End Time field.
- **Specific Start Time** – Specify the start position of a playback segment.
- **Specific End Time** – Specify the end position of a playback segment.

Stop Animation Action

Stop Animation Action ▣ specifies which currently playing animation is to stop when a script is triggered. You can specify the following properties for this action type:

- **Animation** – Select the animation to stop. If you do not have any object animation in your Autodesk Navisworks file, this field is not available.
- **Reset To** – Select the position of the stopped animation:
  - **Default Position** – The animation returns to its starting point.
  - **Current Position** – The animation remains at its end position.

Show Viewpoint Action

Show Viewpoint Action ▣ specifies which viewpoint to use when a script is triggered. You can specify the following property for this action type:

- **Viewpoint** – Select the viewpoint to show. If you do not have any viewpoints in your Autodesk Navisworks file, this field is not available.

Pause Script Action

Actions are executed one after another in a script, but Scripter does not wait for the current action to be completed before moving on to the next. With Pause Action ▣ you can stop the script for a specified amount of time before the next action is run. Alternatively, you can create several scripts to execute actions separately. You can specify the following property for this action type:

- **Delay** – Enter the time period in seconds.

Send Message Action

Send Message Action ▣ writes a message in a text file when a script is triggered. This can be useful when creating multiple interactive scripts to test if a particular script is working, etc. You can specify the following property for this action type:

- **Message** – Enter the message that is going to be sent to a text file. The location of the text file can be configured in the Options Editor.

Procedure: To Configure the Message File Location

1. Click Application Menu ![N icon] > Options > Tools > Scripter.

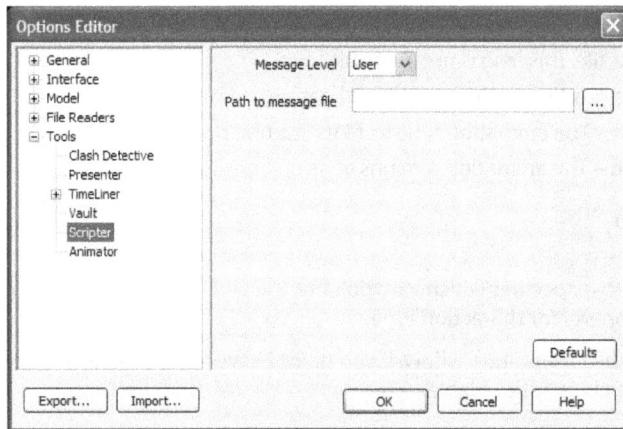

    ![Options Editor dialog showing a tree list on the left with General, Interface, Model, File Readers, and Tools expanded (Clash Detective, Presenter, TimeLiner, Vault, Scripter highlighted, Animator). On the right are Message Level dropdown set to User and a Path to message file field with a browse button. Buttons at bottom: Export..., Import..., OK, Cancel, Help, and Defaults.]

2. In the Scripter options, in the Message Level drop-down list, select the contents of the message file:

    - **User** – The message file only contains user messages (messages generated by message actions).
    - **Debug** – The message file contains both user messages and debug messages (messages generated internally by Scripter). Debugging enables you to see what is going on in more complex scripts.

3. In the Path to message file, enter a file location or click ⬚ to browse to a location.

4. Click OK to save. When a script is triggered, the Send Message action sends the message to the location as configured in step 4.

Set Variable Action

Set Variable Action ![icon] assigns, increases, or decreases a variable value when a script is triggered. You can specify the following properties for this action type:

- **Variable Name** – Specify the alphanumeric name for the variable.
- **Value** – Enter an operand to assign.
    - If you enter a number, for example 0, 400, 5.3, the value is treated as a numeric value. If it has a decimal place, the floating-point formatting is preserved up to the user-defined decimal places.
    - If you enter an alphanumeric string between single or double quote marks, such as "hello" or "testing," the value is treated as a sting.
    - If you enter the word true or false without any quotes, the value is treated as a Boolean (true = 1, false = 0).

- **Modifier** – Enter assignment operators for your variable. You can use any of the following operators with numbers and Boolean values. However, using strings is limited to the Set equal to operator only.
  - Set equal to
  - Increment by
  - Decrement by

Store Property Action

Store Property Action ▣ stores an object property in a variable when a script is triggered. This can be useful if you need to trigger events based on embedded object properties or live data in a linked database. You can specify the following properties for this action type:

- **Selection to get property from** – Click Set, and use the shortcut menu to define the objects, which are used to get the property:
  - **Clear** – Clears the current selection.
  - **Set From Current Selection** – Sets the objects to your current object selection in the main Autodesk Navisworks window.
  - **Set From Current Selection Set** – Sets she objects to your current search set or selection set.

  Note: If your selection contains a hierarchy of objects, the top-level object is automatically used to get the property. For example, if you selected a group called Wheel, which includes two subgroups called Rim and Tire, only the properties that relate to Wheel can be stored.

- **Variable to set** – Enter the name of the variable to receive the property.
- **Category** – Specify the property category. The values in this drop-down list depend on the selected objects.
- **Property** – Specify the property type. The values in this drop-down list depend on the chosen property category.

  Note: For more information about object properties, see Object Properties in Chapter 1.

Load Model Action

Load Model Action ▣ opens a specified file when a script is triggered. You can specify the following property for this action type:

- **File to Load** – Enter the path to the file that is going to be loaded to replace the current one. You might find it useful, if for performance reasons, you cannot append your models together or you would like to delineate phases of a project.

Procedure: To Add an Action

1. In the Scripts pane, select the script.

2. In the Events pane, select the event.

3. At the bottom of the Actions pane, click an action type button to define the action. For example, click Play Animation to create a play animation action.

4. Review the properties in the Properties pane and change the property values, as required.

Procedure: Enabling Scripting

To enable animation scripts in your animations, select the Animation tab and click Enable Scripts on the Script panel. You can now interact with your model.

> When scripts are enabled, you cannot create or edit scripts in the Scripter window. To disable scripting, click Enable Scripts again.

Exercise: Create and Configure Actions

Outer Doors Open Script

1. Continue to work on the file from the previous exercise. Alternatively, if you did not complete that exercise, open the file *C:\Navisworks 2017 Essentials Class Files\Training\Examples\ Animations\KLM 6.nwf.*

2. In the Scripts pane of the Scripter window, expand Entrance Outer Doors and select the Outer Doors Open script.

3. In the Events pane, select the On Hotspot event.

4. In the Actions pane, click Play Animation ▷ to add a play animation action.

5. In the Properties pane, click the Animation field, then select Opening Outer Doors.

6. Select Pause at End.

7. In the Starting At drop-down menu, select Start.

8. In the Ending At drop-down menu, select End.

Outer Doors Close Script

1. Select the Outer Doors Close script.

2. In the Events pane, select the On Hotspot event.

3. In the Actions pane, click Play Animation ▷ to add a play animation action.

4. In the Properties pane, click the Animation field, then select Opening Outer Doors.

5. Select Pause at End.

6. In the Starting At drop-down menu, select End.

7. In the Ending At drop-down menu, select Start.

   Note: The selection in steps 6 and 7 causes the animation to play backwards (close doors).

8. Repeat the steps to apply to the Entrance Inner Doors. Now you have added and configured actions to the hotspots in the scripts. You are ready to see the interactive animations. The created scripts need to be enabled to work with the navigation tools.

Enabling Scripting

1. Select the Animation tab. On the Script panel, click Enable Scripts 📜 . Notice how the Events, Actions, and Properties panes are all disabled.

2. Select the Entrance 1 saved viewpoint.

3. Using the Navigation bar, interact with your model. When navigating towards the entrance doors they should open and then close behind you as you proceed into the building.

4. Save this file in a temporary location with your initials. (For example, *C: \Temp\Animations\ KLM 6JMD.nwf.*)

Quantification

The process of measuring quantities of materials from models, drawings, and specifications prepared by architects, engineers, and other designers is known as takeoff. In the Autodesk Navisworks software, takeoff is carried out using the Quantification feature. Quantification gives you the tools to automatically create material estimates, measure areas, and count components. You can accurately estimate construction and renovation projects, so you spend less time counting and measuring items and more time analyzing projects. The Quantification feature is available for Autodesk Navisworks Manage and Autodesk Navisworks Simulate users.

Objectives

After completing this chapter, you will be able to:

- Identify the key steps in the Quantification workflow.
- Understand how to setup a quantification project in an Autodesk Navisworks file.
- Assign an Item Catalog to a quantification project.
- Define the units of measure for takeoff properties.
- Understand the role of the Item and Resource catalogs in takeoff calculations.
- Access the Item and Resource catalogs.
- Creating Groups and Items in the Item Catalog.
- Creating Resources in the Resource Catalog.
- Adding Resources to the Item Catalog.
- Identify the differences between 3D Model and Virtual Takeoff options.
- Efficiently select objects in the Selection Tree that can be used to generate model takeoff data.
- Conduct a Model Takeoff using objects from the Autodesk Navisworks Scene View to populate the Quantification Workbook.
- Create a Virtual Takeoff in the Quantification Workbook.

- Create takeoff viewpoints and adding redlines to those viewpoints
- Conduct takeoff measurements in the Scene.
- Override takeoff data in the Quantification Workbook.
- Change the columns that are displayed in the Quantification Workbook.
- Sort column contents in the Quantification Workbook.
- Add Comments to Takeoff data.
- Change the takeoff data appearance.
- Control the display of items in the scene view based on whether they have been taken off or not.
- Delete the takeoff data.
- Remove any overrides from takeoff data.
- Use the tools on the 2D Takeoff toolbar to efficiently create Linear Takeoffs on a 2D sheet.
- Use the tools on the 2D Takeoff toolbar to efficiently create Area Takeoffs on a 2D sheet.
- Use the tools on the 2D Takeoff toolbar to efficiently create Count Takeoffs on a 2D sheet.
- Execute an analysis of refreshed Autodesk Navisworks data.
- Understand the status notifications that can appear after a Change Analysis is executed.
- Update changed quantification takeoff data to reflect changes in the model.
- Export Takeoff data from a Quantification Workbook.

Lesson: Quantification Overview

Overview

This lesson provides an overview of the Autodesk Navisworks Quantification tool for measuring quantities of materials from both 3D models and 2D sheets.

Objectives

After completing this lesson, you will be able to:

- Identify the key steps in the Quantification workflow.

Overview of Quantification

The process of measuring quantities of materials from models, drawings, and specifications from either 2D sheets or 3D design data is known as takeoff. In the Autodesk Navisworks software, takeoff is carried out using the Quantification feature. The Quantification feature provides you with the tools to automatically create material estimates, measure areas, and count building components using a 3D model or a 2D sheet. Rather than carrying out manual calculations on paper sheets, you can markup geometry and perform accurate calculations. By enabling you to accurately estimate construction and renovation projects, you spend less time counting and measuring items and more time analyzing projects. Your takeoff data can also be exported to Excel for analysis and shared with other project team members in the cloud using Autodesk BIM 360®, for optimized collaboration.

> The Quantification feature is available for Autodesk Navisworks Manage and Autodesk Navisworks Simulate users.

Supported File Formats

Autodesk Navisworks Quantification project documents can count and measure the item quantities associated with multiple disciplines, including:

- Civil (earth, road, drainage)
- Architecture (doors, walls, windows)
- Engineering (structural, mechanical, electrical, plumbing)

Quantification supports native and derivate file formats for the following applications.

Publishing Application	File Format
AutoCAD Architecture	.DWF, .DWFX
AutoCAD Civil 3D	.DWF, .DWFX
AutoCAD MEP	.DWF, .DWFX
AutoCAD Plant 3D	.DWF, .DWFX
Autodesk Inventor	.DWF, .DWFX
Autodesk Revit	.RVT, .NWC, .DWF, .DWFX
Adobe	.PDF

> For 2D Takeoff only .DWF and .DWFX file formats are supported. Consider converting 2D image files (such as .PDF) to .DWF using print driver software.

Quantification Workflow

A typical workflow begins with a design file created in an Autodesk design application, such as AutoCAD, AutoCAD Architecture, AutoCAD Civil 3D, or Autodesk Revit and then brought into the Autodesk Navisworks software. The general workflow includes the following:

1. Open the file to which a Quantification is to be created in the Autodesk Navisworks software.

2. Set up a project in the Quantification tool.

3. Manage the Item and Resource Catalogs.

4. Create 3D Model and Virtual Takeoffs, as required.

5. Create 2D Takeoffs, as required.

6. Manage takeoff data, as required.

7. Analyze and validate takeoff data as changes are made to the source files.

8. Output takeoff data, as required.

Lesson: Setting up a Quantification Project

Overview

This lesson describes how to use the Quantification Setup Wizard to start a new quantification project and populate the Quantification Workbook with an Item Catalog.

Objectives

After completing this lesson, you will be able to:

- Understand how to setup a quantification project in an Autodesk Navisworks file.
- Assign an Item Catalog to a quantification project.
- Define the units of measure for takeoff properties.

Quantification Projects

The Quantification Workbook is your key workspace in a quantification project. A project is a collection of files and takeoff items that you use to produce detailed material quantities. When you create a project, you select the catalog content to import, and then specify project settings, such as measurement units. The first time the workbook is accessed in an Autodesk Navisworks file you must setup the project. Your project structure is defined by your catalog and the groups, items and resources you create in Quantification. Once created and saved with the Autodesk Navisworks file it is accessed each time the Quantification feature is accessed.

Procedure: To Setup a Quantification Project

1. To access the Quantification Workbook, use one of the following methods:

    - On the ribbon, click the Home tab, then in the Tools menu, click ⊞⊟ (Quantification).

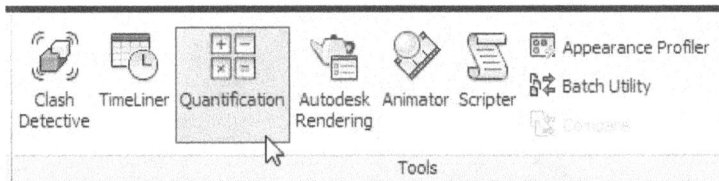

    - On the ribbon, click the View tab, then in the Workspace panel, click the Windows drop-down and select Quantification Workbook.

2. In the Quantification Workbook window, click ⊞ Project Setup... to access the Quantification Setup Wizard. If a project already exists in the Autodesk Navisworks file project, setup is not required.

3. Select an option in the Quantification Getting Started dialog box. This dialog box provides you with the opportunity to review help on Quantification. Select an option to continue.

Note: The Quantification tutorial can also be accessed from Help on the Getting Started with Quantification page in the Quantification User Guide.

4. Select the Item catalog that is to be used for the project. This enables you to assign the takeoff groups and disciplines to be used. The Autodesk Navisworks software provides a few default item catalogs or you can browse to and load any additional item catalog files (.xml). Browse to or select an existing catalog and click Next.

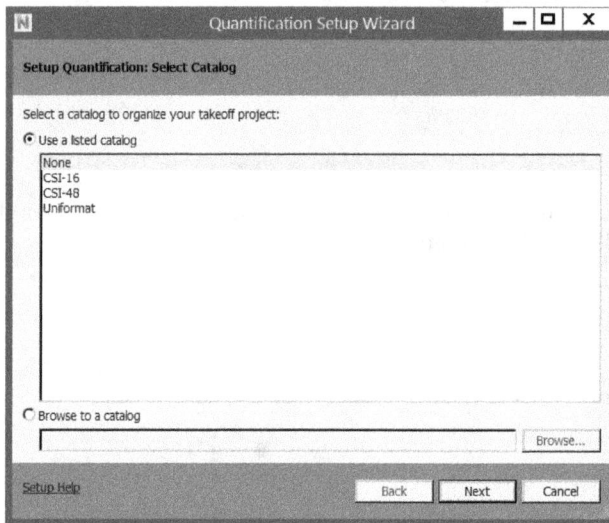

Note: The Listed catalogs can also include company specific catalogs that have been created by an Autodesk Navisworks administrator or other user. If you use a custom catalog it must have the same units and properties as your current project.

5. Select the overall unit type to be used in the project and click Next. The options include:

- **Imperial** – Converts units in the model to imperial, such as feet, pounds, or gallons.
- **Metric** – Converts units in the model to metric, such as meters, kilograms, or liters.
- **Variable** – Uses existing model values. You can change the unit for each individual takeoff property on the next wizard page.

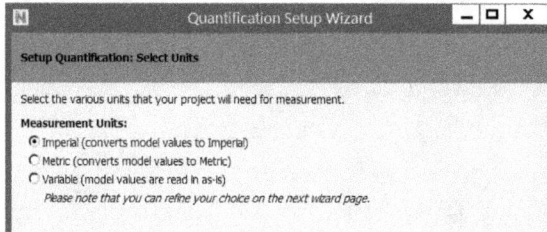

6. Refine the units for specific properties by selecting units in the drop-down lists adjacent to each property. By default, the unit type assigned is consistent with the overall unit type selected in the previous step. Additionally, you can select Show Metric and Imperial units for each takeoff property option, if required, to display both units. Click Next.

7. Click Finish to complete the project setup.

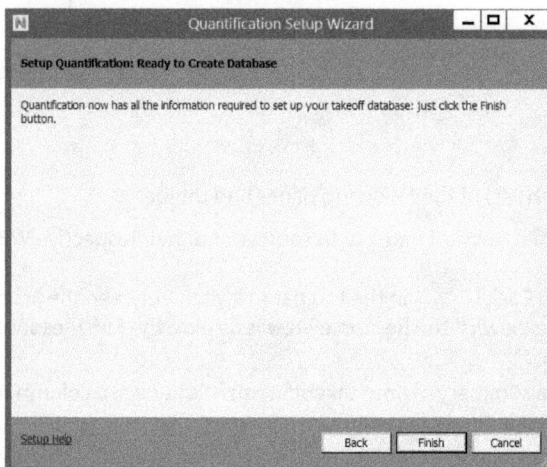

Once the project has been created, the Quantification Workbook updates to display the Item Catalog that was selected or imported.

> Quantification catalogs can be imported after the Quantification Workbook has been created. To import, click ![icon], select Import Catalog, and browse to and open a new catalog. You are prompted if duplicate items are encountered.
>
> **Note:** Import new catalogs with caution. Use existing catalogs that are set up by your IT account administrator or are correctly approved. If you must import a catalog, ensure that it is in .XML format and contains the same units of measurement and properties as those contained in your current project file.

Quantification Workbook

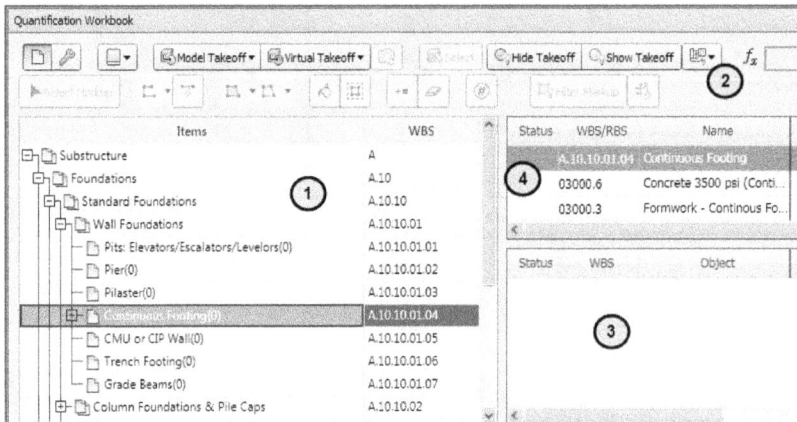

The Quantification Workbook consists of the following panes and toolbar:

- **Navigation pane (1)** – Contains a list of Items or Resources and their respective WBS (Work Breakdown Structure) codes. Click ![icon] in the toolbar to switch between the list of Items (Item View) or Resources (Resource View). If the Resource View is display, the RBS (Resource Breakdown Structure) codes are displayed

- **Rollup pane (2)** – Contains a summary of your takeoff items. Right-click a column header to change the columns displayed in the Rollup pane.

- **Takeoff pane (3)** – Displays all takeoff items. Right-click a column header to change the columns displayed in the Takeoff pane.

- **Toolbar (4)** – Access the main functions of Quantification (3D and 2D) using the toolbar.

Lesson: Item and Resource Management

Overview

This lesson describes the Item and Resource Catalogs and how to populate these catalogs with data that can be used to perform takeoff calculations.

Objectives

After completing this lesson, you will be able to:

- Understand the role of the Item and Resource catalogs in takeoff calculations.
- Access the Item and Resource catalogs.
- Creating Groups and Items in the Item Catalog.
- Creating Resources in the Resource Catalog.
- Adding Resources to the Item Catalog.

Item & Resource Catalog Overview

The Item and Resource catalog information defines the organizational structure of your project and is used to classify the model elements further than the model authoring tools can offer for takeoff data. The Autodesk Navisworks software uses these catalogs to enhance the model information with more construction-related detail for the purpose of generating a more complete quantification of the project, not just counts of objects.

The information that displays in these catalogs is dependent on whether the project has been setup and if resources have been assigned to items in the assigned catalog, or you can create one. When you create a project, you can import a catalog to define the organizational model for your takeoff project. If you base a project on a catalog, the workbook is populated with takeoff groups (such as disciplines) that are derived from the catalog. After you have created a project, you can import additional data from a catalog or spreadsheet to automatically create more takeoff groups and items.

> Once catalogs are created in a project, they should be exported and reused in other projects to ensure consistent use of catalogs in your company's projects.

Item & Resource Catalog Windows

By default, the Item and Resource catalogs are nested together with the Quantification Workbook window. Each can be displayed by selecting their tab name along the bottom of the window. Alternatively, they can be displayed as separate windows by double-clicking on their title bar and double-click again on the title bar to nest them. To toggle these windows on or off, use one of the following:

- On the View tab, in the Workspace panel, expand the Windows drop-down list and select Item Catalog or Resource catalog, as required.
- On the toolbar in the Quantification Workbook, click and select Item Catalog or Resource catalog, as required.
- With either the Item Catalog or Resource Catalog window active, you can click either Resource Catalog or Item Catalog to open the other window.

The Item Catalog and Resource Catalog share a similar structure, a selection tree, variables pane, and general information.

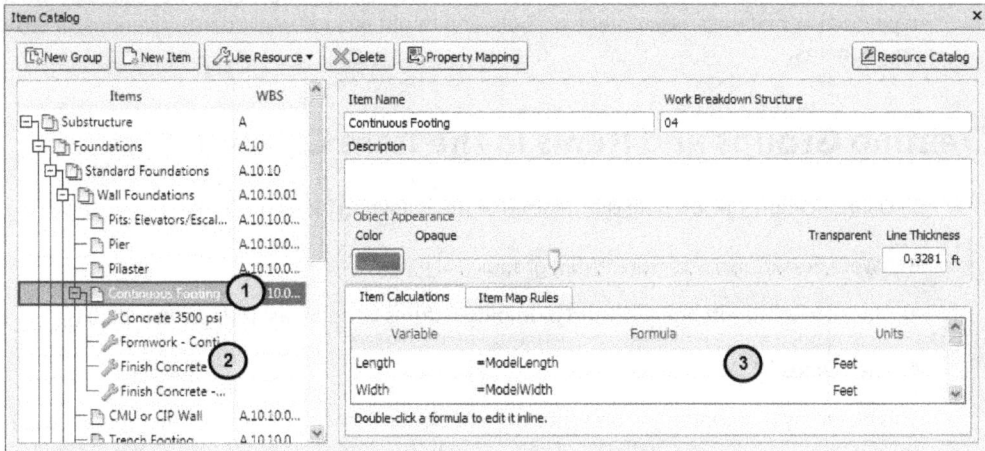

The Item Catalog consists of the following:

- **Items (1)**
- **Resources (2)**
- **Formulas (3)** – The Formula area enables you to link variables with a formula to measure takeoff values.

The Resource Catalog consists of the following:

- **Resource Group (1)**
- **Resource (2)**
- **Formulas (3)** – The Formula area enables you to link variables with a formula to measure takeoff values.

Items in the Item Catalog can be directly associated with a model object, such as a wall or window. Items can exist alone or contain resources. If resources exist, they are listed in the Resource catalog. This catalog is a database of your resources for the project. Resources could be related by function and type, such as materials, equipment, or tools, and might include wall board, coverings, or structural components.

Creating Groups and Items in the Item Catalog

In Quantification, takeoff data is organized in the following hierarchy in the Item Catalog.

- Work Breakdown Structure (WBS) groups ( )
- Items (such as interior walls and plumbing fixtures to be measured and counted) ( )
- Resources ( )

This hierarchy is graphically represented as a navigation tree that supports multiple levels of WBS groups, enabling you to create the organizational structure required for your takeoff project.

Procedure: To Create a New Group

1. In the Item Catalog window, click New Group. If an existing group is selected, the new group is created in that group. To create a new group at the top of the hierarchy, ensure that no groups are currently selected.

   Alternatively, you can right-click in the white space (nothing selected) and select New Group to create a new group at the top of the hierarchy or right-click on an existing group and select New Group to create a new group in it.

2. Enter a name for the group and press ENTER.

Procedure: To Create a New Item 🗅

1. In the Item Catalog window, expand and select the group in which you want to create the item. Once selected, click New Item. The item is created in the group. Items can also be created outside groups by clearing all of the group selections in the Item hierarchy before creating the item.

    Alternatively, you can right-click in the white space (nothing selected) and select New Item to create a new item at the top of the hierarchy or right-click on an existing group and select New Item to create a new item in a selected group.

2. Enter a name for the item and press ENTER.

> 💡 Items and groups can be copied to quickly duplicate items in the Item Catalog. To copy, right-click the required item or group and select Copy. To paste, right-click the Group in which you want the copied Item or Group to sit and select Paste. Once pasted, double-click the copied item or group and enter the new name to rename it. If you copy an existing group or item, its associated resources are also copied.

Creating Resources in the Resource Catalog

In Quantification, takeoff data is organized in the following hierarchy in the Resource Catalog.

- Resource Breakdown Structure (RBS) groups (🗀)

- Resources (🔧)

This hierarchy is graphically represented as a navigation tree that supports multiple levels of RBS groups, enabling you to create the organizational structure required for your takeoff project.

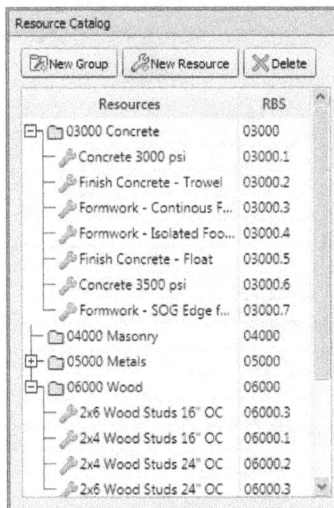

Procedure: To Create a New Resource

1. In the Resource Catalog window, expand the resource grouping in which you want to create the resource. To create a new group in the Resource Catalog, click New Group. Sub-groups can also be created to help further manage the resources required for a quantification project.

    Tip: Groups are only created and used in the Resource Catalog for resource management. The group headings are not used in the Quantification Workbook.

2. Once the required resource group has been selected, click New Resource. The resource is created in the group. Resources can also be created outside groups by clearing all of the group selections in the Resource hierarchy before creating the resource.

    Alternatively, you can right-click in the white space (with nothing selected) and select New Resource to create a new item at the top of the hierarchy or right-click on an existing group and select New Item to create a new item in a selected group.

Adding Resources to the Item Catalog

Resources that are created in the Resource Catalog are not automatically added to the Item Catalog. To be used in the project's Quantification workbook, they must be copied into the Item Catalog.

Procedure: To Copy a Resource to the Item Catalog

1. In the Item Catalog window, expand the item grouping in which to place the new resource.

2. In the Resource Catalog window, expand the resource grouping in which the required resource is located.

3. Select the resource to be copied, right-click and select Add to Selected Catalog Item. Once added, the Item list in the Quantification Workbook also updates and the resource can be used for Takeoff reports.

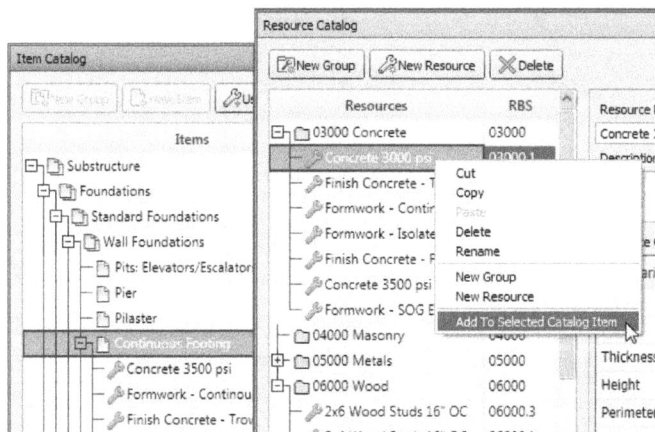

Copying Groups and Items in the Item Catalog

An existing group and item structure that is created in the Item Catalog can be duplicated as required, to create another structure. When copied, all of the groups, items, and resources are also duplicated.

Procedure: To Copy a Resource to the Item Catalog

1. In the Item Catalog window, select the top level that you want to copy. It can contain groups, items, and resources.

2. Right-click and select Copy.

3. Select the level to which you want to paste.

4. Right-click and select Paste.

5. Right-click groups or items in the copied Structure and select Rename.

   Tip: Renaming ensures that all of the catalog items are unique.

Working with the Quantification Windows

The Quantification Workbook, Item Catalog and Resource Catalog are all dockable windows that can be rearranged in the Scene view. Windows can be moved and resized, and either floated in the Scene View or docked (pinned or auto-hidden). Use the following procedures to manipulate the windows:

- To resize a window select and drag on an edge or corner.
- To move a window, click and drag the title bar at the top or side of the window. To prevent a window from automatically docking while you drag it, hold CTRL.
- You can quickly dock and undock a window by double-clicking the window's title bar.
- To pin/unpin a docked window, use and in the title bar.
- To dock in the non-default location, select the title bar and drag to the specific interface

  location. Drop over the docking symbol (e.g.,)

Exercise: Setting up a Quantification Workbook

Setup the Quantification Project

1. Open the file *C:\Navisworks 2017 Essentials Class Files\Training\Examples\Quantification\ Autodesk_Hospital_Quantification.nwf*. The file opens and has both architectural and structural files appended.

2. On the ribbon, click the Home tab, then in the Tools menu, click ⊞⊟⊠⊟ (Quantification) to open the Quantification Workbook, if not already open.

    Note: Alternatively, you can access the Quantification Workbook by selecting Quantification Workbook in the Windows drop-down list on the View tab.

3. Dock the Quantification Workbook at the bottom of the Autodesk Navisworks screen, if it is not already.

    In the Quantification Workbook window, click Project Setup.

4.

5. Select Remind Me Later from the Quantification Getting Started dialog box to continue to the Quantification Setup Wizard.

6. Select Browse to a catalog and click Browse. Browse to and open the *C:\Navisworks 2017 Essentials Class Files\Training\Examples\Quantification\Autodesk_Sample_Hospital - Quantification Catalog.xml*. This XML file is the Item catalog that is used for this project.

7. Click Next and Finish to complete the project setup. The Item Catalog has now been assigned to the file.

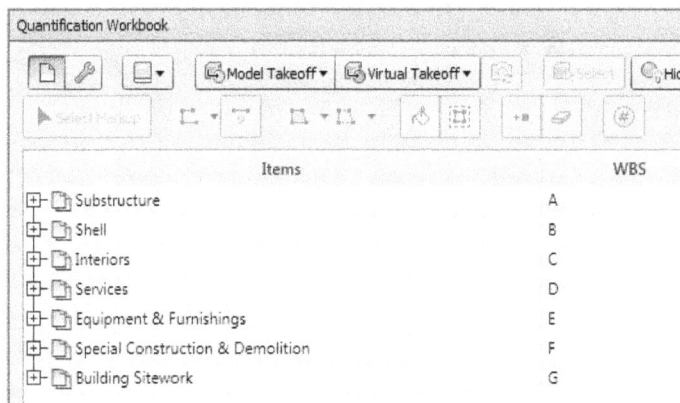

    Note: If one of the default project types was selected, the wizard would prompt for additional unit measurement selections. Because an .XML file was selected the unit definition has already been assigned.

Review the Item and Resource Catalog and Add Items

1. On the Quantification Workbook's toolbar, click ⬚▾ and ensure that the Item Catalog and Resource Catalog items are selected for display.

   Note: Alternatively, you can display the Item Catalog by selecting Item Catalog in the Windows drop-down list on the View tab.

2. By default, the Quantification Workbook, Item Catalog, and Resource Catalog are all included in the window and are individually accessed by selecting the appropriate tab at the bottom of the window, when displayed. You can individually drag out any of the windows, as required, to display them separately.

   Note: Double-clicking on a title bar undocks a docked window.

3. Select the Item Catalog tab, browse the item collections showing the items in the list, the folder structure, and the WBS (work breakdown structure) numbering.

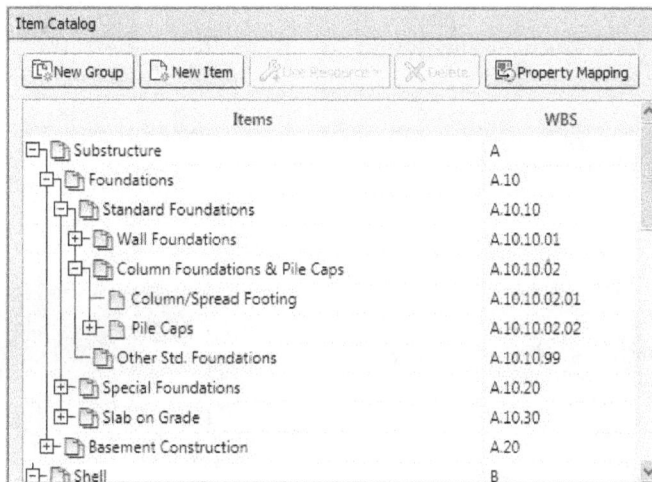

4. In the Item Catalog window, ensure that no groups are currently selected. This ensures that any new groups are added to the top-level of the Item Catalog. Click New Group. Enter **Materials** as the new name for the group and press ENTER.

5. Ensure that the Materials group is selected. In the pane on the right, enter **H** as the Work Breakdown Structure.

6. With the Materials group still selected, click New Group again. Enter **Paint** as the new name for the group and press ENTER.

7. In the Item Catalog window, select the Paint group. Once selected, click New Item. Enter **Blue Paint** as the new name for the item and press ENTER.

8. Select the Paint group and click New Item. Enter **Beige Paint** as the new item.

9. Add **White Paint** and **Red Paint** as two additional items in the Paint group.

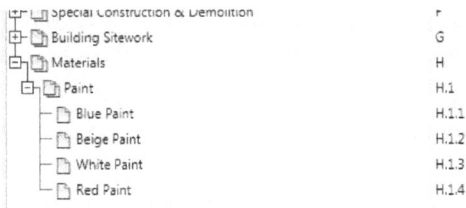

⊞ ⬚ Special Construction & Demolition	F
⊞ ⬚ Building Sitework	G
⊟ ⬚ Materials	H
⊟ ⬚ Paint	H.1
Blue Paint	H.1.1
Beige Paint	H.1.2
White Paint	H.1.3
Red Paint	H.1.4

10. Return to the Quantification Workbook and notice that the new groups and items are now available.

11. Select the Resource Catalog tab. If it is not a listed tab with the Quantification Workbook and Item Catalog, you must display it by clicking ⬚▼ > Resource Catalog in the Quantification Workbook.

12. Browse the resource collections displaying the resources in the list, folder structure, and RBS (resource breakdown structure) numbering.

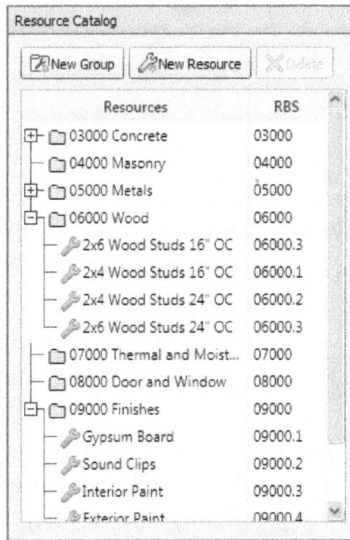

Resource Catalog

New Group	New Resource	✕ Delete

Resources	RBS
⊞ ▢ 03000 Concrete	03000
▢ 04000 Masonry	04000
⊞ ▢ 05000 Metals	05000
⊟ ▢ 06000 Wood	06000
2x6 Wood Studs 16" OC	06000.3
2x4 Wood Studs 16" OC	06000.1
2x4 Wood Studs 24" OC	06000.2
2x6 Wood Studs 24" OC	06000.3
▢ 07000 Thermal and Moist...	07000
▢ 08000 Door and Window	08000
⊟ ▢ 09000 Finishes	09000
Gypsum Board	09000.1
Sound Clips	09000.2
Interior Paint	09000.3
Exterior Paint	09000.4

13. In the Resource Catalog window, expand the 03000 Concrete resource grouping and ensure that it is selected. Click New Group. Enter **Rebar** as the new name for the resource group and press ENTER.

14. Select the Rebar resource group and click New Resource. Enter **Rebar #3** as the new name for the resource and press ENTER.

15. Ensure that the new Resource is selected in the catalog. Notice the default formulas in the Resource Calculations pane. They are used to calculate a takeoff value for this resource once it had been added to the workbook.

Variable	Formula	Units
Length	=ModelLength	Feet
Width	=ModelWidth	Feet
Thickness	=ModelThickness	Feet
Height	=ModelHeight	Feet
Perimeter	=ModelPerimeter	Feet
Area	=ModelArea	Square Feet

16. Return to the Item Catalog window. Expand the Substructure > Foundations > Standard Foundations > Column Foundations & Pile Caps groups. Select the Pile Caps item to identify the location in which to place the new resource.

17. Return to the Resource Catalog window. Expand the 0300 Concrete and Rebar resource groupings.

18. Select the Rebar #3 resource, right-click and select Add to Selected Catalog Item.

19. Return to the Quantification Workbook. Notice that the Rebar #3 Resource is now included in the Item Catalog for the Pile Caps item.

Duplicate Items in the Item Catalog

1.   In the Item Catalog, select the Pile Caps item.

2.   Right-click and select Copy.

3.   Select the parent Column Foundations & Pile Caps group. Right-click and select Paste.

4.   Expand the copied Pile Caps item and notice that all of the resources were copied with it.

5.   Right-click on the first Pile Caps item and select Rename. Enter **Pile Caps-9 Pile** as the new name.

6.   Rename the copied Pile Caps item as **Pile Caps-6 Pile**.

7.   Return to the Quantification Workbook and notice that the changes to the Pile Cap items are reflected in the Navigation pane.

8.   Save the workbook and leave the file open. You will continue working on this file in the next exercise.

Lesson: 3D Model and Virtual Takeoff

Overview

This lesson describes the differences between creating 3D Model and Virtual Takeoffs in an Autodesk Navisworks Quantification Workbook. The procedure for creating both types of 3D takeoffs is described.

Objectives

After completing this lesson, you will be able to:

- Identify the differences between 3D Model and Virtual Takeoff options.
- Efficiently select objects in the Selection Tree that can be used to generate model takeoff data.
- Conduct a Model Takeoff using objects from the Autodesk Navisworks Scene View to populate the Quantification Workbook.
- Create a Virtual Takeoff in the Quantification Workbook.
- Create takeoff viewpoints and adding redlines to those viewpoints
- Conduct takeoff measurements in the Scene.
- Override takeoff data in the Quantification Workbook.

Overview of 3D Model and Virtual Takeoffs

Using the Quantification Workbook, you can perform a 3D model (automatic) takeoff or a virtual (manual) takeoff. The source application determines whether automatic model takeoff is available, and if your files retain their properties and the Globally Unique Identifier (GUID) from the original design file, you can carry out model takeoff. A virtual takeoff can be used for items with no associated model geometry or properties. When exporting from the source application, ensure that you also export the object properties and GUID. If no properties are available or an object has not been mapped from the source file, you can carry out a virtual takeoff.

- **Model takeoff** – Uses the properties embedded in the design source files to create takeoff data. It extracts objects from the model and displays them as Items in the Quantification Workbook.
- **Virtual takeoff** – Perform virtual takeoff to add takeoff items that are not linked to a model object, or where an item displays in the model but does not contain any associated properties. You can use measure tools in conjunction with a virtual takeoff, and associate a viewpoint with the virtual takeoff Item.

Object Selection for Takeoff

To conduct a model takeoff you must select items in the Scene. Selection can be accomplished using any of the following techniques:

- Click an object (group ⊞ or above) in the Scene view.
- Expand items in the Selection Tree and click an object (group ⊞ or above). To select multiple objects in the Selection Tree, press and hold CTRL and SHIFT to select multiple or a range of objects, respectively.
  Tip: If using the Selection Tree, ensure that the display is set to Standard Tree.
- Use the Find Items tool to find objects with the searched criteria. Once found, the objects are automatically selected.
  Tip: Previously found items that were stored as Sets can also be used to select objects.
- To select all of the objects that have the same name or type as an already selected object, you can use the Select Same tool. On the Home tab, in the Select & Search panel, expand Select Same and Same Name or Same Type in the drop-down list.

Model Takeoff

Model takeoff can be used for objects that have properties mapped in the Autodesk Navisworks software. Quantification takes the object properties and GUID from the original publishing application, such as AutoCAD or Autodesk Revit, and creates takeoff items in the Quantification Workbook.

To carry out model takeoff, objects must be a group (⊞) or instance (⚒ or ⚒). If you try to takeoff a model object that is a model (🗎), layer (≋), collection (⁘), item (▱), or if the object does not contain a GUID or properties, an error message is displayed indicating that a selected item cannot be taken off.

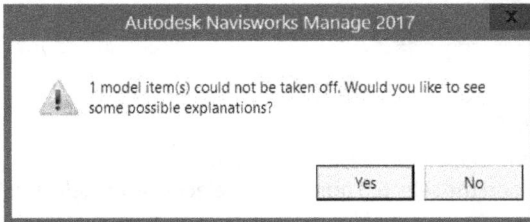

Tip: Ensure that your workbook is in Item view before performing takeoff.

Globally Unique Identifier (GUID)

A Globally Unique Identifier (GUID) is a 16-byte (128 bit number) that is associated with each object in a model. It is commonly split into several fields of varying lengths and written in groups of 8-4-4-4-12 hexadecimal characters (32 characters to represent the 16 bytes or 128 bits). For example, GUIDs might display as follows:

- 71B923D4-ABCD-4BE4-861A-3A26146EF3F0
- 398A60AB-ABCD-48C1-ADEA-70009C3DFAC9

When exporting files from their native application to use in Quantification, ensure that the export settings include object and element property mapping.

Conducting a Model Takeoff

Once objects have been selected in the Scene View, they can be taken off. The following describes the multiple ways in which this can be done.

Procedure: To Assign a Selected Scene Object to an Existing Workbook Item

1. In the Quantification Workbook, select the Item to which you want to assign the Scene object.

2. Use any one of the techniques that have been previously discussed to select objects in the Scene, if not already selected.

3. Add the selected object to the Quantification Workbook using one of the following:

   - Right-click in the Selection Tree and select Quantification > Take off to: *<Name of Existing Item>*. Where *<Name of Existing Item>* represents the name of the Item selected in the Quantification Workbook.

- Right-click a selected object in the Selection Tree and select Quantification > Select Corresponding Takeoff Objects. The corresponding Workbook item must be selected to assign the object(s).

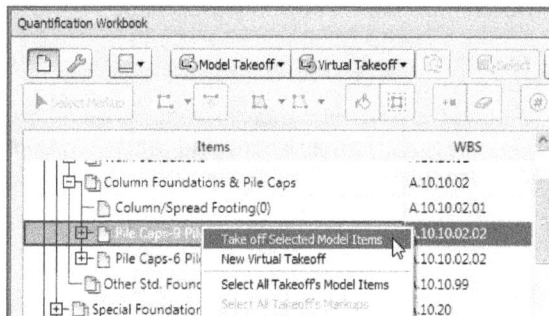

- With the object(s) selected in the Selection Tree, in the Quantification Workbook, right-click the Item to which to add the selected objects and select Take off Selected Model Items.

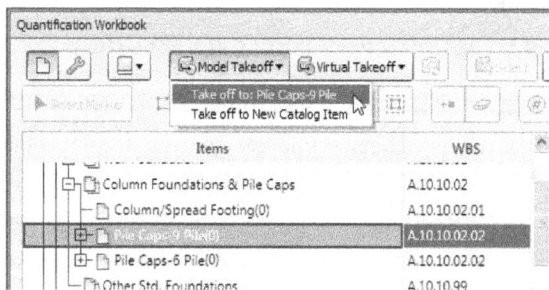

- **Tip:** Ensure that the Quantification Workbook is in Item view to use the Take off Selected Model Items option.

- With the object(s) selected in the Selection Tree, in the toolbar of the Quantification Workbook, click Model Takeoff and select Take off to: *<Selected Item Name>*.

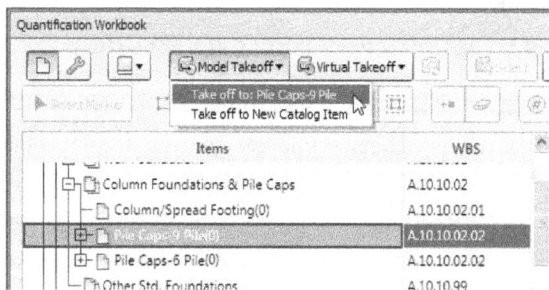

- Drag the selected object(s) into the Quantification Workbook's Navigation pane. When dragging to the Navigation pane, drop the object(s) by releasing the left mouse button on the Item type. The Item type does not need to be selected for this takeoff creation method.

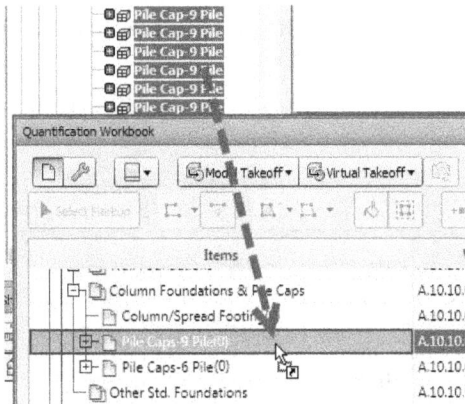

- Drag the selected object(s) into the Quantification Workbook's takeoff pane. When dragging to the Navigation pane, drop the object(s) by releasing the left mouse button on the Item type.

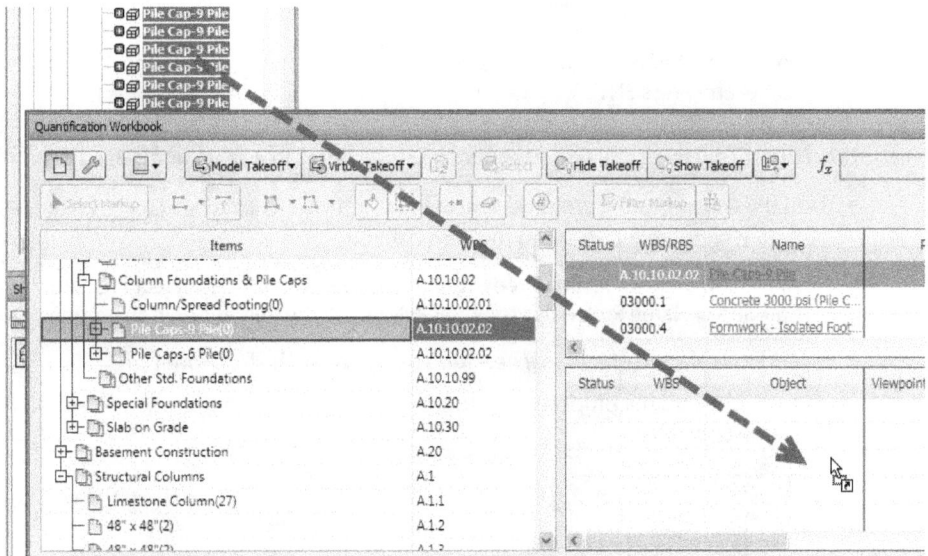

Workbook items might have been imported from an existing catalog as a starting point, or you might need to create items as you are generating the takeoff. This can be done using a number of methods.

Procedure: To Assign a Selected Scene Object to a New Workbook Item

1.   Use any one of the techniques that were previously discussed to select objects in the Scene.

2.   Add the selected object to a new Item using one of the following:

■   Right-click in the Selection Tree and select Quantification > Take off to new catalog item.

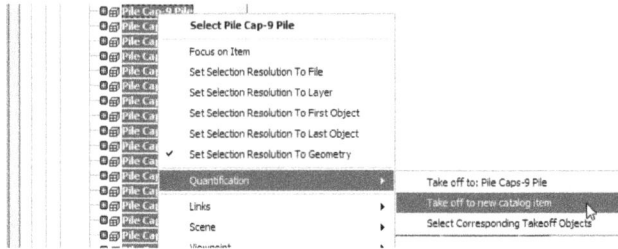

■   With the object(s) selected in the Selection Tree, in the toolbar of the Quantification Workbook, click Model Takeoff and select Take off to new catalog item.

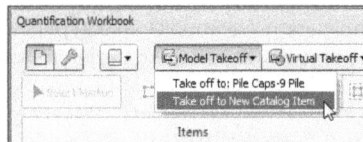

3.   To rename the new Item, double-click the new Item Name in the Item Catalog, enter a new name, and press ENTER.

Procedure: To Use an Object Category to Create Items in a Workbook Group

1.   In the Quantification Workbook, select the Group to which you want to create new items. Create one, if required, using the Item Catalog.

2.   At the top of the Selection Tree expand the view type list and select Properties. Expand Category > Name Properties to obtain a list of all the item types in the model.

3.   Add the selected object to a new Item using one of the following:

■   Right-click the property type to Take off and select Quantification > Take off to: <Group to be added to>.

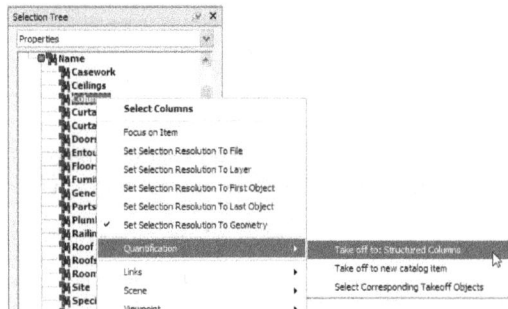

- Without any Items selected in the Quantification Workbook, drag the selected property into the Quantification Workbook's Navigation pane. When dragging, drop the object(s) by releasing the left mouse button on the Item type.

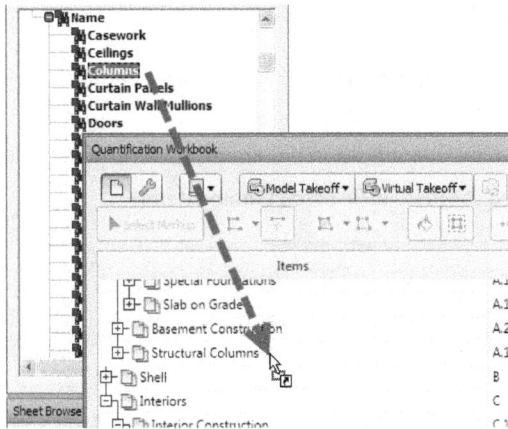

4. New Item types are automatically added to the assigned group and the take off data for each item is automatically populated.

Virtual Takeoff

Virtual takeoff is used to add takeoff objects that are not linked to a model object or item. These situations include:

- Where an object has geometry, but does not have any properties
- Where an object does not have geometry, and does not have any properties

This could be the case if you did not save the properties from the original design application with your file, or if the object that you want to takeoff does not exist in the model. In both cases, you can associate a viewpoint with the virtual takeoff object so you can navigate your way back to it during the takeoff process. Once your virtual object has been taken off, you can begin to add properties by using formulas, which provides quantities for the object.

Conducting a Virtual Takeoff

Once the need for a Virtual Takeoff item has been identified it can be created in the Quantification Workbook and its property values can be customized.

Procedure: To Create a Virtual Takeoff

1. In the Quantification Workbook, click the Item (⬚) that you want to contain the new virtual takeoff (e.g., Wood Door - Single).

2. To add a new Virtual Takeoff to the Quantification Workbook, use one of the following:

    ▪ Click Virtual Takeoff and select Create in Selected Catalog Item.

    ▪ With the Catalog Item selected in the Quantification Workbook, right-click and select New Virtual Takeoff.

3. A new takeoff item is added to the Takeoff pane that includes the following:

    ▪ Takeoff item with a default name.
    ▪ A viewpoint based on the current model orientation.

    Note: Items added to the takeoff virtually are added one at a time.

4. To rename the new takeoff, select it in the Takeoff pane and enter a new name in the f_x field in the Quantification Workbook toolbar.

5. Once the virtual takeoff object has been listed in the Takeoff pane, you can use the measurement tools and formulas to add property details to the Quantification workbook. Alternatively, you can enter values for those objects that might not be physically modeled in the Scene. The takeoff fields that can be populated include: Length, Width, Thickness, Height, Perimeter, Area, Volume, Weight, and Count.

    Refer to Conducting Takeoff Measurements for more information on measuring objects in the Scene.

6. In the Takeoff pane, in the Quantification Workbook, navigate to the takeoff item that you want to associate with the measurement. Double-click the takeoff formula cell that you want to change (i.e., Length or Area) and type the new measurement. Items that contain explicitly measured and entered values are identified with 🔲 in the Status column of the Takeoff pane.

    Tip: Items that are added to the Quantification Workbook using Model Takeoff can also have overwritten values and are identified with 🔲 in the Status column of the Takeoff pane.

Working with Takeoff Viewpoints

By default, a takeoff viewpoint is stored for a takeoff item that is created using Virtual Takeoff. The current orientation of the scene is the viewpoint that is stored when the Virtual Takeoff option is selected. This viewpoint is also stored in the Saved Viewpoints panel.

- To access the viewpoint for a takeoff item, click in the Takeoff pane in the Quantification Workbook or select the viewpoint in the Saved Viewpoints panel.

  Tip: Consider renaming the viewpoint that is stored in the Saved Viewpoints panel from its default name to help identify it.

- To update the viewpoint associated with the virtual takeoff, right-click and select Takeoff's

  Viewpoint > Add/Update. Alternatively, click on the Quantification Workbook toolbar.

- To remove the viewpoint associated with the virtual takeoff, right-click and select Takeoff's Viewpoint > Remove.

Although viewpoints are not automatically created using Model Takeoff, they can be explicitly added to the takeoff item.

- To create a viewpoint for a model takeoff item, select the item in the Item list or in the Takeoff pane

  and click on the Quantification Workbook toolbar. If the Item is selected in the Item list, a viewpoint is created for all of its items. Selecting in the Takeoff pane enables you to select a single

  item. is added to the Viewpoint column in the Takeoff pane and also added to the Saved Viewpoints panel. Explicitly created viewpoints for Model Takeoff items can also be updated and removed using the techniques described above.

  Tip: Consider renaming the viewpoint that is stored in the Saved Viewpoints panel from its default name to help identify it.

Redline markups can also be incorporated with the viewpoints that are stored with Model and Virtual takeoff data.

Procedure: To Create a Redline in a Takeoff Viewpoint

1. Ensure that the viewpoint is active by clicking in Viewpoint column associated with Takeoff.

2. Select the Review tab. Use the tools on the Redline panel to draw and add text as required, and highlight areas in the viewpoint. The redline is only saved with the Takeoff viewpoint.

Conducting Takeoff Measurements

You can add properties to a virtual takeoff by measuring objects in the model and then transposing those properties into a virtual takeoff. You can use measuring tools to make linear, angular, and area measurements, and to automatically measure the shortest distance between two selected objects.

Procedure: To Measure an Object

1. In the Scene View, navigate to the object or area in which you want to conduct the measure.

2. In the Autodesk Navisworks toolbar, select the Review tab to access the Measure tools.

3. Select a measure option in the Measure drop-down list.

4. Select items in the Scene View to conduct the measurement and note the value. When you measure, you must select a point on an item to register a point - selecting the background does not register anything. You can reset a measure command at any time by right-clicking instead of left-clicking in the Scene View. This starts the measure command again with no points registered, as if you had chosen a new measurement type.

   Endpoints of standard measuring lines are represented by small cross symbols in the Scene View.

   Tip: Consider using the Locking tools in the Lock drop-down list in the Measure panel to maintain specific directions when measuring. Refer to the Locking article in the Autodesk Navisworks Help documentation for more information on locking.

Refer to the Measure Tools article in the Autodesk Navisworks Help documentation for more information on measuring.

Lesson: Managing Takeoff Data

Overview

This lesson describes how you can manipulate takeoff data once it has been added to the Quantification Workbook. These techniques help you to become more efficient in viewing and editing takeoff data. You also learn to update this data when changes are made to the source files.

Objectives

After completing this lesson, you will be able to:

- Change the columns that are displayed in the Quantification Workbook.
- Sort column contents in the Quantification Workbook.
- Add Comments to Takeoff data.
- Change the takeoff data appearance.
- Control the display of items in the scene view based on whether they have been taken off or not.
- Delete the takeoff data.
- Remove any overrides from takeoff data.

Managing Takeoff Data

In the Quantification Workbook there are a number of tools that you can use to manage and more efficiently create a takeoff report. The following is possible:

- Change the columns that are displayed in the Quantification Workbook.
- Sort the column contents in the Quantification Workbook.
- Add Comments to Takeoff data.
- Change the takeoff data appearance.
- Control the display of items in the scene view based on whether they have been taken off or not.
- Delete the takeoff data.
- Remove overrides from the takeoff data.

The columns that are shown in the Takeoff or Rollup panes are assigned by default, but they can be customized for a project. Additionally, you can sort columns in ascending or descending order.

Procedure: To Change the Columns displayed in the Takeoff or Rollup Panes

1. In the Quantification Workbook, in the Takeoff or Rollup panes, right-click a column header and select Choose Columns.

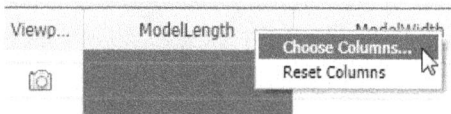

2. In the Choose Objects Columns dialog box, select the columns that you want to display, clear those to be removed, and click OK.

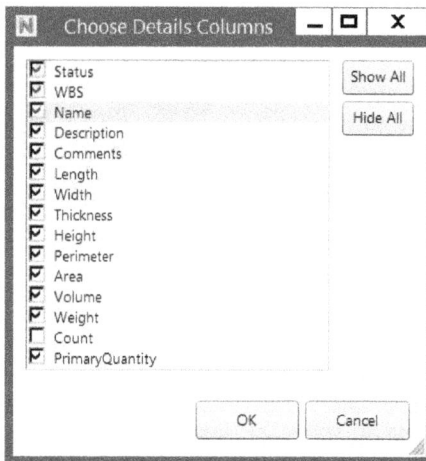

Tip: Click Show All or Hide All to display or suppress all of the columns.

Procedure: To Sort Column Contents in the Quantification Workbook

1. Click a column header to sort alphanumerically, in an ascending order (▲).

2. Click again to sort in descending order (▼).

Comments can be added to Takeoff data to provide further annotation on Takeoff information. Once created, it is assigned a comment number and it is added to the Comments window with any other comments that may exist in the project. You can also use the Find Comments tool to review any comments associated with the Takeoff data.

Procedure: To add a Comment to Takeoff Data

1. In the Quantification workbook, select a takeoff to display its information in the Rollup pane.

2. Right-click the Comments field for the takeoff item and click Add Comment. Alternatively, you can right-click a Name in the Takeoff or Rollup panel and click Add Comment.

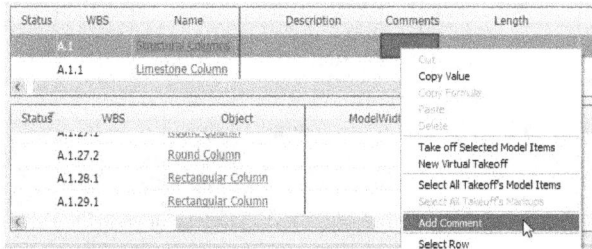

3. Type your comment in the Add Comment dialog box and click OK.

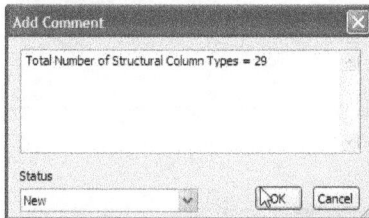

The Comment Number displays in the Comment cell in the Rollup pane and the comment is added to the Comments Window.

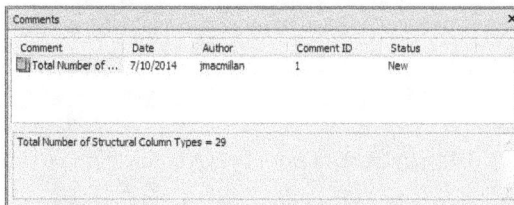

Once a Scene item has been added to the Quantification Workbook, you can control its display appearance (color) in the Scene based on the original model appearance or the takeoff appearance. The original model appearance is based on colors from the source model and the takeoff is the color that was set in the Item catalog for that item.

Procedure: To Change the Takeoff Data Appearance

In the Quantification Workbook, click [icon] and select one of the following:

- Select Reapply Quantification Appearance to set the Scene view to display the specific Item Catalog color for those items that have been taken off. All of the items that have been taken off are displayed with their assigned color and those not taken off remain with their original appearance.
- Select Reapply Original Model Appearance to set the Scene view back to its original appearance (color).

Note: Controlling the appearance using the [icon] options is only available when the model is set to Shaded mode (not Full Render mode).

Autodesk Navisworks files can contain a large number of items that are required to be listed in the Quantification Workbook. As you add model items to the workbook you can use tools in the Quantification Workbook toolbar to clear the display of items from the Scene view as they are added. Doing so enables you to ensure that all of the required items are added to the workbook and nothing is missed.

Procedure: To Control the Scene Display based on Taken Off Items

In the Quantification Workbook, use one of the following toolbar options:

- Click Hide Takeoff to hide the model items that you have taken off and display all other model items.
- Click Show Takeoff to display only the model items that you have taken off, and hide all of the other model items.

Tip: Click these icons a second time to clear the hide or show display option.

Model and Virtual takeoff data can be deleted from the Quantification Workbook, if required.

Procedure: To Delete a Takeoff Item

1. In the Quantification Workbook's Takeoff pane, select the takeoff that you want to delete.

   In the toolbar, click Update and select Delete Selected Takeoff.

2.

   [icon: Update dropdown menu showing Select Row, Update Selected From Model, Remove Overrides From Selected, Delete Selected Takeoff]

Overwritten Model and Virtual takeoff data can be reset from the Quantification Workbook, if required.

Procedure: To Remove Overrides from a Takeoff Item

1. In the Quantification Workbook's Takeoff pane, select the takeoff that you want to reset.

   Tip: Select individual cells in the Takeoff pane or select an entire row to clear all of the overrides in the row. To select an entire row, click Update and Select Row.

   In the toolbar, click Update and select Remove Overrides From Selected.

2.

   Tip: This option is only available if there is an overwritten value for the item. Alternatively, you can right-click a cell and select Remove Override

Exercise: Creating and Working with 3D Model Takeoff Data

Conduct a Model Takeoff

1. Continue to work on the file from the previous exercise. Alternatively, if you did not complete that exercise, open the file *C:\Navisworks 2017 Essentials Class Files\Training\Examples\Quantification\Autodesk_Hospital_Quantification2.nwf*.

2. In the Saved Viewpoints window, select Structure to change the viewpoint.

3. In the Quantification Workbook, expand the Substructure > Foundations > Standard Foundations > Wall Foundations groups. Select the Continuous Footing item. This identifies the item to which the quantification are going to be assigned.

4. Open the Sets window and select the Continuous Footings set. Wall Foundation objects are selected in the Selection Tree.

5. Press and hold the left mouse button on the Continuous Footing Selection set in the Sets window. Drag the set to the Continuous Footing item in the Quantification Workbook and release the left mouse button on the Continuous Footing item to add the take off. Thirteen Wall Foundation items should be added.

Tip: Refer to the Model and Virtual Takeoff topic to test other methods of adding the takeoff.

6. In the Rollup pane of the Quantification Workbook, scroll to the right to review the total Volume of the Continuous Footing.

Status	WBS/RBS	Name	Area	Volume
	A.10.10.01.04	Continuous Footing	0.000 ft²	2,767.375 ft²
	03000.6	Concrete 3500 psi (Conti...	0.000	102.504 yd²
	03000.3	Formwork - Continous Fo	0.000 ft²	0.000 ft²

Notice how the resources were automatically filled out for the Continuous Footing based on the element properties.

7. Close the Sets window.

8. In the Quantification Workbook, expand the Substructure > Foundations > Standard Foundations > Column Foundations & Pile Caps groups. Select the Pile Caps-9 Pile item. This identifies the item to which the next quantification is going to be assigned.

9. On the Home Tab, select Find Items. Conduct a search to locate all of the objects with the name Pile Cap-9.

10. Once the items have been found, the Selection Tree files are expanded to display the selected items.

11. Return to the Quantification Workbook. Ensure that the Pile Caps-9 Pile item is still selected in the Navigation pane.

12. Right-click on any one of the selected Pile Cap-9 Pile objects in the Selection Tree and select Quantification > Take off to: Pile Caps-9 Pile.

Tip: Refer to the Model and Virtual Takeoff topic to test other methods of adding the takeoff.

13. When prompted that one model item could not be taken off, click No. This prompt displays if any item is selected that cannot be taken off (e.g., Collections $\overset{\circ\circ}{\circ}$). This occurs if the Find Items tool is used and locates collection items that cannot be taken off, but do have the name that was being searched for.

14. In the Selection Tree, press and hold the CTRL key and select the Pile Cap-9 Pile Collection to clear it from the selection group.

15. In the Selection Tree, right-click on any one of the selected Pile Cap-9 Pile objects and select Quantification > Take off to: Pile Caps-9 Pile. Thirty-six Pile Caps have been taken off.

16. Select all of the Pile Cap-6 Pile objects using any of the selection techniques.

17. Add the Pile Cap-6 Pile objects to its associated item in the Quantification Workbook. Twenty Pile Caps have been taken off.

18. In the Quantification Workbook, expand the Interiors > Interior Construction > Interior Doors > Standard Interior Doors groups. Select the Wood Door - Single item. This identifies the item to which the quantification is going to be assigned.

19. In the Quick Find field, in the Select & Search panel on the Home tab, enter **flush** to search for a single-flush door.

20. Once one of the Single-Flush doors has been selected in the Selection Tree, select the Select Same drop-down list in the Select & Search panel and select Same Name. All of the Single-Flush objects are selected in the Selection Tree.

21. With the object(s) selected in the Selection Tree, in the toolbar of the Quantification Workbook, click Model Takeoff and select Take off to: Wood Door - Single.

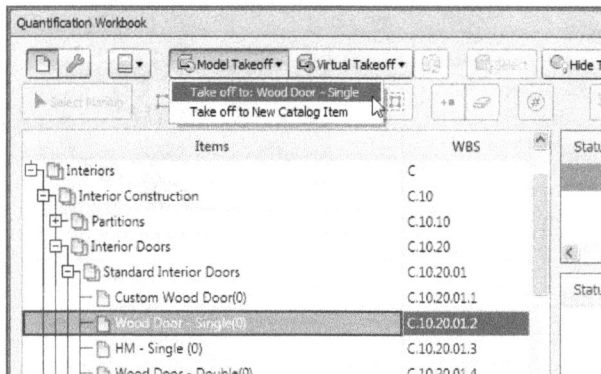

22. Click No when prompted that model items could not be taken off. As an alternative to clearing Collections in the Selection Tree manually, you can run another search that only finds the required Type. Clear all of the items from selection.

23. Open the Find Items window and add the following criteria. Conduct the search. Notice that the search only contains the required items and not the Collection type items.

Category	Property	Condition	Value
Item	Type	Contains	Single-Flush

24. Right-click one of the selected items in the Selection Tree and select Quantification > Take off to: Wood Door - Single. A total of 367 doors have now been added to the workbook.

Partitions	C.10.10
Interior Doors	C.10.20
Standard Interior Doors	C.10.20.01
Custom Wood Door(0)	C.10.20.01.1
Wood Door - Single(367)	C.10.20.01.2
HM - Single (0)	C.10.20.01.3
Wood Door - Double(0)	C.10.20.01.4

25. Close the Find Items window.

Add Catalog Items Directly from the Model

1. In the Item Catalog, select the Substructure group. Click New Group. Enter **Structural Columns** as the new name for the group and press ENTER.

2. In the Selection Tree, expand the View Type list and select Properties. Expand the Category > Name Properties.

3. Select Columns. Notice that the structural columns in the model are now selected.

4. Right-click on the Column property and select and Quantification > Take off to: Structural Columns. A total of 29 new Item types have automatically been added to the Item list and the takeoff data for each has been populated. This approach eliminates having to create the items individually.

Manage the Quantification Data

1. Ensure that no objects are selected in the Scene View.

2. In the Quantification Workbook, click Hide Takeoff. All of the Pile Caps, Continuous Footing, Single-Flush Door, and Structural Column items are cleared from display in the Scene View. This helps you to identify which scene objects are still left to take off.

Note: This might be difficult to see without zooming into the model.

3. Click Hide Takeoff a second time to disable it and display all of the objects in the Scene View.

4. Click Show Takeoff to display only the Pile Caps, Continuous Footing, Single-Flush Door, and Structural Column items in the Scene View. This helps identify which items have already been taken off.

5. On the Viewpoint tab, Render Style panel, set the Mode to Shaded.

6. In the Quantification Workbook, click [icon] and select Reapply Original Model Appearance to set the Scene view back to its original appearance (color).

Note: Controlling the appearance using the [icon] options is only available when the model is set to Shaded mode (not Full Render mode).

7. Click [icon] and select Reapply Quantification Appearance to set the Scene view to display the specific Item Catalog color for those items that have been taken off. All of the items that have been taken off are displayed with their assigned color (e.g., purple for Pile Caps) and those not taken off retain their original appearance.

Click Show Takeoff a second time to disable it.

8.

9. In the Quantification Workbook, navigate to and select the Pile Cap items (Substructure > Foundations > Standard Foundations > Column Foundations & Pile Caps) in the Navigation Pane. Select the Pile Caps-9 Pile item.

10. In the Takeoff pane, select the first Pile Cap item.

11. In the Navigation Bar, in the Zoom tools, click Zoom Selected to navigate to this item. Zoom out and reorient as required to obtain a good view of this first Pile Cap.

12. In the Quantification Workbook toolbar, click [icon] to save a viewpoint for this item. Notice that a Quantification Views folder has been created in the Saved Viewpoints window.

13. Return to the Overall viewpoint. In the workbook's Takeoff pane, click [icon] adjacent to the first Pile Cap-9 Pile item to change to the saved view. As an alternative, you can also select the viewpoint in the Saved Viewpoint window.

Tip: You can select multiple items and create the viewpoints at the same time.

Conduct a Virtual Takeoff

1. In the Saved Viewpoints window, select Missing Door to change the viewpoint.

2. In the Quantification Workbook, expand the Interiors > Interior Construction > Interior Doors > Standard Interior Doors groups. Select the Wood Door - Single item.

   A number of doors have already been added using Model Takeoff. However, an office along this hallway is missing a door. Because it is not included in the source model, a Virtual Takeoff can be done to communicate this information.

   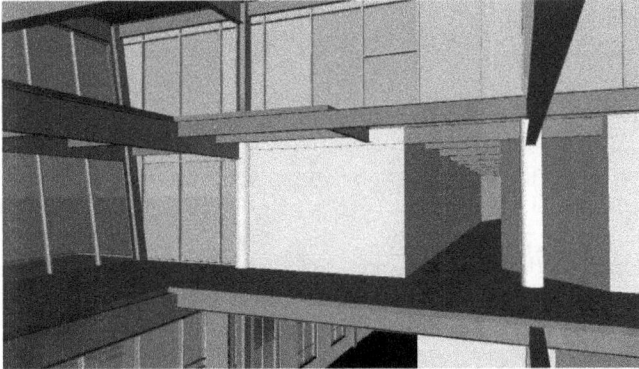

3. In the Quantification Workbook toolbar, click Virtual Takeoff and select Create in: Wood Door - Single.

   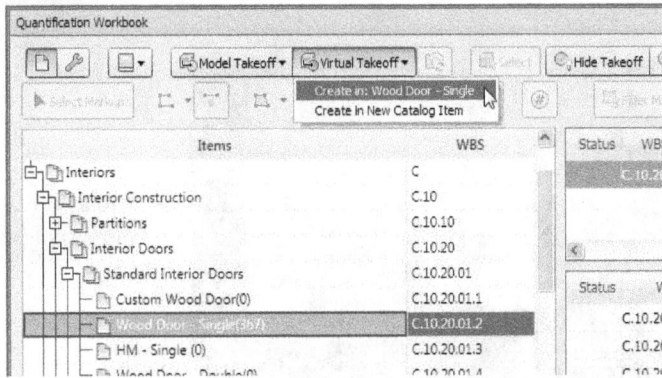

4. A new takeoff item is added to the Takeoff pane that includes the following:

   - Takeoff item with a default name.
   - A viewpoint based on the current model orientation.

   Note: Items added to the takeoff virtually are added one at a time.

5. Select the Name cell for the virtual takeoff. Enter **Missing Door** in the f_x field in the Quantification Workbook toolbar.

6. In the Rollup pane, scroll and review the properties for the 368 doors. The quantity includes the virtual door. However, the model properties do not include the virtual property values as these fields are zero by default.

7. In the columns for the Missing Door takeoff, enter the following property values:

   - ModelWidth = **3.000 ft**
   - ModelThickness = **0.167 ft**
   - ModelHeight = **7.00 ft**

   Note: Additional doors might be missing in this model, but you do not need to add any additional virtual takeoffs at this time.

8. In the Rollup pane, review the properties and notice that the property values have been included in the totals for all 368 doors.

9. Notice that ⬚ displays in the Status column. This indicates that fields in this item have been overwritten.

10. Click ⬚ adjacent to the Virtual Takeoff item to activate it.

11. Select the Review tab, and select Draw > Ellipse.

12. Draw an Ellipse on the office wall similar to that shown below. Select Text, and pick a point inside the Ellipse. Enter **Add Door** as a note in the viewpoint.

13. In the Saved Viewpoints window, select Missing Door to change the viewpoint. Notice that the redline is not included in this view.

14. Click ⬚ adjacent to the Virtual Takeoff item and notice that the redline is included in this view.

15. Save the workbook and leave the file open. You will continue working on this in the next exercise.

Lesson: 2D Takeoffs

Overview

This lesson describes how you can use the tools available on the 2D Takeoff toolbar to add Takeoffs to a Quantification Workbook. The Takeoff types that are discussed include Linear, Area, and Count Takeoff that enable you to add data to the workbook using a 2D sheet.

Objectives

After completing this lesson, you will be able to:

- Use the tools on the 2D Takeoff toolbar to efficiently create Linear Takeoffs on a 2D sheet.
- Use the tools on the 2D Takeoff toolbar to efficiently create Area Takeoffs on a 2D sheet.
- Use the tools on the 2D Takeoff toolbar to efficiently create Count Takeoffs on a 2D sheet.

2D Takeoff Overview

2D Takeoff enables you to measure lines, areas, and counts on a 2D sheet that exists directly in the project. By using the 2D data in the project you can markup geometry and perform accurate calculations for use in the Quantification workbook. Both 2D and 3D quantification takeoffs exist in the same workbook.

2D Takeoff supports native and scanned DWF files. Non-native DWFs files (such as PDFs) can easily be converted to DWF using print driver software for use in 2D Takeoff or Autodesk TrueView. See Supported file formats in the Help documentation. To conduct a 2D Takeoff:

- 2D sheets must exist in the Navisworks project. Click ⬒ (Import Sheets & Models) in the Project Browser.
- The 2D sheets must be prepared/converted for use in the Navisworks project. Right-click a sheet name in the Project Browser and select Prepare Sheet/Model or Prepare All Sheets/Models.
- Ensure the scale of the 2D sheets are the same as the 3D model.

Customizing Sheet Scale

When using 2D dwfx data, it is important that the measurements taken are at the same scale as the data that is in the 3D Model. To customize the sheet scale:

1. Activate a 2D Sheet.
2. Select the View tab > Workspace panel, expand the Windows drop-down list, and select Set Scale by Measure.
3. Click New Measure.
4. On the 2D sheet, trace a line that defines a length of geometry that has a length you already know.
5. In the Enter Value dialog, type the known length and measurement unit and click OK. The average scale displays in the Set Scale by Measurement window. If required, repeat to trace several lines for a more accurate average scale value.

- Select a row, right-click and select Delete to delete a measurement record. Press Delete or right-click a row and select Delete to delete a scale record.

2D Takeoff Tools

Similar to the 3D Takeoff tool, a Quantification project must be setup and the Item Catalog assigned. Additionally, a 2D sheet must be active in the Navisworks project using the Project Browser. By activating the 2D sheet, the 2D Takeoff tools are enabled. The tools are located in the second row of the Quantification workbook's toolbar.

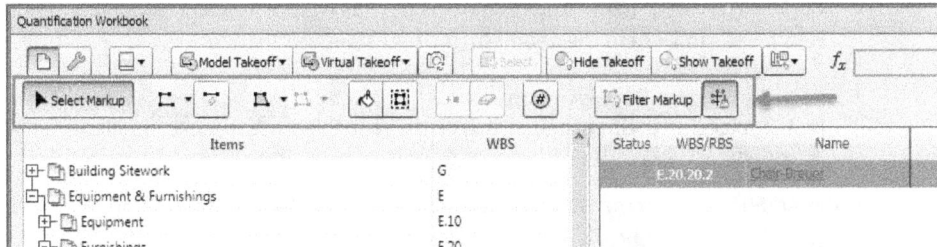

2D Takeoff tools enable you to mark up line geometry on a 2D floor plan or other worksheet. The markup will then appear as an object in the Quantification workbook, displaying properties such as area, perimeter, or length. The measurement is done by tracing linear markups to measure a wall or the perimeter of a room, or use area tools to record the extent of a surface. You can also place markup pins on 2D sheets to perform a Count takeoff.

The following 2D Takeoff types are discussed:

- Linear takeoffs
- Area takeoffs
- Count takeoffs

Linear Takeoffs

There are a number of commands in the 2D Takeoff toolbar that enable you to measure the length or perimeter of individual or multi-line geometry. The values obtained are added to the Quantification workbook. The commands that can be used include:

- Polyline
- Rectangle Polyline
- Quick Line

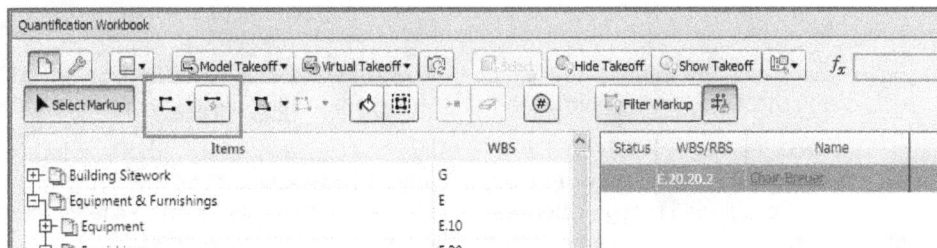

Procedure: To Conduct a Linear Takeoff

1.   Activate the 2D sheet from which measurements will be taken to populate the Takeoff data.

2.   In the Item Catalog, select the item to which the 2D Takeoff will be added.

3.   Select a Linear measurement tool in the 2D Takeoff toolbar.

- Click ⌐ (Polyline) to measure single or multi-line segments when the length or perimeter is required, and where the geometry is a non-standard shape.

- Click ⌑ (Rectangle Polyline) to measure perimeters. The tool creates a square or rectangular shape. Once drawn you can move the vertices to create a different quadrilateral shape.

Note: Additional linear measurement tools are discussed later in this section.

4.   Conduct the measurement on the 2D sheet.

- For a Polyline measurement, click on the sheet to position the start point for the measurement. As you move over existing geometry, the cursor changes to a snap (green vertex). Continue to select entities on the sheet to define the length or perimeter to be measured. To complete the polyline, select the start point a second time.

- For a Rectangle Polyline measurement, click on the sheet to position the start point for the measurement. Select an entity in the opposite corner to define the rectangle.

5.   The measurement is completed when:

- the start point is selected a second time,
- the second point in the Rectangular Polyline is selected, or
- when you press Enter.

The Takeoff item is added to the active Item in the Item Catalog.

To Draw Horizontal or Vertical Lines

To draw a line that is perfectly horizontal or vertical when using the Polyline (⌐) tool, press and hold SHIFT when drawing.

The Quick Line tool on the 2D Takeoff toolbar is another measurement tool that can be used to obtain a linear Takeoff on single or multi-line segments. To use this tool, click ⌑ (Quick Line) and click an entity on the sheet. Depending on the shape of the line, alternative Quick Line options may be

available to more accurately define the measurement of the selected entity (⌑ ⌐ ⌐ ⌑). These options enable you to toggle between the selection of the selected single line segment, a polyline of lines connected to the selected line, a curve, or all connected curves.

Bucket Fill & Quick Box Tools

The Bucket Fill and Quick Box tools enable you to measure both linear and area Takeoff. These topics are discussed later in this Lesson.

Area Takeoffs

Use the Area tools to build up multiple line segments of a polygon, or trace a rectangle straight onto the sheet to obtain the area of the traced entities. Once the entities are traced, the area is automatically measured and a new takeoff item is added into the Quantification Workbook.

Procedure: To Conduct an Area Takeoff

1. Activate the 2D sheet from which the measurements will be taken to populate the Takeoff data.

2. In the Item Catalog, select the item to which the 2D Takeoff will be added.

3. Select an Area measurement tool in the 2D Takeoff toolbar:

    - Click ⬚ (Area) to measure the size (area) of a non-rectangular area.

    - Click ⬚ (Rectangle Area) to measure the size (area) of a rectangular area.

4. Conduct the measurement on the 2D sheet.

    - Click on the sheet to position the start point for the Area measurement. Continue to select entities on the sheet to define the area to be measured. To complete the area, either select the start point a second time or right-click. As you select entities, a blue highlight displays, defining the area. Once drawn, you can move the vertices to create a different quadrilateral shape.

    - Click on the sheet to position the start point for the Rectangle Area measurement. Select an entity in the opposite corner to define the rectangle.

5. The measurement is completed when:

    - the start point is selected a second time,
    - you right-click to automatically close the area,
    - the second point in the Rectangular Polyline is selected, or
    - you press Enter.

    The Takeoff item is added to the active Item in the Item Catalog.

When an Area Takeoff is conducted, there might be an area within the overall area that is not required in the takeoff value. For example, if an office has a column inside it, the column must be omitted to provide an accurate value on the available floor space. To remove a portion of an overall area, use the Backoff commands.

Procedure: To use Backoff to modify an Area Takeoff

1. Ensure that the Area takeoff from which an area will be removed is selected in the Takeoff pane.

2. Select a Backoff tool in the 2D Takeoff toolbar.

    - Click ⌶ (Backoff) to remove a non-rectangular area from a larger Takeoff.

    - Click ⌶ (Rectangle Backoff) to remove a rectangular area from a larger Takeoff.

3. Trace the area on the 2D sheet.

    - Click on the sheet to position the start point for the Backoff. As you move over existing geometry, the cursor changes to a snap (green vertex). Continue to select entities on the sheet to define the length or perimeter to be measured. To complete the backoff, either select the start point a second time or right-click. Once drawn, you can move the vertices to create a different quadrilateral shape.

    - Click on the sheet to position the start point for the Rectangle Backoff. Select an entity in the opposite corner to define the rectangle.

4. The Backoff is completed when:

    - the start point is selected a second time,
    - when you right-click to automatically close the area,
    - the second point in the Rectangular Polyline is selected, or
    - you press Enter.

    The original Takeoff item is updated to reflect the removal of the backoff area.

Bucket Fill and Quick Box tools

The Bucket Fill and Quick Box tools in the 2D Takeoff toolbar provide additional methods of efficiently selecting connected entities to measure length/perimeter or area by making single selections, or drawing sketch lines and boxes. Using these two tools you can create either linear or area Takeoff entries in the Quantification Workbook.

- The Bucket Fill tool enables you to efficiently select within a geometry boundary to define the

  linear or area for a Takeoff item. Click ⬚ (Bucket Fill) and click within an area to select all entities that are required to define a closed area. You can continue to select additional enclosed areas by making multiple selections. A linear measurement is identified (as shown on the left) with the first selection. Select again in the same area to obtain an area measurement. While in the command, the last measurement type (linear or area) is used to define each successive selection. Press Enter to accept the measurement and add it to the selected item in the Quantification Workbook.

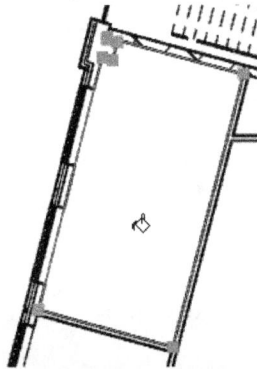

Single Click for Linear **Click twice for Area**

> **Using a Sketch Line with the Bucket Fill tool**
> When using Bucket Fill, you can drag a sketch line through entities on the sheet to automatically find closed areas that intersect the sketched line. This can be used as an alternative to selecting within an area.

- The Quick Box tool enables you to efficiently drag a bounding box over existing geometry to

  select the length of multiple entities or an area for Takeoff measurement. Click ⬚ (Quick Box) and drag a bounding box over existing entities. Depending on the shape of the entities in the bounding box, Quick Box options appear to more accurately define the measurement

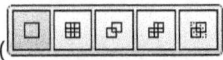

  (⬚ ⬚ ⬚ ⬚ ⬚). These options enable you to toggle between multiple options. Hover over each item to preview its selection. Select the option to add the Takeoff to the selected item in the Quantification workbook. Similar to Bucket Fill, if you select within the enclosed area in the Scene View (prior to finalizing the Takeoff) it toggles the selection from a linear to an area measurement. The available options are as follows:

  - ⬚ (Option 1): Finds the largest boundary area in your selection. This could be a single line segment or a closed polygon, depending on the extent of the Quick Box you draw. This option results in the minimum number of line segments, and hence takeoffs, for the selected geometry.

- (Option 2): Finds the largest boundary area in your selection, plus all line segments (the smallest geometry) within that boundary. This option results in the maximum number of line segments, and hence takeoffs, for the selected geometry.

- (Option 3): Finds the largest boundary area in your selection (similar to Option 1), but also finds geometry areas that are connected to the selection by end-to-end connected lines. All geometries are handled in the same way (finds the minimum number of line segments).

- (Option 4): Largest boundary area, most line segments (similar to Option 2), but also finds geometry areas that are connected to the selection by end-to-end connected lines. All geometries are handled in the same way (finds the maximum number of segments).

- (Option 5): Finds all geometry areas that are connected to or intersect the original selection. For example, if your selection consists of a single room in a corridor, this option may find all other similar areas (rooms) that connect on either side of your selected room.

Count Takeoffs

A Count Takeoff is used to record the number of items. For example, it can be used to count the number of desks in an office. The process involves adding count pins to your 2D sheet. Each pin then becomes a Takeoff value in the Quantification workbook.

Procedure: To conduct a Count Takeoff

1. Activate the 2D sheet from which measurements will be taken to populate the Count Takeoff data.

2. In the Item Catalog, select the item to which the 2D Takeoff will be added.

3. On the 2D Takeoff toolbar, click (Count) to position a count pin.

4. On the 2D sheet, click to position count pin(s). Notice that each pin is numbered sequentially in the Takeoff Pane. The Rollup pane displays the total count.

    Tip: To delete a count pin, select it and press Delete. As an alternative, you can use the Erase tool. Select the count pin so that it displays as blue, click , and select the pin again on the sheet to remove it. The Takeoff value automatically updates.

Counting Items using the Selection Tree

Similar to 3D Quantification (in which you can select and use items directly from the 3D model's Selection Tree), when doing 2D Quantification using a .DWFX file with properties, you can drag items into the Quantification to add a Count Takeoff. Linear and/ or area measurements are not added to the object. This type of Count Takeoff can only be done on .DWFX files that were created with a source 3D CAD model, where the model's properties were maintained in the .DWFX file.

Additional 2D Takeoff Tools

The following additional 2D Takeoff tools can be used to efficiently work with 2D Takeoffs.

- The Select Markup option enables you to activate the selection tool for selecting 2D Takeoffs on a sheet. Once enabled, select a single takeoff to activate it. To select multiple Takeoffs, hold CTRL and click the individual takeoffs on the sheet. Alternatively, drag a box around the takeoffs that you want to select.

- To edit the shape of a linear or area Takeoff, you can select and drag any of the vertices that define the shape. As an alternative you can use the ⊞ (Add Vertex) tool on the 2D Takeoff toolbar and select on an active entity to add additional vertices for dragging. Press ENTER to update the Takeoff values to incorporate the changes to the shape or size.

- The Filter Markup option enables you to clear unselected Takeoffs from the display on the sheet. To use this tool, select a Takeoff in the Takeoff pane (not in the Scene View) or select a Category or item in the Quantification Workbook and use the command. To clear the filter, select the button again. This tool is convenient when multiple Takeoffs are in a small area.

  - When an item is selected, and the Filter Markup option is selected, all but the selected markup is removed from the sheet.

  - When a category is selected, and the Filter Markup option is selected, all items in the selected category remain displayed, while any others outside of the category are removed from the sheet.

- The ⊞ (Hide background and annotations) option can be used to toggle off the display of background images and annotations from a 2D worksheet to assist with visibility. Once enabled, click ⊞ a second time to toggle the background images and annotations on again. This tool will only clear backgrounds and annotations in files that were created with a source 3D CAD model where the backgrounds and annotations are identified as such.

- To quickly review a Takeoff item in the Takeoff pane (when the item is not easily located), you can select the Takeoff in the Scene View, right-click and select Select Corresponding Takeoff Objects.

- To temporarily zoom to a selected Takeoff, select it in the Scene View and press and hold the Space Bar. Once you release the Space Bar, the viewpoint returns to the previous zoom level and location.

Exercise: Creating and Working with 2D Takeoff Data

Conduct Linear and Area 2D Takeoffs

1. Continue to work on the file from the previous exercise. Alternatively, if you did not complete that exercise, open the file *C:\Navisworks 2017 Essentials Class Files\Training\Examples\ Quantification\Autodesk_Hospital_Quantification3.nwf*.

2. Open the Sheet Browser and click ![icon] (Import Sheets & Models). Open *Autodesk_Hospital_Architectural.dwfx* from the Class Files folder. Four 2D Sheets are added to the project.

3. If the four new sheets have the ![icon] icon adjacent to them, they need to be prepared for use in Navisworks. Right-click on one of the sheets in the Sheet Browser, right-click and select Prepare All Sheets/Models.

4. Double-click on the Sheet: A103 - First Floor Plan sheet in the Sheet Browser to activate it.

5. Navigate to the area shown.

6. In the Item Catalog, expand the Interiors > Interior Finishes > Floor Finishes group. Click New Item. Enter **Sheet Vinyl** as the new name for the Item and press ENTER. Add **Office Carpet** and **Ceramic Floor** as additional items.

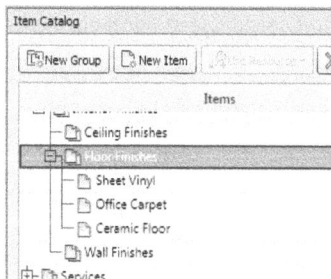

7. Return to the Quantification Workboook and select the Office Carpet item, if not already selected.

8. On the 2D Takeoff toolbar, click ⌐ (Polyline) to measure the perimeter of a non-rectangular shape.

9. Click on the sheet to position the start point for the Polyline measurement, as shown at point 1 below. Continue to select the points (2, 3, 4) that define the shape of this office. To complete the polyline, select the start point (1) a second time. The Takeoff is added to the workbook.

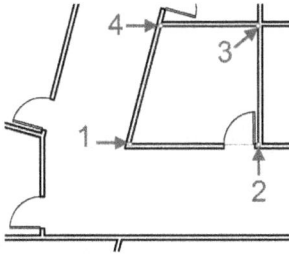

10. In the Quantification Workbook, review the Rollup and Takeoff panes for the newly added quantification data for the office. This quantification value measured the perimeter of the office, not the area which is required for a carpet measurement.

Status	WBS/RBS	Name	Length	Width	Thickness	Height	Perimeter	Area
	C.30.20.2	Office Carpet	44.520 ft	0.000 ft	0.000 ft	0.000 ft	44.520 ft	0.000 ft²

Status	WBS	Object	ModelLength	ModelWidth	ModelThickness	ModelHeight	ModelPerimeter
	C.30.20.2.1	Office Carpet 1	44.520 ft				44.520 ft

Tip: It is always important to review the Takeoff data to ensure that it is reporting the required information.

11. In the Takeoff panel, right-click Office Carpet 1and select Delete Takeoff to remove it from the workbook.

12. On the 2D Takeoff toolbar, click ◪ (Area) to measure the area of a non-rectangular shape.

13. Click on the sheet to position the start point for the Area measurement, as shown at point 1 below. Continue to select the points (2, 3, 4) that define the shape of this office. To complete the area measurement, either select the start point (1) a second time, or right-click the mouse after making the 4th selection.

14. In the Quantification Workbook, review the Rollup and Takeoff panes for the required quantification data that measures the area of the office.

Status	WBS/RBS	Name	Length	Width	Thickness	Height	Perimeter	Area	Volume
	C.30.20.2	Office Carpet	0.000 ft	0.000 ft	0.000 ft	0.000 ft	44.523 ft	121.817 ft²	0.000 ft³

Status	WBS	Object	ModelLength	ModelWidth	ModelThickness	ModelHeight	ModelPerimeter	ModelArea
	C.30.20.2.1	Office Carpet 1					44.523 ft	121.817 ft²

Tip: The ⌐ (Polyline) and ⬚ (Area) tools are measured in the same way, however the results provide different results. Polyline is for linear measurements and Area measures surface area. Ensure that you select the correct command for the required measurement. In a similar way, the ⬚ (Rectangle Polyline) and ⬚ (Rectangle Area) tools produce linear and area measurements, respectively.

15. On the 2D Takeoff toolbar, click ⬚ (Rectangle Area) to measure the area of the rectangular office to the right of the previously measured office. Ensure that the Office Carpet item is still selected. Select two opposing corners in the room to define the area.

16. Click on the sheet to position the start point for the Rectangle Area measurement. Select an entity in the opposite corner to define rectangle. Review the Rollup and Takeoff panes. Notice that two takeoffs now exist.

Status	WBS/RBS	Name	Length	Width	Thickness	Height	Perimeter	Area	Volume
	C.30.20.2	Office Carpet	0.000 ft	0.000 ft	0.000 ft	0.000 ft	85.764 ft	227.442 ft²	0.00

Status	WBS	Object	ModelLength	ModelWidth	ModelThickness	ModelHeight	ModelPerimeter	ModelArea
	C.30.20.2.1	Office Carpet 1					44.523 ft	121.817 ft²
	C.30.20.2.2	Office Carpet 2					41.241 ft	105.625 ft²

17. Pan upwards to the one of the rectangular offices that have a column in it.

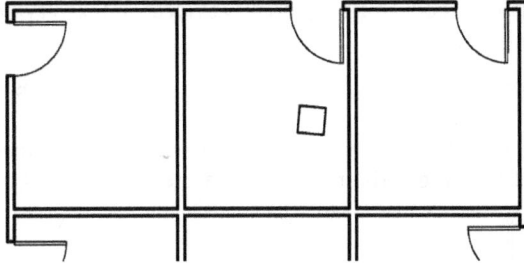

18. On the 2D Takeoff toolbar, click ⬛ (Rectangle Area) and measure the area of entire office. Review the area value on the Takeoff pane.

19. On the 2D Takeoff toolbar, click ⬛ (Backout) and select the 4 vertices that define the outline of the column. Right-click the mouse to clear the selection once the fourth vertex is selected. Review the area on the Takeoff pane. The column's area has been removed.

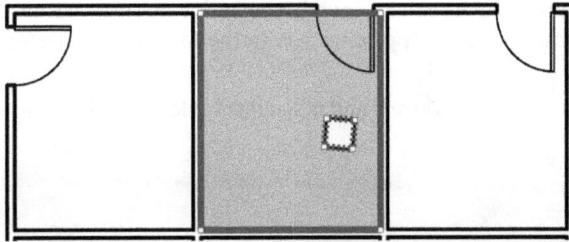

20. In the Quantification Workbook, select the Ceramic Floor item.

21. On the 2D Takeoff toolbar, click ⬛ (Area) and measure the ceramic corridor flooring in the area shown. Zoom in and pan as you are selecting vertices for the Takeoff to accurately make selections.

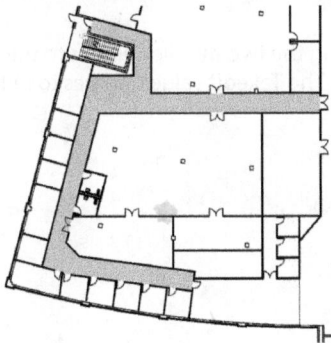

22. In the Quantification Workbook, return to one of the Office Carpet items and select it in the Takeoff pane. The sheet automatically reorients to show these takeoffs. This is a good way to quickly change the view to review the takeoffs.

23. In the Scene View, select the Takeoff that was done in the hallway (Ceramic), right-click and select Select Corresponding Takeoff Objects. Notice that the Quantification Workbook now displays the information on this Takeoff. This is a good way to locate a Takeoff when you don't know its Category.

24. In the Quantification workbook, select the Sheet Vinyl item in the Floor Finishes group.

25. Zoom to the following location and use the ⬜ (Area) command to measure the overall area of the room by defining the four corners. This room will be a kitchen with vinyl flooring.

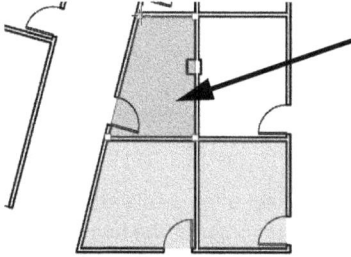

26. An area where the column comes into the room must be removed. This is not an enclosed area in the room so the Backout tool is not appropriate. With the Takeoff still selected, on the 2D Takeoff toolbar, click ⬚ (Add Vertex) and make the 4 selections shown to add four vertices near the column.

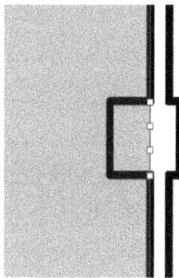

27. Press ESC to clear the Add Vertex command. Drag the two middle vertices to trace the shape of the column. Press Enter to complete the edit. The Takeoff value updates to reflect the change.

28. Zoom out on the drawing to see all of the 5 Takeoffs. Notice that the Carpet, Ceramic, and Vinyl flooring types have different colors. This is because of the color that was defined as the default when the item was created. This can be changed in the item catalog if required.

29. In the Item Catalog, expand the Interiors > Interior Construction group. Click New Item. Enter **Column Closures** as the new name for the Item and press ENTER.

30. Select the Column Closures item in the Quantification workbook, if not already selected.

31. On the 2D Takeoff toolbar, click ⬛ (Quick Box) to quickly measure the perimeter of one of the columns in an office. Zoom to another office with a column.

32. Drag a selection box around the column, as shown.

33. Once you complete the selection the Quick Box tools appear. Notice how the linear perimeter measurement is highlighting. Select again inside the selected area to convert to an Area measurement. The selection highlights in red indicating it is measuring area.

34. Select ⬜ to select the area. It selects the largest boundary area with the least line segments. The area takeoff value is added to the workbook.

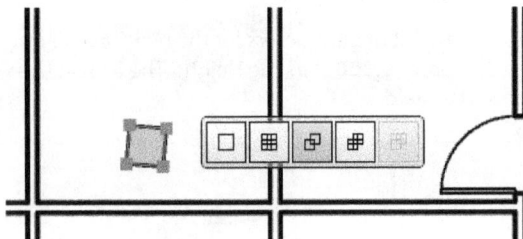

35. Zoom out and using the ⊞ (Quick Box) command use the other options in the Quick Box set to select different entities in the selection box. Notice the Takeoff values that are added with each selection. Undo this action to clear the addition of these test Takeoffs from the workbook.

Tip: Review the Takeoffs that are created to ensure that it is reporting for the entities that are required. If Takeoffs are added that are not required, select it in the Takeoff pane, click Update, and select Delete Selected Takeoff.

Tip: As an alternative you can also use the 🪣 (Bucket) tool to quickly select enclosed areas to Takeoff their perimeters and areas.

36. In the Item Catalog, expand the Interiors > Interior Finishes > Wall Finishes group. Click New Item. Enter **Beige Paint** as the new name for the Item and press ENTER.

37. Zoom to the kitchen that was Taken off using the Sheet Vinyl item. Ensure that the Beige Paint item is selected in the Quantification workbook.

38. On the 2D Takeoff toolbar, click ⌐ (Polyline). Trace the perimeter of the room to Takeoff its perimeter. Ensure that you trace around the column.

39. In the Takeoff pane, scroll through the list of parameters for the new Takeoff until you reach the Height parameter. Select it and enter **9.000 ft** as the Height. The icon in the Status cell indicates that this was an overwritten field.

Status	WBS	Object	Thickness	Height	Perimeter	Area
▣	C.30.10.1.1	Beige Paint 1	0.000 ft	9.000 ft	42.673 ft	0.000 ft²

40. Select the Area parameter field. In the equation field enter **=Height*ModelPerimeter** to obtain the Area value for the paint Takeoff.

f_x | =Height*ModelPerimeter

Status	WBS	Object	Thickness	Height	Perimeter	Area
▣	C.30.10.1.1	Beige Paint 1	0.000 ft	9.000 ft	42.673 ft	384.060 ft²

Conduct a Count Takeoff

1. Double-click on the Sheet: A104 - Second Floor Plan sheet in the Sheet Browser to activate it. On this sheet there are a number of tables that need to be counted. Zoom into the tables.

2. Add a new item called **Round Table - Med** to the Equipment & Furnishings > Furnishings > Moveable Furnishings group. Ensure that this new item is selected in the Quantification Workbook. Also add **Chair-Breuer** as an item.

3. Ensure that the Round Table - Med Item is selected in the Quantification Workbook.

4. On the 2D Takeoff toolbar, click (Count). Select one of the tables on the sheet to position a count pin. Add a total of 21 pins, one on each table, as shown. Press ESC to disable the command.

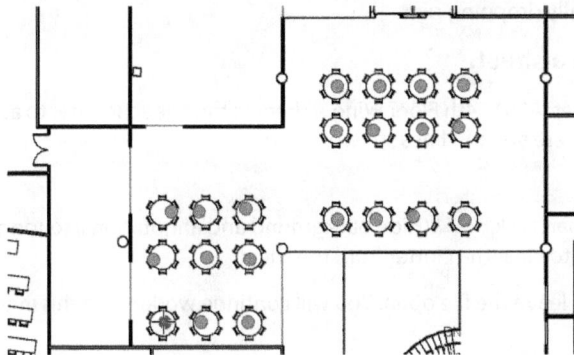

5.   Review the Takeoff and Rollup panes to see the total count. There are 21 medium-sized round tables.

Status	WBS/RBS	Name	Area	Volume	Weight	Count	PrimaryQuantity
	E.20.20.1	Round Table - Med	0.000 ft²	0.000 ft³	0.000 lb	21.000 ea	

Status	WBS	Object	Thickness	Height	Perimeter	Area	Volume	Weight
	E.20.20.1.19	Round Table - Med 19	0.000 ft	0.000 ft	0.000 ft	0.000 ft²	0.000 ft³	0.000 lb
	E.20.20.1.20	Round Table - Med 20	0.000 ft	0.000 ft	0.000 ft	0.000 ft²	0.000 ft³	0.000 lb
	E.20.20.1.21	Round Table - Med 21	0.000 ft	0.000 ft	0.000 ft	0.000 ft²	0.000 ft³	0.000 lb

Tip: To delete a count pin, select it so that the pin displays as blue and then press Delete. The Takeoff value automatically updates.

6.   Ensure that the Selection Tree is displaying the Standard view.

7.   Open the Find Items window and conduct a search using the following criteria. This represents the types of chairs used at the tables that were just counted. Find all instances of this chair: there should be 126 instances located.

Category	Property	Condition	Value
Item	Type	Contains	Chair-Breuer

8.   Ensure that the Chair-Breuer item is selected in the Quantification Workbook.

9.   Right-click on any of the selected items in the Selection Tree and select Quantification > Take off to: Chair-Breuer. Review the Rollup pane and notice that all of these 2D items have been counted. If properties exist for items in the dwfx file, this type of Count Takeoff can be done as an alternative to manually dropping pins.

Clear Annotations from a sheet.

1.   Double-click on the Sheet: A101 - 4th Floor Wing A sheet in the Sheet Browser to activate it. On this sheet, notice that there are grid lines shown.

2.   On the 2D Takeoff toolbar, click [icon] (Hide background and annotations) to toggle off the display of the grid lines to clear the clutter from the sheet.

3.   Save the workbook and leave the file open. You will continue working on this in the next exercise.

Lesson: Analyzing Changes

Overview

This lesson describes how you can analyze changes made to properties of the source files that are being used in the Autodesk Navisworks software and how these changes can be updated in the Quantification Workbook.

Objectives

After completing this lesson, you will be able to:

- Execute an analysis of refreshed Autodesk Navisworks data.
- Understand the status notifications that can appear after a Change Analysis is executed.
- Update changed quantification takeoff data to reflect changes in the model.

Analyzing Takeoff Data

Change Analysis enables you to compare changes to properties between model versions. You can then review the changes to decide whether to give approval. If differences are identified or you make changes to your takeoff data in a project, you receive status notifications in the Quantification Workbook that highlight what has been changed and provides status notification on the type of change that has been made.

The following describe the types of notifications that can be presented:

- A warning flag next to a changed Item or Resource in the Navigation pane .

- Green triangle in the corner of a cell . The triangle indicates an overwritten value. Hover over the corner of the cell (when available) to view a tooltip showing the original and overridden value of the takeoff.

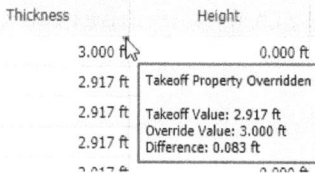

Thickness	Height
3.000 ft	0.000 ft
2.917 ft	Takeoff Property Overridden
2.917 ft	Takeoff Value: 2.917 ft
2.917 ft	Override Value: 3.000 ft
	Difference: 0.083 ft

- Blue triangle in the corner of a cell . The triangle indicates that a model property has changed. Hover over the corner of the cell to display a tooltip showing the old and new values of the model property.

ModelWidth

3.000 ft

Model Property Changed

Old Model Value: 3.000 ft
New Model Value: 6.000 ft
Difference: 3.000 ft

- An icon in the Status column of the Quantification workbook's Takeoff pane. Hover over the icon to display the status in a tooltip. Any number of the status notification "lights" might appear in the Status column for one takeoff item.

Icon	Action	Description
	Override (Green)	When a formula has been overridden and Change Analysis has not been run. Hover over the icon to display a tooltip.
	Change (Blue)	Where a model object has changed and differs from the associated takeoff item in Quantification Workbook. Hover over the icon to display a tooltip.
	Error (Red)	Where there are computation errors with the formula or model item. Hover over the icon to display a tooltip.
	Delete (Black)	Where a takeoff's model item has been deleted. Hover over the icon to display a tooltip.

- The formula bar displays with a red outline (vs. gray) in the Quantification Workbook if an invalid formula was entered. You are prevented from applying the formula.

Procedure: To Analyze and Update Changes in the Quantification Workbook

1. In the Quantification Workbook, click Change Analysis and select Analyze Changes. Change analysis should be executed after appended files in the Autodesk Navisworks file have been refreshed (Home tab > Project panel > Refresh). This ensures that the quantification workbook is accurate.

   Note: Virtual Takeoffs cannot be analyzed because they are not linked to the model.

2. Review the changes that are identified in the Quantification Window . Use any of the following to manipulate the results in the Quantification Workbook.

   - To update the Quantification Workbook with the new changes to the model, select a cell in the row, click Update, and select Update Selected from Model. Items can be updated individually by selecting them in the Takeoff pane or you can select all of the items in a catalog item and update them all at the same time.

   - For any takeoff item that indicates that the model item has been deleted (), select a cell in the row, click Update, and select Delete Selected Takeoff.

   - Once the analysis has finished and you have reviewed all of the notifications, you might want to ignore some of them. Click Change Analysis and Clear Analyze Results if you want to ignore the changes that have been identified.

Lesson: Exporting Takeoff Data

Overview

This lesson describes how to export the data once the project has been completed.

Objectives

After completing this lesson, you will be able to:

- Export Takeoff data from a Quantification Workbook.

Exporting Takeoff Data from the Quantification Workbook

Takeoff data can be exported from the Quantification Workbook for use in other applications using the .XML or excel format.

Procedure: To Export Takeoff Data

1. In the Quantification Workbook, click ⬚▾.

2. In the drop-down list, select an export option. The available options include:

    - Export Catalog to XML
    - Export Quantities to Excel
    - Export Selected Quantities to Excel

    Tip: The ⬚▾ drop-down list can also be used to import a catalog into the Quantification Catalog.

3. In the dialog box, navigate to the preferred save location. Enter a filename, and save the data.

Exercise: Analyzing and Updating Takeoff Data

1.   Save the file, if not already saved.

2.   Click [icon] in the Quick Access toolbar to close the file.

Refresh the Autodesk Navisworks files to Reflect Changes in the Source Model.

1.   Open Windows explorer and navigate to the *C:\Navisworks 2017 Essentials Class Files\Training\Examples\Quantification* folder.

2.   Rename Autodesk_Hospital_Architectural.nwc and enter **Autodesk_Hospital_Architectural_OLD.nwc** as its new name.

3.   Rename Autodesk_Hospital_Architectural_rev2.nwc and enter **Autodesk_Hospital_Architectural.nwc** as its new name.

4.   Return to the Autodesk Navisworks software and open *Autodesk_Hospital_Quantification.nwf*. If you did not complete the previous tasks in this exercise, open the file *Autodesk_Hospital_Quantification4.nwf* instead.

5.   In the Sheet Browser, return to the Autodesk_Hospital_Architectural.nwc file.

6.   Select the Missing Door viewpoint, if not already active. Notice that a door has been added to the model.

    Note: The purpose of renaming the files was to simulate a design change in the Autodesk Revit model as many training environments do not have access to this software. The *Autodesk_Hospital_Architectural_rev2.nwc* file has had a design change. In a normal design environment, when a change is made to the Autodesk Revit model, you can use the Refresh command to incorporate the changes from the source file into the Autodesk Navisworks software.

7.   In the Quantification Workbook, click Change Analysis and select Analyze Changes.

8.   In the Quantification Workbook, expand the Interiors > Interior Construction > Interior Doors > Standard Interior Doors group. Notice that [icon] displays in the Item list helping you to determine where the differences have been found.

9.   Select the Wood Door - Single item.

10.   In the *Autodesk_Hospital_Architectural_rev2.nwc* file, a door has been added where it was initially missing. The Virtual Takeoff is no longer required. In the Quantification Workbook's Takeoff pane, scroll to the bottom of the list and select any cell in the Virtual takeoff row.

11.   In the toolbar, click Update and select Delete Selected Takeoff. Notice that the quantity of Single-Flush doors is once again 367.

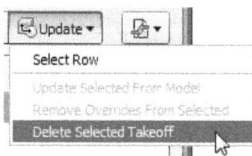

12. Select the Status column header in the Takeoff pane to sort the list. Select again, if required, so that the two changed items are listed at the top of the Takeoff pane. The C.10.20.01.2.110 and C.10.20.01.2.115 objects have been changed.

Status	WBS	Object	Viewp...	ModelLength	ModelWidth	ModelThickness	ModelHeight
	C.10.20.01.2.110	Single-Flush			3.000 ft	0.167 ft	7.000 ft
	C.10.20.01.2.115	Single-Flush			3.000 ft	0.167 ft	7.000 ft
	C.10.20.01.2.1	Single-Flush			3.000 ft	0.167 ft	6.667 ft
	C 10 20 01 2 2	Single-Flush			3 000 ft	0 167 ft	6 667 ft

13. Roll the cursor over the blue triangular icon ▶ for both items and notice that a model property for these objects has changed.

ModelHeight	ModelPerim
7.000 ft	

Model Property Changed
Old Model Value: 7.000 ft
New Model Value: 6.667 ft
Difference: 0.333 ft

6 667 ft

ModelWidth	ModelThickness
3.000 ft	0.167
3.000 ft	0.167

Model Property Changed
Old Model Value: 3.000 ft
New Model Value: 6.000 ft
Difference: 3.000 ft

14. Select the ModelHeight cell for the C.10.20.01.2.110 object. Click Update and select Select Row.

15. In the toolbar, click Update and select Update Selected From Model. The C.10.20.01.2.110 object resorts now that the data is no longer marked as changed.

16. Select the ModelWidth cell for the C.10.20.01.2.115 object. Click Update and select Select Row.

17. In the toolbar, click Update and select Update Selected From Model. It also resorts the list.

Notice that 🔓 no longer displays in the Item list because all of the changes have been updated.

18. It is good practice to review the changed objects to ensure that they still should remain in the takeoff. Scroll to the C.10.20.01.2.110 object in the list. The door remains a Single-Flush door and only the height was changed.

19. Scroll to the C.10.20.01.2.115 object in the list. Notice that the object has updated to a Double-Flush door.

20. Double-Flush doors are not required in this takeoff grouping. Select a cell in the C.10.20.01.2.115 object row, right-click and select Delete Takeoff. There are now a total of 366 doors in the model.

21. The new door that was added to rev2 of the model must be added to the Takeoff. Select the Missing Door viewpoint, if not already active.

22. Change the Selection Priority to First Object and select the new door in the Scene View. The door highlights in the Selection Tree.

23. Drag the new door to the Wood Door-Single(366) item in the Quantification Workbook. The new door is added as the new C.10.20.01.2.115 item and the number of doors update to 367.

Note: When updating and working with the Quantification Workbook, after objects have been added to a model, consider using the Show Takeoff and Hide Takeoff options to help identify the items that need to be added to the Takeoff.

Export the Quantification Workbook

1. In the Quantification Workbook, click [icon] and select Export Catalog to XML. This enables you to save the Item Catalog that was customized for use in another project.

2. In the Export Catalog to XML dialog box, browse to the *C:\Temp* folder, enter **Class Catalog.xml** as the name for the file, and save it.

Note: Consider setting up and saving to a network location so that multiple Autodesk Navisworks users can use the new catalog.

3. In the Quantification Workbook, click [icon] and select Export Quantities to EXCEL. This enables you to save all of the taken off quantities to an excel spreadsheet.

4. In the Export Catalog to Excel dialog box, browse to the *C:\Temp* folder, enter **Hospital Takeoff Report.xlsx** as the name for the file, and save it.

5. Click Yes to open the file once it has been created. This only opens if you have Excel on your computer.

6. Review the Takeoff Quantities that have been added to the file. Close the file.

7. Save the file.

Clash Detective

Autodesk® Navisworks® Clash Detective identifies, inspects, and reports interference clashes in a 3D project model. Clash Detective can eliminate a tedious manual task, with the accompanying risk of human error, to significantly reduce the expensive consequences of incomplete, inaccurate, and poorly coordinated design information. You can use Clash Detective for a quick check for design work that an engineer has just completed, or for an ongoing audit check of the project by the project coordinator.

Clash Detective can also conduct clash tests between traditional 3D geometry (triangles) and laser geometry. Clash test reports can be produced for communicating to other people. Batches of clash tests can be saved and exported to use in other projects.

By Linking Clash Detective and Object Animation together, you can check animated versus animated or animated versus static object clashes. For example, linking a Clash Detective test to an existing animation scene would automatically highlight clashes for both static and moving objects during the animation (for example, a crane rotating through the top of a building or a delivery truck colliding with a work group).

You can also link Clash Detective, TimeLiner, and Object Animation together for clash testing of fully animated TimeLiner schedules. So, instead of visually inspecting a TimeLiner sequence to ensure, for example, that the moving crane didn't collide with a work group, you can run a Clash Detective test.

Objectives

After completing this chapter, you will be able to:

- Conduct a clash test and view the results.
- Select the correct clash type options for the type of clash test required.
- Run a clash test using the Find and Selection Set tools.
- Use existing rules and create new rules to ignore certain clashes.
- View clash results and add comments.

- Create a clash report and review the results.
- Review and edit existing tests, delete, compact, and reset tests, and rerun any existing clash test.
- Conduct a clash test after updating the 3D files and view the results.
- Export a clash test from a project.
- Import a clash test into a project.
- Create and run custom clash tests.
- Run a clash test using laser scan data.
- Use the Hold function to temporarily move objects to a different position.
- Use the SwitchBack function to dynamically update and view clashed objects.
- Run and interpret the results of time-based clashes.

Lesson: Clash Detective Overview

Overview

This lesson describes how to open the Clash Detective window in the Autodesk Navisworks software. It also introduces you to the Select tab for defining and running the clash test, the Results tab for viewing the results, and the Rules tab to customize what information is excluded in a clash test.

Objective

After completing this lesson, you will be able to:

- Conduct a clash test and view the results.
- Select the correct clash type options for the type of clash test required.
- Run a clash test using the Find and Selection Set tools.
- Use existing rules and create new rules to ignore certain clashes.

Conducting a Clash Test

The Clash Detective window enables you to set up rules and options for your clash tests, view the results, sort them, and produce clash reports.

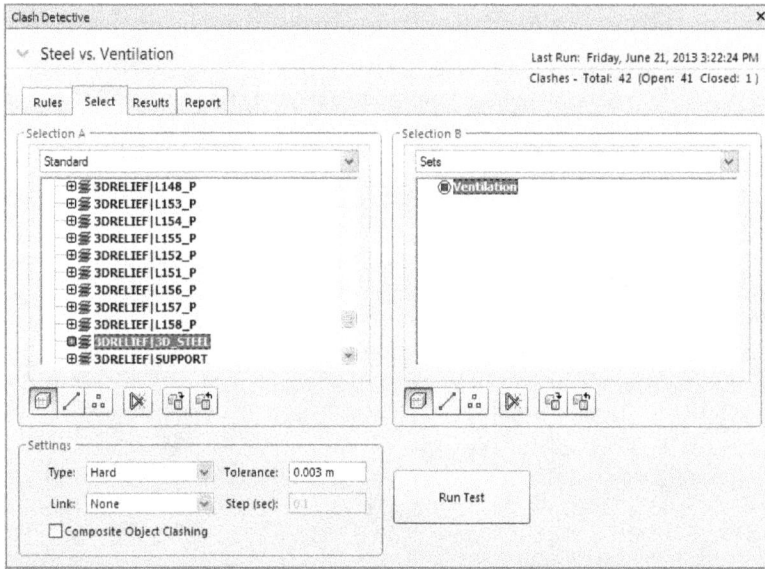

Procedure: To Conduct a Clash Test

1. Select the Home tab and click Clash Detective in the Tools panel.

2. Select the Select tab in the Clash Detective window. There are two identical panes in this tab called Selection A and Selection B. These panes represent the two sets of items that are going to be tested against each other during the clash test.

    The Selection A and Selection B panes in the Clash Detective window can be displayed in four view formats to aid in selecting items for clash testing. To change formats, select the Standard, Compact, Properties, or Sets options in the drop-down list at the top of each pane, as required. The Standard option provides a full, expandable listing of the layers. The Compact option provides a top-level listing of the layers. The Properties option sub-divides the models according to its properties. If there are saved selection or search sets available, a Sets option is also available. Using the Sets option you can select from the lists to define the items to be tested.

3. Click the required geometry type in the Selection A and Selection B panes. Clash tests can be conducted on the following geometry types:

    - **Surfaces** – Clashes item surfaces (default setting).

    - **Lines** – Clashes items with center lines (e.g., pipes).

    - **Points** – Clashes (laser) points. See Laser Scan Data Clashing for more information.

4. In each of the Selection A and Selection B panes, select the items that are to be compared against. To select the items for the clash detection, use one of the following techniques:

   - Select the items directly in the Selection Tree. Consider using the Standard, Compact, or Properties option to change the view formats when making selections.
   - In the Scene View, select an item or set of items to be clashed. If required, press and hold CTRL to select multiple items. In the Clash Detective window, click Use Current Selection

     below the required panes to assign the currently selected items in the Scene View to that pane.
   - Select the Sets option associated with either the Selection A and Selection B panes and select from the saved selection or search sets that already exist in the model.

   Note: Items which have been hidden are not included in a clash test.

   > Clash testing can be faster, more effective, and easily repeatable if you use selection or search sets. Carefully consider which sets of objects need clashing against each other and create selection and search sets accordingly.
   >
   > Creating batch clash tests is another way to speed up clash testing.

5. Clash Detective can clash test a selection against itself, in addition to clash testing against the set in the other pane. Click the Self Intersect option for the Selection A, Selection B, or both panes, as required.

6. Define the Clash type in the Type drop-down menu. There are four types of clashes:

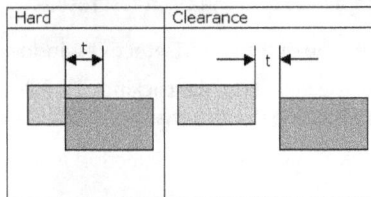

Hard	Clearance
t	t

   t = Tolerance

   - **Hard** – Where two objects actually intersect.
   - **Hard (Conservative)** – This option performs the same clash test as Hard, and also applies a conservative intersection method.
   - **Clearance** – Where two objects come within a specified distance of each other.
   - **Duplicates** – Where two objects are identical, both in type and position.

A standard Hard clash test type applies a Normal Intersection Method, which sets the clash test to check for intersections between any of the triangles defining the two items being tested (all Autodesk Navisworks geometry is composed of triangles). This might miss clashes between items where none of the triangles intersect. Choosing Hard (Conservative) reports all of the pairs of items that might clash. This might give false positives in the results, but is a more thorough and safer clash detection method.

You can use Duplicates testing to clash the entire model against itself by selecting the whole model in both the Selection A and Selection B panes. Use this to detect any items in the scene that might have been duplicated by mistake. For example, a multiple instanced item might have been inserted in the same place twice or a reference file was loaded twice (it was referenced by more than one file in the scene).

If you select Clearance, hard clashes are also detected. Any objects closer than the set tolerance and any interference are obviously less than the set clearance, as shown in the image above.

7. Define the Tolerance that should be used in the test in the Tolerance drop-down menu (for 1mm enter **0.001**).

8. Click Run Test to begin the clash analysis.

   Note: The progress bar that displays during a clash test indicates how far through the test Clash Detective has got. Press Cancel to stop the test at any time. All clashes processed before test termination are reported and the test is saved with a Partial status.

   Tip: Before running a clash test, it might be useful to go to the Rules tab and select one or more of the rule definitions. This filters out unnecessary clashes and makes the results more meaningful. See Setting Clash Rules.

9. Details on the number of clashing instances are identified at the top of the Clash Detective window. Select the Results tab to review a detailed list of the clash test results.

10. The default name for a clash test displays at the top of the Clash Detective window (e.g., Test1).

    To rename the test, expand Test1 at the top of the Results tab by clicking ∨ . Select the default name and press F2 (or slowly double-click) to rename the test that was just created.

    Tip: To add a new test, click Add Test, otherwise changes to the Selection A and Selection B panes reflect in the existing/active clash test.

Linking a Clash Test to TimeLiner or Object Animations

Linking to TimeLiner integrates the features of Clash Detective and TimeLiner, allowing the automation of interference checking throughout the lifecycle of a TimeLiner project. By linking to object animations, interference checking can be done for both static and animated objects. This means that an animated object is checked against the other selected objects through its animated path, not just in its static position (for example, a crane rotating through the top of a building).

Procedure: To Link to a Clash Test

1. On the Select tab, in the Link drop-down list, select TimeLiner or the object animation.

2. In the Step field, enter the interval period (in seconds) that clash checks are made throughout the simulation sequence

> Linking to TimeLiner or object animations takes more time to complete than a normal clash test.

Clash Rules

You can use clash rules to filter out clashes that are not relevant to a particular clash review session. For example, based on specific object properties. A selection of predefined rules are available for use or you can create new rules using a default list of template rules.

Procedure: To Set Pre-Defined Clash Rules

1. In the Clash Detective window, select the Rules tab. The following rules are available for use:

- **Items in same layer** – Items found clashing that are in the same layer are not reported in the results.
- **Items in same group/block/cell** – Items found clashing that are in the same group (or inserted block) are not reported in the results.
- **Items in same file** – Items found clashing that are in the same file (either externally referenced or appended) are not reported in the results.
- **Items with coincident snap points** – Items found clashing that have coinciding snap points are not reported in the results. This can be useful for pipe runs made from cylinders.

2. Select one or multiple predefined rules, as required.

Procedure: To Edit an Existing Clash Rule

1. To edit an existing rule, on the Rules tab, select the rule, and click Edit.

2. In the Rule name area, enter a new name that describes the edited rule.

3. In the Rules Editor dialog box, in the Rule Templates area, select a different rule.

4. In the Rule description area, click an underlined value to assign a new value (if a variable item exists in the current template). Select a value from the drop-down list or enter a new value. Click OK.

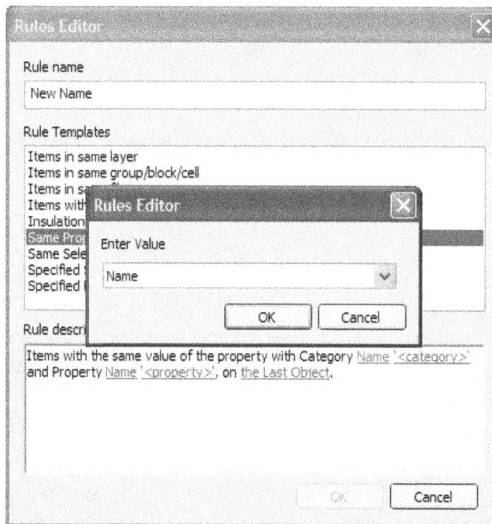

5. Repeat this procedure to change other values in the same rule, and click OK in the Rules Editor.

Note: Not all rules have editable values. Editable values are displayed as underlined blue text, and when selected, are displayed as underlined red text.

Procedure: To Add a New Clash Rule

1. To add a new rule, on the Rules tab, click New.

2. In the Rules Editor dialog box, in the Rule name area, enter a name for the new rule.

   Note: If no name is entered, it automatically names the rule based on the selected rules.

3. In the Rule Templates area, select a rule similar to the requirements of the new rule.

4. In the Rule description area, click an underlined value to assign a new value (if a variable item exists in the current template). Select a value from the drop-down list or enter a new value. Click OK.

5. Repeat to change other values in the same rule. In the Rules Editor, click OK.

   Note: Not all rules have editable values. Editable values are displayed as underlined blue text, and when selected, are displayed as underlined red text.

Exercise: Conduct Simple Clash Tests

Using standard selection to define clash test items.

1. Open the file *C:\Navisworks 2017 Essentials Class Files\Training\Examples\Heating Plant.nwf*.

2. Select the Home tab and click Clash Detective in the Tools panel.

3. When Clash Detective opens, the Select tab is displayed, by default. There are two identical panes in this tab called Selection A and Selection B. These panes represent two sets of items that are tested against each other during the clash test.

4. In the Clash Detective Selection A pane, expand the Heating Plant hierarchy, and select 3DMODULE|X-REF.

   Tip: To sort the list, select the *heating plant.nwd* file in the Selection Tree, right-click and select Scene > Sort. This sorts the list in both the Selection Tree and the Clash Detective.

5. In the Selection B pane, expand the Heating Plant hierarchy, and select COLH|3D_STEEL.

6. Click Application Menu > Options > Interface > Display Units. Change the Decimal Places value to 3, if not already set. Click OK.

7. Under Settings, set Type to Hard and Tolerance to 0.001, if not already set.

8. Click Run Test to run the clash test.

9. Observe that 24 clashes are identified at the top of the Results tab.

10. Review the results in the Results lists, which includes information about each clash. See Clash Results for more information.

11. Expand Test1 at the top of the Results tab by clicking ⌄, if not already expanded. Select Test1 and press F2 (or slowly double-click) to rename the test that was just created. Enter **3dModule vs. 3dsteel** as the new name.

Using the Find and Selection Set tools to define clash test items.

1. In the expanded area, click Add Test. Enter **Steel vs. Ventilation** as the new name.

2. Compress the Clash test list by clicking ∧.

3. On the Home tab, in the Select & Search panel, click Find Items 🔍. You want to locate all of the steel structure in the model.

4. In the Search In area, select *Heating Plant.nwd*.

5. In the Category drop-down list, select Item.

6. In the Property drop-down list, select Name.

7. In the Condition drop-down list, select Contains.

8. In the Value field, enter **steel**.

Category	Property	Condition	Value
Item	Name	Contains	steel
⌄			

☑ Match Character Widths
☑ Match Diacritics
☑ Match Case
☐ Prune Below Result
Search: Default ⌄

9. Clear the checkmark in the Match Case option (to ignore case sensitivity).

10. Click Find All. The entire model is searched for all items containing the word "steel" in their display names in the Selection Tree. All found items are highlighted in the scene and on the Selection Tree.

11. In the Clash Detective window, click the Select tab.

12. In the Selection A pane, click Use Current Selection 📋 to select all steel items that have been found.

13. Return to the Find Items 🔍 window to locate all vents in the model.

    Note: To delete the criteria from the previous search, right-click the Category Item, and click Delete Condition.

14. In the Category drop-down list, select Item.

15. In the Property drop-down list, select Name.

16. In the Condition drop-down list, select Contains.

17. In the Value field, enter **vent**.

18. Verify that the Match Case option is cleared.

19. Click Find All.

    Tip: When conducting this type of search, it might save time to save this search so you can use it later. Remember, search sets automatically update with any changes to the model.

20. On the View tab in the Workspace panel, expand Windows and click Sets to open the Sets window. Right-click in the Sets window and click Save Search.

21. Change the name of Search Set to **Ventilation**.

22. Close the Sets and the Find Items window.

23. In the Selection B pane in the Clash Detective, select Sets in the drop-down list at the top of the pane. Select the Ventilation search set.

    Note: Do not click Use Current Selection option in the Selection B pane. Any items currently selected in the scene are selected instead of the Ventilation Set.

    In the Selection A pane, all the searched steel items are selected, and in the Selection B pane all the ventilation items are selected.

24. Under Settings, for Type, select Hard, to check only for actual interactions.

25. Ensure that the Self Intersect options are cleared in both the Selection A and Selection B panes.

26. In Tolerance, enter **0.005** to set the run tolerance to 5mm.

27. Click Run Test. 34 clashes were found between the steel and the vents.

28. Select the Select tab and in the Tolerance field, change the value to **0.004** to set the run tolerance to 4mm.

29. Click Run Test. There are now 38 clashes found between the steel and the vents. See Clash Results for further information.

30. Save this file with the same name plus your initials to a new location. (For example, *C:\Temp\ Heating PlantJMD.nwf.*)

Lesson: Clash Results

Overview

In the Clash Detective, on the Results tab, you can view clash results, view the clash status, and add comments.

Objective

After completing this lesson, you will be able to:

- View clash results and add comments.

About Clash Results

In Clash Detective, click the Results tab.

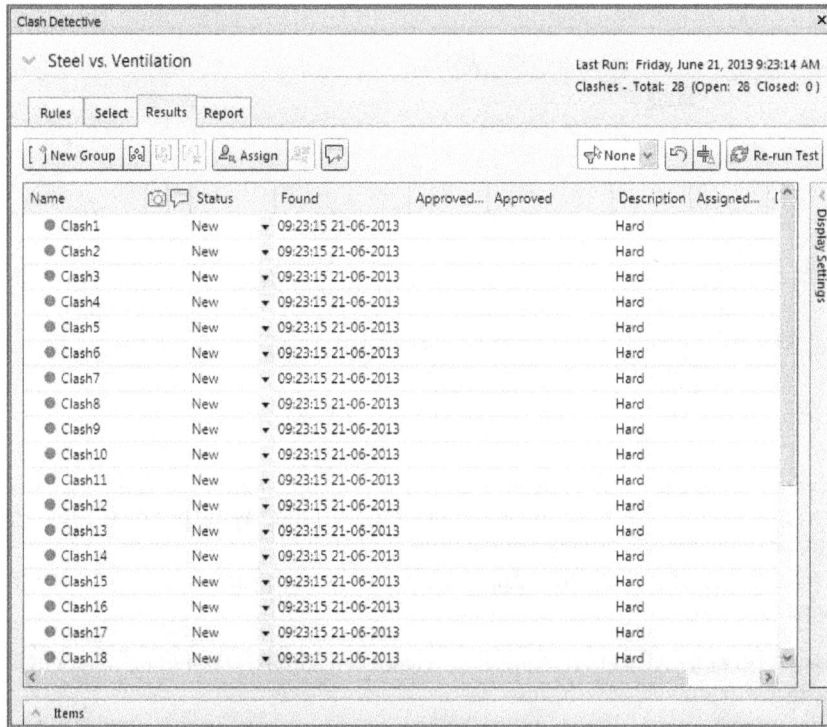

The results of the clash test are listed in alphanumeric order based on the active column. They can be reordered by clicking on any of the column headers.

The list at the top of the window displays the clashes, numbered and sorted by severity, and color coded accordingly. Displayed with each clash result are columns that identify custom viewpoints, number of comments, clash status, date found, who approved it, when it was approved, description, who it has been assigned to, and the clash distance. You have to scroll to see all of the details for a clash item.

Clash Name

Default names are initially provided for each clash result. They can be renamed to provide a more meaningful description. To rename a clash, right-click the clash name and click Rename. Enter a new name for the clash and press ENTER.

Clash Status

Each clash has a current status associated with it. This status is updated automatically each time the same test is run, or can be manually overridden using any of the options in the drop-down menu.

- **New** (Red) – A clash found for the first time in the current run of the clash test.

- **Active** (Orange) – A clash found in a previous run of the test and not resolved.

- **Reviewed** (Cyan) - A clash previously identified and reviewed with no immediate resolution.

- **Approved** (Green) – A clash previously found and approved by someone. If the status is changed to Approved, the user currently logged on is recorded as the person who approved it together with the time of approval.

  Note: If a clash has been changed to Approved, when the clash is run again, if the clash still exists, it remains as Approved.

- **Resolved** (Yellow) – A clash found in a previous run of the test but not found in the current run of the test. It is assumed to be resolved.

  Note: If a clash is manually changed to Resolved, when the clash is run again, if the clash still exists it is changed back to New (Red).

- **Old** – Any clash in an "old" test (parts of the model have changed since the last time the test was run). The icons still have the code of the status from the previous run, but this is a reminder that the current test is old.

> You can change the status of multiple clashes. Either hold CTRL while selecting individual clashes, or use SHIFT to select a range of clashes.

Display Settings Pane

The Display area controls the way in which clashes are displayed in the Scene View. This pane is located to the right of the clash list in the Results tab. It is an expandable pane that can be compressed when not being used to increase the width of the clash list. To expand or compress the Display Settings pane, click the arrow on the pane's name.

Use the following options or any combination of options for an efficient review of clashes:

Highlighting Area:

- **Item 1/Item 2** – Highlights or clears the highlighting on item 1 or item 2 in a selected clash.
- **Use item colors/Use status color** – This drop-down list enables you to customize the colors of clashing objects as their item color or to identify them using the status color for the clash.
- **Highlight all Clashes** – Highlights all clashes found during the test in the scene view.

Isolation Area:

- **Dim Other** – Dims all other objects in the model. (This makes it easier to see the clashed items.)
- **Hide Other** – Hides all other objects in the model.
- **Transparent Dimming** – Renders all items that are not involved in the clash so that they are transparent and gray. Use the Options Editor to customize the level of dimming transparency, and to display items not involved in the clash as wireframes. By default, 85% transparency is used. This option is only available in conjunction with the Dim Other option.
- **Auto Reveal** – Temporarily hides objects that obscure the clashed objects (recommended).

Viewpoint Area:

- **Auto-update** – This option enables you to define a custom viewpoint for a clash. Once repositioned, the custom view is automatically saved with the clash. A camera icon displays in the Results grid to identify that a custom viewpoint has been stored. Use Focus on Clash to return to the original default viewpoint as the saved viewpoint for the clash.

  Note: To delete a saved custom viewpoint, right-click the camera icon in the Results grid and select Delete Viewpoint. Use the Delete All Viewpoints option to delete all of the custom viewpoints from all of the clashes on the Results tab.

- **Auto-load** – This options enable you to reposition a viewpoint to review a clash without saving the viewpoint.

- **Manual** – This option prevents the viewpoint of the model from changing when a clash is selected in the Results grid.

- **Animation Transitions** – Animates the scene view between the selected clashes. Clearing this option leaves the viewpoints static while selecting clashes one by one. Use Auto Zoom or Save Changes with this option to benefit from the effect.

- **Focus on Clash** – Resets the clash viewpoint to that of the original clash point. This is used if the original point has been navigated away from.

Simulation Area:

- **Show Simulation** – Uses time-based and animation clashing. It moves the playback slider in the TimeLiner sequence or an animation scene to the exact point at which the clash occurs enabling you to investigate the events happening immediately before and after the clash. For clash groups, the playback slider is moved to the point in time of the 'worst' clash from the group.

View in Context Area:

- **All** – Zooms so that the entire scene as visible.
- **File** – Zooms so that the files involved in the clash are visible in the scene view.
- **Home** – Resets the scene view to the define Home View.
- **View** – Press and hold View to show the selected view in the scene view.

Adding and Reviewing Comments

You can add a comment to any clash result without having to save a viewpoint. All comments that have been added to various clash results can be reviewed and included in a clash report.

Procedure: To Add a Comment to a Clash Result

1. Right-click the name of the clash and click Add Comment.

    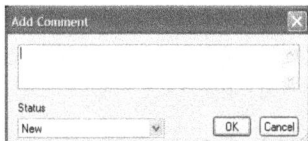

2. In the Add Comment dialog box, enter your comment.

3. In the Status drop-down menu, select a status and click OK.

    Note: The number of clashes added to a clash result are listed in the Comment column in the Results grid.

Procedure: To Review Clash Result Comments

1. Select the Review tab. On the Comments pane, click View Comments ⌐, if the Comments window is not already displayed.

2. In the Clash Detective's Results tab, select the clash name. The comment associated with the selected clash is displayed in the Comments window.

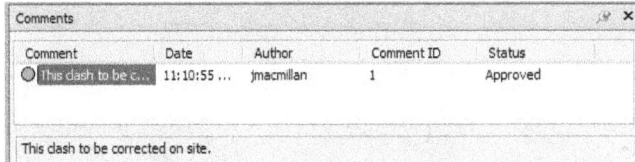

Comment	Date	Author	Comment ID	Status
◎ This clash to be c...	11:10:55 ...	jmacmillan	1	Approved

This clash to be corrected on site.

Procedure: To Find All Clash Results Comments

Use Find Comments to quickly find all comments associated with clash results.

1. On the Review tab, in the Comments panel, click Find Comments ⌐.

2. In the Find Comments dialog box, select the Source tab.

3. Add a checkmark to Clash Detective. Click Find. All comments associated with the Clash Detective results are listed and include the comment text.

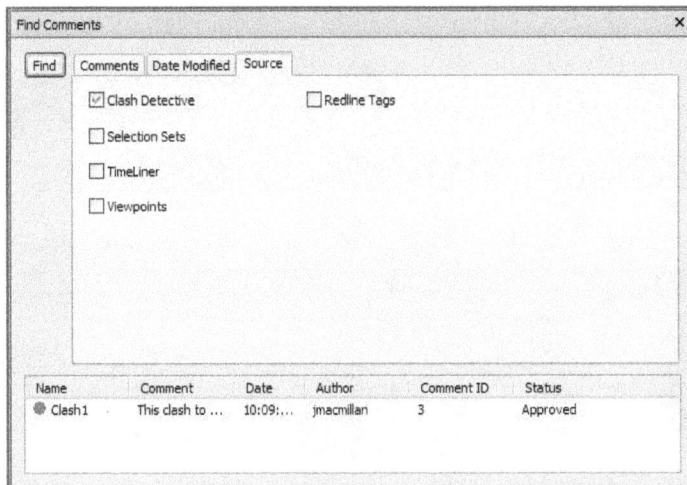

Find Comments

Find | Comments | Date Modified | Source

☑ Clash Detective   ☐ Redline Tags

☐ Selection Sets

☐ TimeLiner

☐ Viewpoints

Name	Comment	Date	Author	Comment ID	Status
● Clash1	This clash to ...	10:09:...	jmacmillan	3	Approved

4. Click on the clash result at the bottom of the Find Comments window to display the comment.

> When using the Find Comments tool, View Comments ⌐ should be enabled so that when you select a clash result in the Find Comments window, it is also displayed in the Comments window.

Clash Groups

You can manage clash results individually or you can create and manage clash groups. Created groups are represented in the Results tab as folders.

Procedure: To Create a Clash Group

1.   On the Results tab, in the Results area, click New Group. A group is added to the Results list. Alternatively, you can right-click the selected clashes and select Group.

2.   Enter a new descriptive name for the clash group and press ENTER.

3.   Select the clashes you want to add to this group, and drag them into the folder.

      Note: Once grouped, a single comment can be added to several items it applies to.

4.   When you click the created clash group, the Item panes in the lower section of the Results tab show all of the clashing items in that clash group, and all corresponding clashes are shown in the Scene View.

      Note: To explode a group, right-click and select Explode Group. Any comments added to a group are removed when exploded.

Exercise: Clash Testing, Viewing Results, & Adding Comments

1. Continue to work on the file from the previous exercise. Alternatively, if you did not complete that exercise, open the file *C:\Navisworks 2017 Essentials Class Files\Training\Examples\ Heating Plant 2.nwf*.

2. Select the Home tab and click Clash Detective in the Tools panel, if it is not already displayed.

3. Click the Select tab. Ensure that the Steel vs. Ventilation clash test is active as indicated at the top of the window. If not, click ⌄ and select the Steel vs. Ventilation clash test. Click ⌃ to compress the list of tests.

4. Select the Select tab, if not already active. Under Settings, set the Tolerance to 0.003.

5. Click Run Test.

6. In the Results tab view all clash results. The results should include New and Active clashes, as identified in the Status column. New clashes are identified with (Red). Active clashes are identified with (Orange).

7. Observe the various clash details available for a clash result by scrolling to the right.

8. Scroll to the first of the Active (Orange) clashes. Right-click on Clash1 and select Rename. Enter **SV1** and press ENTER.

9. Rename Clash2 to **SV2**.

10. In the Status column for SV1, select Resolved from the drop-down menu. The icon for the clash changes to (Yellow).

11. In the Status column for SV2, select Approved from the drop-down menu. The icon for the clash changes to (Green).

12. At the top of the clash list, click Re-run Test.

13. In the Results tab view the results. All the clashes in the last test with New status have changed to Active. The SV1 clash that was manually changed to Resolved has been seen again and therefore marked as New. The SV2 clash manually changed to Approved remains approved even though the clash still exists (shown at the bottom of the list). Notice also that the SV2 clash displays the date approved and who approved it.

14. Click clash result SV2 (at the bottom of the list).

15. Expand the Display Settings pane, if not already active. It is located to the right of the clash list. In the Display pane, clear all options in the Highlighting, Isolation (including the Dim and Hide Other options), Viewpoint, Simulation, and View in Context areas. Scroll to access all of the options, if required.

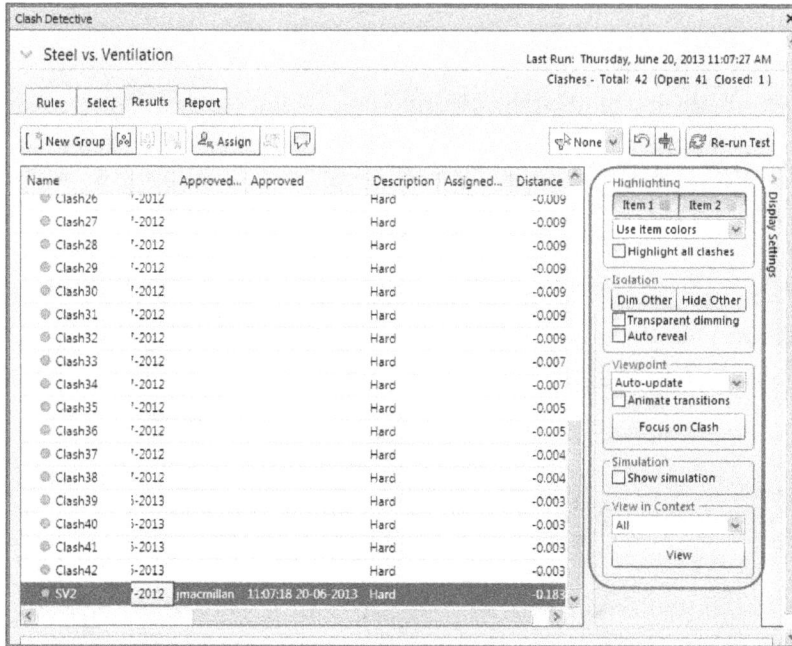

16. Click clash result SV1. The viewpoint that displays is the default that is saved with the clash.

17. In the Display Settings pane, select Hide Other in the Isolation area and observe the effect in the scene.

18. In the Display Settings pane, clear Hide Other and select Dim Other. Observe the effect in the scene.

19. Ensure that Auto-update is the active option in the Viewpoint drop-down list. Using the navigation tools, change the viewpoint for the clash.

20. Click another clash in the list to change to its viewpoint. Notice that the SV1 Viewpoint cell in the Results grid displays a camera icon. This indicates that a custom viewpoint has been created.

21. Click clash result SV1 and notice that the new viewpoint is displayed.

22. With SV1 still active, click Focus on Clash to return to the default viewpoint and save it as the custom viewpoint.

Tip: Right-click on the SV1 clash and select Delete Viewpoint to remove the custom viewpoint and return to the default viewpoint that was created for the clash.

Tip: To reorient a clash's viewpoint without having it save as a custom viewpoint, use the Auto-load option in the Viewpoint drop-down menu.

23. Compress the Display Settings pane to enlarge the viewing area for the clash list.

24. Right-click clash SV2, and then click Add Comment.

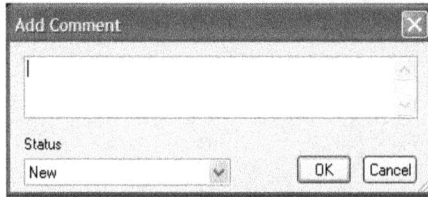

25. In the Add Comment dialog box, enter **This clash to be corrected on site**.

26. Change Status to Approved, and then click OK.

27. On the Review tab in the Comments pane, click View Comments ⬚ , if the Comments window is not already displayed. Note that the comment is displayed at the bottom.

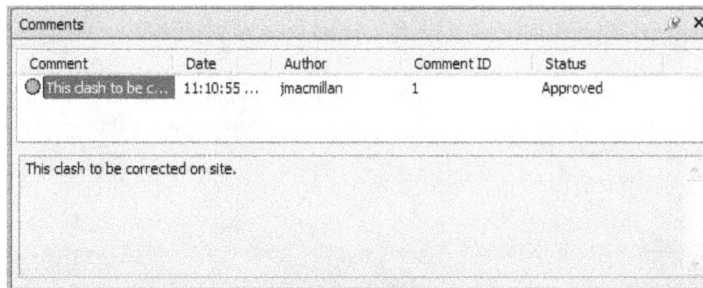

28. Return to the Clash Detective window. Notice that the SV2 Comment cell in the Results grid indicates that one comment has been added for this clash.

29. Select SV1. Notice that there are no comments identified in the Results grid or displayed in the Comments window. The Comments are only displayed for the selected clash result.

30. On the Review tab, in the Comments panel, click Find Comments 🔍.

31. In the Find Comments window, select the Source tab.

32. Clear all but the Clash Detective option and click Find.

Find Comments						×
Find	Comments	Date Modified	**Source**			
	☑ Clash Detective		☐ Redline Tags			
	☐ Selection Sets					
	☐ TimeLiner					
	☐ Viewpoints					

Name	Comment	Date	Author	Comment ID	Status
◉ SV2	This clash to ...	3:15:3...	jmacmillan	1	Approved

The comment associated with the clash SV2 result is listed and includes the comment text.

33. Click on clash result to display the comment in the Comments window.

34. Save this file with the same name and your initials to a new location. (For example, *C:\Temp\ Heating Plant2JMD.nwf*.)

Lesson: Clash Test Reporting

Overview

In the Clash Detective window, the Report tab is used to create reports containing details of all the clash results found in the current test. You can produce a report in the form of a text file, an HTML report, or an XML report, or you can simply save it as a list of viewpoints for review. With the As viewpoints reporting format, a folder with the same name as the Clash test is created in the Saved Viewpoints window that contains a viewpoint for each clash that was detected in the test. The HTML option creates an HTML file that contains a JPG viewpoint of each clash result alongside their details.

Objective

After completing this lesson, you will be able to:

- Create a clash report and review the results.

Report Contents

In the Clash Detective window, select the Report tab.

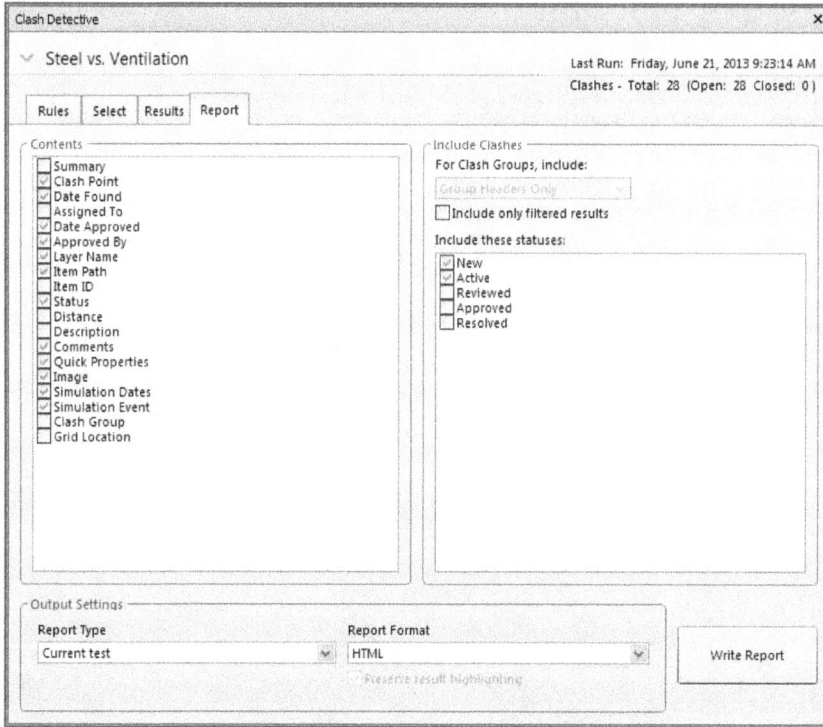

Contents

The Contents area defines the contents of the report for the active Clash test. This can include Quick Properties properties relating to the items involved in the clash, how to find them in the Selection Tree, whether images or TimeLiner task information should be included, etc.

> By only including "need to know" information, the report is shorter and easier to read than a report that includes all possible information.

Include Clashes

The Include Clashes area defines which clashes, according to their status, should be included in the report. If clash groups are available, you have additional control over whether groups are included or not.

Report Type

Select the type of report from the Report Type drop-down menu.

- **Current test** – Creates a single file for the current Batch test.
- **All tests (combined)** – Creates a single file containing all results from all Batch tests.
- **All tests (separate)** – Creates a separate file for each Batch test containing all results.

Report Format

Select the format of the report from the Report Format drop-down menu.

Important: When selecting XML, HTML, or Text format options, a separate folder is created for all the JPEG files that are created as part of the report. The folder is created in the folder where the report is stored.

- **XML** – Creates an XML file containing all the clashes and a JPEG image of each of their viewpoints alongside their details. All images are stored in a subfolder.
- **HTML** – Creates an HTML file containing all the clashes and a JPEG of each of their viewpoints alongside their details. All images are stored in a subfolder.
- **HTML (Tabular)** - Creates an HTML (tabular) file with the clash test(s) displayed as a table. This report can be opened and edited in Microsoft Excel 2007 onwards.
- **Text** – Creates a single TXT file and JPEG files (stored in a subfolder) for each of the clashes. The text file contains all of the details for the clashes with reference to the image filenames.
- **As viewpoints** – Creates a folder in the Saved Viewpoints window. The folder has the same name as the Batch test. Each clash is saved as a viewpoint in this folder, with a comment attached containing the clash result details. You can rename the clash test folder. Use the Preserve result highlighting option to maintain the transparency and highlighting for each viewpoint. You can adjust the highlighting in the Results tab and Options Editor.

> Use As Viewpoints if you want to add markups on the viewpoints to provide additional information about the clash in the form of redline measurements or tags.

Procedure: To Write a Report

1. In the Clash Detective window, select the Report tab.
2. In the Contents area, select the content information to include in the report.
3. In the Include Clashes area, select the Clash Status types to include in the report and how to deal with groups, if present in the clash test.
4. In the Report Type drop-down menu, select from the Current or All test options.
5. In the Report Format drop-down menu, select the output format.
6. Click Write Report.
7. In the Save As dialog box, select the location and filename, and click Save. The report is created and saved in the selected location.

Procedure: To Read a Report in XML Format

1. Open MS Excel. Browse for and select the XML report file.

2. When the Open XML dialog box is displayed, select the As a read-only workbook option, and click OK. The report is displayed in Excel or an XML viewer.

Procedure: To Read a Report in HTML Formats

1. Open My Computer. Browse for the HTML report file.

2. Double-click the file. The file opens in Internet Explorer.

Procedure: To Read a Report in Text Format

1. Open My Computer. Browse for the text report file.

2. Double-click the file. The file opens in Notepad. Alternatively, open MS Word. Browse and open the text report file.

Procedure: To Read a Report in the As Viewpoints Format

1. Select the View tab and expand the Windows option in the Workspace panel. Select Saved Viewpoints in the drop-down menu to enable the Saved Viewpoints window, if it is not already displayed.

2. In the Saved Viewpoints window, find the clash reports folder. Expand the folder to display the listed clash viewpoints.

3. Select the Review tab. On the Comments pane, click View Comments , if the Comments window is not already displayed.

4. In the Saved Viewpoints window, select the clash viewpoint. The clash details are displayed in the Comments window and the Scene View updates with the image of the clash.

Exercise: Clash Testing and Creating a Report

1. Continue to work on the file from the previous exercise. Alternatively, if you did not complete that exercise, open the file *C:\Navisworks 2017 Essentials Class Files\Training\Examples\ Heating Plant 3.nwf*.

2. On the Home tab in the Tools panel, click Clash Detective in the Tools panel, if it is not already displayed.

3. In the Clash Detective window, select the Select tab.

4. Ensure that the Steel vs. Ventilation clash test is active as indicated at the top of the window. If not, click and select the Steel vs. Ventilation clash test. Click to compress the list of tests.

5. In the Settings area, set the Tolerance to 0.015.

6. Click Run Test.

7. In the Results tab, review all clash results. Only 6 clashes are found with these settings.

8. Select the Report tab.

9. In the Contents area, clear all but the following options: Clash Point, Date Found, Date Approved, Approved By, Layer Name, Item Path, Status, Comments, and Image.

10. In the Include Clashes area, clear all but the following options: New, Active, Approved, and Resolved.

11. In the Output Settings area in the Report Type drop-down menu, select Current test.

12. In the Output Settings area in the Report Format drop-down menu, select HTML.

13. Click Write Report.

14. In the Save As dialog box, create a temporary folder in a suitable location on the computer (for example, *C:\Temp*), then enter a filename, **Plant_clashes**, and click Save.

    A subfolder is automatically created in the *Temp* folder, where all the JPG images for each clash are stored.

15. Open Windows Explorer and browse for *Plant_clashes.html*. Double-click the file to view how the clash data and images are displayed.

16. Save this file with the same name plus your initials to a new location. For example, *C:\Temp\ Heating Plant3JMD.nwf*.

Lesson: Working with Clash Tests

Overview

In Clash Detective, you can create batches of clash tests, group them together, and save in a single file. This can either be done in an NWD or NWF file.

Objective

After completing this lesson, you will be able to:

- Review and edit existing tests, delete, compact, and reset tests, and rerun any existing clash test.

> If saving clash tests for future use, it is recommended to save them in an NWF file, as this references the files that are used to build up the 3D model and does not get overwritten when files are changed or re-published.

View Clash Tests

In Clash Detective, expand the list of tests at the top of the Clash Detective window by clicking ⌄. This provides a list of all clash tests currently set up in the file.

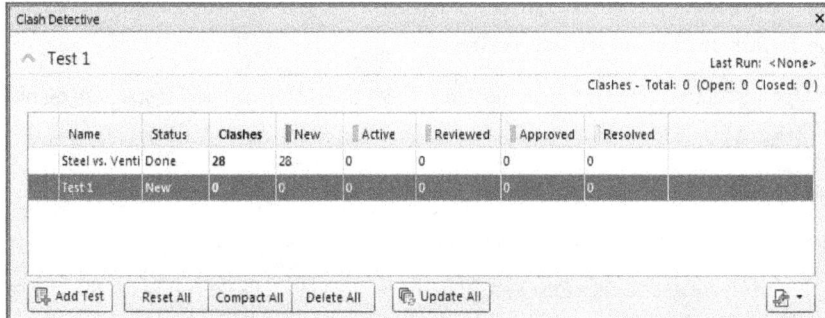

If no clash tests have been set up, a test that has not been run called Test 1 is displayed. When a clash test is run from the Select tab, the results data is added.

Using the Clash Test Options

Procedure: To Add a New Clash Test

1. Click Add Test in the expanded clash test list to add a new Clash test to the current batch of tests.

2. Select the new clash test, and press F2 to rename it, if required.

3. Select the new clash test and use the Select and Rules tabs to define its options.

Procedure: To Edit a Clash Test

1. Select the clash test to be edited in the expanded clash test list.

2. Press F2 to rename, if required.

3. Select the Select and Rules tabs, as required, to edit its options.

Procedure: To Delete a Single or Multiple Clash Tests

1. Select the clash test to be deleted in the expanded clash test list.

2. Right-click and select Delete or press <Delete>. The clash test is deleted. Alternatively, click Delete All to delete all clash tests in the list.

Procedure: To Compact a Clash Test

1. Select the clash test to be compacted in the expanded clash test list.

2. Right-click and select Compact. All resolved clashes are deleted, which is useful if the clash list is too large. Alternatively, click Compact All Tests to compact all clash tests in the list.

Procedure: To Reset a Clash Test

1. Select the clash test to be reset in the expanded clash test list.

2. Right-click and select Reset. The status of clash test is reset to New on the Batch tab and all clashes are cleared. Alternatively, click Reset All Tests to reset all clash tests in the list.

Procedure: To Run or Re-run All Clash Tests

1. Click Update All to run or re-run all the listed clash tests. The updated results are displayed against each test.

Procedure: To Run or Re-run a Single Clash Test from a Batch

1. Select the clash test to be re-run in the expanded clash test list.

2. Select the Select tab and click Run Test, or in the Results tab click Re-run Test. Only the selected test is re-run.

> Be careful when executing the delete, compact, clear all, and reset functions in the Clash Detective. When executing these commands there is no warning that this is going to adversely affect your ability to track the entire lifecycle of clashes.

Lesson: Audit Checks

Overview

Clash Detective can also save the clash test setup options and the results, so the test can be run again later and compared as the work progresses. Each clash test has a set of Run, Rule, and Display options associated with it. The test is saved in an NWD or NWF file that can be used again later.

Objective

After completing this lesson, you will be able to:

- Conduct a clash test after updating the 3D files and view the results.

> If saving clash tests for future use, it is advisable to save them in an NWF file, as this references the files that are used to build up the 3D model (NWD, DWG, 3DS) and does not get overwritten when files are changed or re-published.

Conducting Clash Audit Checks

Clash Detective can be used as an ongoing audit check through the lifecycle of a project.

Procedure: To Conduct a Clash Audit

1. Open the file to be clash tested.

2. Expand the list of tests at the top of the Clash Detective window by clicking ∨ . Click Delete All to clear any existing tests.

3. Click Add Test. Enter a new name for the clash. Press ENTER. Click ∧ to compress the list.

4. Select the Rules tab and set the rules, as required.

5. Select the Select tab. Define the items that are being clash tested and set the Settings. Click Run Test to run the clash test.

6. Select the Results tab, if not automatically activated.

7. Rename the clashes to provide a descriptive name. To rename, select the clash name, press F2, and rename it. Define the expanded Display Setting options, as required.

8. Save the Clash test as an NWF file.

9. Return to the source application file and resolve the clashing problems.

10. On the Home tab, in the Project panel, click Refresh ⟳ to refresh the NWF file to include the revisions made in the source application file.

11. Run the clash test again.

    Note: If there was more than one clash test listed, Update All re-runs all tests.

12. In the Results tab the original renamed clashes remain. However, their status has been automatically updated to Resolved   (Yellow) if the clash has been corrected.

Exercise: Clash Testing After Clashes are Corrected

1. In Windows Explorer, open the folder *C:\Navisworks 2017 Essentials Class Files\Training\Examples*. Copy the files *Clash.nwd* and *Clash2.nwd* to a temporary location for example, *C:\Temp*.

2. From the temporary location, open *Clash.nwd* in the Autodesk Navisworks software.

3. On the Home tab in the Tools panel, click Clash Detective ✏️, if it is not already displayed.

4. Expand Test1 at the top of the Clash Detective window by clicking ⌄ .

5. Select Test 1. Press F2 and in the clash name field, enter **Piping2 & Steel** as the new name. Press ENTER.

6. Click ⌃ to compress the list of tests.

7. Select the Rules tab. Clear all Ignore Clashes Between options, if not already cleared.

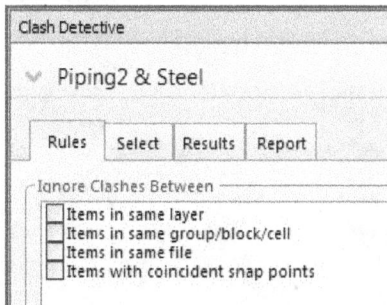

8. Select the Select tab. Expand *Clash.nwd* in both panes.

9. Select Steel in the Selection A pane and Piping_2 in the Selection B pane.

10. Under Settings, set Type to Hard and the Tolerance to 1mm (enter a value of 0.001m).

11. Click Run Test to run the clash test.

12. In the Results tab, rename the two clashes as **One** and **Two** respectively by clicking a clash name, pressing F2, and then renaming it.

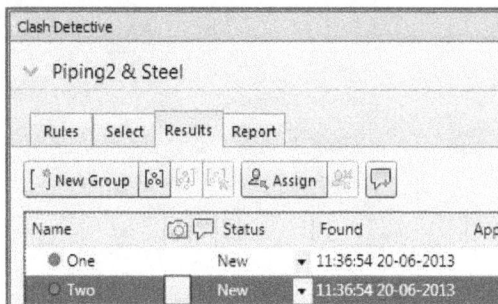

13. Save the file as an NWF file, in the temporary location, for example, *C:\Temp\clash.nwf*.

    In a real scenario, now that the items clashing in the model are known, they would be corrected in the model using the source application file.

    For the purposes of this exercise, you are replacing the *Clash.nwd* file with *Clash2.nwd*, which has these items already repositioned for you.

14. Start a new Autodesk Navisworks file to clear the previously used files from the session.

15. In Windows Explorer, navigate to the temporary folder, *C:\Temp,* and rename *Clash.nwd* to *Clash.old.nwd*.

16. Rename *Clash2.nwd* to *Clash.nwd*.

17. Open *clash.nwf* (*C:\Temp\clash.nwf*).

    The NWF file contains the Piping2 & Steel clash test, but references the replaced *Clash.nwd* file, which has the piping re-routed to avoid the clashes.

18. Run the clash test again.

19. In the Results tab notice that the two original clashes, named One and Two, remain, but their

    status has been automatically updated to Resolved   (Yellow).

20. Start a new Autodesk Navisworks file to clear the previously used files from the session. Do not save the file.

Lesson: Exporting and Importing Clash Tests

Overview

Exporting Clash Tests

Clash tests can be set up based on generic properties then exported to be later imported and used in other projects. They also can be exported and used as a basis for custom clash tests.

Objective

After completing this lesson, you will be able to:

- Export a clash test from a project.
- Import a clash test into a project.
- Create and run custom clash tests.

> Any clash tests based on specific item selections are not exported. For example, clashing one layer against another is not a valid test for exporting. You can use the Find Items function to search for each layer based on a specific property (Item, Name). These searches can be saved as search sets and selected in the Selection A and Selection B panes in the Clash Detective window.

Export and Import Clash Tests

Procedure: To Export Clash Tests

1. Select the Output tab and in the Export Data panel, click Clash Tests 🔲. Alternatively, in the expanded list of tests at the top of the Clash Detective window, select Export Clash Tests from the Import/Export Clash Tests drop-down menu 🔲 ▾.

2. In the Export dialog box, select the location, assign a filename, and click Save.

Procedure: To Import Clash Tests

1. Open the NWD or NWF project file that the clash tests are to be imported into.

2. In the expanded list of tests at the top of the Clash Detective window, select Import Clash Tests from the Import/Export Clash Tests drop-down menu 🔲 ▾.

3. In the Import dialog box, locate and select the XML file to be imported. Click Open.

   The XML file is imported, including all clash test information.

> 💡 If the clash test to be imported contains a search set as one of the clash selections, then the search set is also imported along with all other test rules, options, and selection information.

Setting up Custom Clash Tests

Exported clash tests can be used as a basis to define custom clash tests. If there is a common set of clash tests that you reuse on multiple projects, you can change it into a custom clash test. Once installed as a custom clash test, the entire batch of tests can be selected and run directly from the Select tab. An additional benefit is that the results from all tests are combined and presented as the results of the custom clash test. The name of each test is displayed in the Description field of the results.

Procedure: To Use a Custom Clash Test

1. Export the clash tests to an XML file in a temporary location. The name of the file is used as the default name of the custom test.

2. Create a new folder called *C:\Program Files\Autodesk\Navisworks Manage 2017 \custom_clash_tests* and copy the exported XML file to this folder. Alternatively, any of the following directories can also be used to store the XML file associated with a custom test. The file location is dependent on your operating system.

    ▪ *C:\Documents and Settings\user\Application Data\Navisworks\custom_clash_tests* (user is the name of the current user and only accessible to that user) - prior to Windows 7

    ▪ *C:\Documents and Settings\All Users\Application Data\Navisworks\custom_clash_tests* (accessible to all users) - prior to Windows 7

    ▪ *C:\Users\username\AppData\Roaming\Autodesk Navisworks Manage 2017\ custom_clash_tests* (username is the name of the current user and only accessible to that user) - Vista and Windows 7

    Note: The *Application Data* or *App Data* folders referred to above are "hidden" folders by default and need to be "unhidden" in Windows Explorer.

3. If already open, close and then restart the Autodesk Navisworks software and open the file that is going to be tested. Clash Detective searches these directories on startup looking for custom tests.

4. In the Clash Detective window, select the Select tab.

5. In the Settings area, the custom clash test is listed in the Type drop-down menu. Once a custom clash test is selected, most options in the Select tab are grayed out and cannot be selected because they are predefined as part of the custom clash test.

6. Click Run Test to run the custom clash test. All clash tests in the custom clash test are run and the results are displayed in the Results tab as one list.

7. Select the Results tab to view the results of the custom clash test. The name of each test is displayed in the Description column.

Exercise: Exporting, Importing, and Custom Clash Tests

Export a Clash Test

1. Open the file *C:\Navisworks 2017 Essentials Class Files\Training\Examples\Heating Plant.nwd*.

2. On the Home tab, in the Select & Search panel, click Find Items [icon]. You want to locate all of the steel structure in the model.

3. In the Search In area, select *Heating Plant.nwd*.

4. In the Category drop-down menu, select Item.

5. In the Property drop-down menu, select Name.

6. In the Condition drop-down menu, select Contains.

7. In the Value field, enter **steel**.

8. Clear the Match Case option, and then click Find All.

9. Select the View tab. On the Workspace panel, expand Windows and click Sets to open the Sets window, if it is not already displayed.

10. Right-click in the Sets window and click Save Search. Rename this search set as **Steel**.

11. In the Find Items window, change the value steel to vent. Click Find All again.

12. Right-click in the Sets window and click Save Search. Rename this search set as **Vents**.

13. Close the Find Items window.

14. Select the Home tab and click Clash Detective [icon] in the Tools panel, if not already active.

15. In the Clash Detective window, select the Select tab.

16. In the Selection A pane in the Clash Detective, select Sets in the drop-down list at the top of the pane. Select the Steel search set. In the Selection B pane, select the Vents search set.

17. Under Settings, set the Type to Hard and the Tolerance to 0.005m.

18. Click Run Test to run the clash test.

19. Expand the list of tests at the top of the Clash Detective window by clicking ∨. Select Test1 and rename the clash test to **Steel - Vents**.

20. Select the Output tab and in the Export Data panel, click Clash Tests [icon]. Alternatively, in the expanded list of tests at the top of the Clash Detective window, select Export Clash Test from the Import/Export Clash Tests drop-down menu [icon].

21. Browse to a temporary directory (for example, *C:\Temp*) and save the file as *Steel_Vents_ClashJMD.xml*.

Import a Clash Test

1. In the Autodesk Navisworks software, start a new Autodesk Navisworks file without saving *Heating Plant.nwd* to clear the file from the session.

2. Open the file *C:\Navisworks 2017 Essentials Class Files\Training\Examples\Heating Plant.nwd* again.

3. In the expanded list of tests at the top of the Clash Detective window, notice that only the empty Test1 clash is listed because the Steel-Vents test was not saved with the file.

4. In the expanded list of tests at the top of the Clash Detective window, select Import Clash Test from the Import/Export Clash Tests drop-down menu .

5. In the Import dialog box, browse to the saved XML file and click Open to import the file.

6. In the list of tests at the top of the Clash Detective window, select the imported clash test and select the Select tab. Click Run Test to run the imported clash test in this project file.

7. Close the file without saving.

Save a Custom Clash Test

1. Close the Autodesk Navisworks software.

2. Browse to the temporary directory (e.g., C:\Temp) and copy the previously exported file *Steel_Vents_ClashJMD.xml* to a new directory called *C:\Program Files\Autodesk\Navisworks Manage 2017\custom_clash_tests*.

3. Restart the Autodesk Navisworks software.

4. Open the file *C:\Navisworks 2017 Essentials Class Files\Training\Examples\Heating Plant.nwd* again.

5. In the expanded list of tests at the top of the Clash Detective window, notice that only the empty Test1 clash is listed because the Steel-Vents test was not saved with the file.

6. In the Clash Detective window, select the Select tab.

7. Under Settings, in the Type drop-down menu, select the custom clash test Steel_Vents_ClashJMD. Notice that most options in the Select tab are grayed out and cannot be selected.

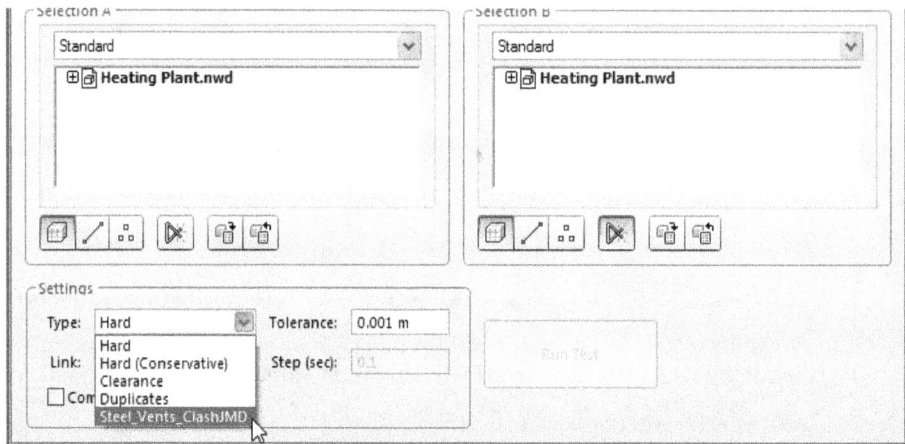

8. Click Run Test to run the custom clash test.

9. Select the Results tab to view the results of the Custom Clash test.

10. Close the file without saving.

Lesson: Laser Scan Data Clashing

Overview

Increasingly, users are bringing laser scan data into the Autodesk Navisworks software alongside traditional geometry based models. Laser scan data usually comes into the Autodesk Navisworks software as a point cloud. You can use Clash Detective with these two types of data to check for interferences.

Objective

After completing this lesson, you will be able to:

- Run a clash test using laser scan data.

Running a Clash Test with Laser Scan Data

The value of being able to clash as-built point clouds with new-build designs is immense.

Traditional hard clash testing of surfaces involves looking for intersections of triangles (that the 3D surfaces are made from). Similarly, when hard clashing points against lines with surfaces, there must be an interaction in order for a clash to be recognized. This can be difficult with points (laser point cloud). Even if the point is on the surface, it is not registered as a clash, as is not large enough to pass through the surface.

For this reason, when clashing points and surfaces, a clearance type test is used to specify a tolerance around each point. This better represents the point cloud and therefore it identifies any clashes.

Procedure: To Run a Clash Test with Laser Scan Data

1. In the Clash Detective window, select the Select tab.

2. Define the files that are to be clash tested. In one pane, select the point cloud data file and click Points ⬚ to clash test the point cloud. Clear the other clash items. In the second pane, select the surface model and click Surfaces ⬚ to clash test the point cloud data against surface data.

3. In the Settings area, set Type to Clearance and assign the required Tolerance value.

4. Click Run Test to run the clash test.

Exercise: Clash Testing Geometry Against Laser Scan Data

1. Open the file *C:\Navisworks 2017 Essentials Class Files\Training\Examples\Misc\Point Cloud Surface Clash.nwd.*

2. In the Saved Viewpoints window, click the Clash viewpoint.

3. Select the Home tab and click Clash Detective in the Tools panel, if it is not already displayed.

4. In the Clash Detective window, select the Select tab.

5. In the Selection A pane, expand Point Cloud Surface Clash.nwd and select *PointCloud Facade.nwd.* Click Points to clash test the point cloud. Clear the other clash items.

6. In the Selection B pane, expand Point Cloud Surface Clash.nwd and select *Simple Duct Model.nwd.* Click Surfaces to clash test surface items. Clear the other clash items.

7. In the Settings area, set Type to Hard and Tolerance to 0.000m.

8. Click Run Test to run the clash test.

   Zero clashes are found even though you can see the ducting coming through the façade of the building.

9. In the Select tab, in the Settings area, change Type to Clearance and set the Tolerance to 0.001m.

10. Click Run Test again. This time 1 clash is found.

11. In the Results tab notice that the section of ducting has now been detected as being within 1mm of a point on the surface of the building.

12. Close the file without saving.

Lesson: Methods for Testing and Resolving Clashes

Overview

The Hold function in the Autodesk Navisworks software can be extremely useful in conjunction with Clash Detective. You can pick up objects and move them about the model to check for any clashes (for example, to see if a piece of machinery can be moved in or out of a building for maintenance or replacement). As an alternative you can also use SwitchBack to return to the source data, make changes, and update the changes in the Autodesk Navisworks software to resolve clashes.

Objective

After completing this lesson, you will be able to:

- Use the Hold function to temporarily move objects to a different position.
- Use the SwitchBack function to dynamically update and view clashed objects.

> SwitchBack requires the source CAD package to be on the same computer and running when SwitchBack is used.

Holding and Releasing Objects

When you navigate around a model in the Autodesk Navisworks software, it is possible to pick up or hold selected items and move them around the model. This tool is best for working through what-if scenarios to adjust objects to resolve clashing. For example, you might want to relocate an item and rerun a clash test based on its new position.

Procedure: To Hold and Release Objects

1. Select the objects you want to hold in either the Scene View or the Selection Tree.

2. Select the Item Tools context-sensitive tab. On the Hold panel, click Hold ![icon]. The selected objects are now held and move with you through the model when you use navigation tools, such as Walk, Pan, etc.

3. To release the held objects, in the Item Tools tab, on the Hold panel, click Hold ![icon] again.

    Tip: If you want to reset the objects to their original positions, on the Item Tools tab, in the Transform panel, click Reset Transform ![icon].

Using SwitchBack in Clash Detective

SwitchBack is a feature that you can use in multiple tools in the Autodesk Navisworks software. By using SwitchBack in Clash Detective, you can run a clash test, step through the clash results, and switch directly back to the originating CAD package for any items you need to change to resolve the clash.

Procedure: To Use the SwitchBack Test Option

1. Launch the file's source software package and the Autodesk Navisworks software.

2. Prepare the source software to enable switchback.

    -   **AutoCAD -** At the command line, enter **NWLOAD**.
    -   **Microstation -** Click Utilities > Key In. In the Key-In dialog box, enter **mdl enter nwexport11** to load the nwexport plugin.
    -   **Autodesk Inventor -** Open the Autodesk Inventor software.
    -   **Autodesk Revit -** To initialize in the Autodesk Revit software, open a project or start a new one, and click Add-Ins tab > External Tools > Navisworks SwitchBack to enable it. You can now close the project, but do not close the Autodesk Revit software.

3. In the Clash Detective window, select the Results tab.

4. Select the result to be reviewed.

5. Expand the Items area at the bottom of the Results tab. The clashing Items from the selected clash are highlighted. Reselect items in the Item 1 pane, if required. Click SwitchBack. The file is opened in its source software application.

6.   Make the required changes in the source application file and save it.

7.   Return to the Clash Detective Results tab again. Reselect the item in the Item 2 pane, if required, and click Switchback to edit this item.

8.   Make the required changes in the source application file and save it.

9.   Return to the Autodesk Navisworks software and Refresh the file so that the Autodesk Navisworks file reflects the changes made in the source application file. Re-run the clash test, as required.

Exercise: Clash Testing and Moving Objects

1. Open the file *C:\Navisworks 2017 Essentials Class Files\Training\Examples\Ship Complete.nwd*.

2. Select the Home tab and click Clash Detective in the Tools panel, if it is not already displayed.

3. In the Clash Detective window, select the Select tab. This clash test checks for all interferences with the piping against the entire ship.

4. In the Selection A pane, select the _150_M layer. This selects all of the yellow piping.

5. In the Selection B pane, select *ShipComplete.nwd* to select the entire ship.

6. Click Surfaces in both panes to clash test surface items.

7. In the Settings area, select a Hard clash Type and set a Tolerance of 5mm (0.005m).

8. Select the Rules tab. Add a checkmark to Items in same layer (the piping is all drawn on the same layer).

9. Select the Select tab. Click Run Test to run the clash test.

10. In the Results tab, 28 clashes are listed.

11. Scroll to and select Clash26. The flange passes through the floor.

12. Under the Display Settings pane, expand the Viewpoint drop-down list and select Manual. The Manual option enables you to navigate the scene without overwriting the view of this clash.

13. Pan the scene to see the top of the flange through the floor.

14. Select the Home tab and expand the Select & Search panel. Set the resolution to Layer from the Selection Resolution drop-down menu.

15. Select the flange (which includes all the pipe work in the layer).

16. In the Saved Viewpoints window, select PipingSystemToMove.

17. Select the Item Tools tab. On the Hold panel, click Hold to hold all of the selected items (for example, the section of the piping system above the floor).

18. Use Pan to raise the floor above the section of piping. (Note that there is a top and bottom surface to the floor. Both need to be moved above the piping system.)

19. In the Item Tools tab, on the Hold panel, click Hold again to release the held items.

    By moving these objects, the model has effectively changed.

20. In Clash Detective, run the clash tests again on the modified model. Depending on how you moved the floor, you might have more or fewer clashes.

21. In the Results tab, notice that some clashes are Resolved ⟳ as a result of lowering this section of piping. However, other Active clashes have been added.

This method obviously does not alter the original CAD drawings. However, it is a quick and simple way to test a possible solution after discovering a clash. The design team could then be advised to revise this section of piping by lowering it a specified distance.

Lesson: Time-Based Clashing

Overview

Time-based clashing combines the main functions of TimeLiner and Clash Detective to provide an additional cost saving feature. Project models can now include the representation of temporary items such as work packages, ships, cranes, installations, etc. Such objects are added into the TimeLiner project and scheduled to appear and disappear at particular locations, over specific periods of time.

As these work package objects "move" around a project site based on a TimeLiner schedule, two work package objects could, at some point in the schedule, take up the same space, or "clash." With Time-based clashing, this can be checked automatically throughout the lifetime of a project. The time and cost savings could be considerable.

When a time-based clash session is run, at each step of a TimeLiner sequence, Clash Detective is used to check to see if a clash has occurred. If it has, a date of when that clash took place is logged, along with the task that caused the clash. Work package objects can be rescheduled to eliminate such a clash.

Objective

After completing this lesson, you will be able to:

- Run and interpret the results of time-based clashes.

Preparation

- Each work package needs to be modeled covering the area or volume required (for example, semi-transparent blocks).

- These work packages are also created as tasks in the project scheduling software and linked to TimeLiner (see Linking to a Project File), or the work package tasks can be created manually (see Creating Tasks).

- In TimeLiner, task types need to be created in the Configure tab, to represent the different work package types (similar to the task types of Construct and Demolish), for example, Create a task type WP1, Start Appearance (Red 90%), End Appearance (Hide), etc.

Procedure: To Run a Time-Based Clash Test

1. Open the project model file that includes the work package tasks.

2. On the Home tab in the Tools panel, click TimeLiner ⬚, if the TimeLiner window is not already displayed.

3. Select the Tasks tab. Verify that the work package tasks are displayed (active).

4. Select the Configure tab, verify the task types have been created to match the work packages.

5. Select the Simulate tab. Play the simulation to view the work packages and verify that they are displayed in the correct location and during the correct periods of time.

6. Select the Home tab and click Clash Detective ⬚ in the Tools panel, if not already displayed. (keep TimeLiner open). Select the Select tab. At the top of the Selection A and Selection B panes, select Sets in the drop-down list. Select the Work Package Sets that were created.

7. In the Settings area, select TimeLiner from the Link drop-down menu.

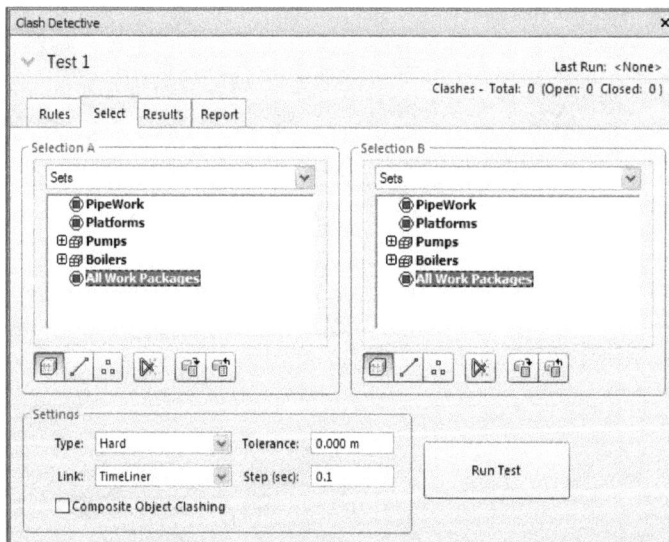

8. Click Run Test. The number of clashes are displayed on the Results tabs.

9. In the Display Settings area, select options as required (suggested options include: Auto Reveal, Hide Other, and Simulation).

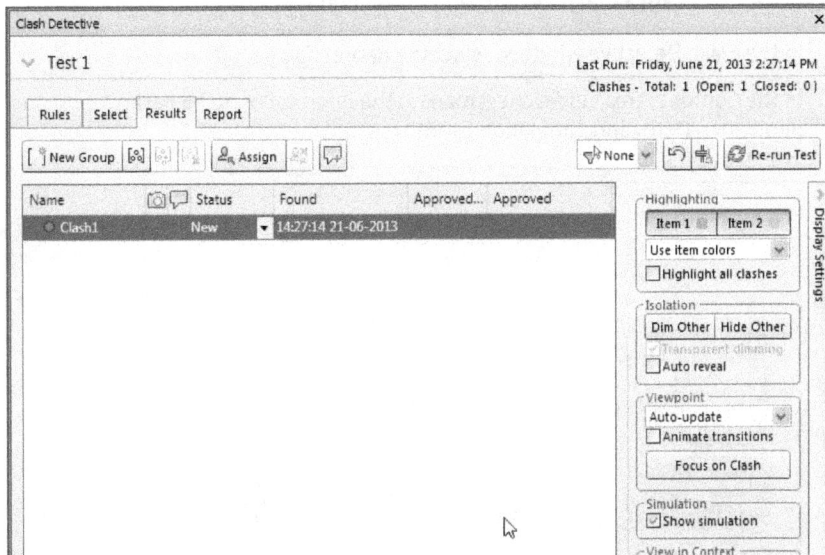

10. Select a clash and scroll the results area to the right to see its details. Continue to review the remaining clashes, as required.

As with other task scheduling issues, the work package tasks can be rescheduled to avoid clashes.

Note: The selected clash is displayed in the scene and in the Simulate tab, where its position on the timeline is displayed.

Clash Detective with TimeLiner Report

You can produce a Clash Detective report that includes information so that planners can adjust the project schedules independent from the Autodesk Navisworks software.

Procedure: To Create a Clash Report with TimeLiner Data

1. In the Clash Detective window, select the Report Tab.

2. In the Contents area, add a checkmark to the information to be in the report, including Simulation Dates and Simulation Event.

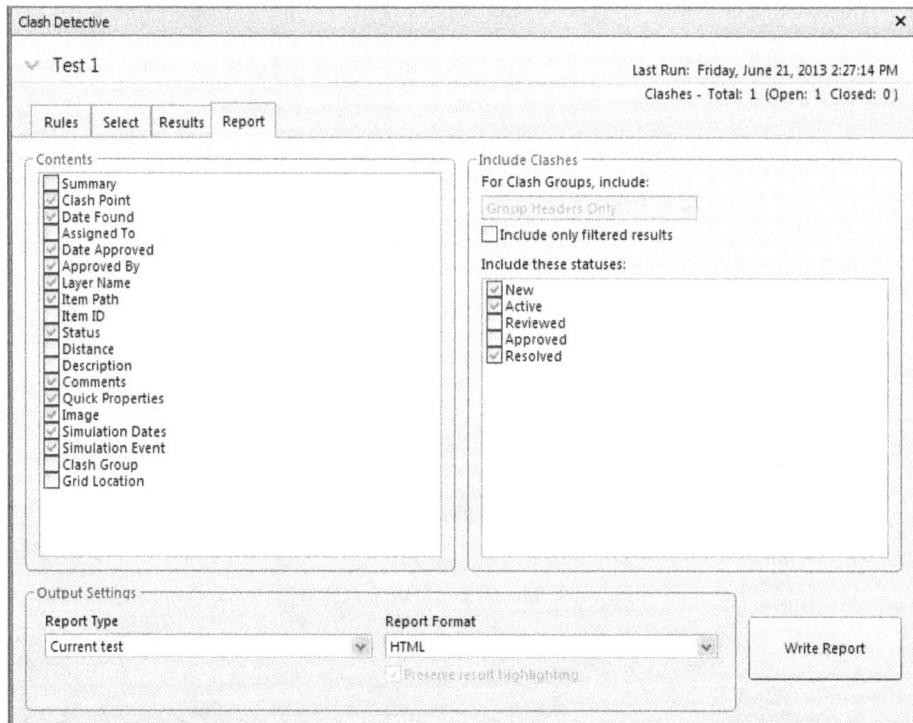

Tip: By only including "need to know" information, the report is shorter and easier to read than one including all possible information.

Note: The options selected in the Contents area are maintained for future use.

3. In the Include Clashes area, add a checkmark to those clashes required for the report.

4. Select a Report Type from the drop-down menu.

5. Select a Report Format (suggest HTML) from the drop-down menu.

6. Click Write Report.

7. In the Save As window, select the location, enter a filename, and click Save. The report can be viewed in the appropriate software.

   Tip: It might be helpful to include information in the report about each work package in the clash, in addition to the details of the clash. This can be set up in Global Options.

Procedure: To Use the Global Option Settings

1. Click Application Menu ![N] > Options > Interface > Quick Properties > Definitions.

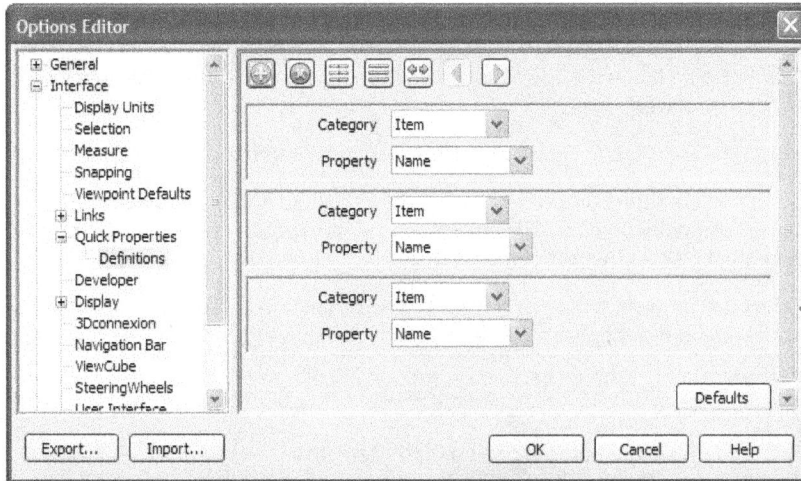

2. In the Options Editor dialog box, in the first Category field, select TimeLiner.

3. In the first Property field, select Attach to Task: 1.

4. Continue to add definitions with TimeLiner in the Category field. Under Properties, select other properties from the drop-down list as required (for example, Attach to Task Start (Actual): 1).

   Tip: To add additional definition fields, click ![icon].

5. Click OK.

   The information in the selected properties is included in reports for all relevant work package tasks if Quick Properties is included in the Report contents list.

Exercise: Conducting and Reporting a Time Based Clash Test

1. Open the file *C:\Navisworks 2017 Essentials Class Files\Training\Examples\Boiler Room\ Boiler Room.nwd*.

2. In the Saved Viewpoints window, click the Work Package Maintenance Schedule viewpoint to view the work packages. These have been modeled as semi-transparent flat red, yellow, purple, and green blocks on the floor.

   The red blocks are WP1, the purple blocks are WP2 (2a and 2b, one task for each boiler by the same people), WP3 is yellow, and WP4 is green.

3. On the Home tab in the Tools panel, click TimeLiner , if the TimeLiner window is not already displayed.

4. Select the Tasks tab to view tasks that have been created to simulate a maintenance schedule.

5. Select the Configure tab. In the Task list, view the Start and End appearance settings specific to these temporary objects (WP1->WP4). Also view the Start and End Appearance for the Construct task for the rest of the model.

6. Select the Simulate tab. Click Play to run the simulation and display the Work packages appearing and disappearing when scheduled to do so.

   At the top right of the scene, there is an overlap between WP2b and WP4 (deliberately difficult to see).

7. Select the Tasks tab before opening Clash Detective.

8. Select the Home tab and click Clash Detective in the Tools panel, if it is not already displayed (keep TimeLiner open).

9. Select the Select tab in the Clash Detective. In both panes, select the Sets option in the drop-down list. Select the All Work Packages set in both panes to run a clash between all work packages.

10. Click Run Test to run the clash test. Five clashes are found. This is inaccurate, as these work packages are not all in the scene at the same time.

11. Select the Select tab. In the Settings area, select TimeLiner from the Link drop-down menu.

12. Click Run Test again to run the time-based clash test. This time only 1 active clash is found. This is an accurate result based on the temporary nature of the work packages.

13. In the Results tab, select Clash 2 and clear all Display Settings options. The clash identifies two colliding work packages, WP2b and WP4, in the scene.

14. In the Display Settings area, select Hide Other in the Isolation drop-down and select Show simulation in the Simulation area. (In the TimeLiner simulation, this displays the point at which the clash occurs.)

15. Select the TimeLiner Simulate tab. Notice the simulation scroll bar is moved to the point at which the clash occurs. The work packages that have clashed are listed under Active Tasks.

Create a Time-Based Clash Report

1. In the Clash Detective window, select the Report tab to define the report contents and write a report.

2. In the Contents area, select the Simulation Dates and Simulation Event options to also include this information in the report.

3. In the Include Clashes area, select New, Active, and Resolved.

4. In the Report Type area, select Current test.

5. In the Report Format area, select HTML.

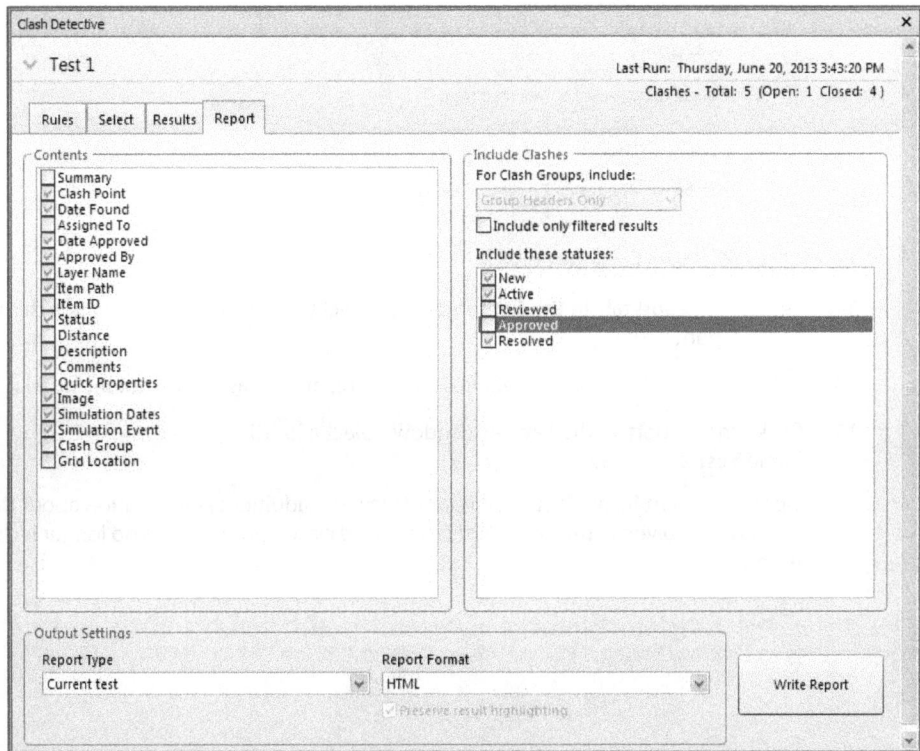

6. Click Write Report. In the Save As window, select a location, (for example, *C:\Temp*) and save with the name **Test 1**.

7. Use Windows Explorer to locate and open the report in Internet Explorer. The report displays information about the active and resolved clashes. It might be helpful for the report to include Start and End time information for each work package involved in the clash.

8. Click Application Menu ⬛ > Options > Interface > Quick Properties > Definitions.

9. Ensure that three definition fields are listed, if not, click ⬚ to add one.

10. In the Options Editor, in the first Category field, select TimeLiner. In the first Property field, select Attached to Task: 1.

11. In the second Category field, select TimeLine. In the second Property field, select Attached to Task Start (Actual): 1.

12. In the third Category field, select TimeLiner. In the third Property field, select Attached to Task End (Actual): 1.

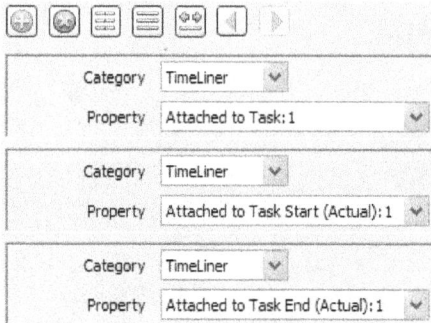

13. Click OK to save these settings.

14. Select the Report tab. In the Contents area, select Quick Properties to include this information in the report.

15. In the Include Clashes area, clear Resolved so resolved clashes are not included.

16. Click Write Report. In the Save As window, select a location, for example, *C:\Temp* with the name **Test 2**.

Open the report in Internet Explorer and view the additional information about the work packages involved in the clash. Notice resolved clash information is no longer included in this report.

Autodesk Rendering

Autodesk Rendering is a general-purpose rendering tool that enables you to customize a model to create physically correct renderings. Rendering shades the model's geometry using the lighting you have set up and materials you have applied, and incorporates sun and sky environment settings that you have selected.

Objectives

After completing this chapter, you will be able to:

- Open the Autodesk Rendering window and understand its interface.
- Identify the key steps in the rendering workflow.
- Understand the panels in the Autodesk Rendering window's Materials tab and their purpose.
- Select materials from the Autodesk Material Libraries and add them to the document library.
- Apply document materials to objects in a model.
- Open the Material Editor and understand its interface.
- Create a new material using the Material Editor window.
- Edit a material using the Material Editor.
- Understand the fields in the Autodesk Rendering window's Material Mapping tab and their purpose.
- Edit material mapping values for a material.
- Understand the fields in the Autodesk Rendering window's Lighting tab and their purpose.
- Create lights in an Autodesk Navisworks scene.
- Edit lights in an Autodesk Navisworks scene.
- Understand how natural lighting can be controlled and used in a scene.
- Understand the fields in the Autodesk Rendering window's Environment tab and their purpose.
- Enable the use and display of the sun and sky lighting effects in the Scene view.

- Edit the properties associated with the sun.
- Edit the sky properties to account for atmospheric conditions.
- Understand how exposure can be controlled and used in a scene.
- Understand the fields in the Autodesk Rendering window's Environment tab that deal with exposure and their purpose.
- Enable the use exposure in the Scene view.
- Edit exposure properties.
- Append a ground plane to a model and move it to the correct position.
- Render and save photorealistic images using the Autodesk Rendering tool in both Autodesk Navisworks and Autodesk A360.

Lesson: Autodesk Rendering Overview

Overview

This lesson describes how to open the Autodesk Rendering window in the Autodesk Navisworks software. It also introduces you to the tabs available in this window. Additionally, the overall process of rendering a photorealistic image is introduced.

Objectives

After completing this lesson, you will be able to:

- Open the Autodesk Rendering window and understand its interface.
- Identify the key steps in the rendering workflow.

Overview of the Autodesk Rendering Environment

The Autodesk Rendering window enables you to create, edit, and apply materials, lights, and environments to your Autodesk Navisworks files. To open the Autodesk Rendering window, select the

Home tab and click Autodesk Rendering 🖼 in the Tools panel. Alternatively, on the View tab, expand the Windows options and click Autodesk Rendering in the drop-down menu. You can also

select the Render tab and click Autodesk Rendering 🖼 on the System panel. The Autodesk Rendering window contains multiple commands and tabs. Each tab is broken into areas, as shown below for the Materials tab.

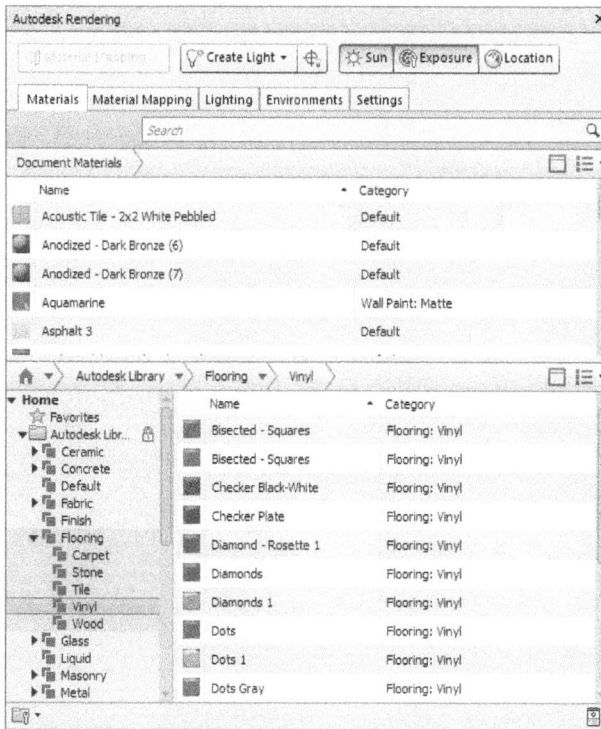

Autodesk Rendering Window Layout

The Autodesk Rendering window contains the Rendering toolbar and the following five tabs:

- **Materials** – Enables you to navigate and manage material collections, known as libraries, provided by Autodesk, or create custom libraries for specific projects. The default material library includes a variety of materials, which can be selected and applied to your model. You can also use this tab to create new materials based on already existing materials or edit existing materials.

- **Material Mapping** – Enables you to adjust the orientation of the texture to fit the shape of the object. This feature is only recommended for advanced users.

- **Lighting** – Enables you to view the lights already added to the model and to customize the lighting properties.
- **Environments** – Enables you to customize the Sun, Sky, and Exposure properties.
- **Settings** - Enables you to change the Render Style presets. You can select from a range of default quality presets, or customize the render settings.

The buttons along the top of the Autodesk Rendering window, in the Rendering toolbar, enable you to define material mapping, create lights, toggle light glyphs, or enable/disable sun, exposure, and location settings. Selecting any of these options directly activates the appropriate tab for the button.

Overview of the Rendering Workflow

Using the Autodesk Rendering tools available in the Autodesk Navisworks software enables you to create highly detailed and photorealistic images. The rendered output displays directly in the Scene View and can be exported for use in presentations or other software applications.

Procedure: To Render an Autodesk Navisworks Scene

1. Open the Autodesk Rendering window.

2. Set up the scene.

    - Apply materials and material mappings to the model geometry. You can apply materials to objects selected in the Scene View.
    - Add artificial and natural lights to the model. Photometric lights (artificial lighting) accurately define lights in a scene. Sun and Sky lighting simulates the effect of sunlight and sky illumination (natural lighting).
    - Customize the exposure settings to control how real-world luminance values are converted into an image.
    - Orient the Scene view with the required orientation and zoom level.

3. Select the rendering quality.

4. Render the image.

5. Save the rendered image.

> In previous versions of the Autodesk Navisworks software, there was another rendering environment called Presenter. This tool has been removed from the software. Any materials that were assigned using the Presenter tool will have to be reassigned using Autodesk Materials.

Lesson: Adding Materials to a Model

Overview

This lesson describes the interface for working with materials, how to add library materials to the document, and how to apply materials to items in the model.

Objectives

After completing this lesson, you will be able to:

- Understand the panels in the Autodesk Rendering window's Materials tab and their purpose.
- Select materials from the Autodesk Material Libraries and add them to the document library.
- Apply document materials to objects in a model.

Materials Overview

The materials available in the Autodesk Navisworks software and other Autodesk products represent actual materials, such as concrete, wood, and glass. These materials can be applied to a model to give objects a more realistic appearance and behavior. Autodesk provides a library of predefined materials. Use the Materials tab on the Autodesk Rendering window to browse materials and apply them to your model. You can also create and modify textures to suit your needs. Once materials have been assigned to a model they are displayed in views and rendered images.

The Materials Tab

In the Autodesk Rendering window, select the Materials tab. The Materials tab enables you to navigate and manage materials. When active, the Materials tab provides you with access to the following:

- Document Materials Panel
- Library Panel

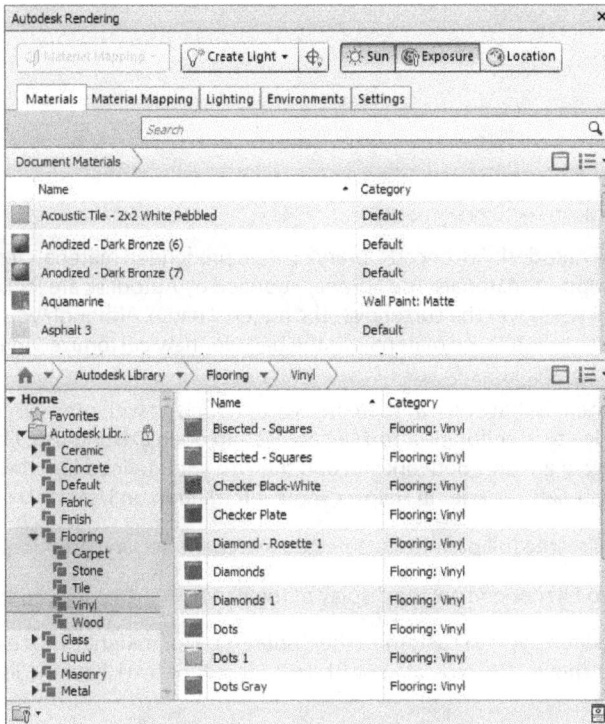

Library Panel

The Library panel in the lower half of the Autodesk Rendering dialog box provides access to the library of materials (standard and advanced) that are provided with the Autodesk Navisworks software. Materials are located in the Library and are then added to the current model for use. To navigate the Library panel, expand the Autodesk Library or Autodesk Advanced Library folders in the left-pane and then further expand any required nodes to find the required material categories. Select the category in the pane on the left to display its list of materials. Once a material has been located, select it in the pane on the right. The buttons for applying or editing the material become available when you hover the cursor over the material swatch. The list of materials can be sorted by selecting the column headers in this panel.

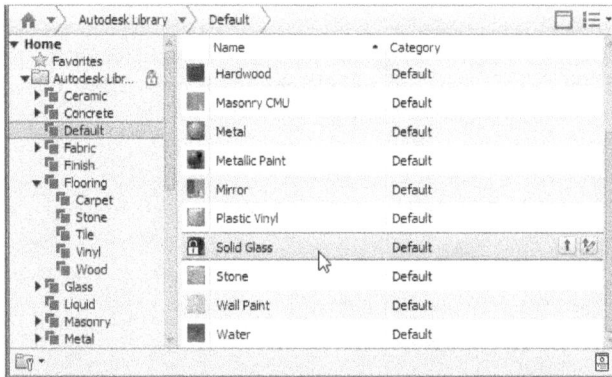

The following libraries are available in the Library panel:

- The Autodesk Library and the Autodesk Advanced Library contain predefined materials for use by Autodesk applications that support materials. The libraries supplied by Autodesk are locked, as indicated by a lock icon when you hover the cursor over the material name. Although you cannot edit the Autodesk library, you can use these materials as the basis for new customized materials that you can save in the user library.

- The User Library contains materials that you can share between models or with other users. You can copy, move, rename, or delete user libraries. You can access and open existing user libraries that have been created locally or are on a network and add them to your defined libraries on the Materials tab. Refer to Use Materials Libraries in Help for more information on User Libraries.

The header for the Library panel lists the full path to the selected material category. Additionally, the header provides ☐ and ☰▾ to filter or control the display of the panel. ☐ enables you to show and hide the Library tree. ☰▾ enables you to customize the display type for materials. For example, you can control the library that is shown, the type of view (thumbnail, list, or text), how the list is sorted, and the thumbnail size.

Document Materials

The upper portion of the Autodesk Rendering dialog box lists the materials that have been included for use in the document. These materials can consist of materials that have been applied or have not yet been applied. Library materials must be added to the Document Materials panel if they are to be used in the model.

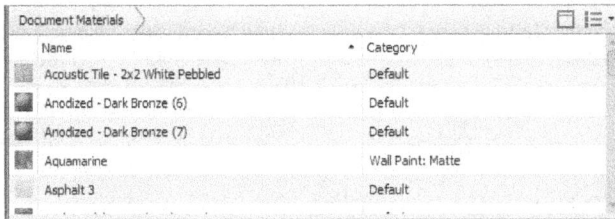

The header for the Document Materials panel also contains and . These icons enable you to show or hide the Document Materials panel and customize the display type for the document materials, respectively.

Adding Materials to the Document

When a model is first created in the Autodesk Navisworks software it does not contain any materials, unless they are brought in with the source CAD file. To assign materials to objects in the model, materials must be selected from a library and added to the document.

Procedure: To Add Materials to the Document Materials Panel

1. Browse to the required material in the library folder.

    Tip: Consider using the Search field at the top of the Materials tab to locate specific materials in the library. The search is conducted in both panels at the same time and can be used to locate both the library and document materials.

2. Select the material in the pane on the right and click to add the material to the current document. Alternatively, right-click the material and select Add to > Document Materials. A copy of this material is now available in the Document Materials panel for use in the current model.

    Note: If an object has been preselected in the scene, the material is also assigned to that object.

    Tip: Click to add the material to the current document and immediately open the material in the Material Editor. If an object is selected, it also applies it. Refer to the Lesson: Creating and Editing Materials for more information on editing materials.

Applying Material to Model Objects

Once a model has been brought into the Autodesk Navisworks software and materials have been added to the document, you can add materials to the objects in the model. You can apply materials to objects that have been selected in the Scene View or in the Selection Tree.

> Materials are applied to an item, layer, etc., depending on the resolution setting of the Selection tool. To change the selection setting, expand the Select & Search panel on the Home tab and set the resolution from the Selection Resolution drop-down menu, as required. Select the panel heading to collapse the panel.

Procedure: To Apply a Material to Items in the Scene

1. Select items in the scene using any of the following techniques:

   - Select individual items directly in the Scene View, or press and hold CTRL to select multiple files.
   - Select individual items directly in the Selection Tree, or press and hold CTRL to select multiple items in the Selection Tree. To select a range of files, press and hold SHIFT while selecting two items to select both items and all of the items listed between them.
   - Select all of the items included in a Selection or Search Set by selecting a name in the Sets window.

   Tip: Using search sets has the added benefit of materials being easily applied to items that are added to the model at a later stage.

2. In the Autodesk Rendering window, use either of the following techniques:

   - In the Document Materials panel, right-click the required material and click Apply to Selection.
   - In the Library panel, navigate to and select the required material and click 🔼 . Once selected, the material is copied to the Document Materials panel and assigned to the model if an object is selected.
   - Click and drag the required material directly onto an item from either the Document Materials panel or the Library panel. If you click and drag from the Library panel, the material is also added to the Document Materials panel.

3. Press <ESC> to clear item selection and view the item(s) with the applied materials.

Once a model has had materials assigned to it, that material can be overwritten with another material by selecting the object again and assigning a new material. Alternatively, you can remove the material that was previously assigned by selecting the object, right-clicking and selecting Reset Item>Reset Appearance.

Rename and Manage Materials

Materials that are copied from the library panel to the Document Materials panel, have the same name as the one in the library by default. Once copied to the document you can maintain this name or rename it to something more recognizable for easy reference, reuse, and management. Renaming materials is recommended if a library material is edited to help identify that it is different than the material in the library. Once materials have been customized in the Document Materials panel, they can be saved for reuse in other documents using the Favorites library.

Procedure: To Rename a Material

1.   Right-click the material in the Document Materials panel and select Rename.

2.   Enter a descriptive name and press ENTER.

Procedure: To Manage Materials in the Favorites Library

1.   Right-click the material in the Document Materials panel and select Add to > Favorites.

2.   Navigate to the top of the Library tree and select the Favorites library node. The added Document Material displays in the pane on the right.

3.   To further organize materials in the Favorites library, right-click the Favorites node and select Create Category to create a new category. Right-click and select Rename and enter a new descriptive name for the category. Sub-categories can also be created. Materials can be dragged and dropped between categories, as required.

   Tip: Once a category has been added to the Favorites library you can add to the top-level or a category when you use the Add to option in the Document Materials panel.

Materials that are deleted from the Document Materials panel are also cleared from any object to which it has previously been assigned.

Lesson: Creating and Editing Materials

Overview

This lesson describes the overall process of creating a new material and editing it. Additionally you learn about the Material Editor interface that is used to create and edit materials.

Objectives

After completing this lesson, you will be able to:

- Open the Material Editor and understand its interface.
- Create a new material using the Material Editor window.
- Edit a material using the Material Editor.

Material Editor

A material is defined by its properties. The available properties depend on the selected material type. Use the Material Editor to review and edit the properties of a material. You cannot modify materials in the Autodesk materials library, but you can use them as a basis for new materials. To open the Material Editor, use one of the following techniques:

- Double-click a material in the Document Materials panel.
- Right-click a material in the Document Materials panel and select Edit.
- Select a material in the Autodesk Library, and click 🖫. This option adds the material to the Document Materials panel and opens the Material Editor at the same time. If an object is selected it also assigns it to the model.

The Material Editor contains two tabs: Appearance and Information.

Appearance Tab

The Appearance tab contains the controls for editing the material properties. The options available on this tab change depending on the type of material that is selected.

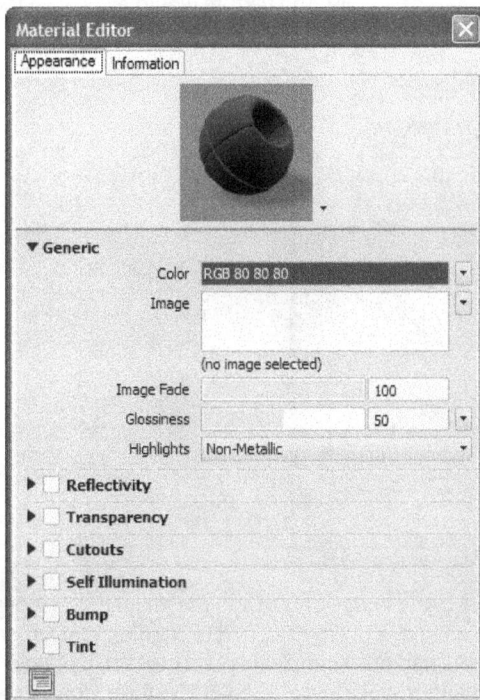

The following are consistent tools that are available for all material types when using the Materials Editor:

- Click ⬚ adjacent to the thumbnail image to access a list of options for changing the shape and render quality of the thumbnail preview.

- ▤ at the bottom of the Material Editor enables you to toggle the display of the Autodesk Rendering window on and off.

The following categories can be customized to fully define a material's properties. The Generic category is a required entry, but the remaining categories can be selected to activate them or not and then values can be assigned for them by expanding them.

- **Generic**
  - **Color** – Assigns the color of the material. Select in the field to open the Color dialog box to define the color.

    Tip: The color of a material on an object is different in different areas of the object. For example, when you look at a red sphere, it does not appear to be uniformly red. The sides away from the light appear to be a darker red than the sides facing the light. The reflection highlight displays the lightest red. In fact, if the red sphere is very shiny, its highlight might appear to be white.

  - **Image** – You can assign textures to a material's color. The texture would display on the assigned material color. Two types of textures can be used: Image (1) and Procedural-based (2).

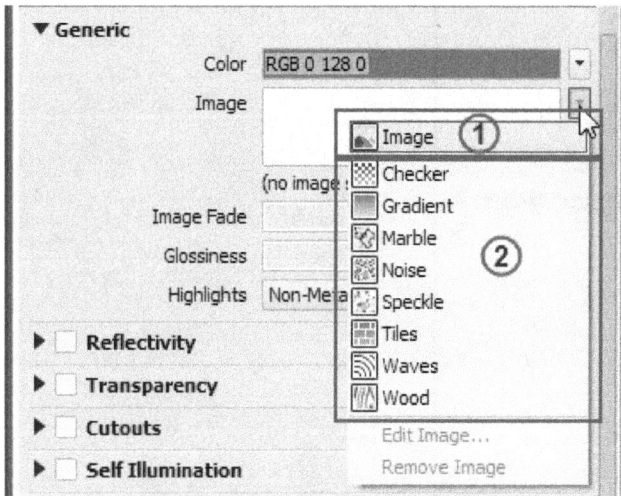

  - Image textures (1) are assigned using the Image option and use an image to represent a texture. For example, you can use an image of wood, concrete conglomerate, metal, or carpet. You can edit the texture scale and other properties to customize it to your model. The product provides a library of images that you can use with textures. You can also add your own textures (BMP, RLE, DIB, GIF, JFIF, JPG, JPEG, PCX, PNG, TGA, or TIFF).

- Procedural- based textures (2) are selected from the predefined list. They are generated using a mathematical algorithm to represent repetitive textures, such as tiles or wood. You can adjust the texture properties for the required effect. For example, you can adjust tile size and mortar spacing for a brick material or change the spacing of the grain in a wood material. The types of settings for a procedural texture vary. You nest them to add depth and complexity to the material.

Marble   Checker   Speckle   Noise

> The Autodesk Navisworks software has a Texture Editor that can be used to edit either image or procedural-based textures. To open the Texture Editor, double-click the image field when a texture has been assigned. Refer to The Texture Editor in Help for more information on using the Texture Editor.

- **Image Fade** – Controls the composite between the base color and the image. The image fade property is only editable if an image is used.
- **Glossiness** – The reflective quality of the material defines the degree of glossiness or dullness. To simulate a glossy surface, the material has a small highlight, and its specular color is lighter, perhaps even white. A duller material has a larger highlight that is closer to the main color of the material.
- **Highlights** – Controls the means of deriving specular highlights of the material. The Metallic setting disperses light according to the angle of the light on the object (anisotropic). Metallic highlights are the color of the material. Non-metallic are the color of the lights hitting the material.

■ **Reflectivity** – Reflectivity simulates a scene reflected on the surface of a shiny object. For reflectivity maps to render well, the material should be shiny, and the reflection image itself should have a high resolution (at least 512 by 480 pixels). The Direct and Oblique sliders control the level of reflections and the intensity of the specular highlight on surfaces.

- **Transparency** – A completely transparent object allows the passage of light through it. At 1.0, the material is completely transparent, and at 0.0, the material is completely opaque. The effect of transparency is best previewed against a patterned background. The Translucency and Index of Refraction properties only become editable when the Transparency value is greater than 0. A translucent object, such as frosted glass, lets some light pass through and scatters some light in the object. At 0.0, the material is not translucent and at 1.0, the material is as translucent as possible. The index of refraction controls the degree to which light rays are bent as they pass through the material and thus distort the appearance of objects on the other side of the object. For example, at 1.0, the object behind the transparent object is not distorted. At 1.5, the object is greatly distorted, as if it were seen through a glass marble.

- **Cutouts** – Cutout maps make the material partially transparent, giving a perforation effect based on a grayscale interpretation of a texture. You can select an image file to use for cutout mapping. Lighter areas of the map render as opaque and darker areas render as transparent. When you use transparency for frosting or translucent effects, reflectivity is maintained. Cutout areas are not reflective.

- **Self-illumination** – Self illumination maps make portions of an object appear to glow. For example, to simulate neon without using a light source, you could set a self illumination value greater than zero. No light is cast on other objects and the self-illuminated object does not receive shadows. White areas of the map render as fully self illuminating. Black areas render with no self illumination. Gray areas render as partially self illuminating, depending on the grayscale value.

  - Filter Color creates the effect of a color filter over the illuminated surface.
  - Luminance causes a material to simulate being lit in a photometric light source. How much light is emitted is determined by a value that you select in this field. The value is measured in photometric units. No light is cast on other objects.
  - Color temperature sets the color of the self illumination.

- **Bump** – You can select an image file or procedural maps to use for mapping. Bump mapping makes an object appear to have a bumpy or irregular surface. When you render an object with a bump-mapped material, lighter (whiter) areas of the map appear to be raised and darker (blacker) areas appear to be low. If the image is in color, the gray-scale value of each color is used. Bump mapping increases rendering time significantly but adds to the realism.

  - Use the Amount slider and value field to adjust the degree/height of bumpiness. Higher values render as higher relief and low values render as low relief. Grayscale images make effective bump maps.

  Tip: Use bump maps when you want to take the smoothness off a surface, or to create an embossed look. However, the depth effect of a bump map is limited because it does not affect the profile of the object and cannot be self-shadowing. If you want extreme depth in a surface, you should use modeling techniques instead. The bumps are a simulation created by perturbing face normals before the object is rendered. Because of this, bumps do not appear on the silhouette of bump-mapped objects.

- **Tint** – Sets the hue and saturation value of the color mixed with white.

> When creating or editing materials other than the Generic type, the list of available options for customizing the material might vary slightly.

Information Tab

The Information tab contains general information on the material and its type.

- **Information** – This area enables you to specify the material name, provide a description of the material, and enter keywords or tags for the material. The keywords are used to search and filter materials displayed on the Materials tab.
- **About** – This area displays the type, version, and location of the material.
- **Texture Paths** – Displays the file path of the texture files associated with the material attribute.

Note: The About and Texture Paths areas are not editable, and the Texture Path information is only listed for those materials that have textures associated with them. The image below displays a generic material that does not have a texture.

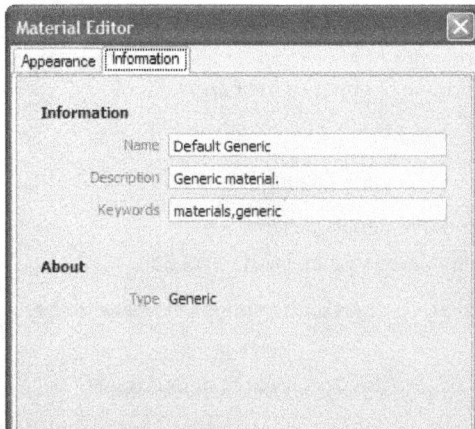

Creating Materials

As an alternative to using Autodesk Library or Autodesk Advanced Library materials in your models, you can also create your own custom materials to more accurately resemble the material finish of the items in a project.

Procedure: To Create a New Material

1. To initiate the creation of a new material, select an existing material from a library and add it to the Document Materials List using one of the following techniques:

    - Select the material in the pane on the right and click 🔼 to add the material to the current document.

    - Select the material in the pane on the right and click 📝 to add it to the current document and immediately open it in the Material Editor for editing.

    - Right-click the material and select Add to > Document Materials.

2. Double-click on the Material in the Document Materials list to open the Material Editor. If you used the 📝 icon to add the material, the Material Editor will already be open.

3.   Click the Appearance tab and modify the options in all of the required categories. The options available on this tab are dependent on the type of material being created. Ensure that the required categories are enabled by selecting the checkbox adjacent to its name.

4.   In the Material Editor, click the Information tab, and enter a name, description, and any required keywords for the material.

5.   Close the Material Editor to save the material to the Document Materials panel.

     Tip: Consider copying the material to a Favorites library for reuse in other documents.

Editing Materials

Materials can be edited at any time once they have been added to the Document Materials panel. Editing materials enables you to adjust the properties of Autodesk Library materials or any of the custom materials that have been created to improve or enhance their appearance.

Procedure: To Edit an Applied Material

1.   To open the Material Editor, use one of the following techniques:

     ▪   Double-click a material in the Document Materials panel.

     ▪   Right-click a material in the Document Materials panel and select Edit.

2.   Using the Material Editor, make the required changes to the options available in the Appearance and the Information tabs.

3.   Close the Material Editor to save the material to the Document Materials panel.

     Tip: If the material has been assigned to the model, its appearance updates to reflect the change.

Lesson: Material Mapping

Overview

This lesson describes the process of how to customize the default settings for how a material is mapped to an object in the Autodesk Navisworks scene. Adjusting material mapping is considered advanced functionality.

Objectives

After completing this lesson, you will be able to:

- Understand the fields in the Autodesk Rendering window's Material Mapping tab and their purpose.
- Edit material mapping values for a material.

Material Mapping Overview

Texture space describes the way in which a texture is applied to an item. For example, applying a cylindrical texture space to a pipe causes textures on the pipe to be rendered more naturally. An item's texture space might have been assigned from the original CAD application and stored in the native CAD file, or set up using the Material Mapping feature with the options of Box, Planar, Cylindrical, or Spherical. Each texture space option applies an imaginary bounding geometry around the item and *shrink-wraps* the texture as accurately as possible to the geometry under this bounding geometry.

When you have applied a texture to an item, the program determines the best fit from the following five available texture spaces:

- **Planar mapping** – Maps the image as if it were projected onto a 2D surface. The image is not distorted in the direction of projection, but is distorted if projected onto a curved surface and viewed from the side. The image is not scaled to the object. This is commonly used for flat faces.

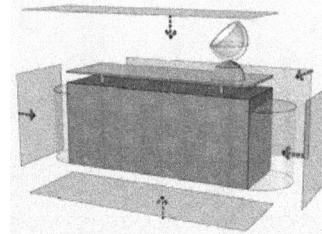

- **Box mapping** – Maps an image onto a box-like shape. The image is repeated on each side of the object.

- **Spherical mapping** – Maps an image onto a spherical object. The top and bottom edges of the map are compressed to a point at the *north and south poles* of the sphere.

- **Cylindrical mapping** – Maps an image onto a cylindrical object. The horizontal edges are wrapped together, but not the top and bottom edges. The height of the image is scaled along the cylinder axis.

- **Explicit mapping** – For objects that have explicit texture coordinates as a default part of their geometry, Autodesk Rendering uses these explicit textures rather than a texture space material mapping. Use this command to enable the Explicit texture coordinate rendering. This option is unavailable if the selected object doesn't have explicit UV coordinates.

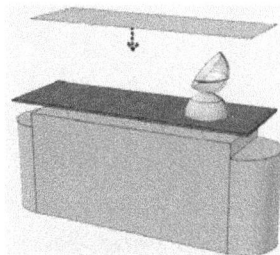

Planar Mapping   **Box Mapping**

Spherical Mapping   **Cylindrical Mapping**

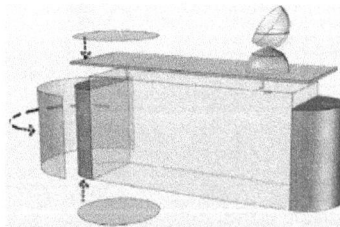

If the resulting map is not what is intended, you can edit the texture space using the options in the Material Mapping tab. The options available for editing depend on the selected material mapping option.

Material Mapping Tab

The texture space that is used when a textured material is assigned to an object is determined by the Autodesk Navisworks software. To change the type of texture space used, you must select the object in the scene and use the mapping type drop-down list. To edit the assigned texture space's setting, use the options on the Material Mapping tab. When an object has been selected in the scene and the Material Mapping tab is selected, you have access to the following:

- Material Mapping drop-down
- Material Mapping settings

Material Mapping Drop-Down

The Material Mapping drop-down list enables you to identify the current texture space setting used on the object and assign a new type. The current type is displayed by default in the Rendering toolbar. Select the drop-down list to access and select another type.

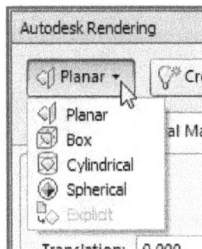

Material Mapping Settings

The Material Mapping tab provides fields that can be customized to further refine the mapping settings. The available fields are dependent on the active texture space setting. Changing the current texture space settings is only recommended for advanced users.

Adjusting Material Mapping

To adjust the material mapping you can change the texture space setting in the Rendering toolbar by selecting a new option in the Material Mapping drop-down. You can also adjust the fields that define the current mapping to adjust how a material map is placed, oriented, and scaled. You can only adjust material mapping for a single geometry item at a time. Geometry items are indicated on the Selection Tree using the following icons: ⚘ and ⬜.

Procedure: To Adjust the Material Mapping Settings

1. Select a geometry item in the Scene View or on the Selection Tree.

2. If no material has been previously added to the selected geometry, select the Materials tab in the Autodesk Rendering window, select a material, right-click and select Assign to Selection. Alternatively, you can click and drag the required material onto the item.

3. The current texture space setting is listed in the Rendering toolbar. (e.g., Box, Cylindrical, Spherical, Planar, or Explicit). If this current setting is not appropriate, select a new type appropriate for the geometry.

4. Use the fields on the Material Mapping tab to further adjust the mapping, as required. The results are available in the Scene View in real time.

> Refer to Adjusting Material Mapping in Help for more advanced information on material mapping.

Exercise: Adding Materials to a Model

Note: As of the printing of this training guide (September 2016), a noticeable software slowdown has been identified when completing this exercise. The slowdown occurs when selecting components in Navisworks Manage 2017 SP1&2. Autodesk will be resolving the issue in a later release of Navisworks.

1. Open the file *C:\Navisworks 2017 Essentials Class Files\Training\Examples\Rendering\ Autodesk_Hospital_Rendering.nwf.*

2. In the Home tab, in the Tools panel, click Autodesk Rendering 🗒 to open the Autodesk Rendering window.

    Tip: If the model opens and the grid lines appear, clear the grid from the display. To do this,

    select the View tab, and on the Grids & Levels panel, click Show Grid ⚓ .

Navigate to a Viewpoint and Add Materials.

1. In the Saved Viewpoints window, select Cafe to change the viewpoint to an internal view of one of the rooms in the model.

2. Select the Viewpoint tab. In the Render Style panel, expand Lighting and select Scene Lights. The Scene Lights option uses the lights that were defined in the source CAD model.

3. In the Render Style panel, expand Mode and select Full Render to ensure a smooth rendering that includes all of the materials.

4. In the Autodesk Rendering window, select the Materials tab. The Document Materials pane is populated with the materials that have been brought in from the source Autodesk Revit model.

5. In the Scene View, select the wall on the left side of the room. Ensure that the Selection Resolution is set to Geometry so that only the wall is selected.

6. In the Library panel of the Materials tab, expand the Autodesk Library and select the Wall Paint category. In the pane on the right, right-click the Aquamarine color and select Assign to Selection.

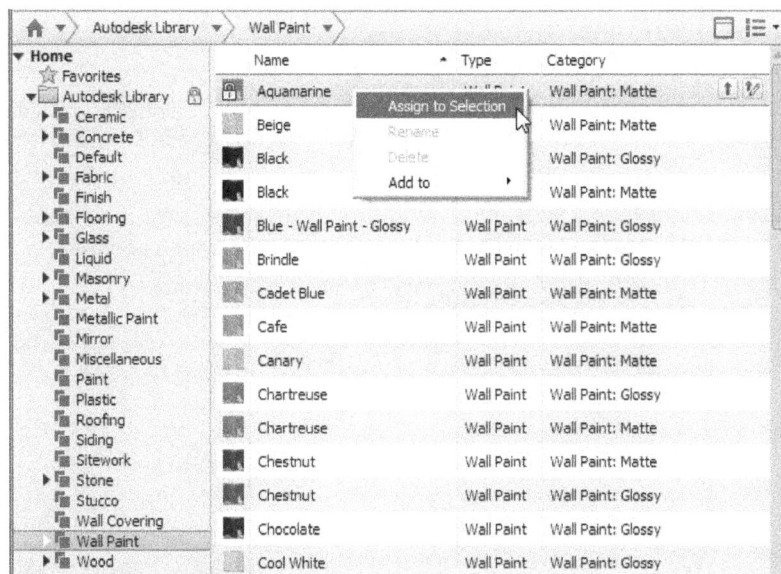

7. Clear the selection in the Scene View and notice that the Aquamarine Wall Paint material has been added to the wall. It has also been added to the Document Materials list near the top of the Materials tab.

8. In the Selection Tree, expand the Level 2 Furniture and select the Laminate-Linen, Matte object in one of the round dining tables.

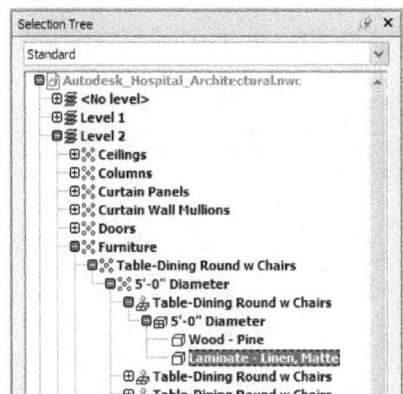

9. Select the Home tab. In the Select & Search panel, expand Select Same and select Same Name. All of the tables in the room are selected.

10. In the Material Library, expand the Stone > Marble categories. In the pane on the right, right-click the Coarse Polished-White material and select Assign to Selection.

11. In the Scene View, select the floor above (top of the scene). In this room, there is currently no ceiling. Only the beams and the floor above are showing.

12. In the Material Library, select the Stucco category. In the pane on the right, right-click the Exterior-Beige material and select Assign to Selection.

13. Clear the selection of the floor above (top of the scene).

14. In the Document Materials panel, scroll to the Metal - Steel - ASTM A992 (1) material. Right-click on this material and select Select Object Applied To. All of the beams are selected in the Scene View.

15. Double-click the Metal - Steel - ASTM A992 (1) material in the list to open the Material Editor. This material is Anodized Aluminum, which is a reflective material. Close the material Editor.

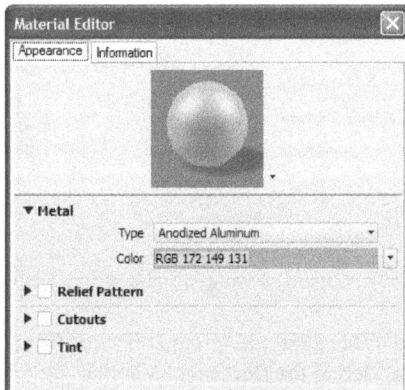

16. In the Material Library, select the Metal category. In the pane on the right, double-click the Bronze-Satin Hammered material to open the Material Editor. This material is not a reflective material. Close the material Editor.

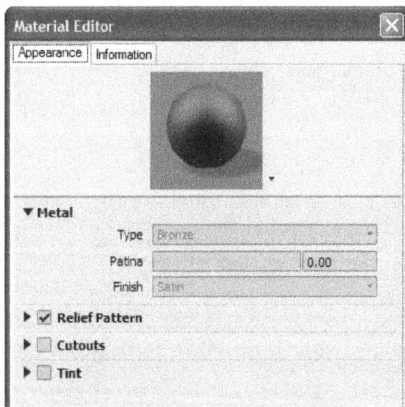

17. Ensure that all the beams are still selected in the Selection Tree. In the Material Library, right-click the Bronze-Satin Hammered material and select Assign to Selection.

18. In the Scene View, select the floor.

19. In the Material Library, expand the Flooring > Vinyl categories. In the pane on the right, right-click the Checker Black-White material and select Assign to Selection.

20. Clear the selection of the floor in the Scene View. Notice that the checked pattern is too small for the model.

21. Select the floor again. Verify in the Selection Tree that the Concrete-Normal Weight-5 ksi object is selected.

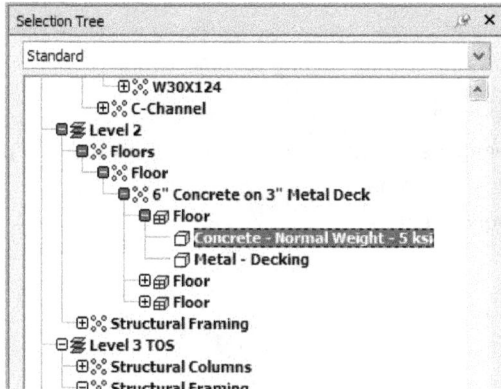

22. In the Autodesk Rendering window, select the Material Mapping tab.

23. In Material Mapping drop-down list, select Planar to change the mapping type for the floor.

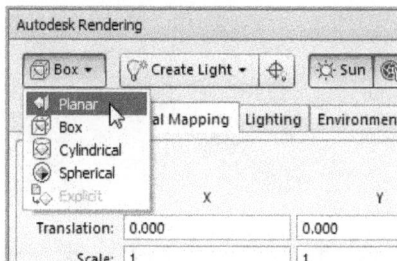

24. In the Material Mapping Settings, change the scale values in the General settings to **.2** for the X, Y, and Z directions. This produces less tiling and a larger pattern.

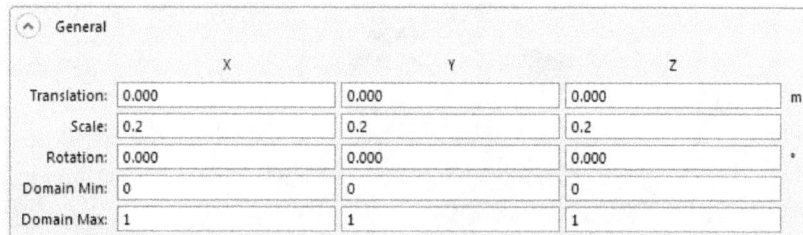

25. Clear the selection of the floor and notice the larger checkered pattern.

26. Leave the file open. You will continue working on this in the next exercise.

Lesson: Lighting

Overview

This lesson describes the process of how to create and edit lights that are used in the Autodesk Navisworks scene.

Objectives

After completing this lesson, you will be able to:

- Understand the fields in the Autodesk Rendering window's Lighting tab and their purpose.
- Create lights in an Autodesk Navisworks scene.
- Edit lights in an Autodesk Navisworks scene.

Lighting Overview

Lighting is used in models to create a more realistic appearance for rendering. Lighting enhances the clarity and three-dimensionality of a scene. There are multiple types of lights that can be incorporated into a scene, including:

- Artificial Lights
- Natural Lights

Your choice of lighting depends on whether your scene simulates natural or artificial illumination.

Artificial Lights

Scenes illuminated with point, spot, distant, or web lights are using artificially illuminated light sources. Artificial lights are subdivided into two types: Photometric and Standard.

- Photometric lights use photometric (light energy) values that enable you to define lights more accurately, as they would be in the real world. Point, Spot, and Web lights are Photometric lights.
  - **Point Light** – A point light radiates light in all directions from its location. A point light does not target an object, but illuminates everything around it. You can use them for general lighting effects.
  - **Spot Light** – A spot light emits a directional cone of light. A spot light distribution casts a focused beam of light, such as a flashlight or headlight. Spot lights are useful for highlighting specific features and areas in your model. A Spot light has a hotspot and falloff cone area that are defined by an angular value that radiates from the source:
    - The Hotspot cone angle defines the brightest part of a light beam.
    - The Falloff cone angle defines the full cone of light.
    - The greater the difference between the hotspot and falloff angles, the softer the edge of the light beam. If the hotspot and falloff angles are near equal, the edge of the light beam is sharp. You can adjust these values directly with the light's gizmo.
  - **Web Light** – A web light (web) is a 3D representation of the light intensity distribution of a light source. Web lights can be used to represent anisotropic (non-uniform) light distributions derived from data provided by manufacturers of real-world lights. This gives a far more precise representation of the rendered light than either spot or point lights.

You can set a light's distribution, intensity, color, and other characteristics. For web lights, you can also import specific photometric files (IES standard file format), which are available from lighting manufacturers to design lighting based on commercially available lights. If you do not use IES files, the effect of using web lights is the same as if you were using point lights.

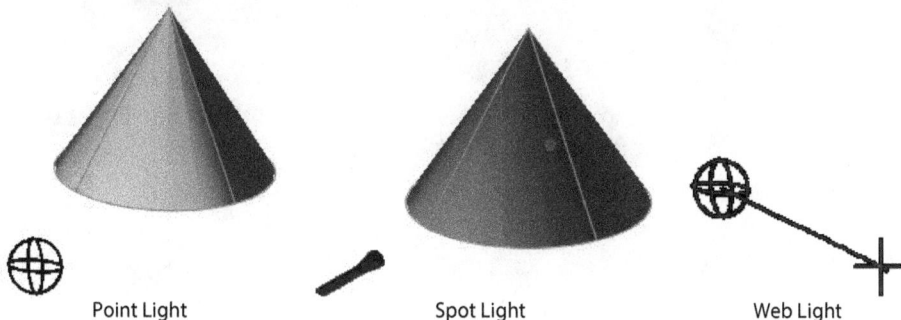

| Point Light | Spot Light | Web Light |

- Standard lights are computer calculated objects that mimic lights in a rendered image. The Distant light type is a Standard light. You can set its intensity and color values.

    - **Distant Light** - Emits uniform parallel light rays in one direction only. The intensity of a distant light does not diminish over distance. It is as bright at each face it strikes as it is at the source. Distant lights are useful for lighting objects or for lighting a backdrop uniformly, but are not physically accurate.

Distant Light

When the light glyphs are displayed, web lights are represented the same way as distant lights, that is as wireframe balls in the Scene View. Both have a From and a To point to define the direction of the light.

Use standard lights when you want to create and control a required effect in rendering and use photometric lights to enable the scene to render based on how the lights would look in the real world.

You can create point lights, spot lights, web lights, and distant lights to achieve the effects you want using the Rendering toolbar and the Lighting tab.

Natural Light

Natural light includes the Sun and Sky lighting system. The options for this are controlled on the Environments tab and the Rendering toolbar. Refer to Sun and Sky Lighting for more information on this type of lighting for your scene.

Lighting Units

The Autodesk Navisworks software supports both International (SI), and American lighting units. Both lighting units can be used in a photometric workflow. American differs from International in that illuminance values are formatted in foot-candles rather than lux. The lighting units are read from the original CAD file, and cannot be modified, unless you change them in the original file, and re-open the file in the Autodesk Navisworks software.

Lighting Tab

The Autodesk Rendering window enables you to manage lights in a model. The creation, use, and settings for those lights are managed using the following interface items:

- Rendering Toolbar
- Lights Panel
- Properties Panel

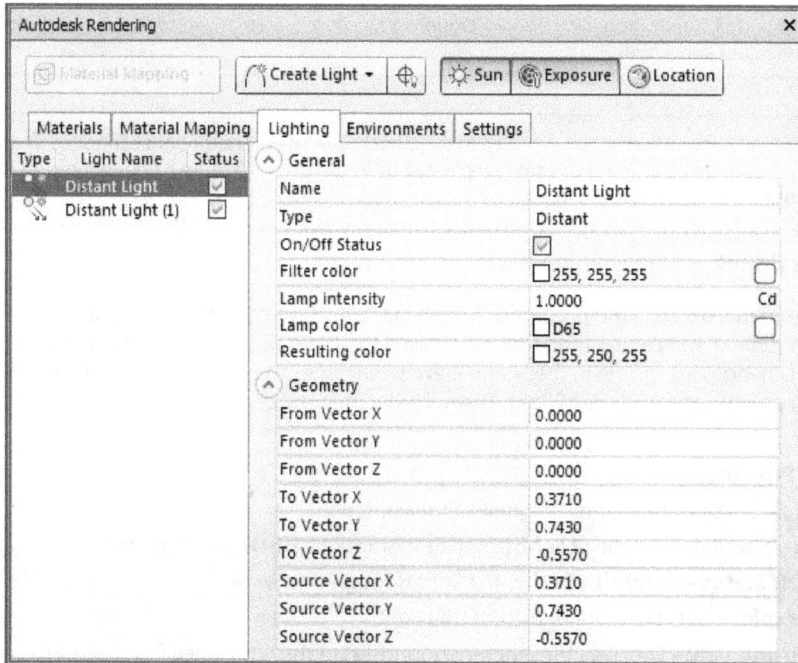

Rendering Toolbar

The Create Light drop-down list, located in the Rendering toolbar, enables you to create light sources in the Scene View. The available light types include:

- **Point** $\mathring{V}$ – Selects the Point Light tool and opens the Lighting tab.

- **Spot** $\mathring{V}$ – Selects the Spot Light tool and opens the Lighting tab.

- **Distant** $\mathring{\searrow}$ – Selects the Distant Light tool and opens the Lighting tab.

- **Web** $\mathring{(}$ – Selects the Web Light tool and opens the Lighting tab.

Lights (point, spot, distant, and web) are each represented by a different light glyph (a symbol in the model showing the location of the light). You can toggle the display of light glyphs on or off while you work. To toggle their display, use ⊕ in the Rendering toolbar. This only controls the display of glyphs representing the light sources in the current viewpoint, it does not toggle the light sources on or off.

Lights Panel

The Lights panel is on the left side of the Lights tab. Each light that is added to the model is listed in the Lights panel by name and type. The Status check box, adjacent to each light's name, enables you to toggle the lights on and off, as required. Clicking a light, selects it, and displays its properties in the Properties panel. A light selected in the Lights panel is also selected in the model (if the glyphs are displayed) and vice-versa.

> By default, unlimited number of lights are used in your model. To limit the lights used to eight lights, click Application Menu [icon] > Options > Interface > Display >Autodesk > and clear the Use Unlimited lights option.

> The sun and sky light is not included in the Lights panel. Its properties are controlled in the Environments tab. The sun is not represented by a light glyph because it does not have a discrete position and affects the entire scene.

Properties Panel

The Properties panel displays the properties for the currently selected light. These properties are initially set by default, but can be modified as required to obtain the required lighting for the scene. The effects of changes are visible in the Scene View in real time. The properties that are displayed in this panel are unique for each type of light. The following general properties are available for artificial light types:

- **General Properties**
    - **Name** – Specifies the name assigned to the light.
    - **Type** – Specifies the type of light: point light, spotlight, distant light, or web.
    - **On/Off Status** – Controls whether the light is toggled on or off.
    - **Filter color** – Sets the color of the emitted light.
    - **Lamp intensity** – Specifies the inherent brightness of the light. Specifies the intensity, flux, or illuminance of the lamp.
    - **Lamp color** – Specifies the lamp color as a CIE standard illuminant (D65 standard daylight) or as a Kelvin color temperature.
    - **Resulting color** – Displays the resulting color of a light that is the product of the lamp color and the filter color as RGB component values. This is a read-only field.
    - A spot light has the added Hotspot and Falloff angle fields that specifies the angle of the brightest cone of light (range is 0 to 159) and specifies the outer extremity of the light, where it meets the darkness (range 1 to 160), respectively.
        - For a Web light, a field is provided to define the IES filename and its location, and to define the rotational offset of the web about the optical X, Y, and Z axis.
- **Geometry** – Geometry properties enable you to enter specific values to control the location of the light. If the light is a spot light or web light, additional target point properties are available.

Creating Lights

The procedure for creating the four types of artificial lights is similar and involves the initial use of the Create Light drop-down list in the Rendering toolbar.

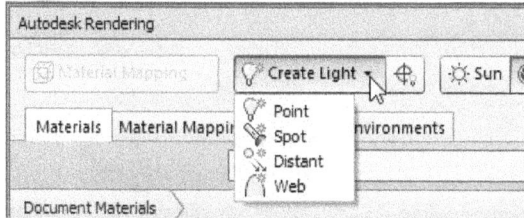

Procedure: To Add a Point light

1. On the Autodesk Rendering window, in the Rendering toolbar, in the Create Light drop-down, click Point .

2. Click in the Scene View to specify a location for the light. When the light gizmo is displayed, use it to adjust the light's position in the model.

3. Use the Properties panel on the Lighting tab to adjust the light's properties, if required.

Procedure: To Add a Spot light

1. On the Autodesk Rendering window, in the Rendering toolbar, in the Create Light drop-down, click Spot .

2. Click in the Scene View to specify a location for the light.

3. Click to specify a target for the spot light. When the light gizmo is displayed, use it to adjust the location and direction of the spotlight.

4. Use the Properties panel on the Lighting tab to adjust the light's properties, if required.

Procedure: To Add a Distant light with a Manufacturer's IES File

1. On the Autodesk Rendering window, in the Rendering toolbar, in the Create Light drop-down, click Distant .

2. Click in the Scene View to specify a location for the light.

3. Click to specify a direction. When the light gizmo is displayed, use it to adjust the distant light's position and target.

4. Use the Properties panel on the Lighting tab to adjust the light's properties, if required.

Procedure: To Add a Web light with a Manufacturer's IES File

1. On the Autodesk Rendering window, in the Rendering toolbar, in the Create Light drop-down, click Web.

2. In the scene view, click to specify a location for the light.

3. In the scene view, click to specify a direction. When the light gizmo is displayed, use it to adjust the web light's position and target.

4. On the Autodesk Rendering window, in the Lighting tab, click ☐ in the Web file field and browse to and open an IES file. The light properties update to use the web settings from the IES file.

5. Use the Properties panel, on the Lighting tab to adjust the light's properties, if required.

Editing Lights

Lights can be edited directly in the scene view or by using the Properties panel on the Lighting tab. When a light is selected in the model or in the Lights panel, a triad displays on the light's glyph. In the case of a Spot light, hotspot and falloff cones also appear. The triad and cones can be manipulated to move and adjust the light. Additional property modification (i.e., lamp settings and color) is done using the General properties on the Lighting tab. You can see the effect on the model as you change the properties of a light.

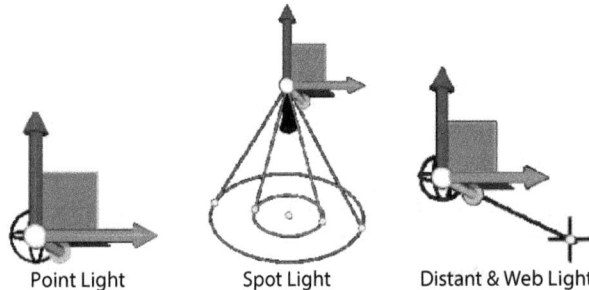

| Point Light | Spot Light | Distant & Web Light |

- Select any of the direction arrows on the triad to translate the glyph (light) in that direction.
- Select the planar rectangle between arrows to move the glyph (light) in a plane.
- Select and drag the center of the triad to freely move the glyph (light) in the scene.
- Select the yellow dots that lie on the perimeter of the hotspot (inner) and falloff (outer) cones for a Spot light and drag them to adjust their angle.
- Select the yellow dot that lies at the center of the cones for a Spot light to relocate the target location. If the yellow dot is not visible ensure that the Targeted option is enabled in the Geometry properties area.
- For Distant and Web lights, enter values in the Geometry properties area to change the location of the target.

You can also adjust a light's location and light's hotspot and falloff angle settings in the Properties view. The light's location values are in the Geometry properties and the angles for a Spot light can be edited in the General properties area.

Filter Color

The filter color sets the color of the emitted light. The default color for a light's filter is white. To modify this color, click ⬜ and change the color using the Color dialog box that displays. Click OK to confirm and assign the new color for the line.

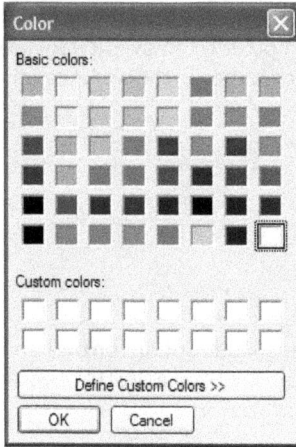

Lamp Settings

A lamp's intensity and color can be modified from its default values to customize the light's appearance.

- Lamp intensity represents the luminous intensity or power in a specific direction. Clicking ⬜ adjacent to the Lamp Intensity field in the General properties area a activates the Lamp Intensity dialog box. Adjust the units to modify the brightness of the lamp for the photometric light.

- Lamp color can also be specified by clicking ⬜ adjacent to the Lamp Color field in the General properties area. Use the Lamp Color dialog box to modify the lamp color for a photometric light.

> Refer to Lamp Intensity Dialog Box in Help for more information on customizing the Lamp Intensity and Lamp Color, respectively.

Deleting Lights

To delete an existing light in an Autodesk Navisworks scene, right-click the light's name in the Lights panel and select Delete.

Controlling Lights in the Scene View

Lights in the Scene view can be controlled in the Autodesk Rendering window or controlled globally.

Disabling Lights in the Autodesk Rendering Window

As an alternative to deleting lights from the scene, you can selectively disable lights that are not required. Disabling a light enables it to remain in the file, but temporarily removes it from use in the scene. To disable an existing light, in the Lights panel, clear the checkbox in the status column, as shown for the Spot Light below.

Controlling Lights for the Scene

The light in the Scene view can also be controlled using the Lighting Mode options on the Render Style panel of the Viewpoint tab. A scene consists of lights imported from the Source CAD file, and any lights that are created in the Autodesk Rendering environment.

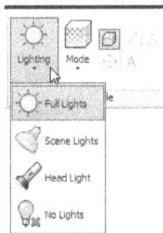

The following controls can be used to achieve the required lighting appearance.

Icon	Name	Description
	Full Lights	Uses lights that have been defined with Autodesk Rendering. This mode takes into account the lights that are enabled on the Lighting tab of the Autodesk Rendering window.
	Scene Lights	Uses the lights defined and imported from the source CAD model. If there are none available, two default opposing lights are used. To change the intensity of the scene lights, click File Options in the Project panel on the Home tab. In the File Options dialog box, select the Scene Lights tab. Move the slider to adjust the ambient intensity.
	Head Lights	Uses a single directional light located at the camera (viewer) in addition to an ambient light. To change the effects of the head lights, click File Options in the Project panel on the Home tab. In the File Options dialog box, select the Head Light tab. The Ambient slider changes the overall brightness of the scene and the Head Light slider changes the brightness of the directional light.
	No Lights	Switches off all lights including any defined in the model. The model is shaded with flat rendering.

Exercise: Adding Lights to a Model

1. Continue to work on the file from the previous exercise. Alternatively, if you did not complete that exercise, open the file *C:\Navisworks 2017 Essentials Class Files\Training\Examples\ Rendering\ Autodesk_Hospital_Rendering2.nwf.*

2. In the Home tab, in the Tools panel, click Autodesk Rendering to open the Autodesk Rendering window, if not already open.

Add Lights to the Scene

1. In the Autodesk Rendering window, select the Lighting tab. Notice that there are two distant lights in the scene. These lights were brought in from the source Autodesk Revit model.

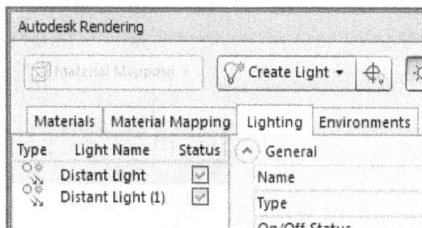

2. On the Autodesk Rendering window, in the Rendering toolbar, in the Create Light drop-down, click Point .

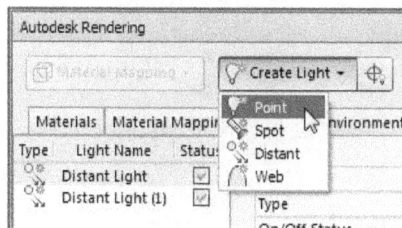

3. In the Scene View, select on a beam in the center of the room to place the point light.

4. Select the green axis on the gizmo and drag the light toward the stair area. Notice that the cursor displays as a hand when moving a light.

5. In the Create Light drop-down, click Spot .

6. In the Scene View, select a beam in the center of the room to place the spot light and select the table top as the target.

7. Select the yellow dot on the outside of the inner ring that is centered on the target and drag by selecting the arrow to make it smaller. This is Hotspot angle. Notice how the Hotspot angle changes in the General properties for this light.

8. Select the yellow dot on the outside of the outer ring that is centered on the target and drag by selecting the arrow to make it smaller. This is Falloff angle. Notice how the Falloff angle changes in the General properties for this light.

9. Adjust the values for the Hotspot and Falloff angle in the General properties for the Spot light. Enter **17** as the hotspot value and **36** as the Falloff value.

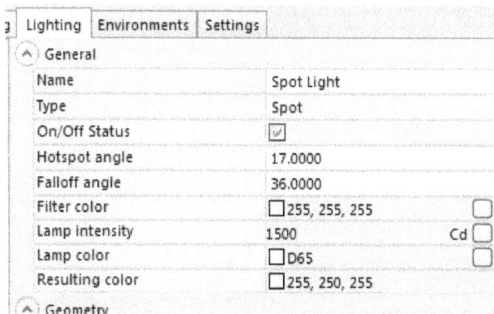

Lighting	Environments	Settings	
General			
Name		Spot Light	
Type		Spot	
On/Off Status		☑	
Hotspot angle		17.0000	
Falloff angle		36.0000	
Filter color		☐ 255, 255, 255	☐
Lamp intensity		1500	Cd ☐
Lamp color		☐ D65	☐
Resulting color		☐ 255, 250, 255	
Geometry			

10. In the Create Light drop-down, click Web ⌂.

11. In the Scene View, select the second beam from the wall to place the web light and select the table beneath it as the direction reference.

12. On the Autodesk Rendering window, in the Lighting tab, click ☐ in the Web file field and browse to and open the 482T12.ies file in the *C:\Navisworks 2017 Essentials Class Files\Training\ Examples\Rendering* folder. The light properties update to use the web settings from this IES file.

13. In the Rendering toolbar, click ⊕. This turns off the display of glyphs representing the light sources in the current viewpoint only, it does not toggle the light sources on or off.

14. Select the Viewpoint tab. In the Render Style panel, expand Lighting and notice that the Full Lights is now active. The Full Lights option uses the lights that were defined in the Autodesk Rendering environment. As soon as new lights are created, this option is enabled.

Tip: Disabling the Full Light option and returning to Scene Lights temporarily eliminates the use of the lights created in the Rendering environment of the scene.

15. Leave the file open. You will continue working on this in the next exercise.

Lesson: Sun and Sky Lights

Overview

This lesson describes the process of creating and editing sun and sky environments that represent the natural lighting used in the Autodesk Navisworks scene.

Objectives

After completing this lesson, you will be able to:

- Understand how natural lighting can be controlled and used in a scene.
- Understand the fields in the Autodesk Rendering window's Environment tab and their purpose.
- Enable the use and display of the sun and sky lighting effects in the Scene view.
- Edit the properties associated with the sun.
- Edit the sky properties to account for atmospheric conditions.

Sun and Sky Overview

One special light is available to simulate the effect of sunlight and sky illumination (natural lighting).

The rays of the simulated sunlight are parallel and have the same intensity at any distance. The angle of the light from the sun is controlled by a geographic location specified in the model, along with a specified date and time of day setting.

The rays of the sun are a yellowish hue, but the light cast from the atmosphere comes from all directions and is distinctly bluish in color. The sky effects are visible in the Scene View for both realistic and photorealistic visual styles.

Environments Tab

The Environments tab in the Autodesk Rendering window enables you to manage sunlight and sky illumination in a model. The settings are saved per file. The creation, use, and settings for these systems are managed using the following interface items in the scrolling Environments tab:

- Sun panel
- Sky Panel

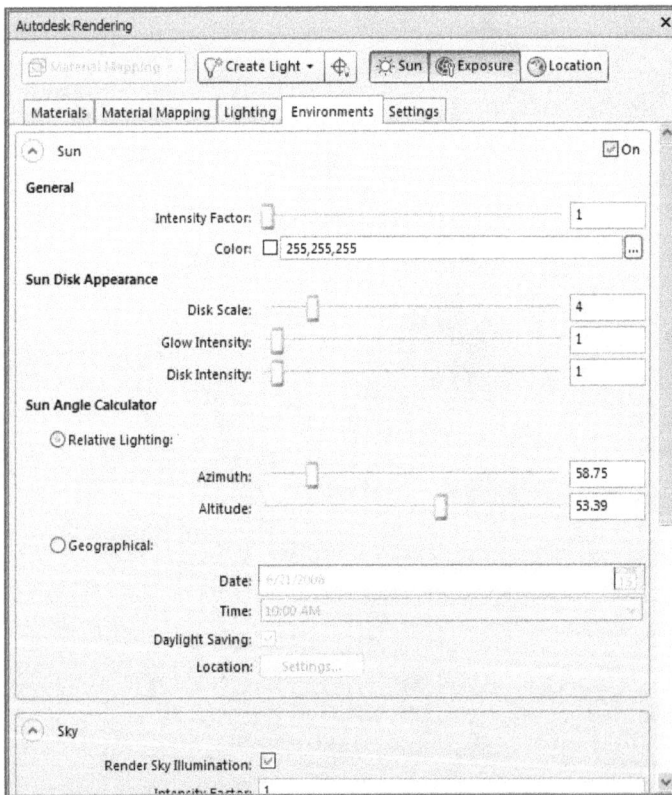

The options in the Sun and Sky panels enable you to customize the effect that these systems have in the scene.

Working with the Sun and Sky Environments

To add the sun and sky light to your model, use the following overall workflow:

1. Toggle on the sun light environment in the scene view.

2. Set the location of the sun.

3. Adjust the sun properties, as required.

4. Adjust the sky properties, as required.

Enabling the Sun Light System (Step 1)

Enabling the sun light environment in the scene requires you to both toggle on the sun and then enable sky illumination. Enabling the sun allows you to set the specific sun characteristics, such as its intensity, color, and disk and angle values. To display the defined sun light in the scene view, the Render Sky Illumination option must be enabled. Further customization of how the sun displays in the scene can be controlled with the settings in the Sky panel.

> Refer to the Adjusting Sun Properties and Adjusting Sky Properties sections for more information on the options available for customization.

Procedure: Enabling the Sun Light System in the Scene View

1. On the Autodesk Rendering window, Rendering toolbar, click Sun ☼ Sun . Alternatively, you can also select the Environments tab and enable the Sun checkbox in the Sun panel. Enabling this option enables the use of the Sun light in the scene.

2. By default, when the Sun light is enabled the sun light effect is visible in the Scene view. The sun's display in the Scene view can be enabled/disabled as required to control the use of the natural light in the Scene view. To ensure that the sun light effect is displayed in the Scene view, select the Render Sky Illumination checkbox in the Sky panel. To toggle it off, clear this option.

    Tip: If the Render Sky Illumination checkbox is not available, the Sun light must be enabled first.

3. The Sun and Sky effects are only visible in the Scene view if the exposure is toggled on. By default, the Exposure is enabled when the Sun light is enabled, but it can also be disabled independently by clearing Exposure option in the Exposure panel. If disabled, the background in the Scene View displays as white. Ensure that this option is enabled to see the affect of the Sun light in the Scene view.

Setting the Sun Location (Step 2)

Setting the Sun Location is done using the Geographic Location dialog box and the Sun Calculator Settings in the Sun Panel. The position and angle of the sun can be defined using one of two methods:

- Relative Lighting
- Geographical Lighting

To define the sun's position, select one of these two options in the Sun Angle Calculator area of the Environments tab. The default option is Relative Lighting, where you define the horizontal azimuth coordinate and the altitude or elevation above the horizon. The Geographical option defines the sun's position with a specific geographic location, as well and the date and time of day settings.

Procedure: To Set the Relative Lighting

1. In the Autodesk Rendering window, in the Environments tab, select Relative Lighting in the Sun Angle Calculator area.

2. Drag the Azimuth slider or enter a specific value in the entry field to define the horizontal azimuth position of the sun. The value can range between 0 and 360 degrees.

3. Drag the Altitude slider or enter a specific value in the entry field to define the elevation above the horizon. The value can range between 0 and 90.

Procedure: To Set the Geographic Position

1. In the Autodesk Rendering window, in the Environments tab, select Geographical in the Sun Angle Calculator area.

2. Click Settings in the Geographical area. As as alternative, on the Autodesk Rendering window, in the Rendering toolbar, click Location.

3. The latitude and longitude for the sun can be specified using two different measurement types: decimal values (Decimal Lat/Long) or as degrees, minutes, and seconds (Degree Minutes Seconds Lat/Long). Regardless of the measurement selected, enter the coordinates to locate the sun in the scene.

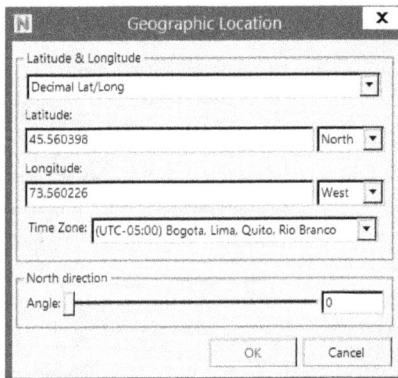

4. In the Time Zone drop-down list, set the time zone.

5. In the North direction area of the dialog box, move the Angle slider to define the angle from 0 for the north direction. The range is 0 to 360 and controls the position of the sun in the Scene View.

    Tip: This setting does not have any effect on the model's coordinate system or the ViewCube compass direction.

6. Click OK to close the Geographic Location dialog box.

7. In the Geographical area, enter a Date and Time value for the sun. Additionally, you can select whether Daylight Savings should be taken into account.

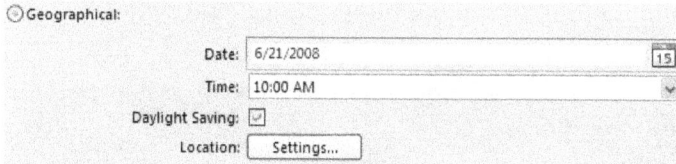

Adjusting the Sun Properties (Step 3)

Once the sun light has been enabled and the sun's position defined you can further customize the default settings that are assigned for the sun using the General and Sun Disk Appearance options in the Sun panel. The following properties are available to define the sun:

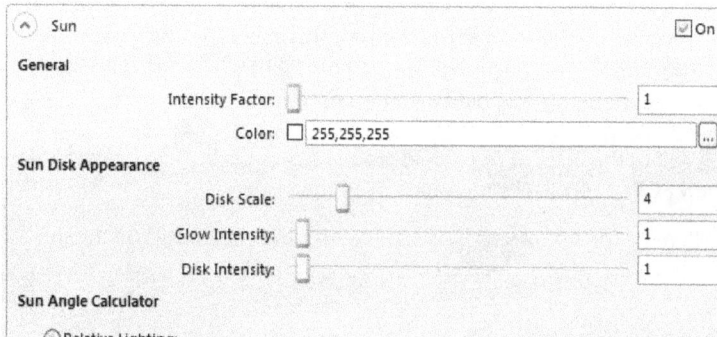

- **General Properties**
  - **Intensity Factor** – Specifies the intensity value for the sun's brightness. The higher the number, the brighter the light.
  - **Color** – Specifies the color of the sun light. By default, the sun light displays as white (RGB of 255,255,255). Click to use the Color dialog box to specify a new RGB value or select a color.

- **Sun Disk Appearance Properties**
  - **Disk Scale** – Specifies a scale value to define the size of the sun disk's appearance in the scene (1.0 = correct size).
  - **Glow Intensity** – Specifies the intensity value for the sun's glow (ranges from 0.0 - 25.0).
  - **Disk Intensity** – Specifies the intensity value for the sun's disk (ranges from 0.0 - 25.0).

Adjusting the Sky Properties (Step 4)

The actual affect that all of the specified sun properties has on the scene can be further controlled with the properties that are available in the Sky panel. These options take into account the actual atmospheric conditions that are going to affect the sun and how it is displayed in the scene. The following properties are available to define the sun:

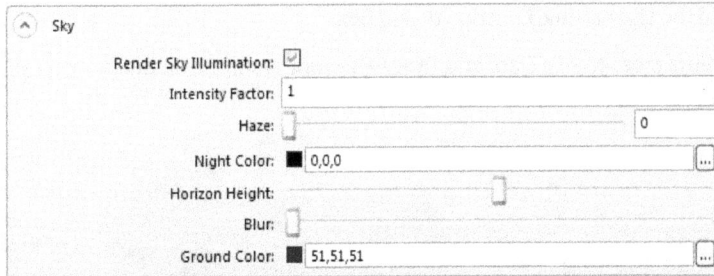

- **Intensity Factor** – Enables you to magnify the intensity value for the sun's brightness.
- **Haze** – Specifies the amount of haze in the air. The range is from 0 (a completely clear day) to 15 (extremely overcast).
- **Night Color** – Specifies the night color and represents the minimum color of the sky (the sky never becomes darker than this value). By default, the night color is black (RGB of 0,0,0). Click ⬚ to use the Color dialog box to specify a new RGB value or select a color.
- **Horizon Height** – Specifies the position of the horizon. This affects not only the visual representation of the horizon (ground plane), but also the point where the sun sets.
- **Blur** – Specifies the amount of blurring between ground plane and sky.
- **Ground Color** – Specifies the color of the virtual ground plane. Click ⬚ to use the Color dialog box to specify a new RGB value or select a color.

Note: The Render Sky Illumination option can be disabled as required, to toggle off the sun light effect in the scene view.

Lesson: Exposure Control

Overview

This lesson describes the overall process of how using the exposure options further customizes the lighting in a scene to incorporate real-world luminance values.

Objectives

After completing this lesson, you will be able to:

- Understand how exposure can be controlled and used in a scene.
- Understand the fields in the Autodesk Rendering window's Environment tab that deal with exposure and their purpose.
- Enable the use exposure in the Scene view.
- Edit exposure properties.

Exposure Overview

Exposure controls how real-world luminance values are converted into a rendered image. You can adjust exposure settings before or after rendering. If you know the required exposure settings, you can set them before rendering the image, otherwise they can be changed after you have reviewed the rendering and determined that changes to the exposure are required.

> The sun and sky effects are only visible if the exposure is toggled on, otherwise the background in the Scene View becomes white.

Environments Tab

Exposure settings are set on the Environments tab and the effects are immediately visible in the Scene View. These settings are saved with the model. The use and settings for Exposure control are managed using the following interface item in the Environments tab:

- Exposure panel

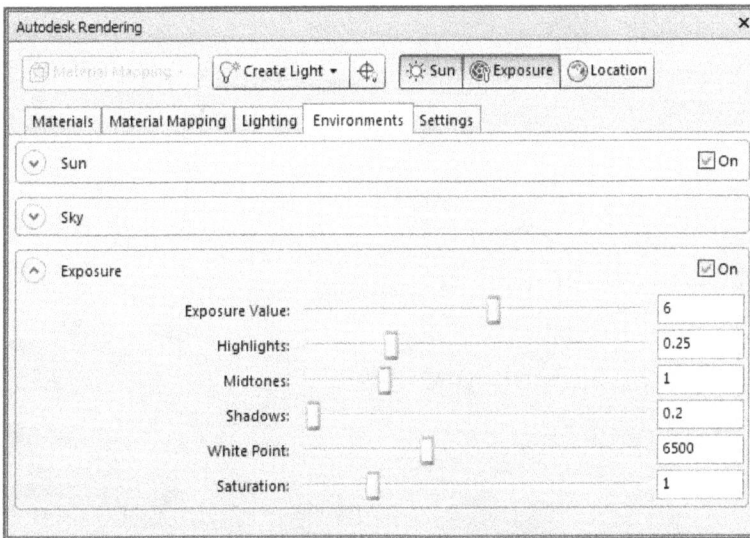

The options in the Exposure panel enable you to enable or disable the use of exposure and customize the affect that it has in the scene.

- **On** – Controls whether exposure (or tone mapping) is enabled or disabled in the Scene view. The effects are visible for both realistic and photorealistic visual styles. If you clear this check box, the scene background is white, and sun and sky simulation are not shown.
- **Exposure Value** – Specifies the overall brightness of the rendered image. This setting is comparable to the exposure compensation setting in cameras with automatic exposure. Enter a value between -6 (brighter) and 16 (darker). The default value is 6.
- **Highlights** – Specifies the light level for the brightest areas of the image. Enter a value between 0 (darker highlights) and 1 (brighter highlights). The default is 0.25.

- **Midtones** – Specifies the light level for areas of the image whose brightness lies between the highlights and the shadows. Enter a value between 0.1 (darker mid tones) and 4 (brighter mid tones). The default is 1.
- **Shadows** – Specifies the light levels for the darkest areas of the image. Enter a value between 0.1 (lighter shadows) and 4 (darker shadows). The default is 0.2.

> Shadows are more distinct the clearer the day is, and can be essential for bringing out the three-dimensionality of a naturally lit scene.

- **White Point** – Specifies the color temperature of the light sources that should display as white in the rendered image. This setting is similar to the White Balance setting on digital cameras. The default value is 6500.
- **Saturation** – Specifies the intensity of colors in the rendered image. Enter a value between 0 (gray/black/white) and 5 (more intense colors). The default is 1.

Enabling and Adjusting Exposure

Adjusting the exposure of the scene enables you to refine the results of the rendering to obtain a more real-world effect.

Procedure: To Adjust the Exposure in a Scene

1. On the Autodesk Rendering window, in the Rendering toolbar, click Exposure. Alternatively, you can also select the Environments tab and select On in the Exposure panel.

2. Use the Exposure Value slider to control overall brightness of the rendered image (range is between -6 (brighter) and 16 (darker)).

3. Use the Highlights slider to adjust the light level for the brightest area of the image (range is between 0 (darker highlights) and 1 (brighter highlights)).

4. Use the Midtones slider to adjust the light level for areas of the image whose brightness lies between the highlights and the shadows (range is between 0.1 (darker mid tones) and 4 (brighter mid tones)).

5. Use the Shadows slider to adjust the light levels for the darkest areas of the image (range is between 0.1 (lighter shadows) and 4 (darker shadows)).

6. Use the White Point slider to control the color temperature of the light sources that should display as white in the rendered image.

    Tip: If the rendered image looks too orange, reduce the White Point value. If the rendered image looks too blue, increase the White Point value.

7. Use the Saturation slider to modify the intensity of the colors in the rendered image (the range is between 0 (gray/black/white) and 5 (more intense colors)).

Lesson: Ground Planes

Overview

This lesson describes how to use ground planes to provide a visual base for a model. It also introduces you to the process of moving a ground plane to a specific position.

Objective

After completing this lesson, you will be able to:

- Append a ground plane to a model and move it to the correct position.

About Ground Planes

Ground planes provide a visual base that the model appears to sit on. This can be useful when you are creating presentations and can enhance the materials, backgrounds, and lighting effects in the model. They can also hide the foundation geometry of a model.

You can append the ground planes that have been created in CAD software to the model files in the Autodesk Navisworks software.

Procedure: To Add a Ground Plane

1. On the Home tab in the Project panel, click Append ⬚. Browse, select, and open the required ground plane file.

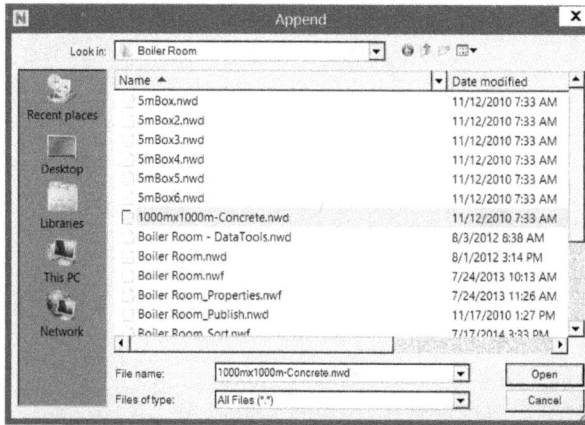

The appended ground plane might not be aligned with the model, but can be adjusted using the Override Transform function.

2. In the Scene View, right-click the ground plane and select Override Item > Override Transform.

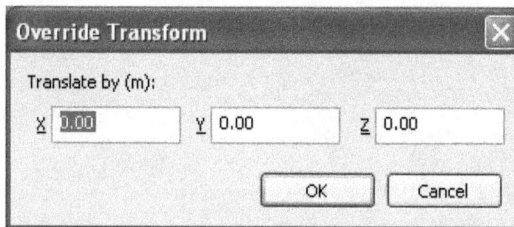

Alternatively, you can also move the ground plane by selecting it, right-clicking and selecting File Units and Transform. In the Units and Transform dialog box, change the scale or location of the ground plane, as required.

3. In the Override Transform dialog box, change the X, Y, and Z dimensions, as required.

4. Click OK to save the changes and close this window.

Lesson: Photorealistic Rendering

Overview

This lesson discusses the specific steps in the process for rendering a photorealistic image.

Objectives

After completing this lesson, you will be able to:

- Render and save photorealistic images using the Autodesk Rendering tool in both Autodesk Navisworks and A360.

Rendering Overview

Rendering creates highly detailed and photorealistic images in the Autodesk Navisworks software. The renderings are created using all of the materials, lights, and environments that were applied to the Scene view using the Autodesk Rendering dialog box. Rendering can be run in the Autodesk Navisworks software (Autodesk Rendering), or it can be done using A360 (Render in Cloud). Rendering involves complex calculations that can keep your computer busy for a long time, which may help you decide which render location is best.

Once rendered, small changes to the scene might be required to further refine it, which requires rendering again. This makes creating photorealistic images a potentially very time-consuming process.

Autodesk Rendering

When the Autodesk Rendering option is enabled on the Render tab, the viewpoint is rendered directly in the Autodesk Navisworks software. During rendering, the output displays directly in the Scene View, along with a progress indicator indicating the completed rendering percentage.

Rendering in the Cloud

When the Render in Cloud option is enabled on the Render tab, A360 is used to create photorealistic images and panoramic renderings without using the resources on your system, enabling you to continue working in your local software. To render using A360, Autodesk Navisworks creates a version of the project containing just the information required to render and then transmits it to the rendering service. By accessing the online render gallery, you can access your renderings, re-render images as panoramas, or re-render with other settings. Additionally, you can preview and download the rendered image.

Using either of these rendering methods you can save or export rendered scenes as images, and use them in presentations, on websites, in print, etc.

Defining the Render Style

When rendering in the Autodesk Navisworks software you must define the render style that is to be used. The following describes the preset and custom settings available.

Render Style

The key to successful rendering is finding a balance between the required visual complexity and an acceptable rendering speed. The highest quality images typically take the most time to render. To work efficiently, consider producing images of acceptable quality. For the final photorealistic finish, you can select a high quality rendering style to create the final image. The following six render styles are available for use:

- **Low Quality** – Anti-aliasing is bypassed. Sample filtering and ray tracing are active. Shading quality is low. Use this render style if you want to quickly see the effect of the materials and lighting that you have applied to the scene. The produced image contains small inaccuracies and imperfections (artifacts).

- **Medium Quality** – Anti-aliasing is active. Sample filtering and ray tracing are active with increased reflection depth settings when compared to the Low Quality render style. Use this render style for a final preview of the scene, before exporting your final rendered output. The produced image is of satisfactory quality, with few artifacts.

- **High Quality** – Anti-aliasing, sample filtering, and ray tracing are active. The image quality is high, and includes all of the reflections and transparencies, anti-aliasing on edges, reflections, and shadows. This render quality requires the most time to produce. Use this render style for the final export of your rendered output. The produced image is of high fidelity with minimum artifacts.

- **Coffee Break Rendering** – Sets a rendering time of 10 minutes with a simplistic lighting calculation and standard numerical precision.

- **Lunch Break Rendering** – Sets a rendering time of 60 minutes with an Advanced lighting calculation and standard numerical precision.

- **Overnight Rendering** – Sets a rendering time of 720 minutes with an Advanced lighting calculation and High numerical precision.

Custom Render Settings

The six render styles that are provided in the Autodesk Navisworks software may not provide the exact rendering settings that you require. For these situations you can customize the settings using the Settings tab in the Autodesk Rendering window. As an alternative you can also click Custom Settings in the list of render styles.

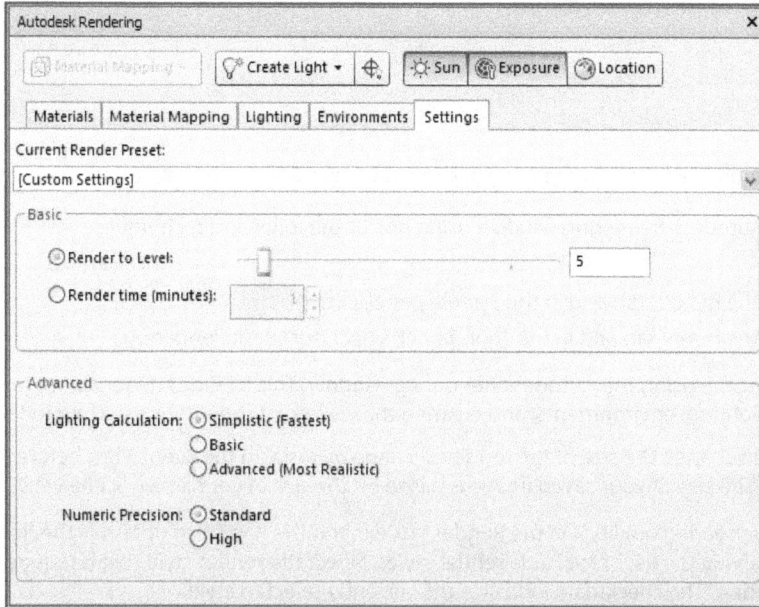

- **Current Render Preset** – Specifies the render style or custom style that is currently assigned in the model. The style can be assigned here or from the Render tab. The values in the Basic and Advanced fields update to show the preset values for the active render styles. If changes are made to a preset render style, it is changed to a custom style.

- **Basic Properties**
  - **Render to Level** – Specifies the render level from 1 to 50. The higher the level, the higher the quality of the rendering.
  - **Render Time (minutes)** – Specifies the rendering time in minutes. When you render animations, this setting controls how long it will take to render the whole animation, not individual animation frames.

- **Advanced Properties**
  - **Lighting Calculation** – Specifies the complexity of the lighting calculation (Simplistic, Basic, and Advanced). Select Simplistic for the fastest calculations and Advanced for the longest but more realistic.
  - **Numeric Precision** – Specifies numeric precision (Standard or High).

Rendering Workflows

The process for rendering directly in the Autodesk Navisworks software or using the A360 cloud service are slightly different. To access either rendering methods, use the Render tab in the Autodesk Navisworks Ribbon.

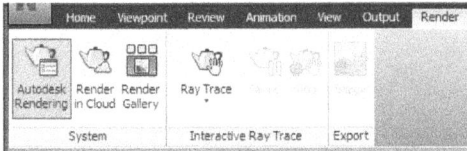

Procedure: To Render a Scene in the Autodesk Navisworks Software

1. Open the Autodesk Rendering window using one of the following techniques:

   - Select the Render tab and in the System panel, click .
   - Select the Home tab and in the Tools panel, select Autodesk Rendering.

2. Set up the scene using the Autodesk Rendering window. This includes materials, material mapping, lighting, environments, and creating the viewpoint (orientation and zoom level).

   Tip: You can change the size of the rendered image by resizing the Scene view before rendering. The size of your saved image is based on the size of your active Scene view.

3. Select the rendering quality. On the Render tab, expand the Ray Trace option in the Render panel to provide the list of available render styles. Select the render style that is required for your rendering. The checkmark indicates the currently selected style.

   Tip: The Low Quality style is the fastest to render and High Quality is the slowest to render.

4. On the Render tab, in the Render panel, click to start rendering. Click (Pause) if you need to temporarily pause the process.

5. Save the rendered image. When the scene is rendered, click (Save) on the Render tab. In the Save As dialog box, select the required file format from the Save As Type drop-down list (.PNG, .JPG, .BMP), browse to a storage location, and enter a name for the file. Click Save.

6. Click (Stop) to return to a realistic visual style.

Real-time navigation is supported during the photorealistic rendering. For example, you can orbit, zoom, and pan your model. However, each interaction with your model restarts the rendering process from the beginning.

Procedure: To Render a Scene using A360

1. Open the Autodesk Rendering window using one of the following techniques:

    ■ Select the Render tab and in the System panel, click [icon].
    ■ Select the Home tab and in the Tools panel, select Autodesk Rendering.

2. Set up the scene using the Autodesk Rendering window. This includes materials, material mapping, lighting, environments, and creating the viewpoint (orientation and zoom level).

3. On the Render tab, in the Render panel, click [icon] to access A360 to render the image. Login to the service if you have not already logged in.

4. In the Render in Cloud window, define the render settings and click Start Rendering. If you want the system to email you when the rendering is complete, select Email me when complete. The file is uploaded to the cloud where the rendering process is completed.

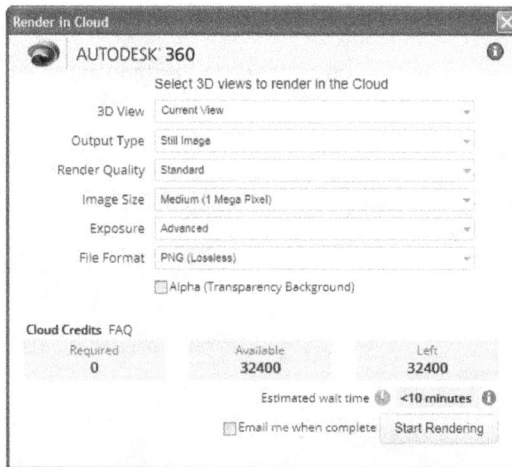

Tip: A360 renders the Navisworks viewpoints in a project, by making it the current view before starting the Render in Cloud command. The service does not work with 2D views.

Tip: A360 Rendering is a highly optimized engine. It is not the same as the rendering engine used in Navisworks. You may find minor differences in the appearance of materials.

Tip: A360 automatically applies advanced exposure controls to simulate real-world lighting conditions. You can adjust this in the Render in Cloud dialog box. To use native exposure control settings instead of the default advanced exposure, render the image from the Render Gallery and select Exposure > Native.

5. Click Render Gallery on the Render tab to review the file in A360 once it has been rendered. The following describes what can be done with the file.

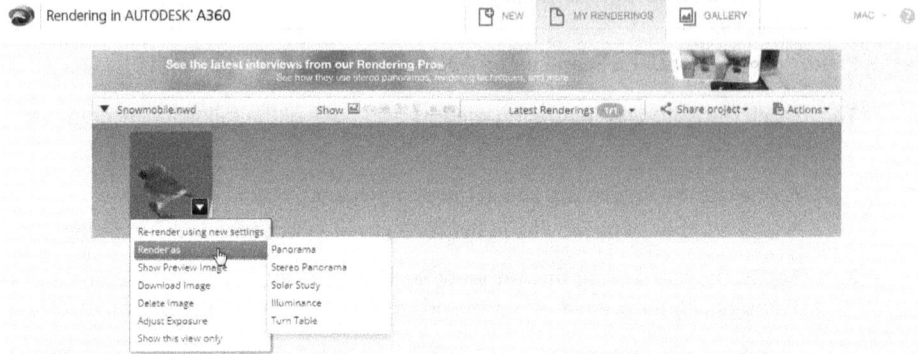

- Select Re-render using new settings to define new render settings and re-render the file.
- Select a Render As setting:
  - Create panoramas of your scene, so that you and your clients can interactively navigate 360 degrees through the scene. Stereo Panoramas can also be created for stereoscopic viewing in Autodesk Navisworks. This allows the viewing of the 3D model through stereo-enabled hardware, including active and passive stereo viewing glasses in conjunction with both CRT screens and dedicated projectors.
  - Perform solar studies of designs in progress, so you understand the effects of the total amount of solar radiation (insolation) and shading during the day.
  - Perform illuminance simulations of scenes to better understand the effects of natural and artificial lighting.
  - Create turntable animations of your model for presentations.
- Show or hide the preview image.
- Download the image.
- Delete the image from A360.
- Adjust the exposure settings using the Adjust Exposure option. Drag the sliders, as required, to adjust the settings.

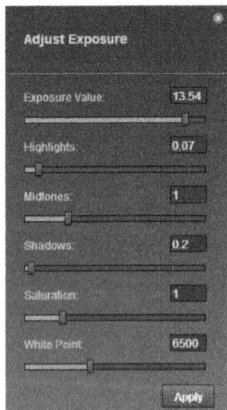

Exercise: Rendering a Model

Render the Scene and Make Adjustments

1. Continue to work on the file from the previous exercise. Alternatively, if you did not complete that exercise, open the file *C:\Navisworks 2017 Essentials Class Files\Training\Examples\ Rendering\ Autodesk_Hospital_Rendering3.nwf.*

2. Select the Render tab in the Ribbon to access the rendering tools.

3. On the Interactive Ray Trace panel, expand the Ray Trace option and select Medium Quality. This sets the rendering quality as medium.

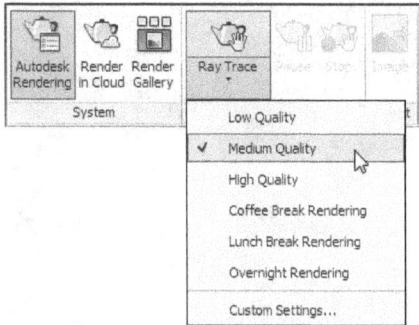

Tip: The Low Quality style is the fastest to render and High Quality is the slowest to render. It is recommended that you begin rendering using a lower quality as you are developing appropriate material and lighting settings and then render at the higher quality once done. Consider using the other options for specific rendering settings based on time.

4. On the Interactive Ray Trace panel, click ![icon] to start rendering.

5. As the rendering is progressing, notice that the lighting is displaying as too white. In the Interactive Ray Trace panel, click ![icon] (Stop) to return to the realistic visual style.

6. In the Lighting tab on the Autodesk Rendering window, select the Point light to access its properties.

7. Click ![icon] adjacent to the Lamp color property. In the Lamp Color dialog box, select Quartz Cool in the Standard colors dialog box. Click OK.

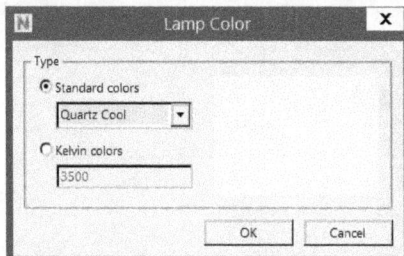

8. In the Lighting tab on the Autodesk Rendering window, select the Spot light to access its properties.

9. Click ☐ adjacent to the Lamp color property. In the Lamp Color dialog box, select Quartz Cool in the Standard colors dialog box. Click OK.

10. On the Render panel, click to render. Depending on your system this rendering might take anywhere from 20 to 60 minutes to render. The following image is provided to show you a final rendering of this scene. Yours might vary slightly depending on the placement of your lights.

11. Stop the rendering to continue with the exercise. To review a saved image of this final rendering, navigate to the *C:\Navisworks 2017 Essentials Class Files\Training\Examples\ Rendering* folder and open *Autodesk_Hospital_Rendering_Cafe.png*.

Tip: During rendering you can Pause and Save the current rendering using the Image option on the Export panel. This enables you to create an image file mid-way through rendering, where the Stop option returns you to the original visual style.

Tip: Rendering using A360 enables you to take advantage of its powerful rendering engine and tools. To review an image of the Cafe rendered using the Cloud and some of its settings, navigate to the *C:\Navisworks 2017 Essentials Class Files\Training\Examples\ Rendering* folder and open *Cafe_Cloud_Rendering.png*.

Navigate to an Exterior Viewpoint and Prepare the Scene

1. In the Saved Viewpoints window, select Outside to change the viewpoint to an external view of the model. If you did not stop the rendering it begins rendering this new viewpoint.

2. Select the Home tab. In the Project panel, click Append. In the Append dialog box, navigate to and select the *C:\Navisworks 2017 Essentials Class Files\Training\Examples\ Rendering\Autodesk_Hospital_Site.nwc*. This is the ground plane that is going to be used in the rendering.

3. On the Autodesk Rendering window, in the Rendering toolbar, click Location. In the Geographic Location dialog box, set the Time Zone to (UTC-05:00) Eastern Time (US & Canada). Click OK.

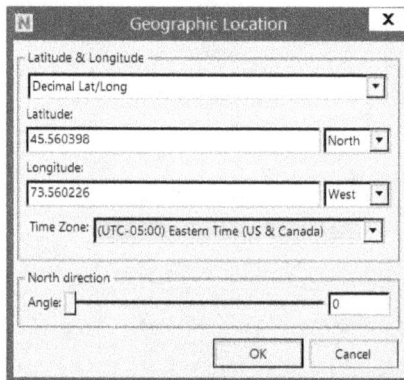

4. On the Autodesk Rendering window, in the Rendering toolbar, ensure that the Sun option is enabled so that the Sun is toggled on in the Scene view.

5. On the Autodesk Rendering window, select the Environments tab. Make the following changes to the Sun properties.

- Enter **4** as the Intensity Factor.
- Select the Geographical option and enter the current date in the Date field.
- Enter **1:45** PM as the Time.

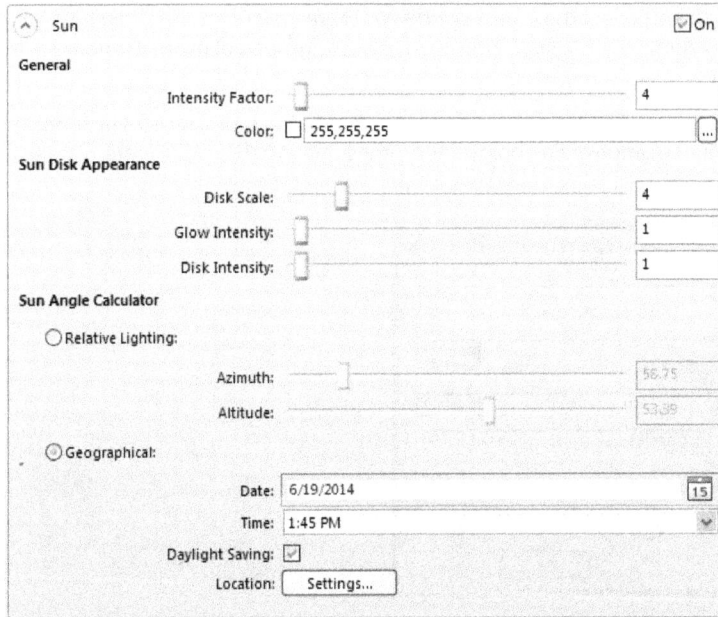

6. On the Environments tab make the following changes to the Sky properties.

- Enter **.9** as the Haze Factor.
- Lower the Horizon using the slider.
- Increase the Blur using the slider.
- Change the Ground Color to a dark Green.

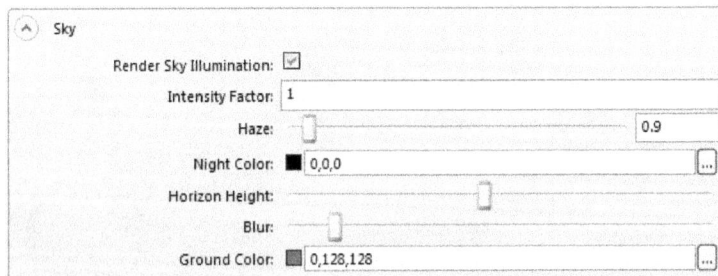

7. On the Environments tab make the following changes to the Exposure properties.

   - Enter **4** as the Exposure Value.

Exposure		☑ On
Exposure Value:		4
Highlights:		0.25
Midtones:		1
Shadows:		0.2
White Point:		6500
Saturation:		1

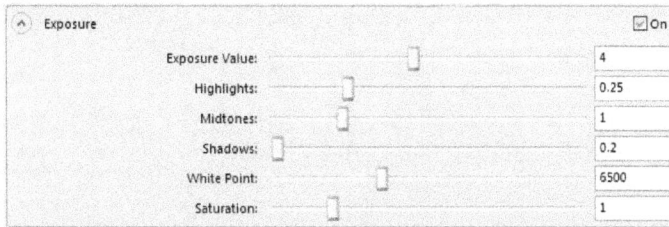

8. Select the Render tab on the Ribbon. On the Render panel, click [icon] to start rendering. A sample of the final rendering displays similar to the following. To review a saved image of this final rendering, navigate to the *C:\Navisworks 2017 Essentials Class Files\Training\Examples\Rendering* folder and open *Autodesk_Hospital_Rendering_Outside.png*.

   Tip: In this exterior view, the default materials that existed in the model and the ground plane were used and only the Sky and Environment setting were customized. To further refine the scene you can manipulate the materials, as required.

9. When the scene is rendered, click [icon] (Save) on the Render tab. In the Save As dialog box, select .PNG in the Type drop-down list, browse to your *C:\Temp* storage location, and enter **Hospital Outside.png** as the name for the file. Click Save.

10. Save the Autodesk Navisworks file.

Data Tools

You can connect to external databases directly from your Autodesk® Navisworks® files, and create links between objects in the scene and fields in the database tables to bring through extra properties.

Objectives

After completing this lesson, you will be able to:

- Use Data Tools to link to an external database and select the data fields to be viewed from in the Autodesk Navisworks Properties window.

Lesson: Database Support (Data Tools)

Overview

This lesson describes how the Autodesk Navisworks Data Tools feature works. It also introduces you to the process used to connect the Autodesk Navisworks software to an external database and view its properties in the Autodesk Navisworks software.

Objective

After completing this lesson, you will be able to:

- Use Data Tools to link to an external database and select the data fields to be viewed from in the Autodesk Navisworks Properties window.

About Database Support

Databases are commonly used to store large amounts of data, such as equipment specifications, catalog data, and maintenance manuals. With Data Tools, you can create a link between the stored data file and the model file.

Procedure: To Link to External Database Files

1.   To display the Properties window, if is not visible, select the View tab, expand the Windows

   option, and enable Properties, or click Properties ▦ in the Display panel on the Home tab.

   Note: The properties for the objects in the model brought in from the CAD application must include unique identifiers to the data in the data file to be linked to.

   Tip: It might be useful to create a custom properties tab, name it Entity Handle, and insert a new Property String linked to the unique identifier in the model objects.

2.   On the Home tab in the Project panel, click File Options ⬚. Select the Data Tools tab.

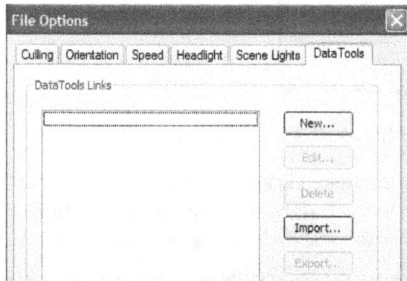

3.   In the File Options dialog box, click New to create a new link.

4.   In the New Link dialog box, in the Name field, enter a name for the new link (for example **Maintenance Details**). This is the name of the tab that displays in the Properties dialog box.

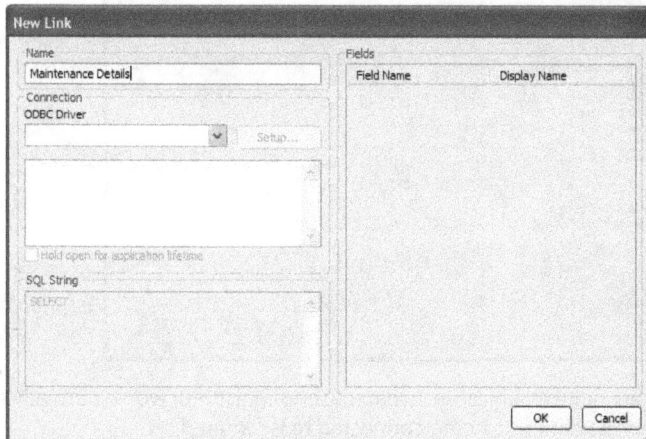

5. Under Connection, select the appropriate ODBC Driver from the drop-down list. This defines the type of database to link to.

Tip: There are several similar options here, so take care to choose the correct one.

6. Click Setup.

7. In the ODBC Microsoft Access Setup dialog box, under Database, click Select to select the database.

8. In the Select Database dialog box, under Directories, navigate to the folder that contains the database file to be linked to. Then select the file in the left pane.

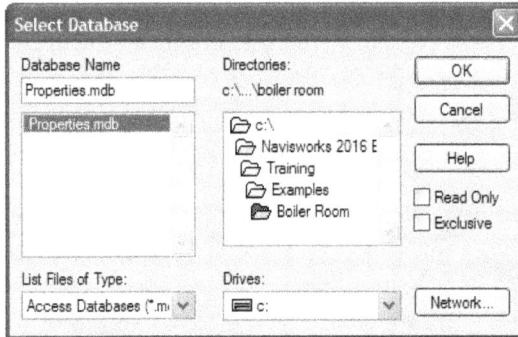

9. Click OK. And then click OK in the ODBC Microsoft Access Setup dialog box.

10. In the New Link dialog box, under SQL String field, click in the window after SELECT and enter the query string. This defines which table in the database to query (or question). For example, enter:

SELECT * FROM tblBoilerData WHERE "NWUniqueID"=%prop("Entity Handle","Value")

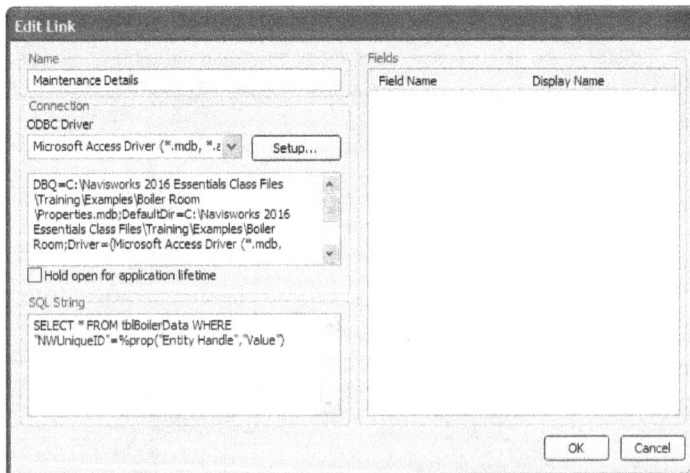

Tip: SQL queries are quite technical and a database administrator would normally set these up, as a knowledge of the database being connected to is required.

All queries start with SELECT and are followed by "what" is to be selected from "where" and with "which" conditions. The * signifies to look at all columns in the specified table. (If only specific columns are required, they would be stated here).

- tblBoilerData is the name of the table in the database that is to be used.
- NWUniqueID refers to the column in the table that is to be the unique identifier.
- %prop signifies that the unique identifier in the table (NWUniqueID) is to link to a category/property pair in the 3D model.
- Entity Handle and Value define the category and property pair in the 3D model.

Tip: There are several example queries in the *Navisworks User Guide*. Some of the queries are relatively simple when they are broken down.

11.   Double-click in the Fields pane to define the columns to be looked at for answers when the table is queried.

12.   In Field Name, enter the name of the field. (Enter the name exactly as displayed in the database column name. e.g., PartName) Press ENTER.

The Display Name (which is the category name displayed in the Properties dialog box) is automatically completed.

13.   If required, double-click the Display Name to edit it.

This is the first question of the query (look for the name of the part that has the specified ID).

14.   Double-click under the previous Field Name that was added and enter the next required column name from the database.

15.   Repeat the above process until all the column names to be queried are listed under Field Name with the appropriate Display Names.

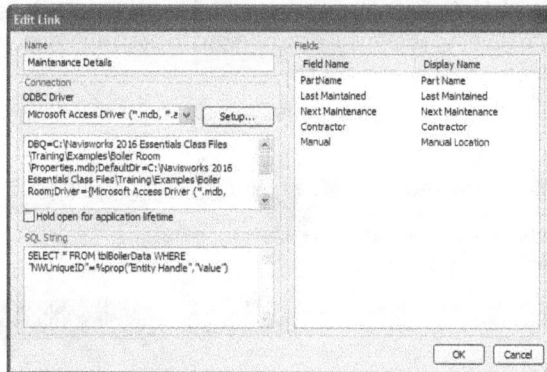

16.   Click OK to save the new link.

17.   Add a checkmark to the new link (for example, Maintenance Details) and then click OK to finish.

The model is now linked to an external data source. Look at the model properties to see what this has added.

Exercise: Linking to an External Database

> There is currently a limitation in Microsoft Access that is creating a Microsoft 32/64 bit ODBC compatibility issue. Autodesk understands that the issue is resolved in Office 2010, although the user may need to download the installer from the following link.
>
> http://www.microsoft.com/downloads/en/details.aspx?familyid=C06B8369-60DD-4B64-A44B-84B371EDE16D&displaylang=en

1. Open *C:\Navisworks 2017 Essentials Class Files\Training\Examples\Boiler Room\ Boiler Room – DataTools.nwd.*

2. In the Saved Viewpoints window, select Boiler Database Properties to access a saved view of the file.

3. To display the Properties window if is not visible, select the View tab, expand the Windows option, and enable Properties or click Properties ▣ in the Display panel on the Home tab.

4. Select the Home tab. Expand the Select & Search panel and select Last Unique from the Selection Resolution drop-down menu.

5. On the Home tab in the Select & Search panel, click Select ▷. Click on one of the large white boilers. Notice that the property tabs from the CAD application (Item, Material, and Entity Handle) are visible.

    The Entity Handle property is the unique identifier in the model, which will be used to link this 3D model to the externally stored data.

    The external database (*Properties.mdb*) contains two tables. One of the tables lists some of the unique IDs (Entity Handles), each of which relates to a single object in the 3D model. There are also columns in this table containing additional data relevant to each object in the model.

6. Set up a link to the database. On the Home tab in the Project panel, click File Options ▭. Select the Data Tools tab.

7. In the File Options dialog box, click New to create a new link.

8. In New Link dialog box, in the Name field, enter **Maintenance Details**. This is the name of the tab that will appear on the Properties window.

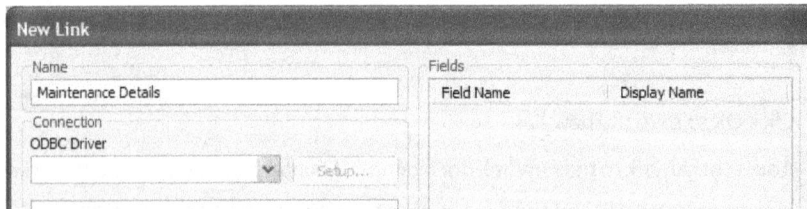

9. Under Connection, in the ODBC Driver drop-down list, select Microsoft Access Driver (*.MDB). This defines the type of database to link to.

    Note: There are several similar options here; be sure to choose the correct one.

10. Click Setup.

11. In the ODBC Microsoft Access Setup dialog box, click Select to select the database to be linked to.

12. Navigate to *C:\Navisworks 2017 Essentials Class Files\Training\Examples\Boiler Room* then in the left pane, select *Properties.mdb*.

13. Click OK, and then click OK in the ODBC Microsoft Access Setup dialog box.

14. In the New Link dialog box, in the SQL String field, click after SELECT in the SQL String area. Enter the following string exactly so that the SQL String field is as shown below making sure spaces are added correctly:

Note: Spaces are vital; to help you add spaces in the correct places, replace the following backslashes \ with a space (for example, SELECT * FROM).

SELECT*\\FROM\\tblBoilerData\\WHERE\\"NWUniqueID"=%prop("Entity\\Handle","Value")

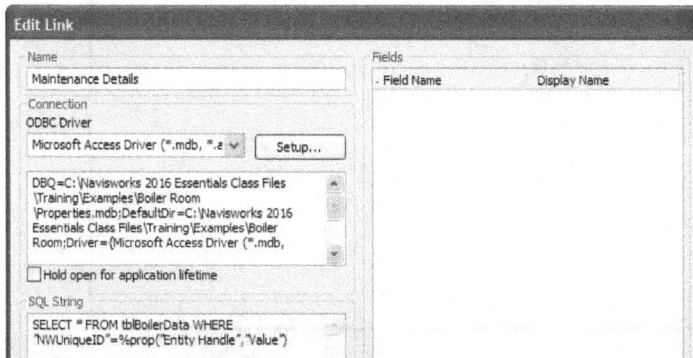

Note: The string defines which table to look in and what to look for in that table. This will be in the form of a query.

15. Double-click in the Fields pane under Field Name and enter **PartName** (no space between), and then press ENTER.

The Display Name (which will be the category name displayed in the Properties window) is automatically completed.

16. Double-click the Display Name to edit it. Edit the Display Name so that it reads, **Part Name**.

This is the first question (to look for the name of the part that has the specified ID).

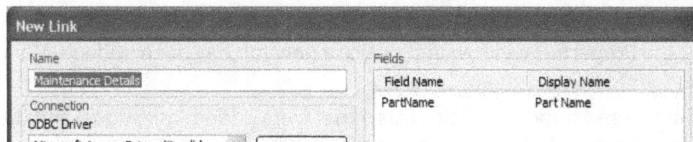

17. Continue to add the following questions:

- Double-click under Field Name to add the next field name. Enter **Last Maintained**, then press ENTER.

- Double-click on the next row under Field Name. Enter **Next Maintenance**, then press ENTER.

- Double-click on the next row under Field Name. Enter **Contractor**, then press ENTER.

- Double-click on the next row under Field Name. Enter **Manual,** then press ENTER.

- Double-click on Manual under the Display Name column to edit it. Enter **Manual Location**, then press ENTER.

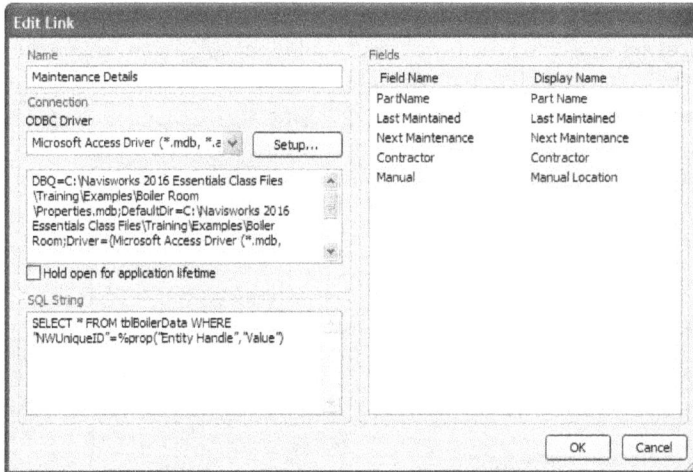

18. Click OK to save the new link.

19. The new link is listed on the Data Tools tab. Add a checkmark to the link, and then click OK to finish.

   The 3D model is now successfully linked to the external data source.

   Tip: If the link cannot be made, check that the link string is correct and the Field Names are correct to the column names in the external data file.

20. Have a look at the model again to see what this has added:

- On the Home tab in the Select & Search panel, click Select and click on one of the large white boilers.

- Look at the Properties window and notice a new tab has been added – Maintenance Details.

- Click this tab and notice the fields listed that were added (questions) and the values (answers) associated with the selected object.

21. Save this file with the same name plus your initials to a new location, for example, *C:\Temp\Boiler Room-Data ToolsJMD.nwf)*.

www.ingramcontent.com/pod-product-compliance
Lightning Source LLC
Chambersburg PA
CBHW080140220326
41598CB00032B/5127